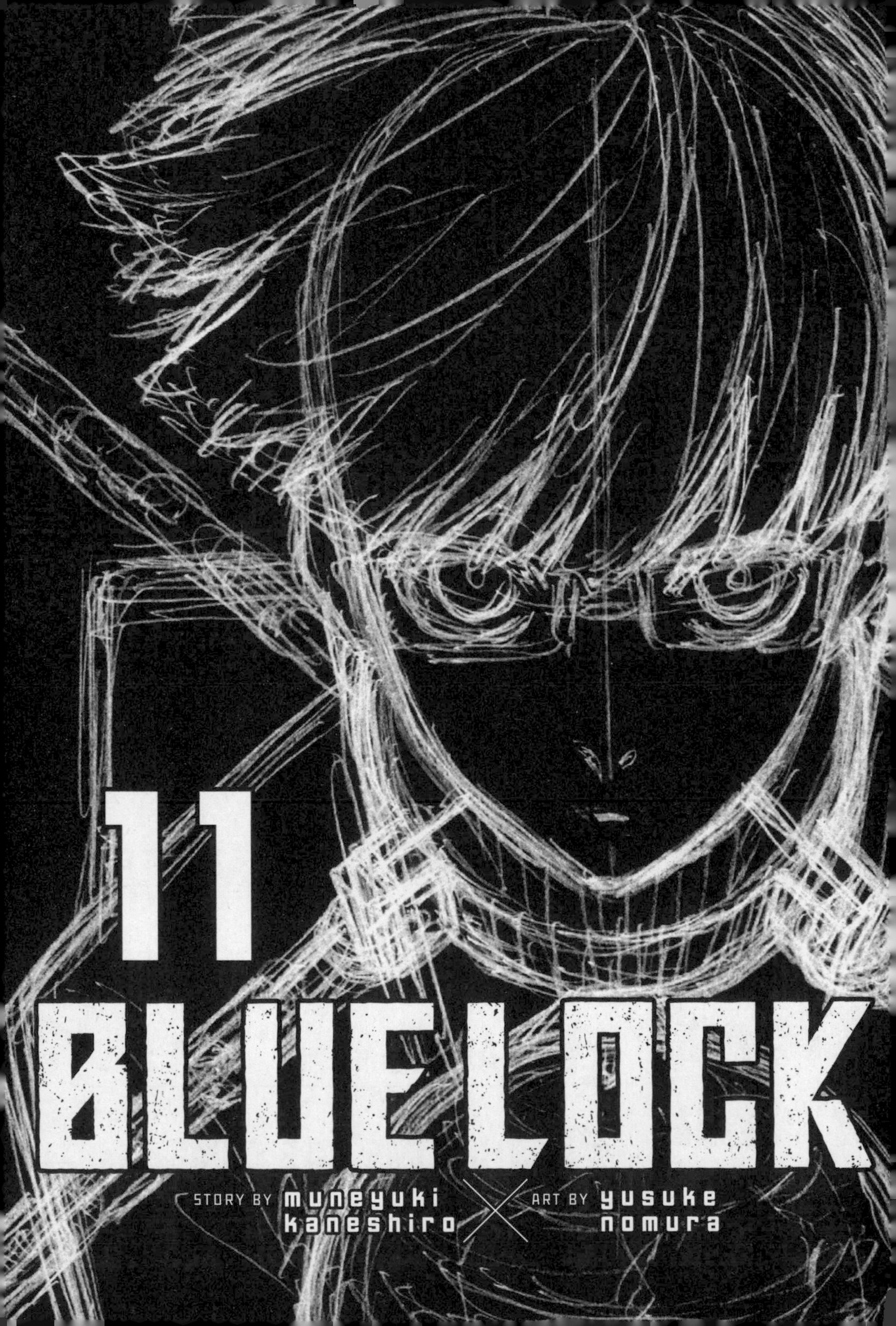
11
BLUE LOCK
STORY BY muneyuki kaneshiro
ART BY yusuke nomura

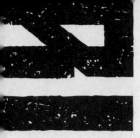

C O N T E N T S

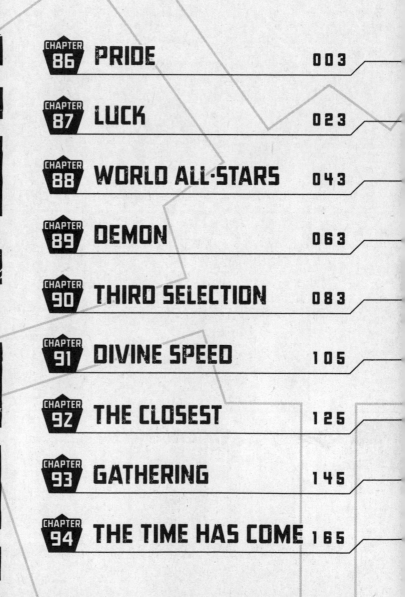

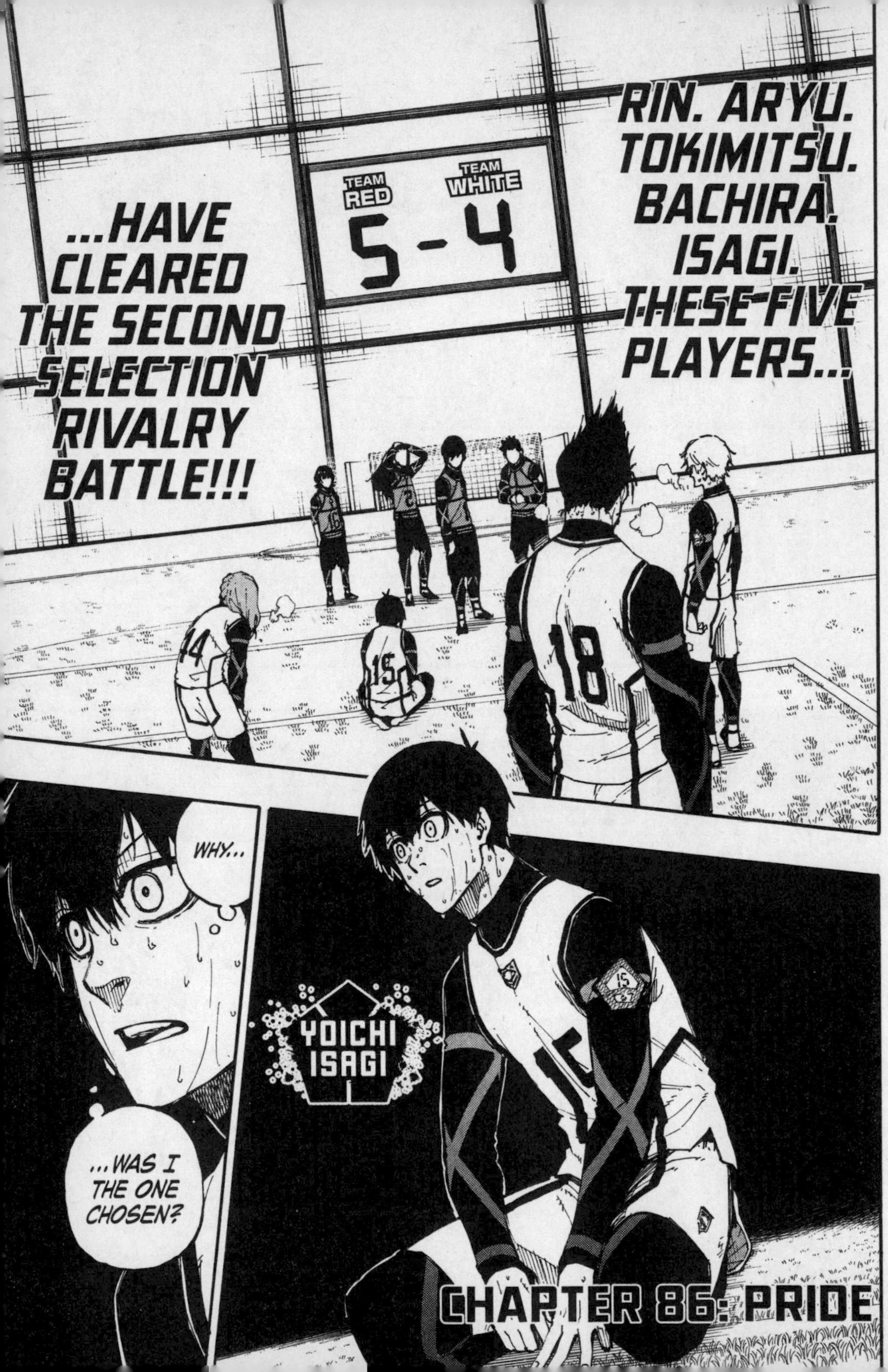
RIN. ARYU. TOKIMITSU. BACHIRA. ISAGI. THESE FIVE PLAYERS...
TEAM RED
TEAM WHITE
5 - 4
...HAVE CLEARED THE SECOND SELECTION RIVALRY BATTLE!!!
YOICHI ISAGI
CHAPTER 86: PRIDE
WHY...
...WAS I THE ONE CHOSEN?

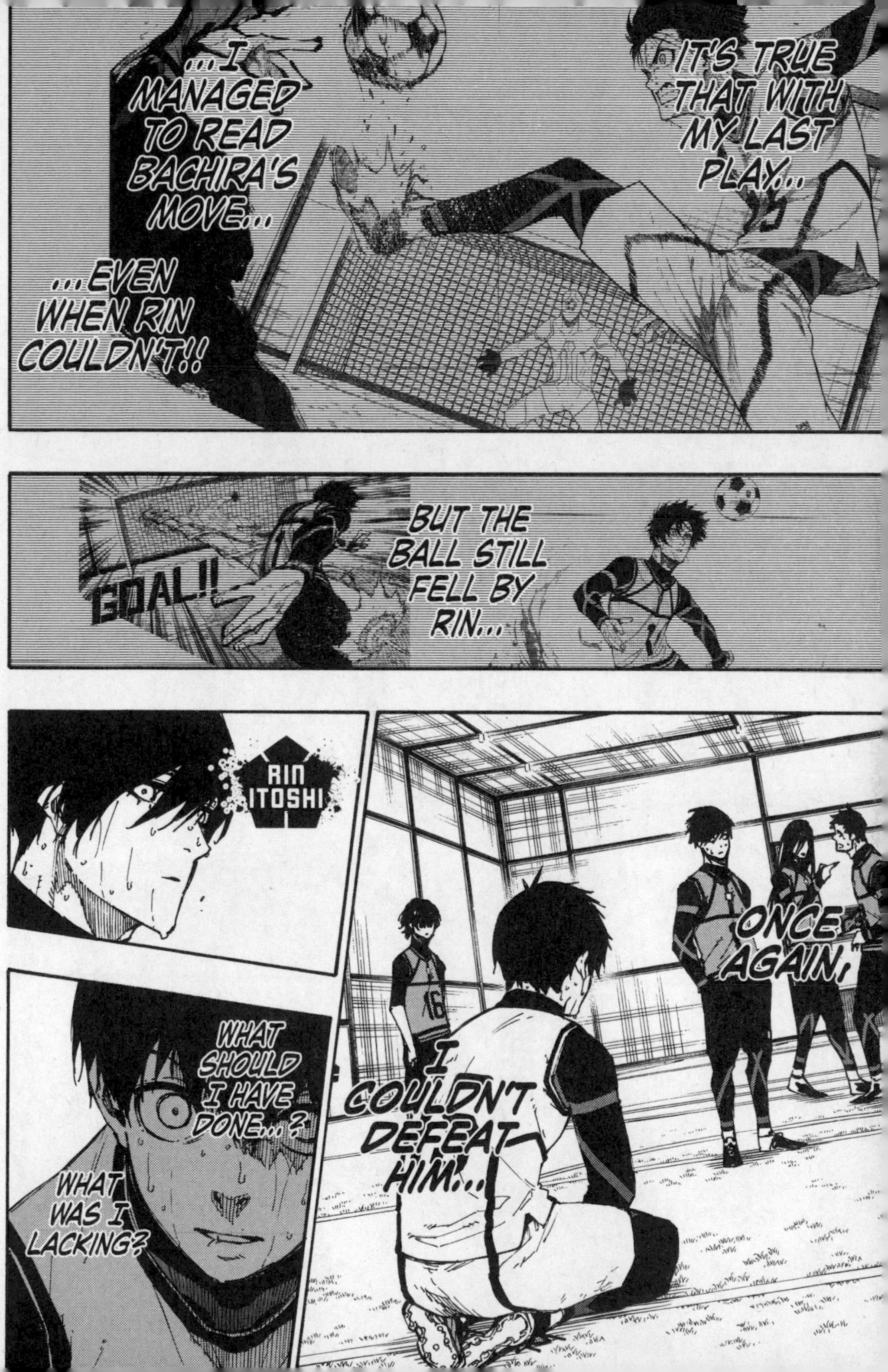
IT'S TRUE THAT WITH MY LAST PLAY...
...I MANAGED TO READ BACHIRA'S MOVE...
...EVEN WHEN RIN COULDN'T!!
BUT THE BALL STILL FELL BY RIN...
GOAL!!
ONCE AGAIN,
I COULDN'T DEFEAT HIM...
RIN ITOSHI
WHAT SHOULD I HAVE DONE...?
WHAT WAS I LACKING?

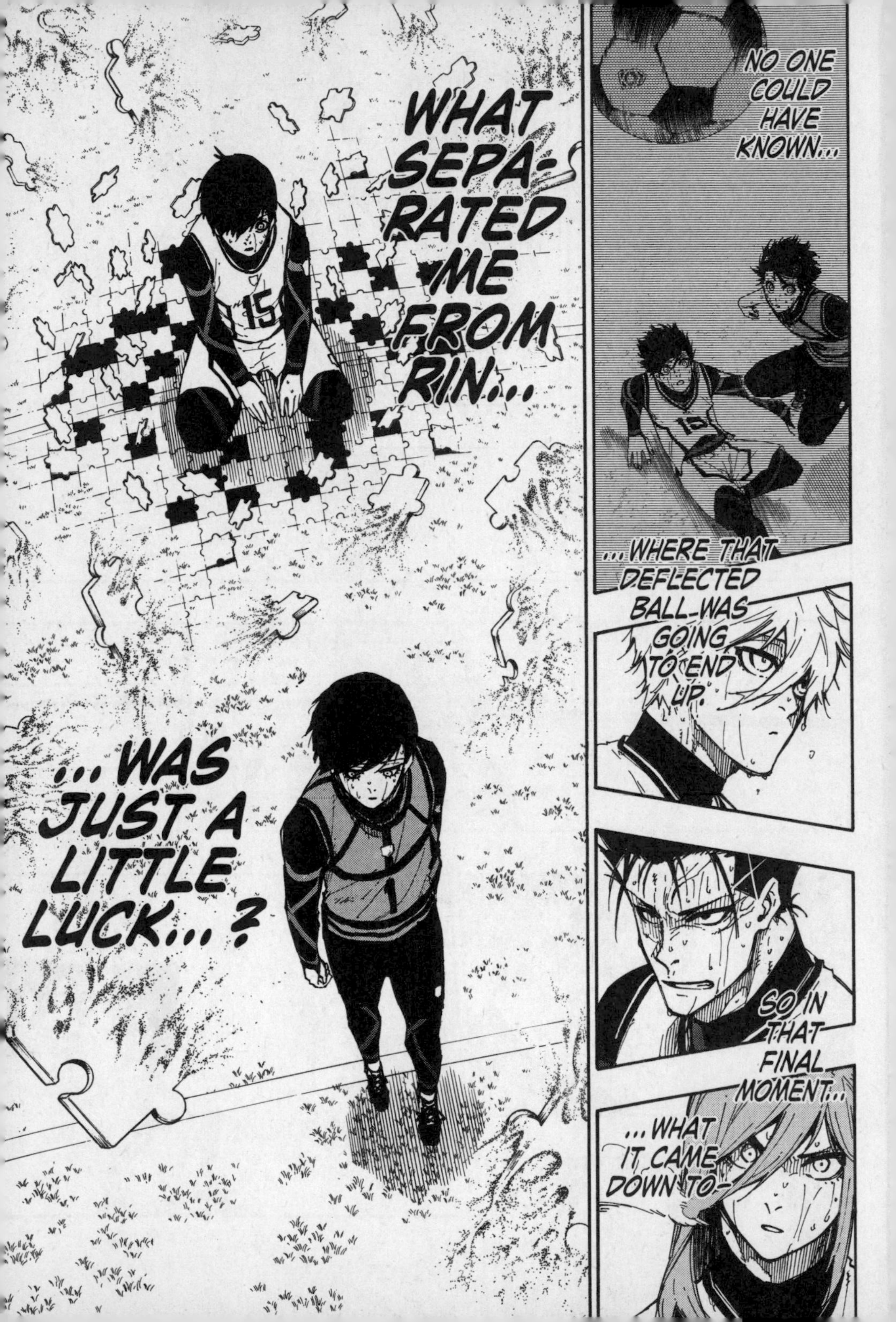
NO ONE COULD HAVE KNOWN...
...WHERE THAT DEFLECTED BALL WAS GOING TO END UP.
SO IN THAT FINAL MOMENT...
...WHAT IT CAME DOWN TO-
WHAT SEPA-RATED ME FROM RIN...
...WAS JUST A LITTLE LUCK...?

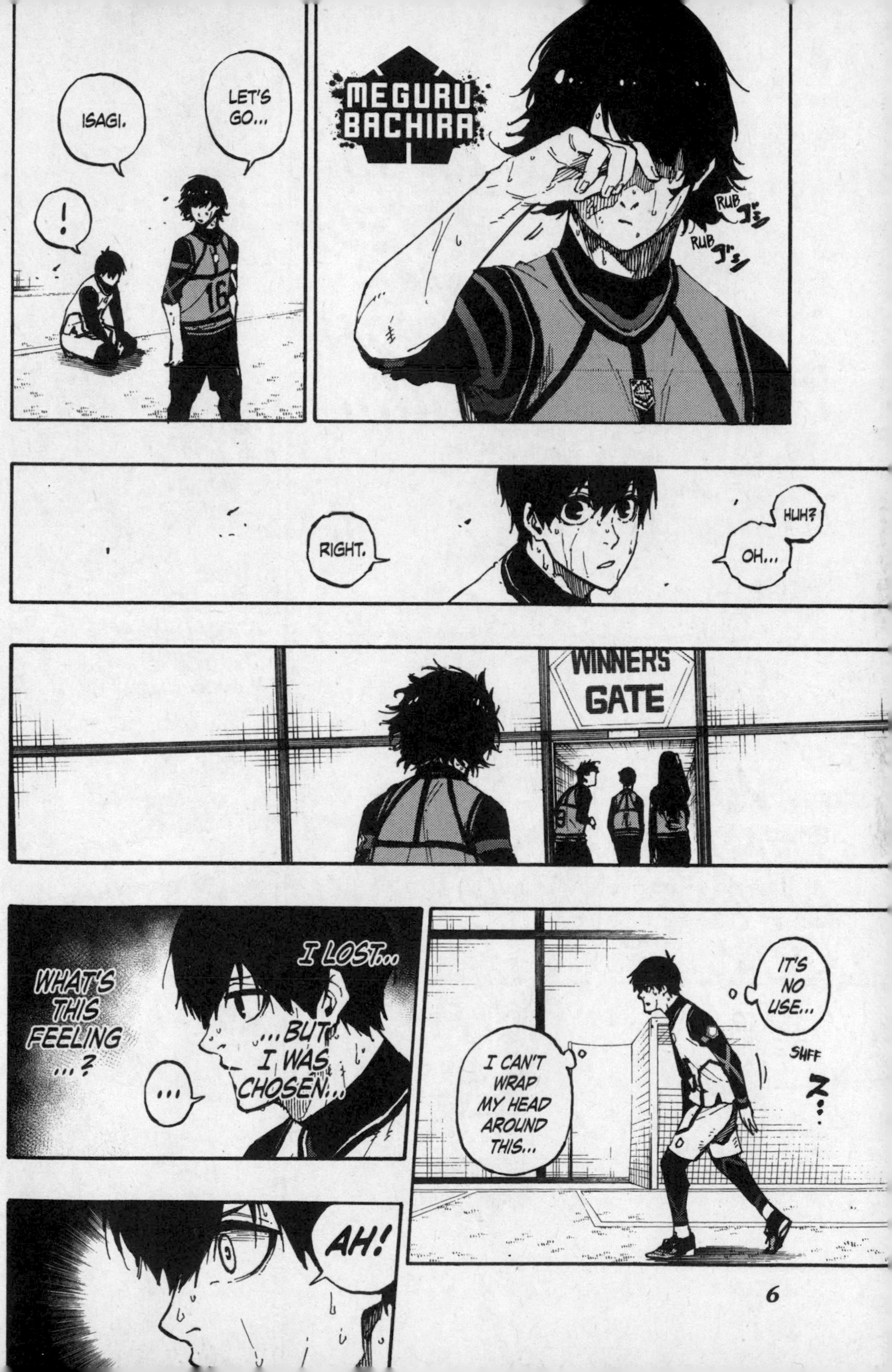
MEGURU BACHIRA
RUB
RUB
LET'S GO...
ISAGI.
!
HUH?
OH...
RIGHT.
WINNERS GATE
IT'S NO USE...
SHFF
I CAN'T WRAP MY HEAD AROUND THIS...
I LOST...
WHAT'S THIS FEELING ...?
...BUT I WAS CHOSEN...
...
AH!

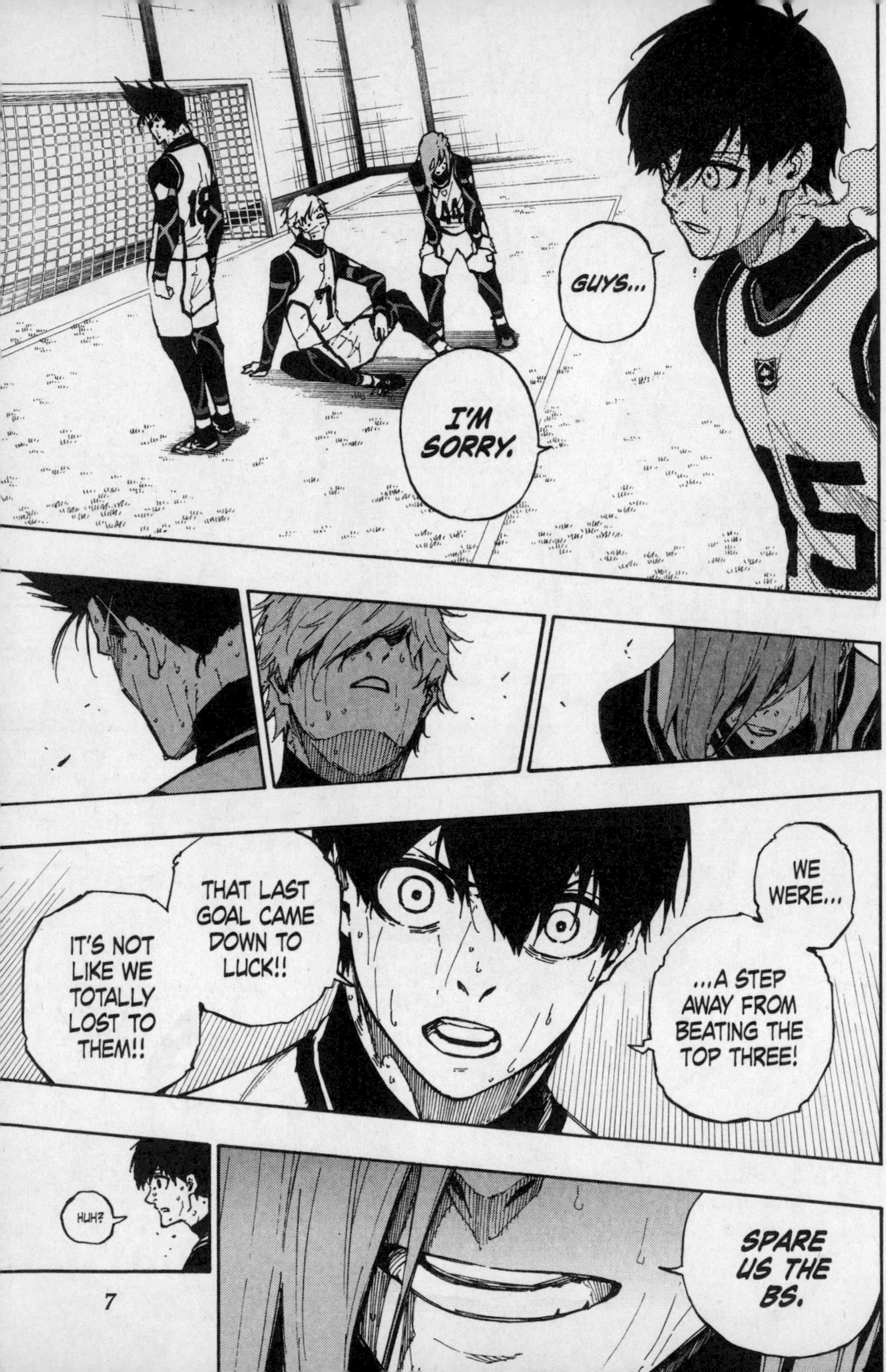
GUYS...
I'M SORRY.
WE WERE...
...A STEP AWAY FROM BEATING THE TOP THREE!
THAT LAST GOAL CAME DOWN TO LUCK!!
IT'S NOT LIKE WE TOTALLY LOST TO THEM!!
SPARE US THE BS.
HUH?

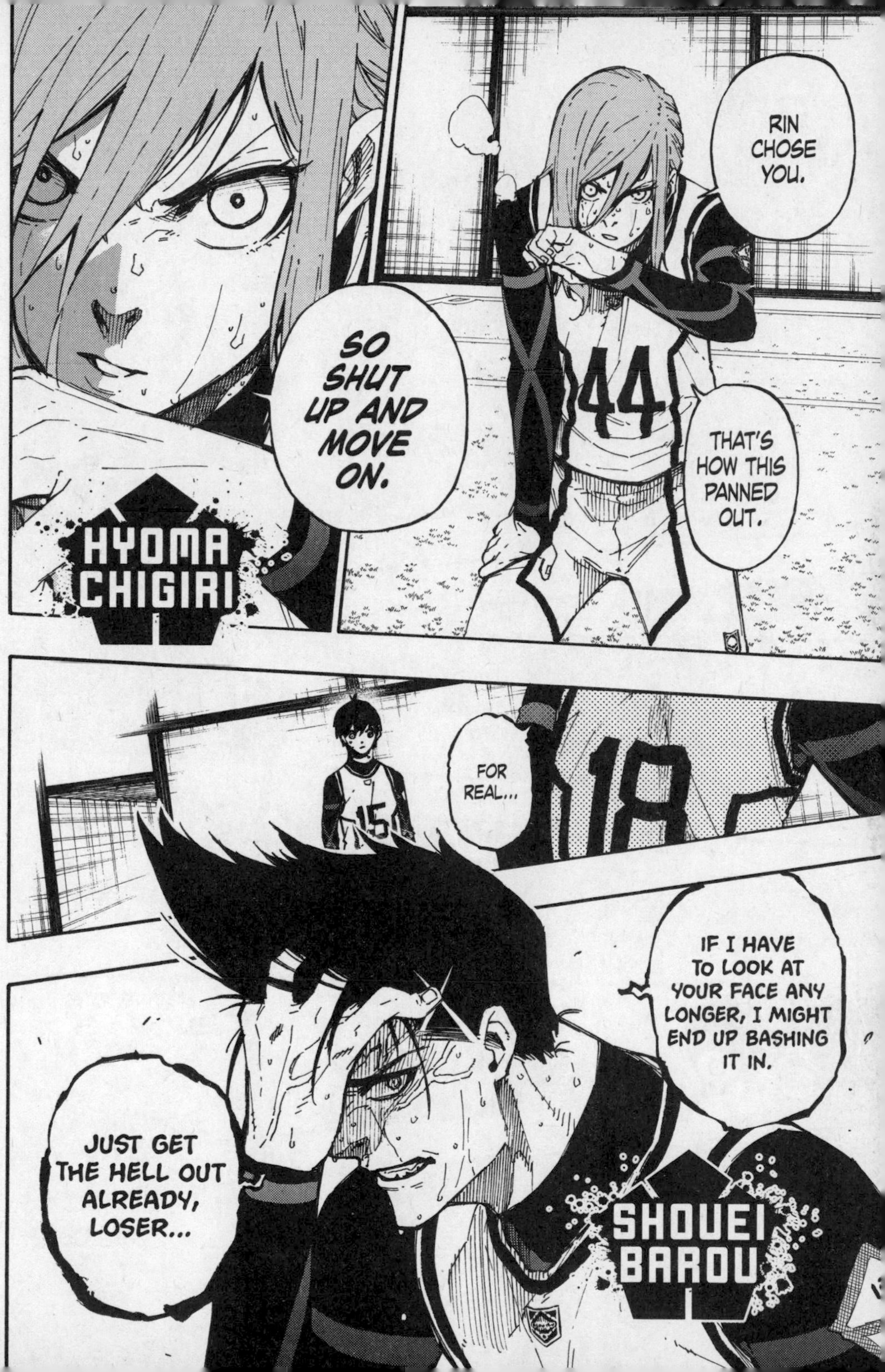
RIN CHOSE YOU.
THAT'S HOW THIS PANNED OUT.
SO SHUT UP AND MOVE ON.
HYOMA CHIGIRI
FOR REAL...
IF I HAVE TO LOOK AT YOUR FACE ANY LONGER, I MIGHT END UP BASHING IT IN.
JUST GET THE HELL OUT ALREADY, LOSER...
SHOUEI BAROU

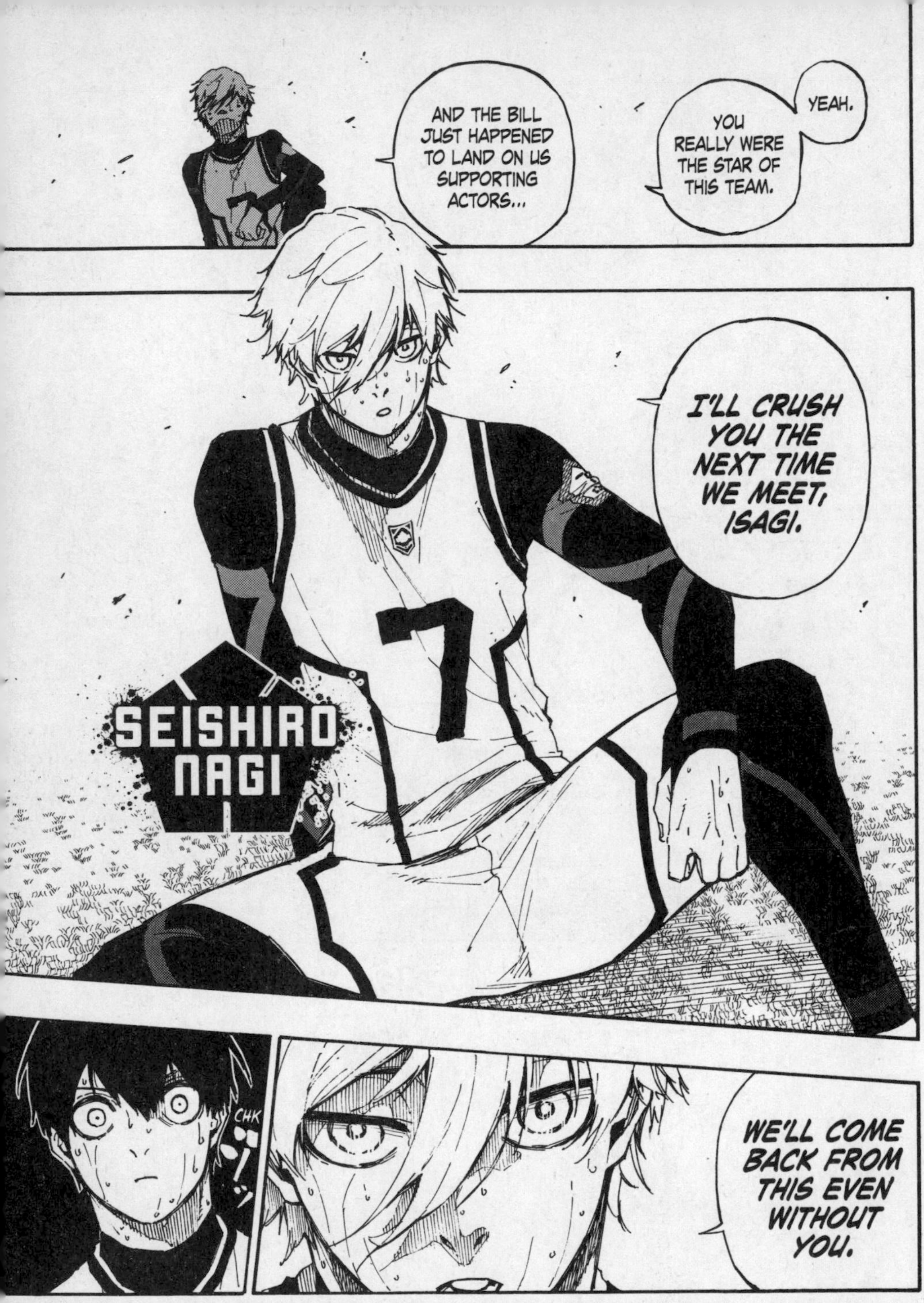
YEAH.
YOU REALLY WERE THE STAR OF THIS TEAM.
AND THE BILL JUST HAPPENED TO LAND ON US SUPPORTING ACTORS...
I'LL CRUSH YOU THE NEXT TIME WE MEET, ISAGI.
SEISHIRO NAGI
WE'LL COME BACK FROM THIS EVEN WITHOUT YOU.
CHK

WITHOUT THESE GUYS...I NEVER...

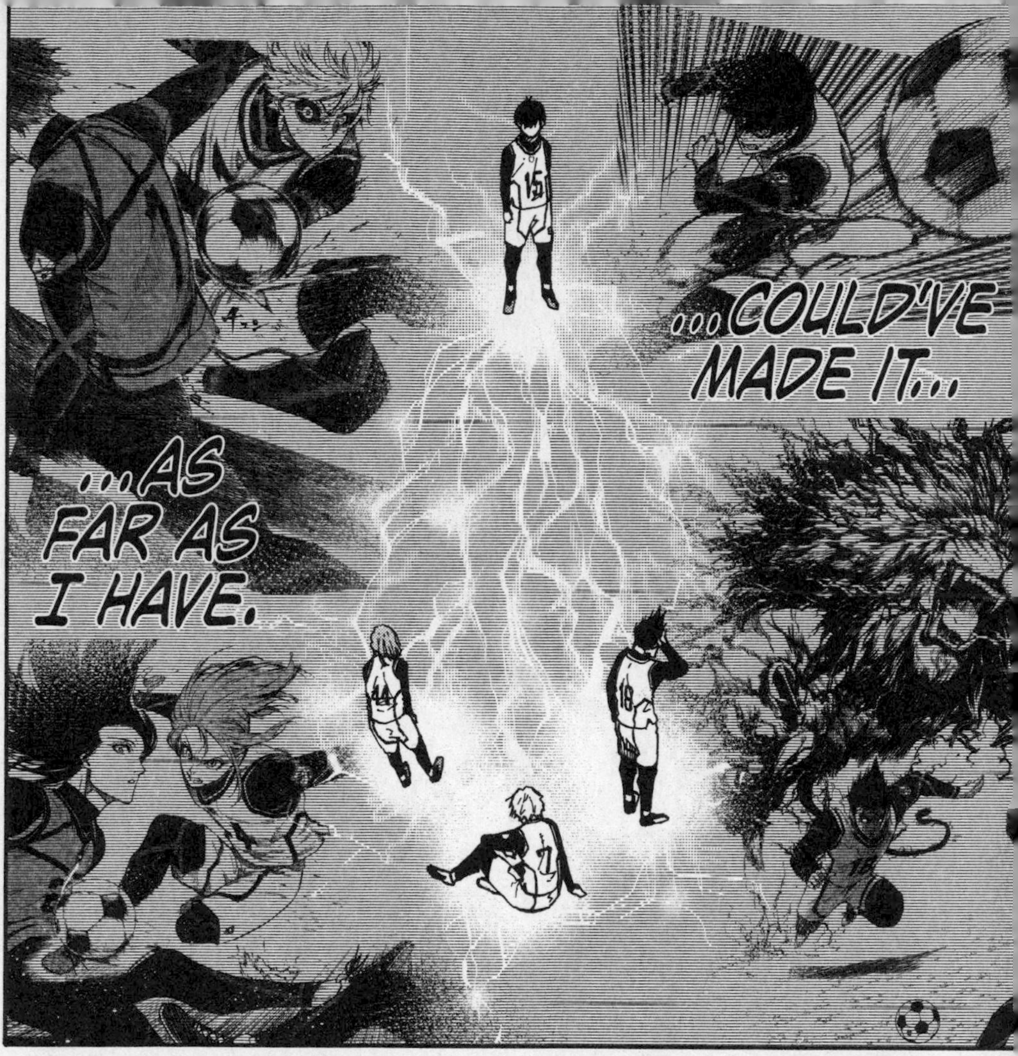
...COULD'VE MADE IT...
...AS FAR AS I HAVE.

THIS WAS SUCH AN INTENSE TIME FOR US...

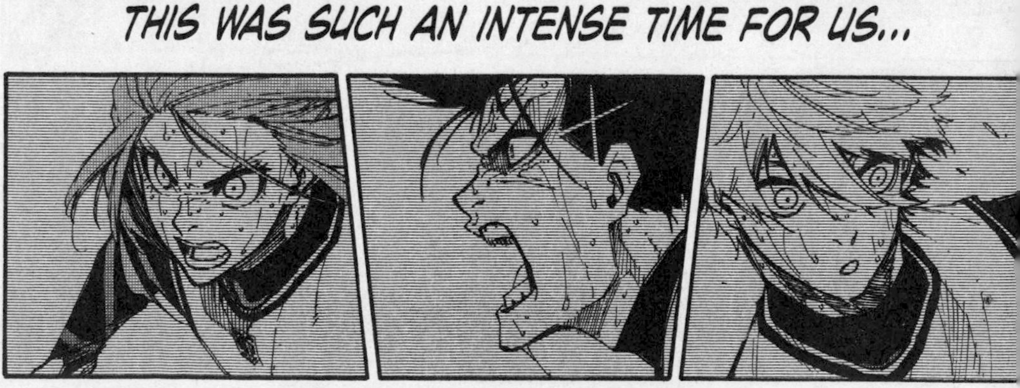

THE FACT THAT I WAS ABLE TO FIGHT ALONGSIDE YOU ALL...

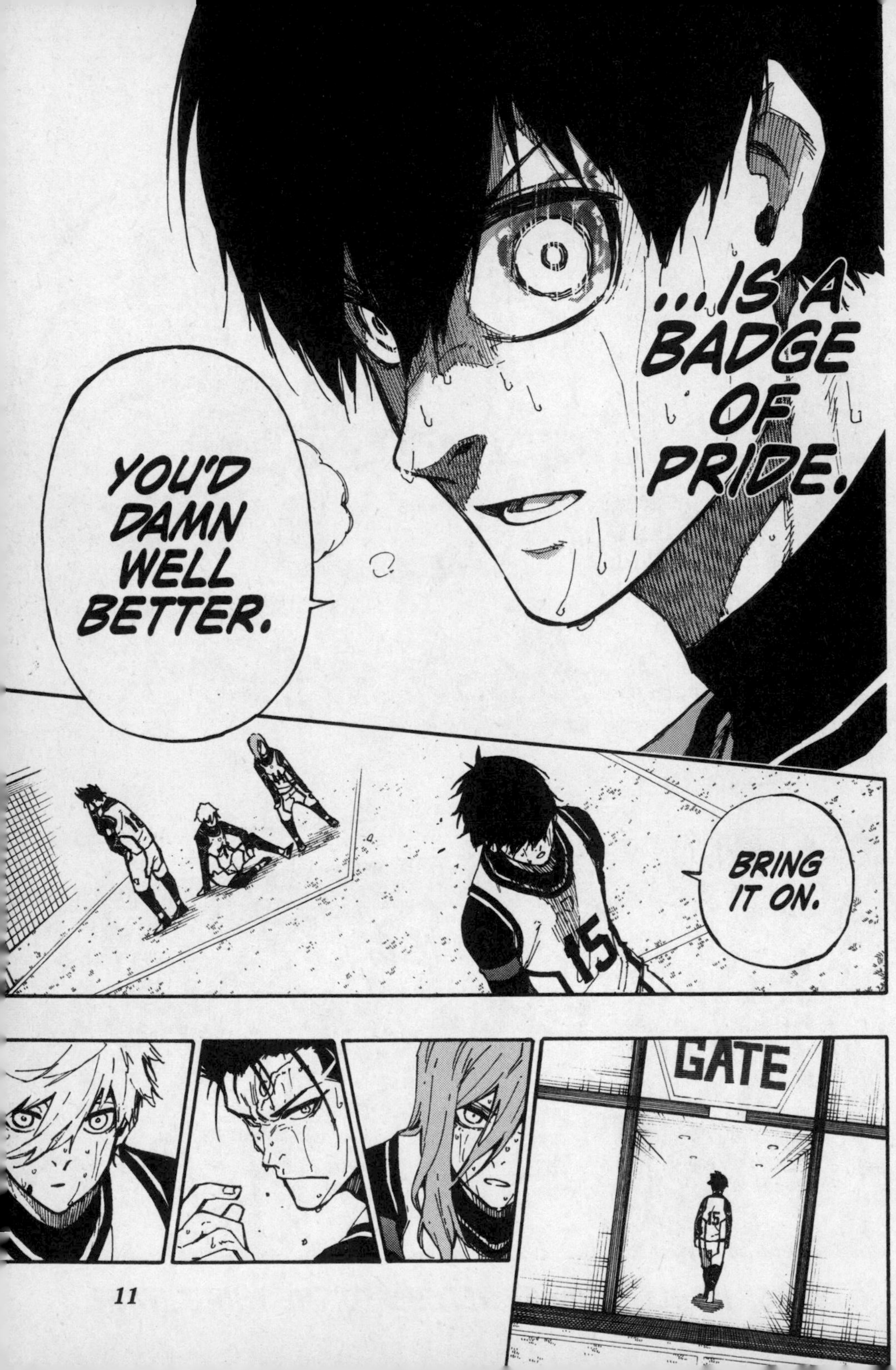
...IS A BADGE OF PRIDE.
YOU'D DAMN WELL BETTER.
BRING IT ON.
GATE

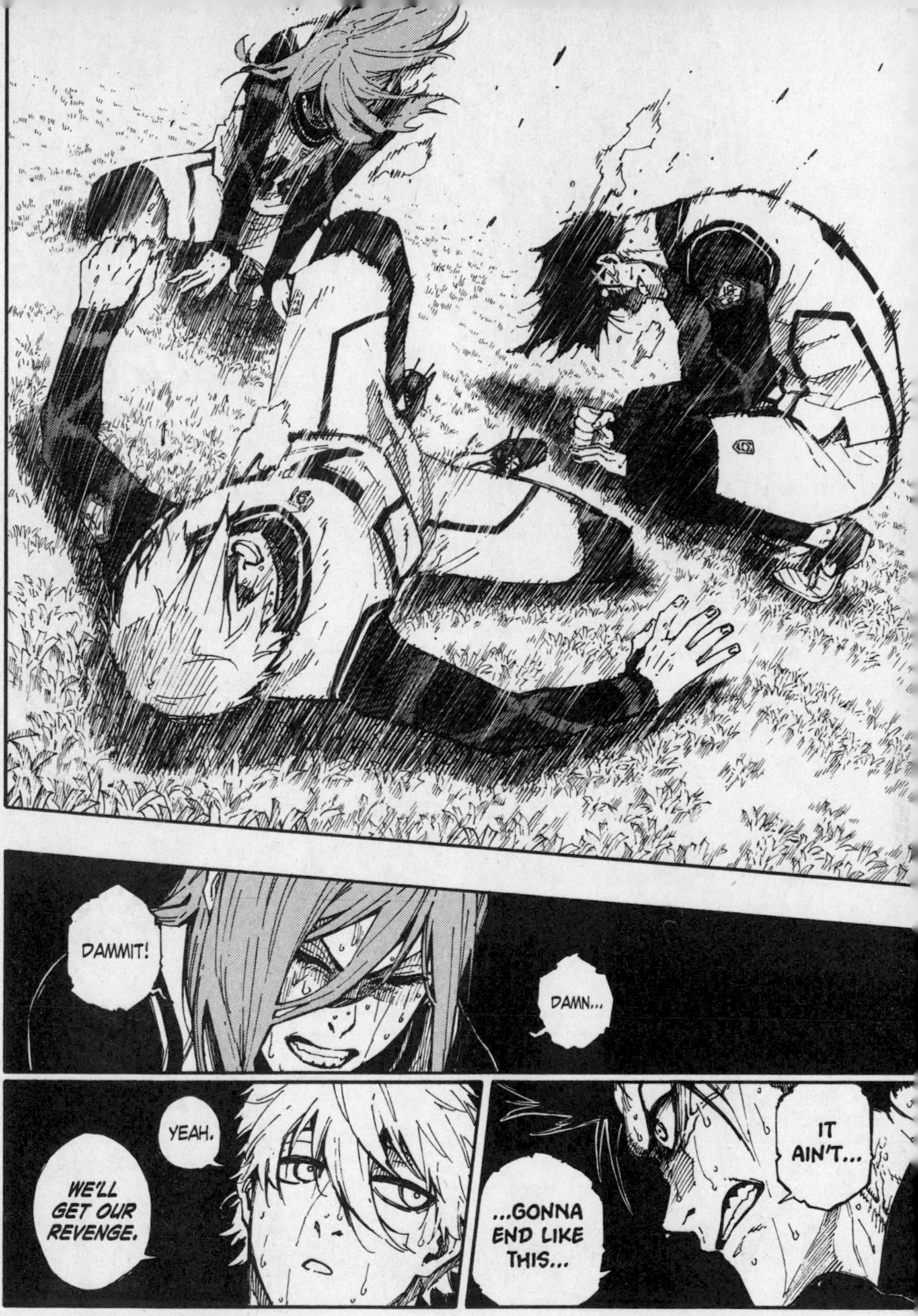
DAMN...
DAMMIT!
IT AIN'T...
...GONNA END LIKE THIS...
YEAH.
WE'LL GET OUR REVENGE.

NAGI, BAROU, CHIGIRI: RETURN TO THE THIRD STAGE...

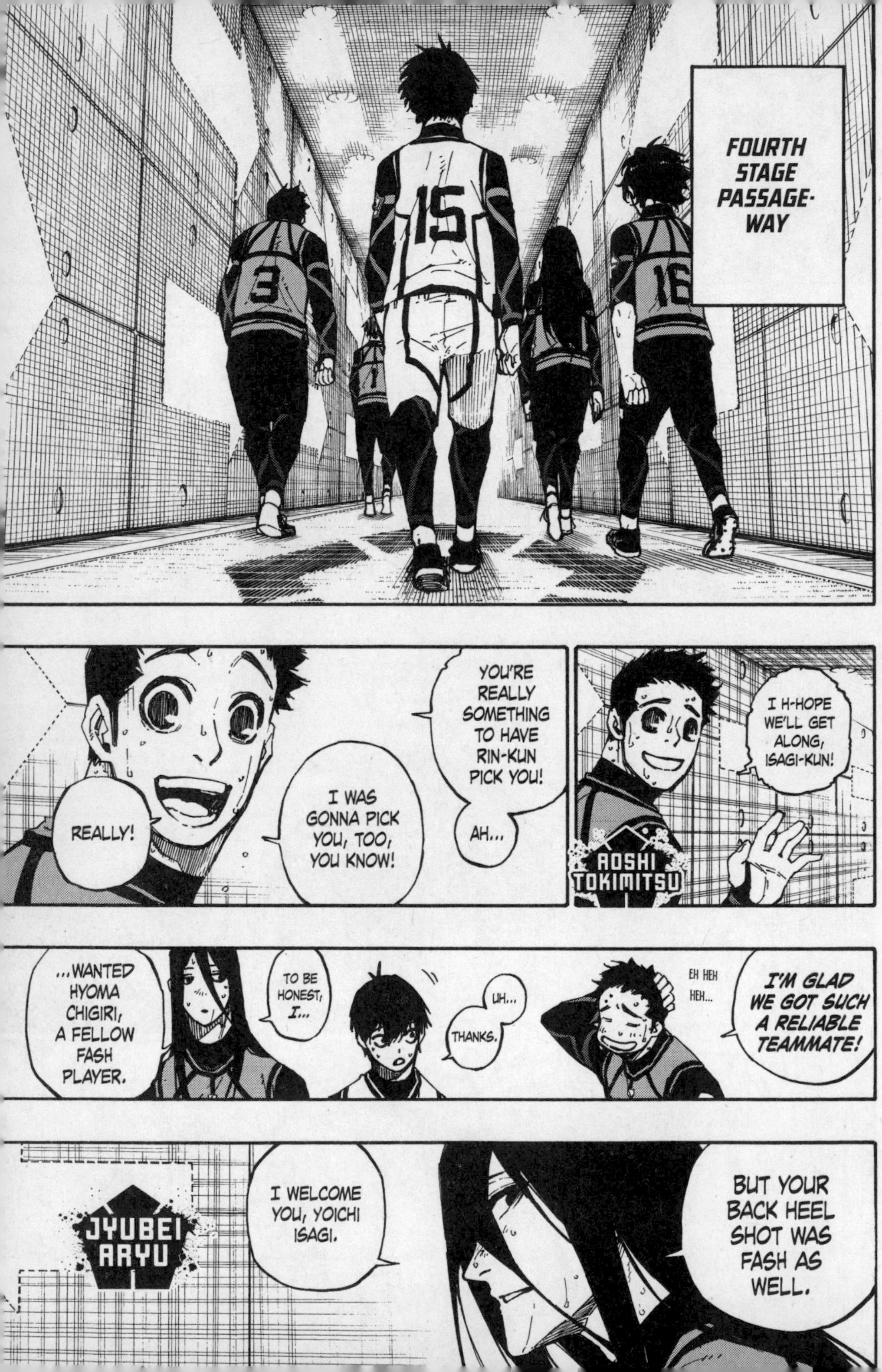
FOURTH STAGE PASSAGE-WAY
I H-HOPE WE'LL GET ALONG, ISAGI-KUN!
AOSHI TOKIMITSU
YOU'RE REALLY SOMETHING TO HAVE RIN-KUN PICK YOU!
AH...
I WAS GONNA PICK YOU, TOO, YOU KNOW!
REALLY!
I'M GLAD WE GOT SUCH A RELIABLE TEAMMATE!
EH HEH HEH...
UH...
THANKS.
TO BE HONEST, I...
...WANTED HYOMA CHIGIRI, A FELLOW FASH PLAYER.
BUT YOUR BACK HEEL SHOT WAS FASH AS WELL.
I WELCOME YOU, YOICHI ISAGI.
JYUBEI ARYU

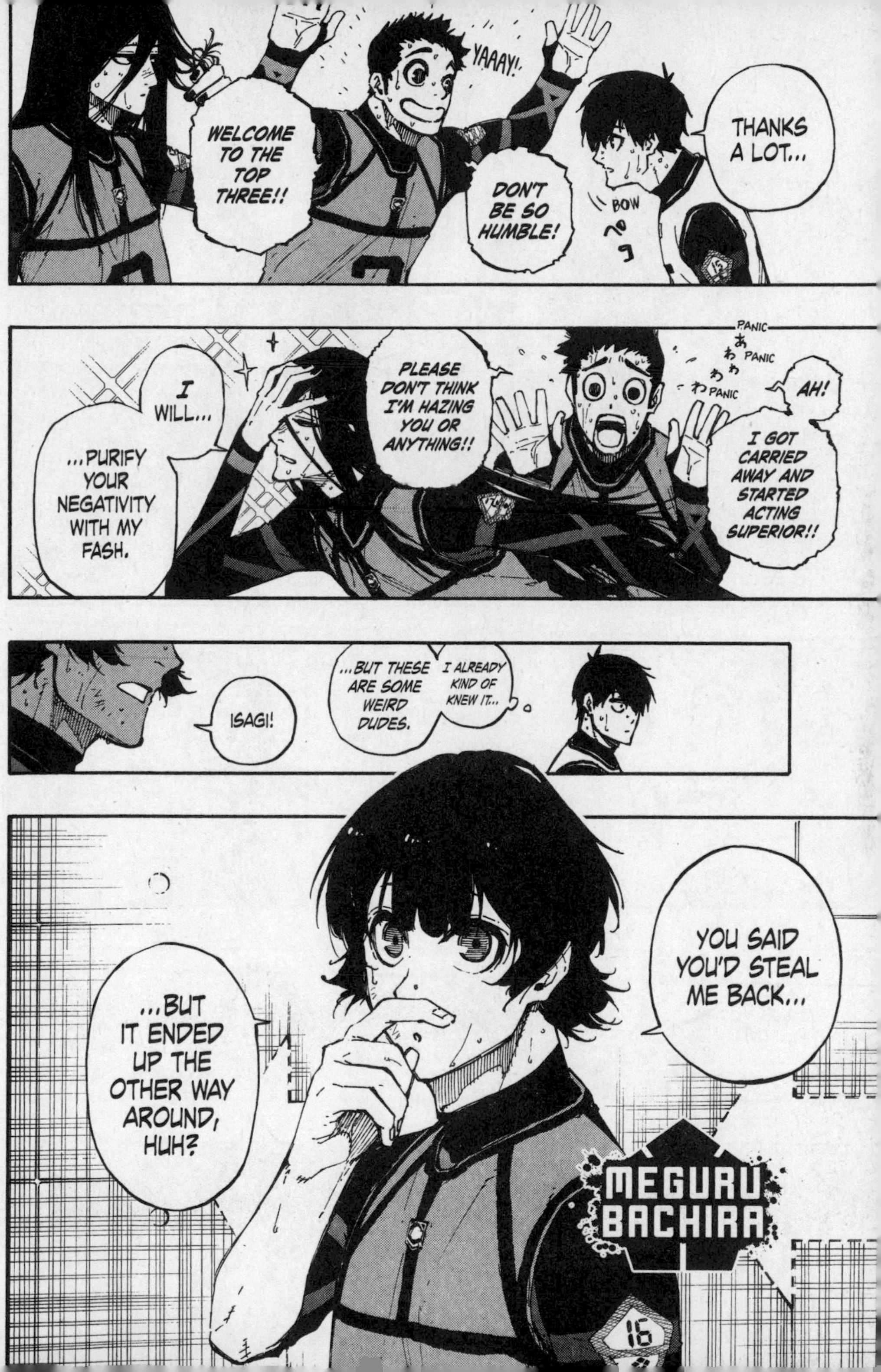
THANKS A LOT...
BOW
YAAAY!!
WELCOME TO THE TOP THREE!!
DON'T BE SO HUMBLE!
PANIC PANIC PANIC
AH!
I GOT CARRIED AWAY AND STARTED ACTING SUPERIOR!!
PLEASE DON'T THINK I'M HAZING YOU OR ANYTHING!!
I WILL...
...PURIFY YOUR NEGATIVITY WITH MY FASH.
I ALREADY KIND OF KNEW IT...
...BUT THESE ARE SOME WEIRD DUDES.
ISAGI!
YOU SAID YOU'D STEAL ME BACK...
MEGURU BACHIRA
...BUT IT ENDED UP THE OTHER WAY AROUND, HUH?

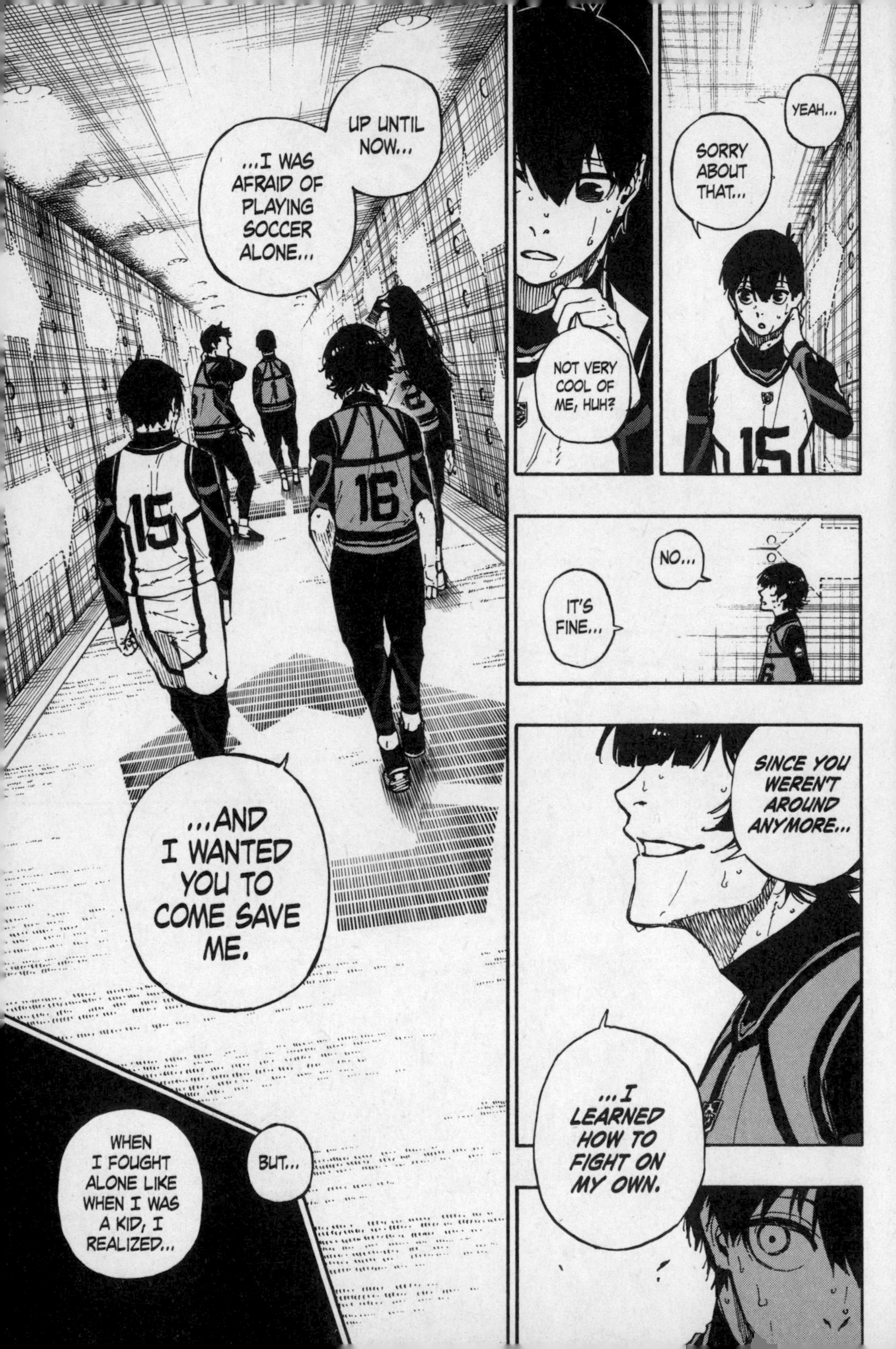
YEAH...
SORRY ABOUT THAT...
NOT VERY COOL OF ME, HUH?
NO...
IT'S FINE...
SINCE YOU WEREN'T AROUND ANYMORE...
...I LEARNED HOW TO FIGHT ON MY OWN.
UP UNTIL NOW...
...I WAS AFRAID OF PLAYING SOCCER ALONE...
...AND I WANTED YOU TO COME SAVE ME.
BUT...
WHEN I FOUGHT ALONE LIKE WHEN I WAS A KID, I REALIZED...

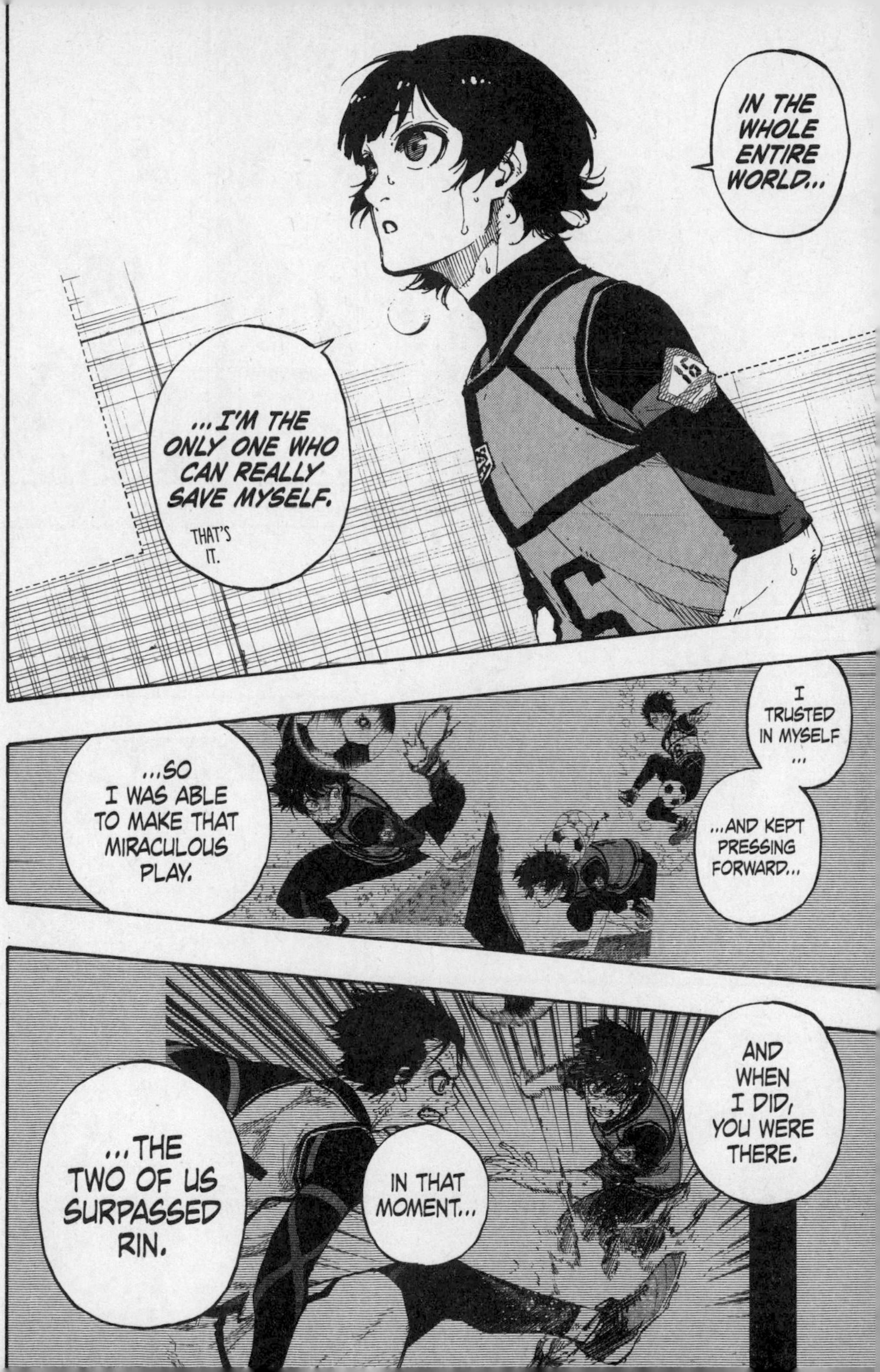
IN THE WHOLE ENTIRE WORLD...
...I'M THE ONLY ONE WHO CAN REALLY SAVE MYSELF.
THAT'S IT.
I TRUSTED IN MYSELF...
...AND KEPT PRESSING FORWARD...
...SO I WAS ABLE TO MAKE THAT MIRACULOUS PLAY.
AND WHEN I DID, YOU WERE THERE.
IN THAT MOMENT...
...THE TWO OF US SURPASSED RIN.

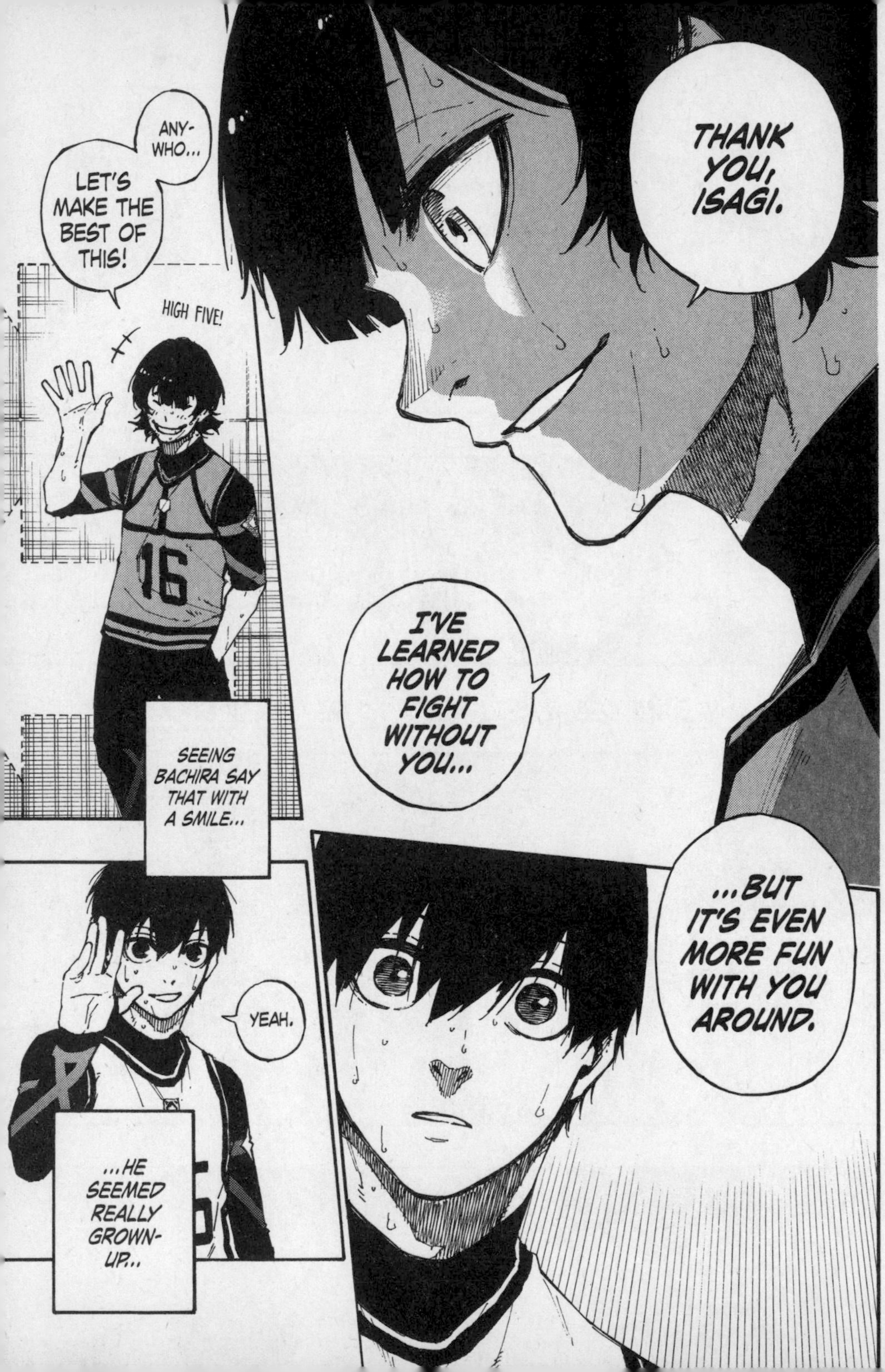
THANK YOU, ISAGI.
I'VE LEARNED HOW TO FIGHT WITHOUT YOU...
...BUT IT'S EVEN MORE FUN WITH YOU AROUND.
ANY-WHO...
LET'S MAKE THE BEST OF THIS!
HIGH FIVE!
SEEING BACHIRA SAY THAT WITH A SMILE...
YEAH.
...HE SEEMED REALLY GROWN-UP...

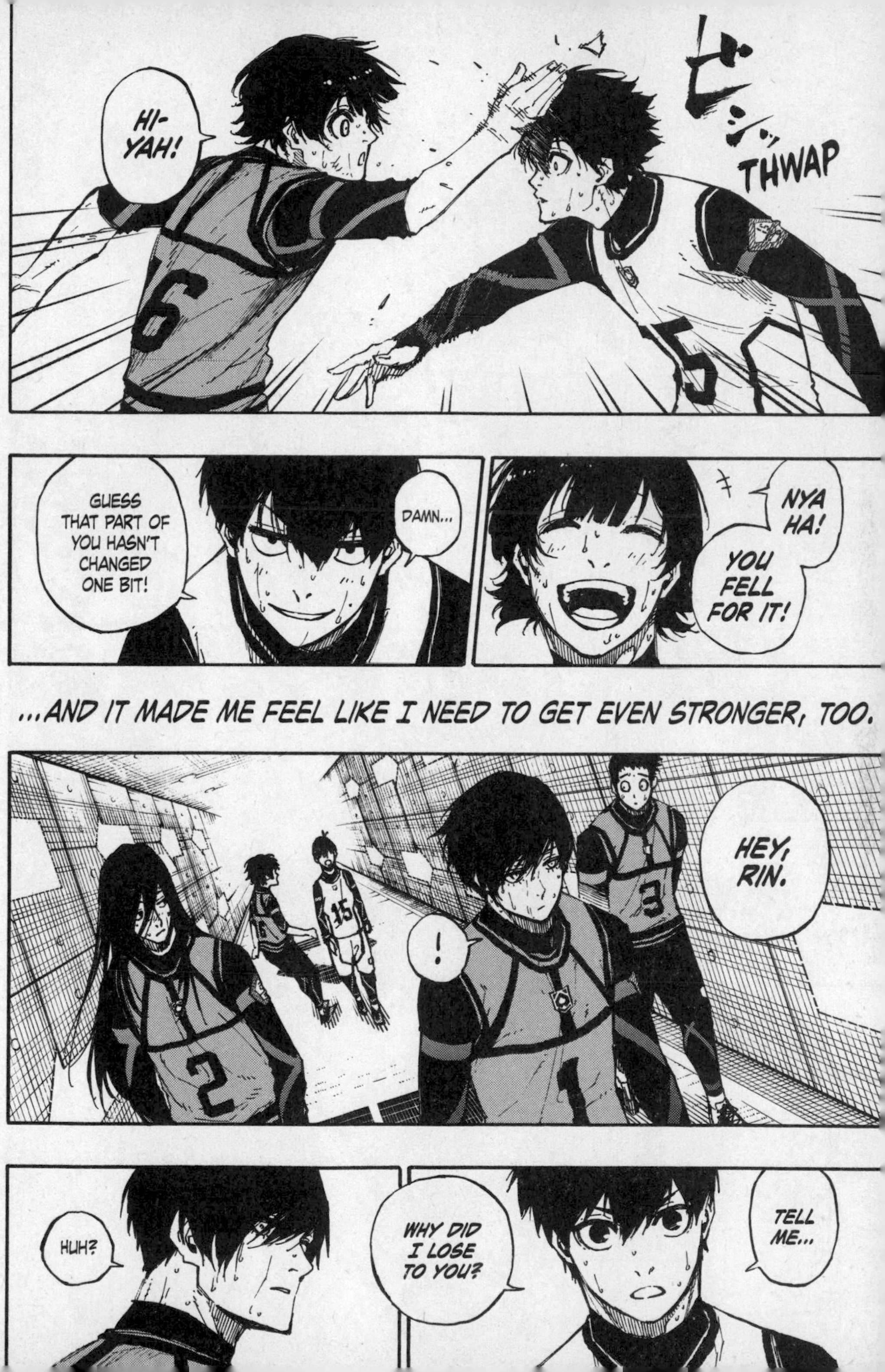
THWAP
HI-YAH!
NYA HA!
YOU FELL FOR IT!
DAMN...
GUESS THAT PART OF YOU HASN'T CHANGED ONE BIT!
...AND IT MADE ME FEEL LIKE I NEED TO GET EVEN STRONGER, TOO.
HEY, RIN.
!
TELL ME...
WHY DID I LOSE TO YOU?
HUH?

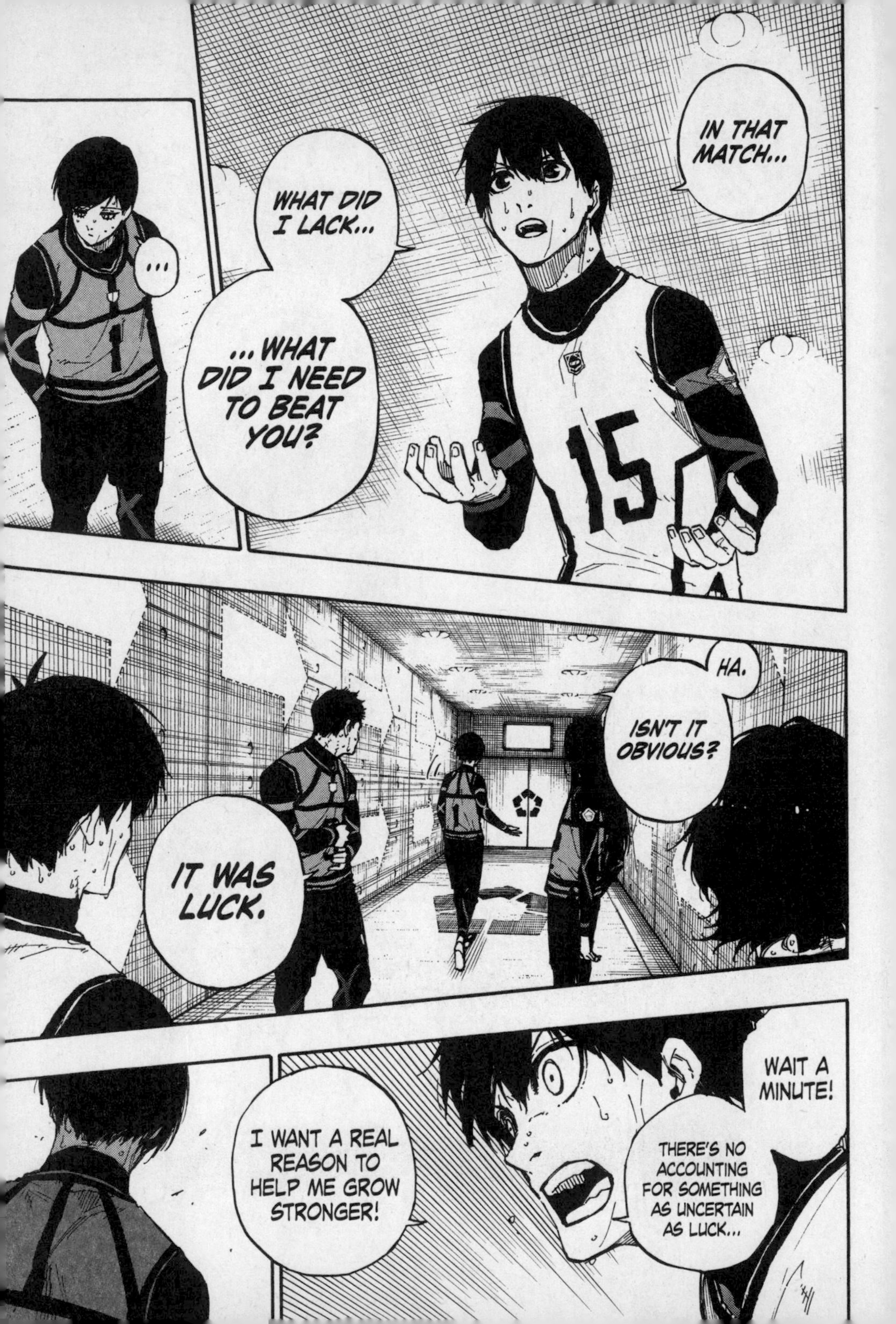
IN THAT MATCH...
WHAT DID I LACK...
...WHAT DID I NEED TO BEAT YOU?
...
HA.
ISN'T IT OBVIOUS?
IT WAS LUCK.
WAIT A MINUTE!
THERE'S NO ACCOUNTING FOR SOMETHING AS UNCERTAIN AS LUCK...
I WANT A REAL REASON TO HELP ME GROW STRONGER!

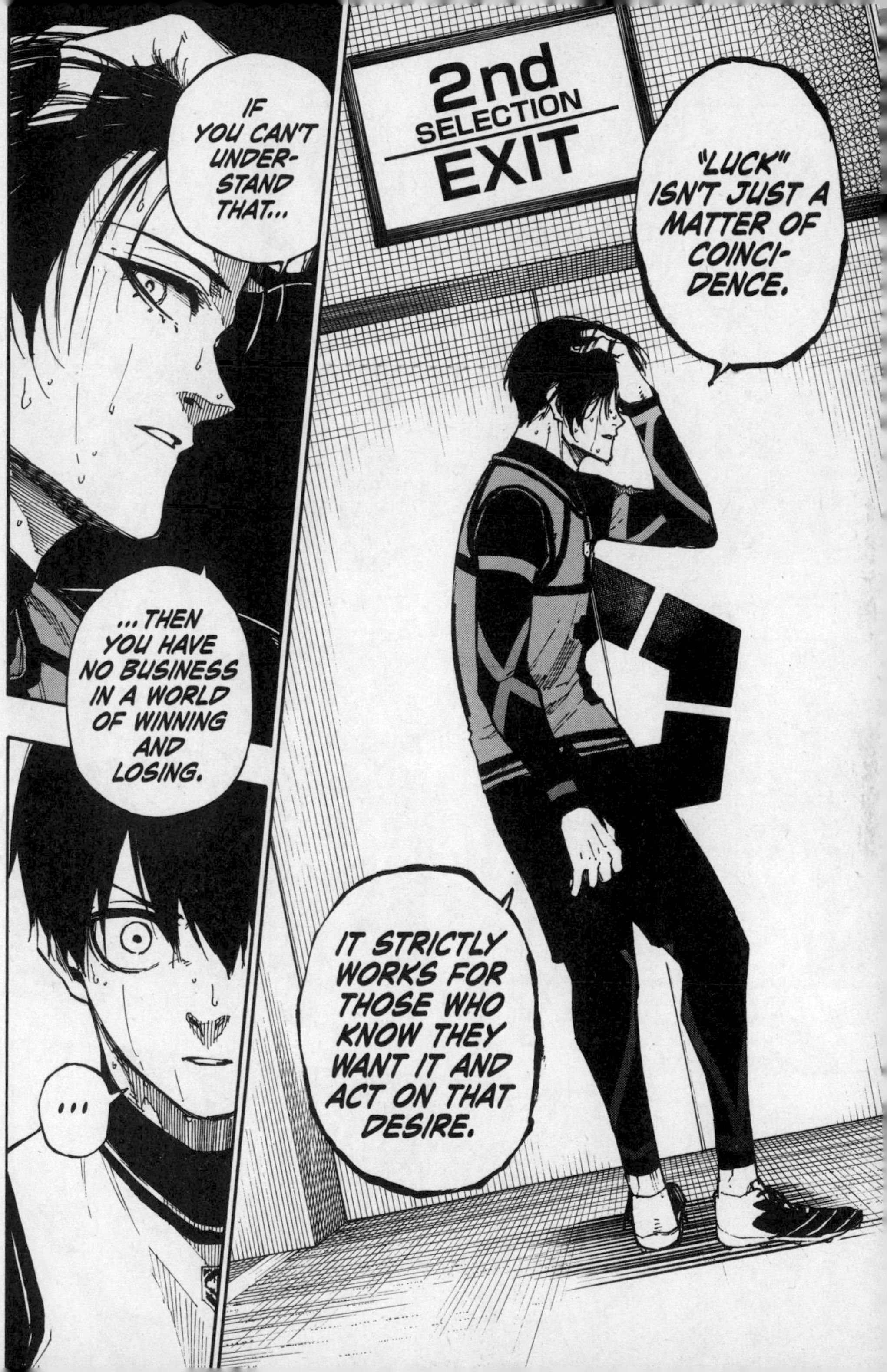
"LUCK" ISN'T JUST A MATTER OF COINCI-DENCE.
2nd SELECTION EXIT
IT STRICTLY WORKS FOR THOSE WHO KNOW THEY WANT IT AND ACT ON THAT DESIRE.
IF YOU CAN'T UNDER-STAND THAT...
...THEN YOU HAVE NO BUSINESS IN A WORLD OF WINNING AND LOSING.
...

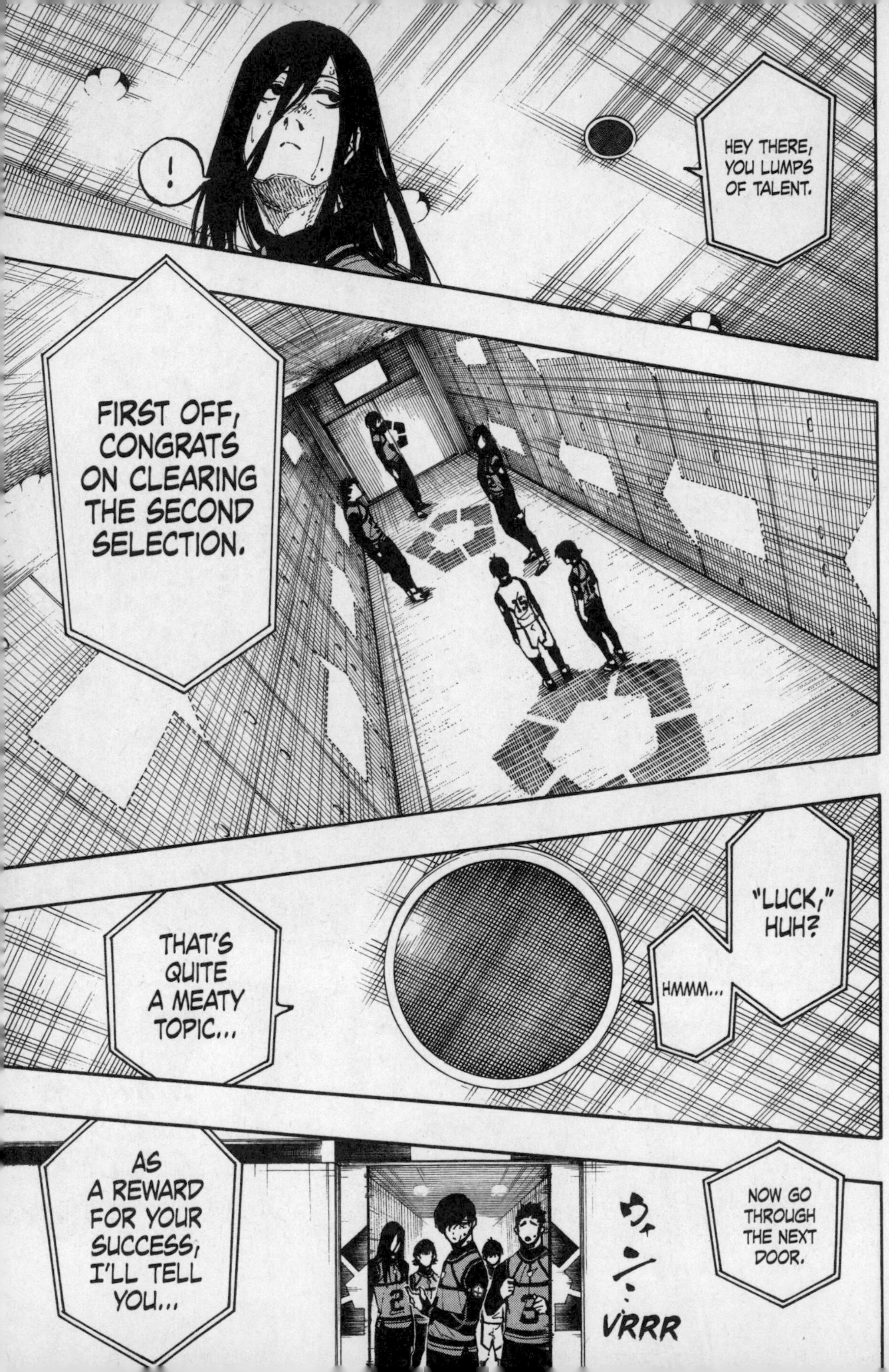
HEY THERE, YOU LUMPS OF TALENT.
!
FIRST OFF, CONGRATS ON CLEARING THE SECOND SELECTION.
"LUCK," HUH?
HMMM...
THAT'S QUITE A MEATY TOPIC...
NOW GO THROUGH THE NEXT DOOR.
ウィーン…
VRRR
AS A REWARD FOR YOUR SUCCESS, I'LL TELL YOU...

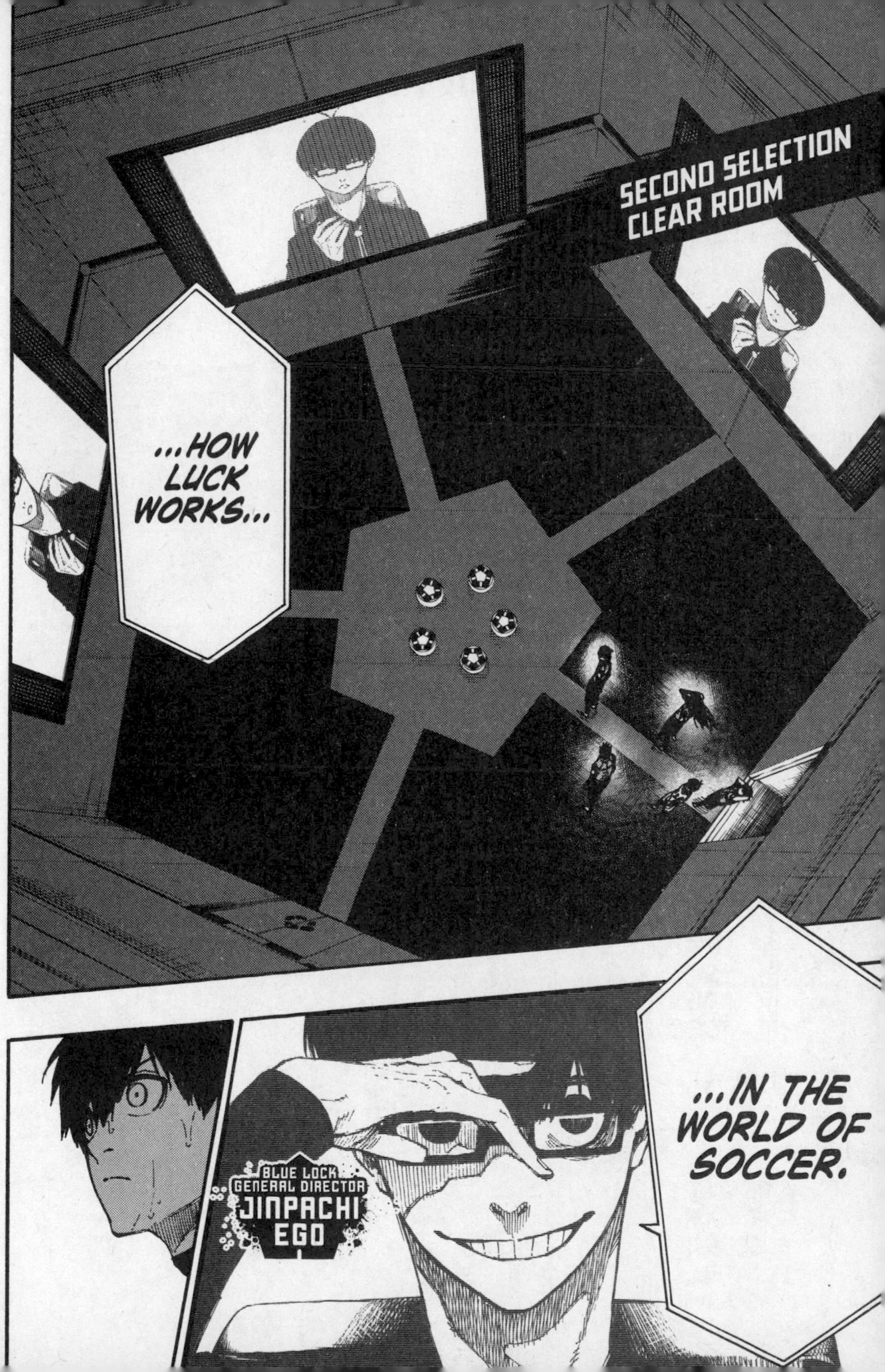
SECOND SELECTION CLEAR ROOM
...HOW LUCK WORKS...
...IN THE WORLD OF SOCCER.
BLUE LOCK GENERAL DIRECTOR JINPACHI EGO

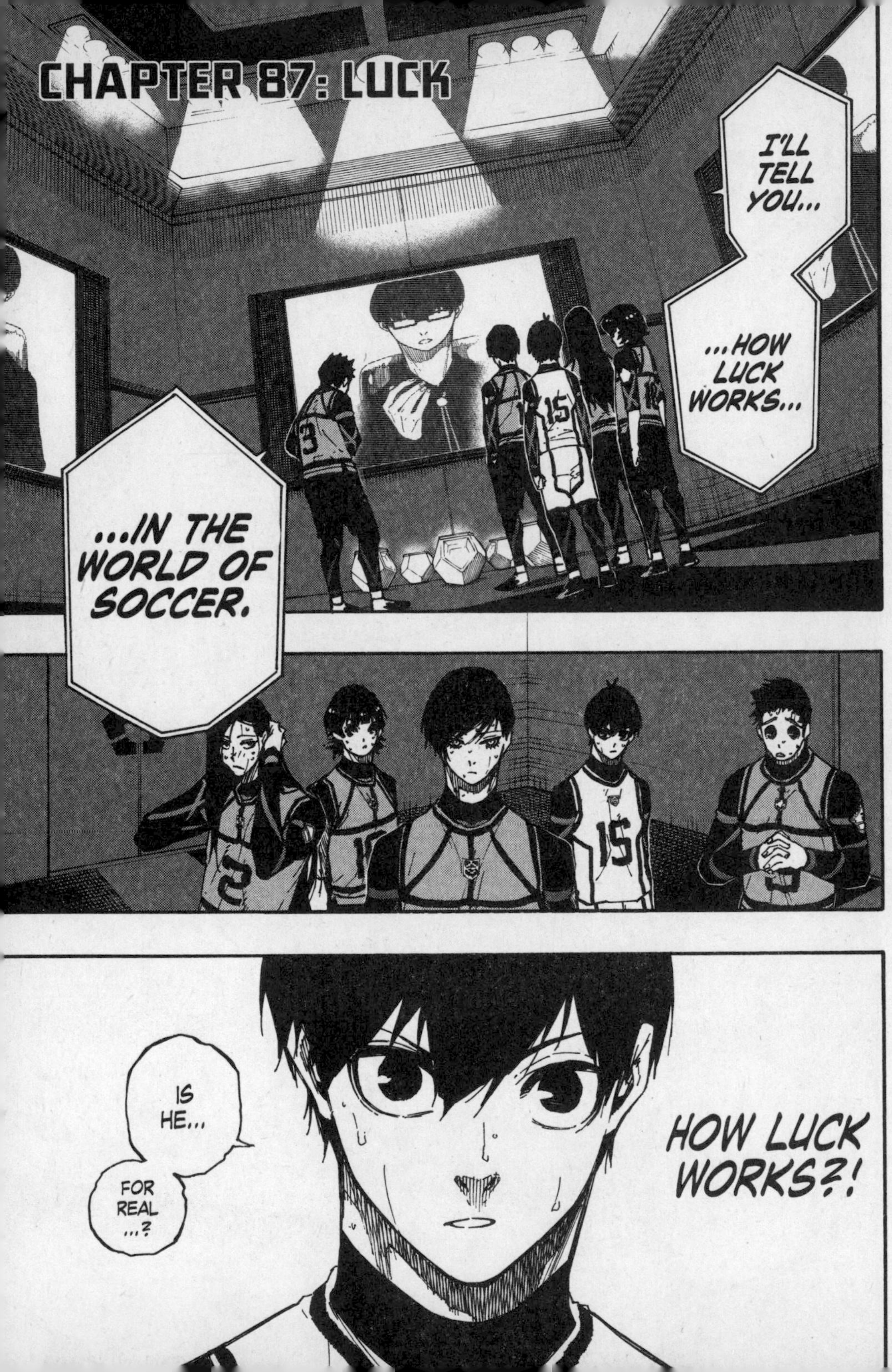
CHAPTER 87: LUCK
I'LL TELL YOU...
...HOW LUCK WORKS...
...IN THE WORLD OF SOCCER.
HOW LUCK WORKS?!
IS HE...
FOR REAL ...?

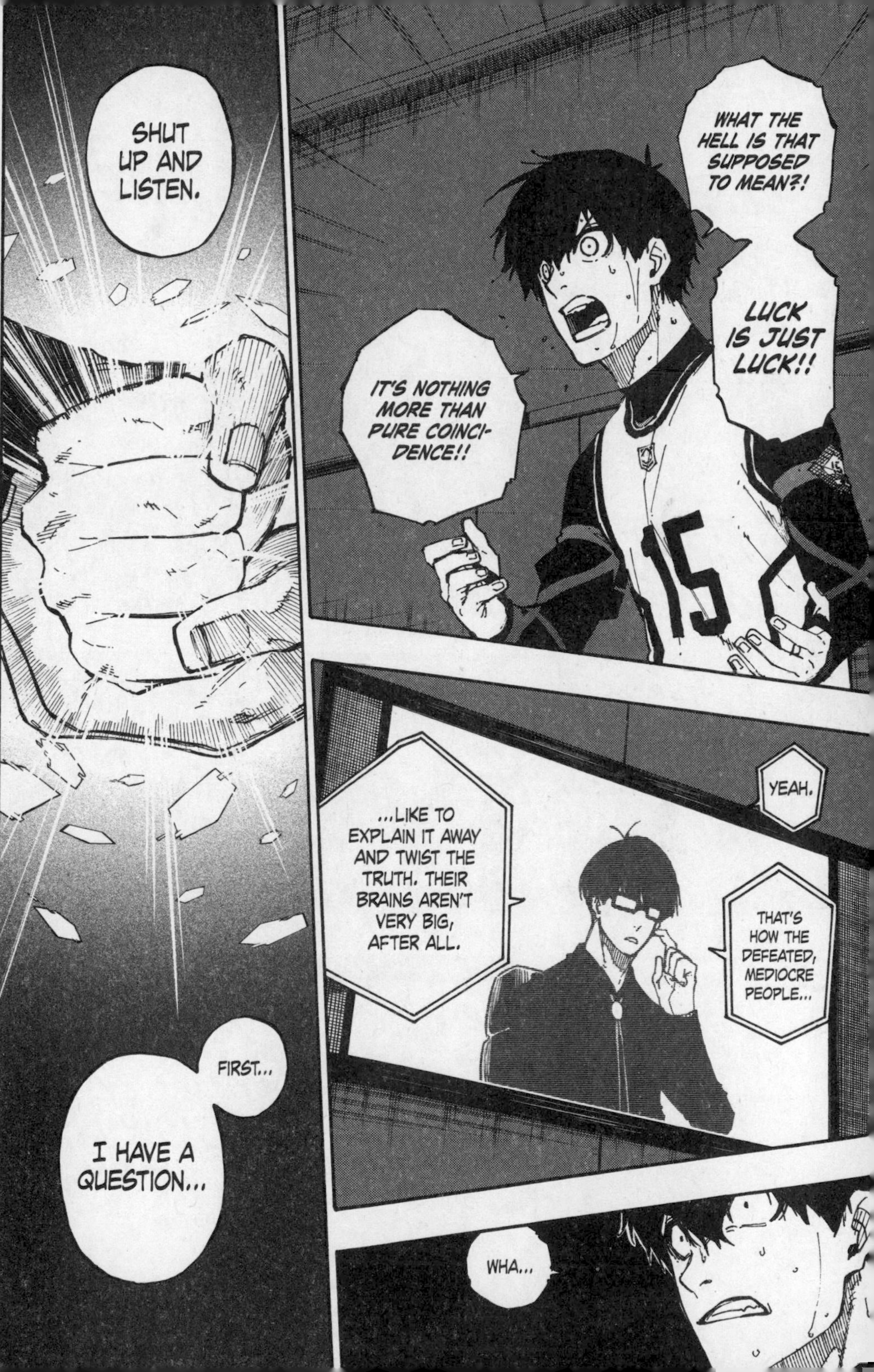
WHAT THE HELL IS THAT SUPPOSED TO MEAN?!
LUCK IS JUST LUCK!!
IT'S NOTHING MORE THAN PURE COINCI-DENCE!!
YEAH.
THAT'S HOW THE DEFEATED, MEDIOCRE PEOPLE...
...LIKE TO EXPLAIN IT AWAY AND TWIST THE TRUTH. THEIR BRAINS AREN'T VERY BIG, AFTER ALL.
WHA...
SHUT UP AND LISTEN.
FIRST...
I HAVE A QUESTION...

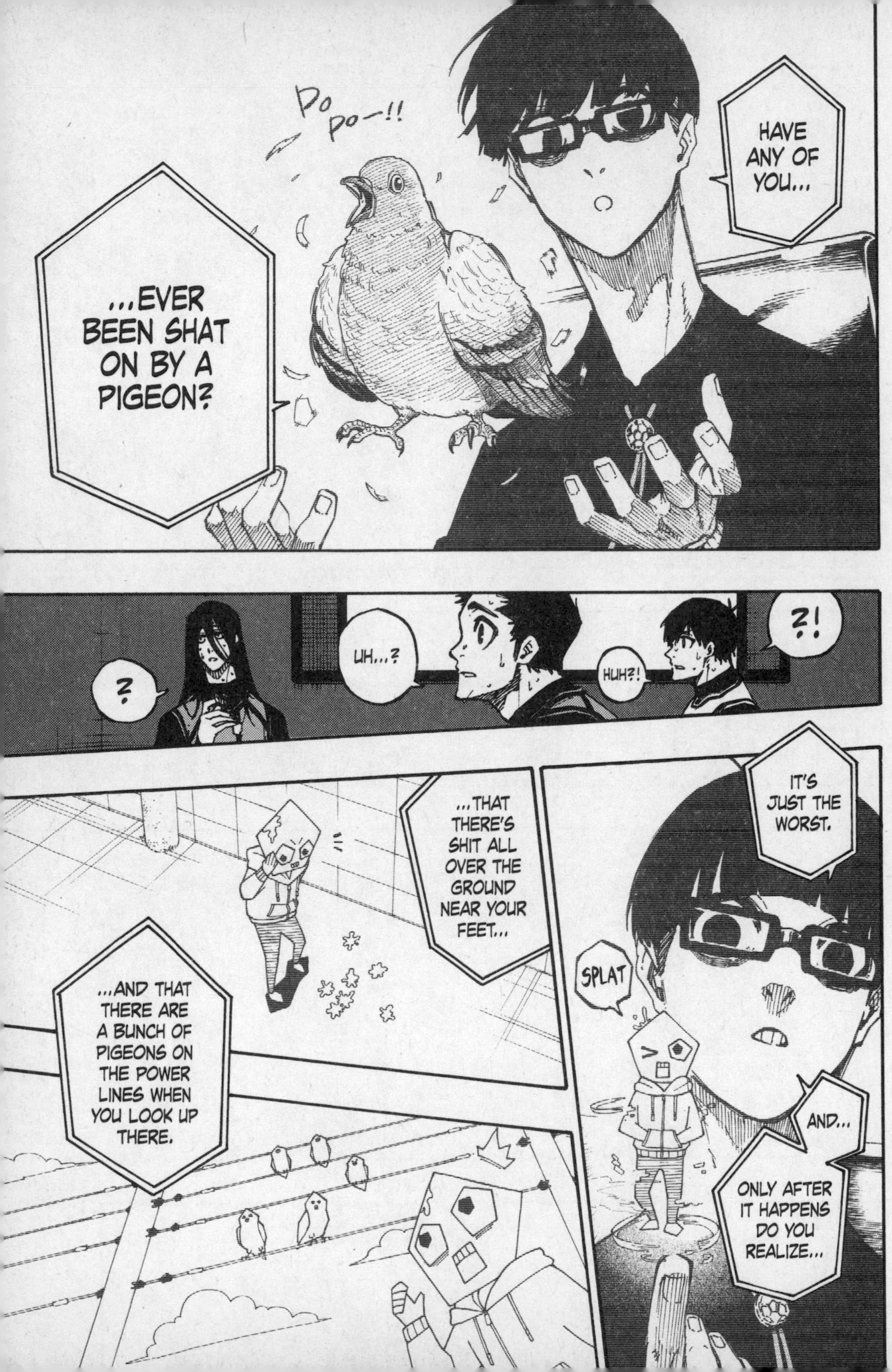
HAVE ANY OF YOU...
Do po—!!
...EVER BEEN SHAT ON BY A PIGEON?
?!
HUH?!
UH...?
?
IT'S JUST THE WORST.
SPLAT
AND...
ONLY AFTER IT HAPPENS DO YOU REALIZE...
...THAT THERE'S SHIT ALL OVER THE GROUND NEAR YOUR FEET...
...AND THAT THERE ARE A BUNCH OF PIGEONS ON THE POWER LINES WHEN YOU LOOK UP THERE.

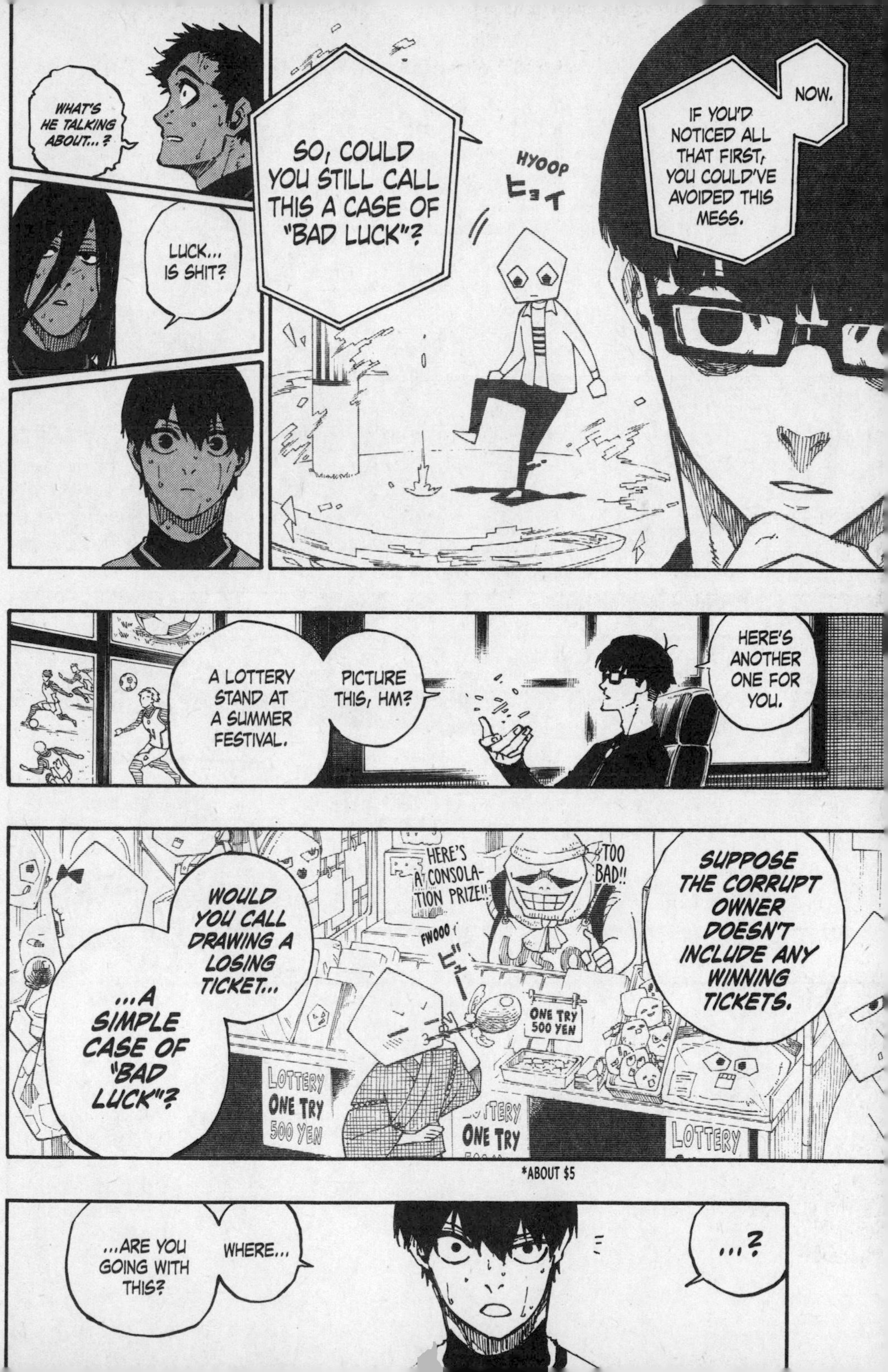
NOW.
IF YOU'D NOTICED ALL THAT FIRST, YOU COULD'VE AVOIDED THIS MESS.
HYOOP
ヒョイ
SO, COULD YOU STILL CALL THIS A CASE OF "BAD LUCK"?
WHAT'S HE TALKING ABOUT...?
LUCK... IS SHIT?
HERE'S ANOTHER ONE FOR YOU.
PICTURE THIS, HM?
A LOTTERY STAND AT A SUMMER FESTIVAL.
SUPPOSE THE CORRUPT OWNER DOESN'T INCLUDE ANY WINNING TICKETS.
TOO BAD!!
HERE'S A CONSOLATION PRIZE!!
ONE TRY 500 YEN
FWOOO
ピー
WOULD YOU CALL DRAWING A LOSING TICKET...
...A SIMPLE CASE OF "BAD LUCK"?
LOTTERY ONE TRY 500 YEN
LOTTERY ONE TRY
LOTTERY
*ABOUT $5
...?
WHERE...
...ARE YOU GOING WITH THIS?

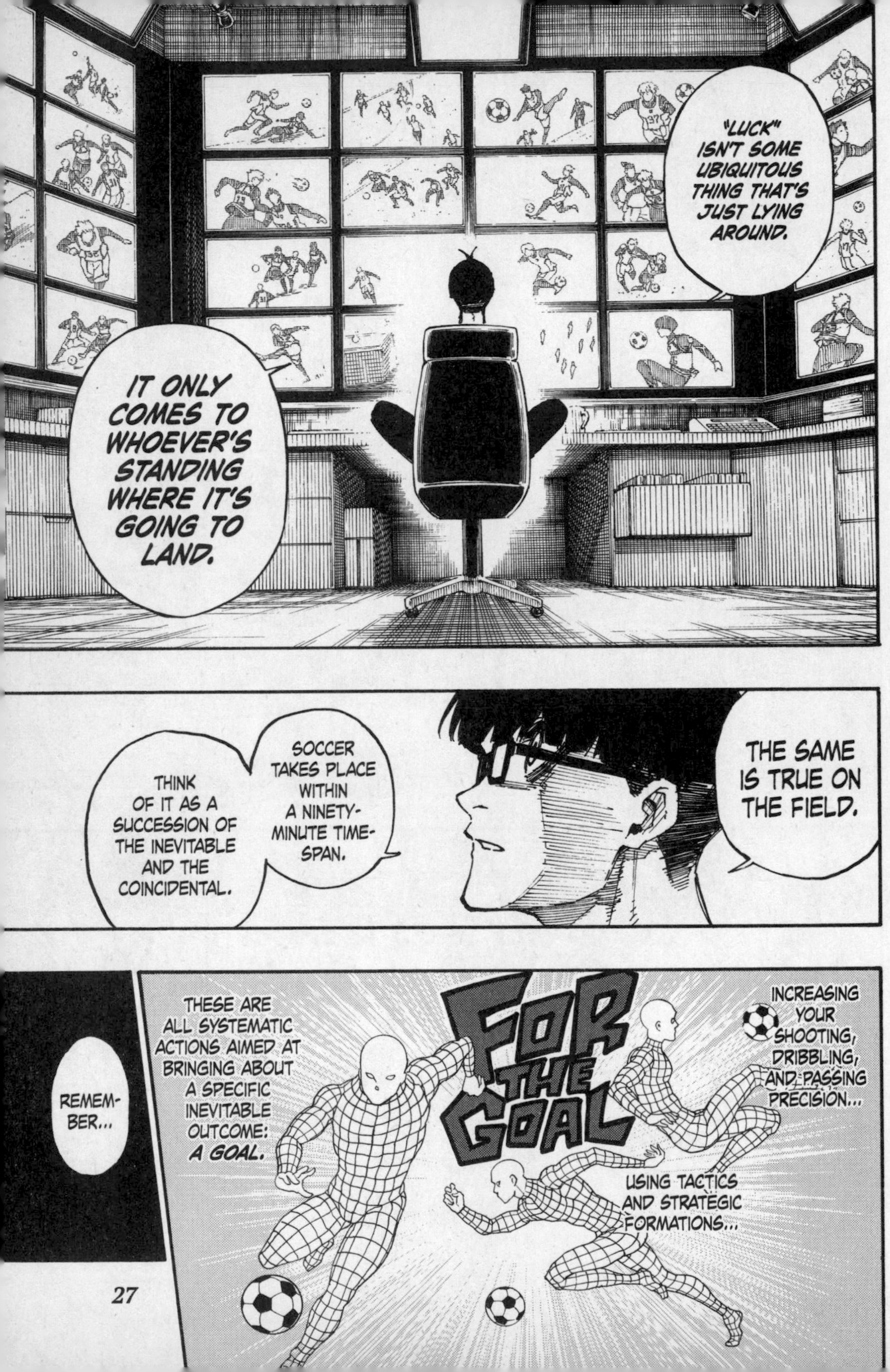
"LUCK" ISN'T SOME UBIQUITOUS THING THAT'S JUST LYING AROUND.
IT ONLY COMES TO WHOEVER'S STANDING WHERE IT'S GOING TO LAND.
THE SAME IS TRUE ON THE FIELD.
SOCCER TAKES PLACE WITHIN A NINETY-MINUTE TIME-SPAN.
THINK OF IT AS A SUCCESSION OF THE INEVITABLE AND THE COINCIDENTAL.
INCREASING YOUR SHOOTING, DRIBBLING, AND PASSING PRECISION...
FOR THE GOAL
USING TACTICS AND STRATEGIC FORMATIONS...
THESE ARE ALL SYSTEMATIC ACTIONS AIMED AT BRINGING ABOUT A SPECIFIC INEVITABLE OUTCOME: *A GOAL.*
REMEMBER...

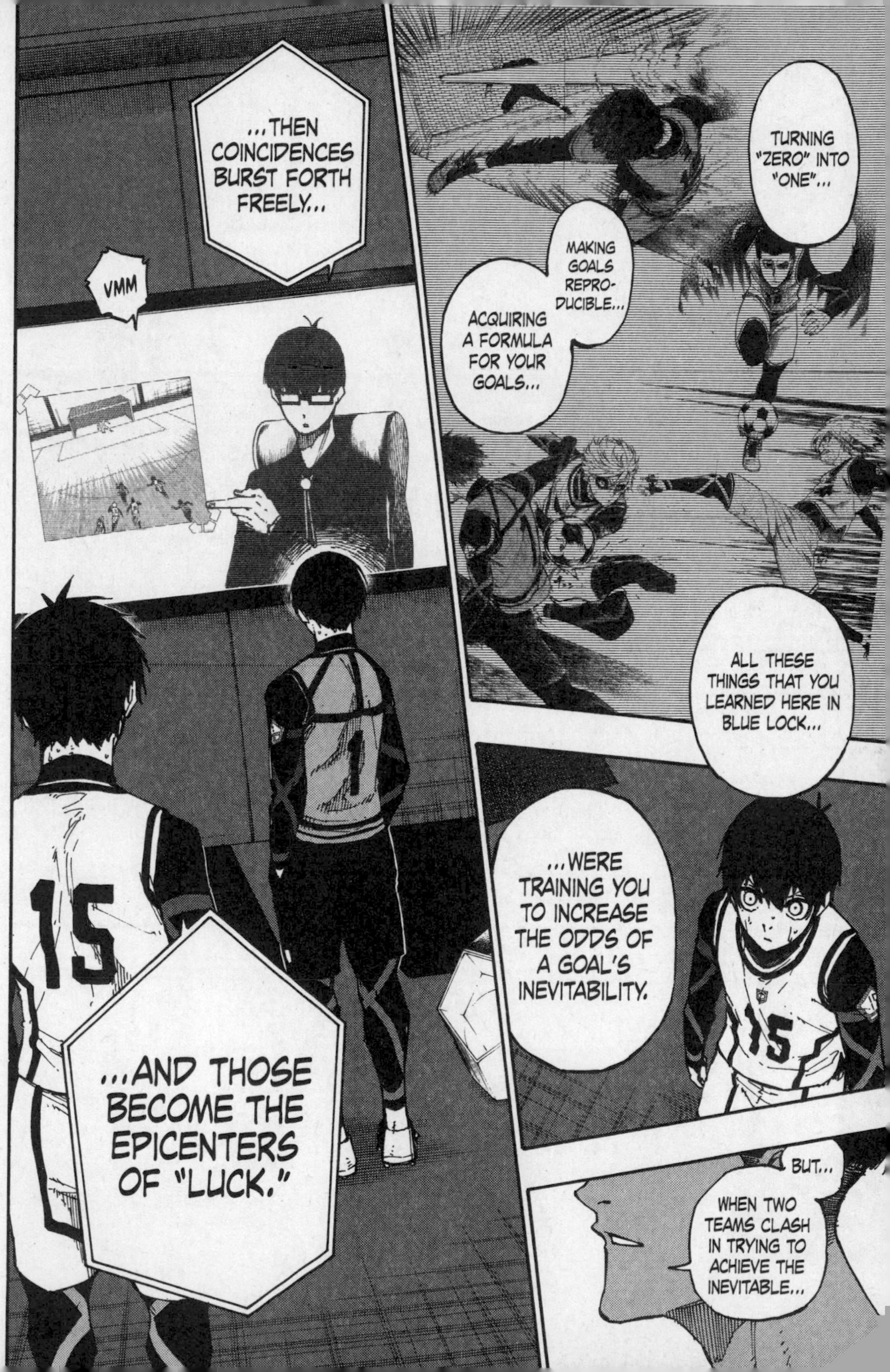
TURNING "ZERO" INTO "ONE"...
MAKING GOALS REPRO-DUCIBLE...
ACQUIRING A FORMULA FOR YOUR GOALS...
ALL THESE THINGS THAT YOU LEARNED HERE IN BLUE LOCK...
...WERE TRAINING YOU TO INCREASE THE ODDS OF A GOAL'S INEVITABILITY.
BUT...
WHEN TWO TEAMS CLASH IN TRYING TO ACHIEVE THE INEVITABLE...
...THEN COINCIDENCES BURST FORTH FREELY...
VMM
...AND THOSE BECOME THE EPICENTERS OF "LUCK."

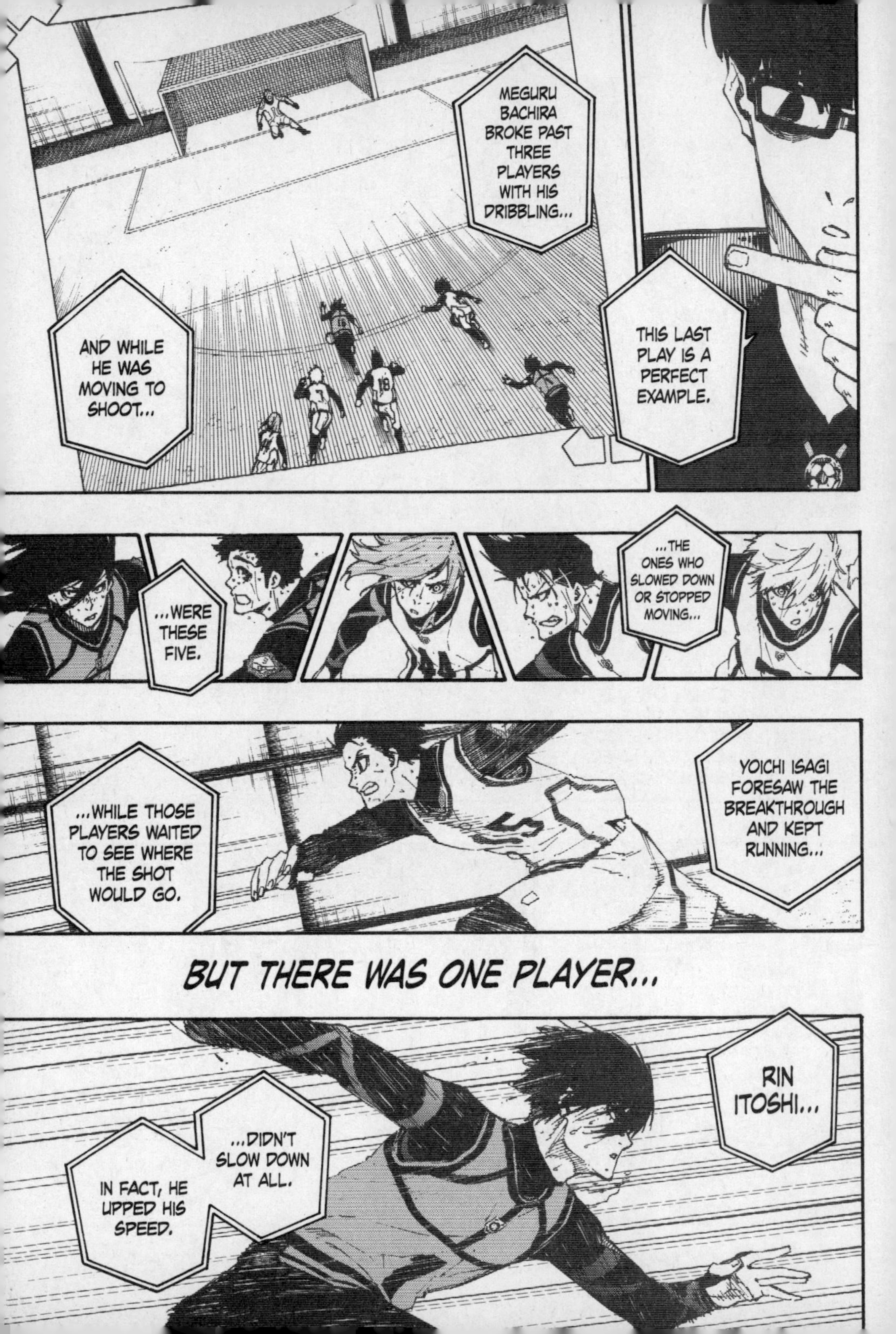
THIS LAST PLAY IS A PERFECT EXAMPLE.
MEGURU BACHIRA BROKE PAST THREE PLAYERS WITH HIS DRIBBLING...
AND WHILE HE WAS MOVING TO SHOOT...
...THE ONES WHO SLOWED DOWN OR STOPPED MOVING...
...WERE THESE FIVE.
YOICHI ISAGI FORESAW THE BREAKTHROUGH AND KEPT RUNNING...
...WHILE THOSE PLAYERS WAITED TO SEE WHERE THE SHOT WOULD GO.
BUT THERE WAS ONE PLAYER...
RIN ITOSHI...
...DIDN'T SLOW DOWN AT ALL.
IN FACT, HE UPPED HIS SPEED.

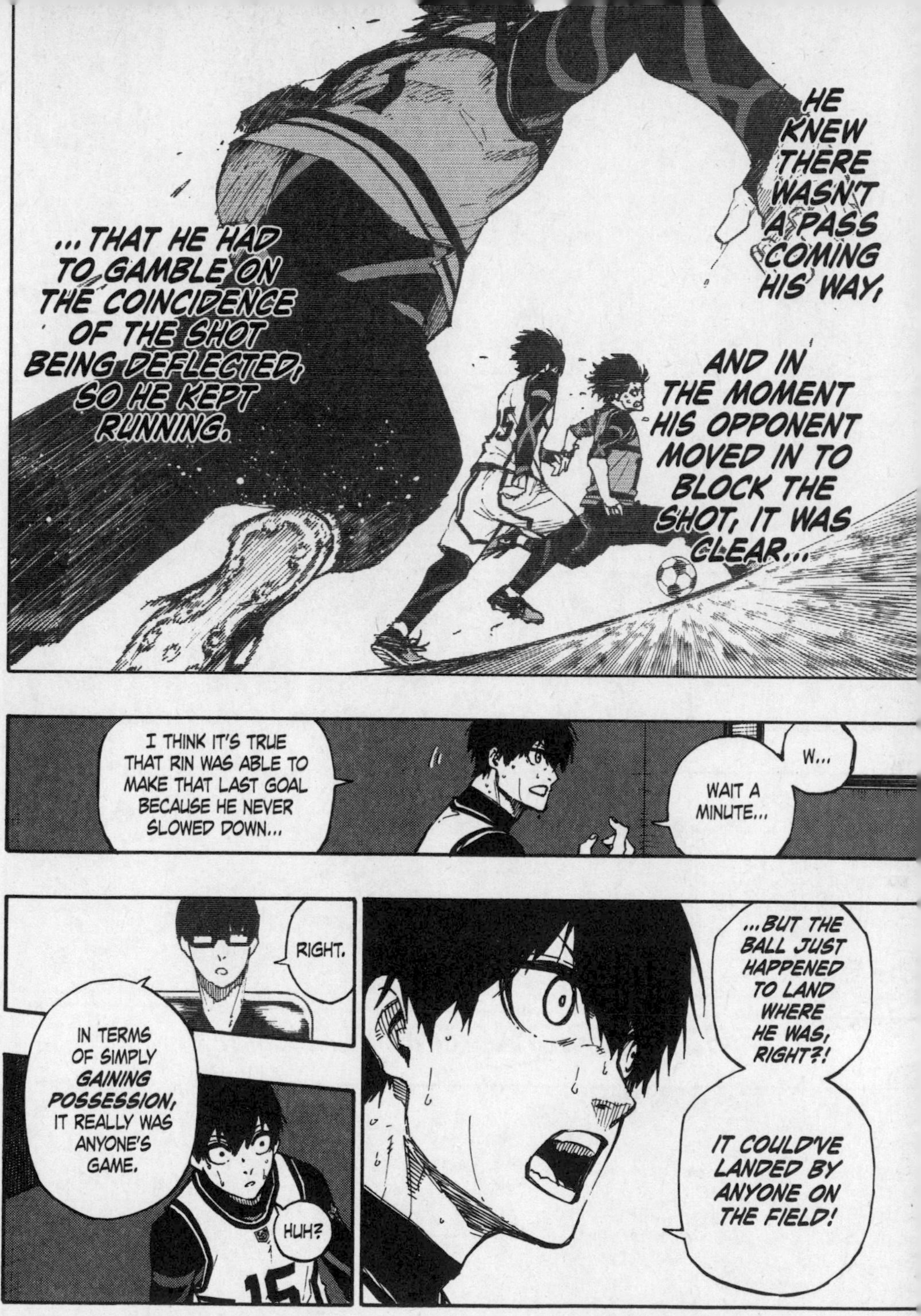
HE KNEW THERE WASN'T A PASS COMING HIS WAY,
AND IN THE MOMENT HIS OPPONENT MOVED IN TO BLOCK THE SHOT, IT WAS CLEAR...
...THAT HE HAD TO GAMBLE ON THE COINCIDENCE OF THE SHOT BEING DEFLECTED, SO HE KEPT RUNNING.
W...
WAIT A MINUTE...
I THINK IT'S TRUE THAT RIN WAS ABLE TO MAKE THAT LAST GOAL BECAUSE HE NEVER SLOWED DOWN...
...BUT THE BALL JUST HAPPENED TO LAND WHERE HE WAS, RIGHT?!
IT COULD'VE LANDED BY ANYONE ON THE FIELD!
RIGHT.
IN TERMS OF SIMPLY GAINING POSSESSION, IT REALLY WAS ANYONE'S GAME.
HUH?
TO A STRIKER, THAT'S LIKE DRAWING A LOSING TICKET...

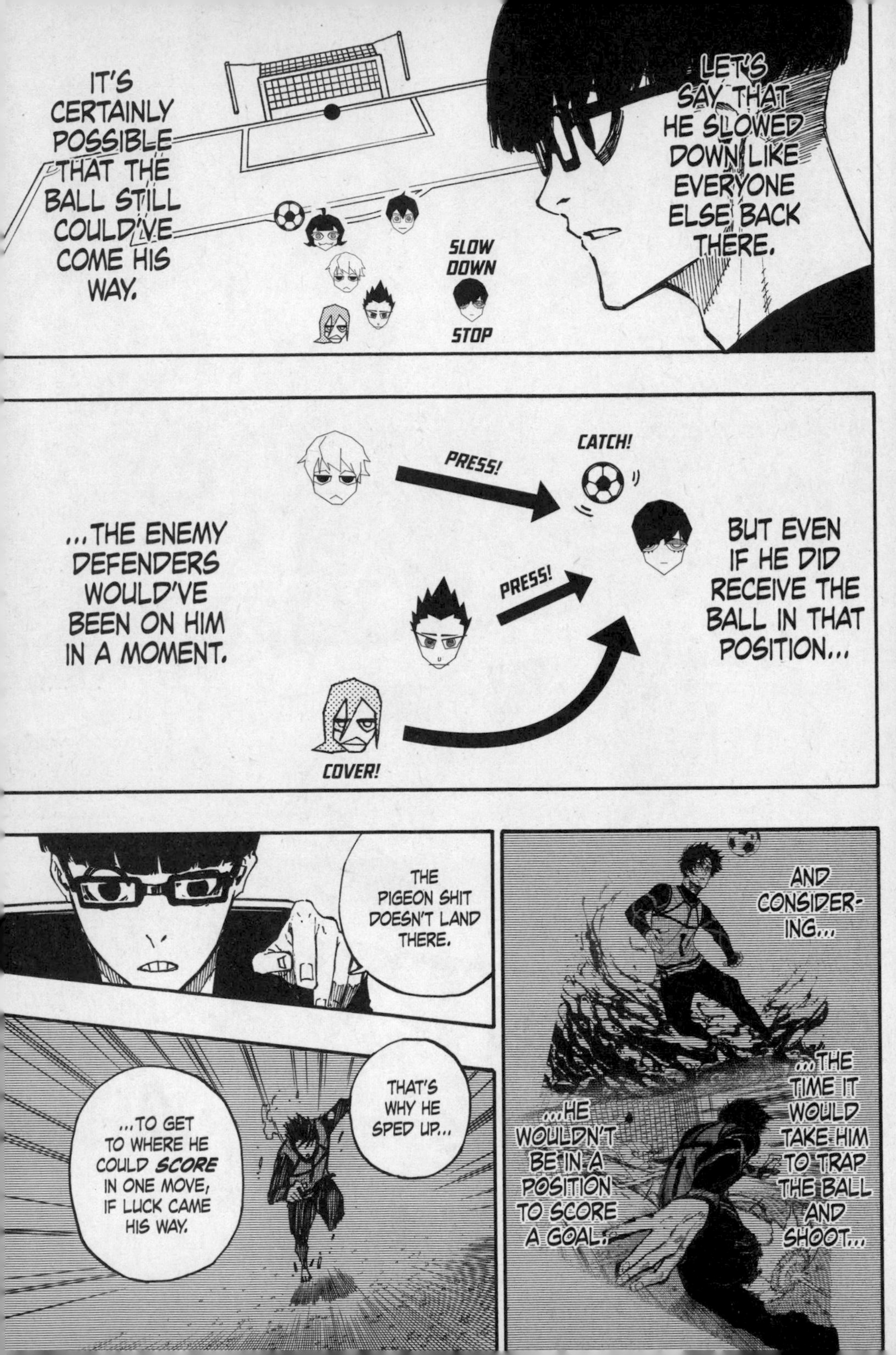

LET'S SAY THAT HE SLOWED DOWN LIKE EVERYONE ELSE BACK THERE.
IT'S CERTAINLY POSSIBLE THAT THE BALL STILL COULD'VE COME HIS WAY.
SLOW DOWN
STOP
BUT EVEN IF HE DID RECEIVE THE BALL IN THAT POSITION...
CATCH!
PRESS!
PRESS!
...THE ENEMY DEFENDERS WOULD'VE BEEN ON HIM IN A MOMENT.
COVER!
AND CONSIDERING...
...THE TIME IT WOULD TAKE HIM TO TRAP THE BALL AND SHOOT...
...HE WOULDN'T BE IN A POSITION TO SCORE A GOAL.
THE PIGEON SHIT DOESN'T LAND THERE.
THAT'S WHY HE SPED UP...
...TO GET TO WHERE HE COULD SCORE IN ONE MOVE, IF LUCK CAME HIS WAY.

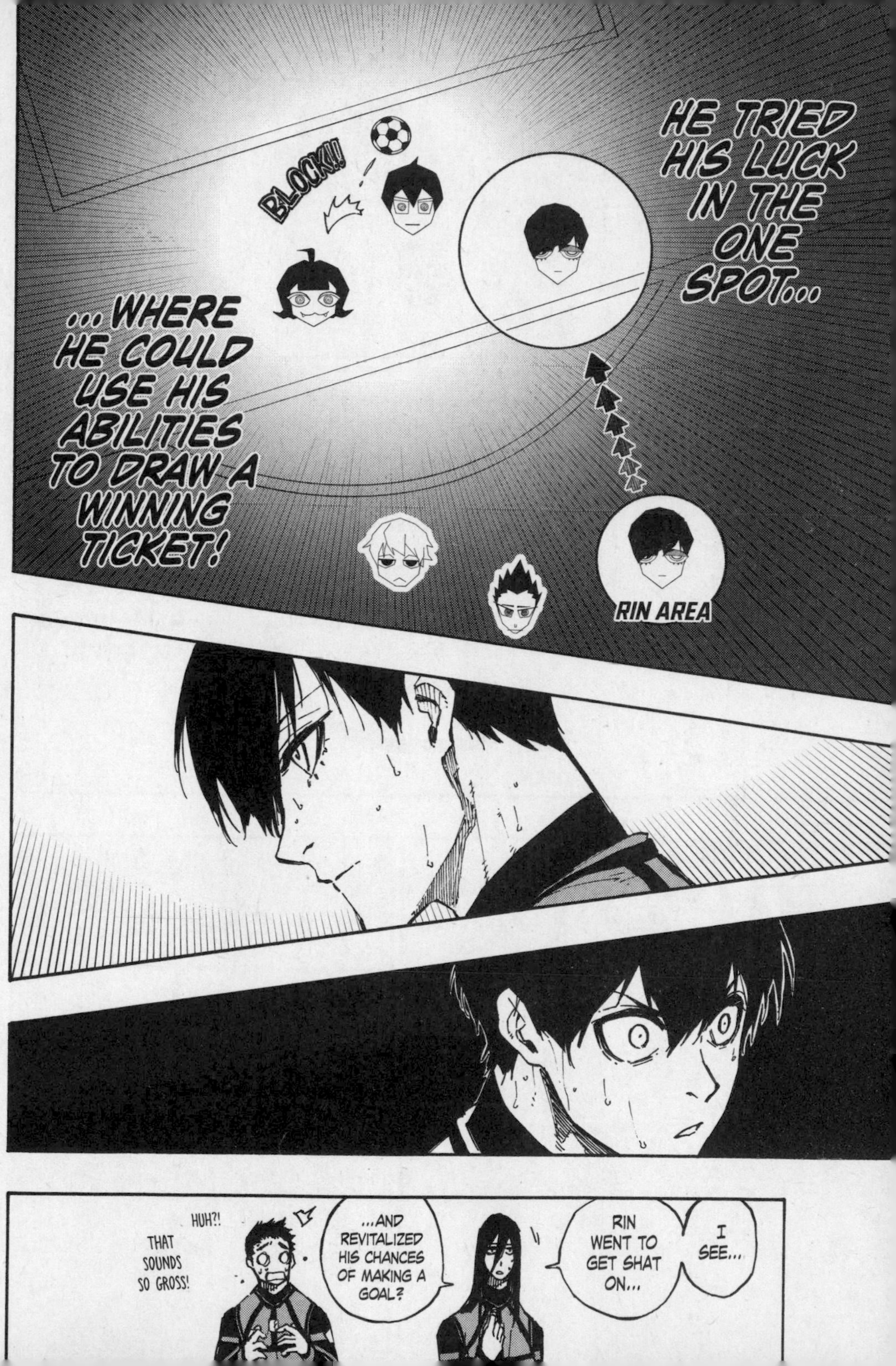
HE TRIED HIS LUCK IN THE ONE SPOT...
BLOCK!!
...WHERE HE COULD USE HIS ABILITIES TO DRAW A WINNING TICKET!
RIN AREA
I SEE...
RIN WENT TO GET SHAT ON...
...AND REVITALIZED HIS CHANCES OF MAKING A GOAL?
HUH?!
THAT SOUNDS SO GROSS!

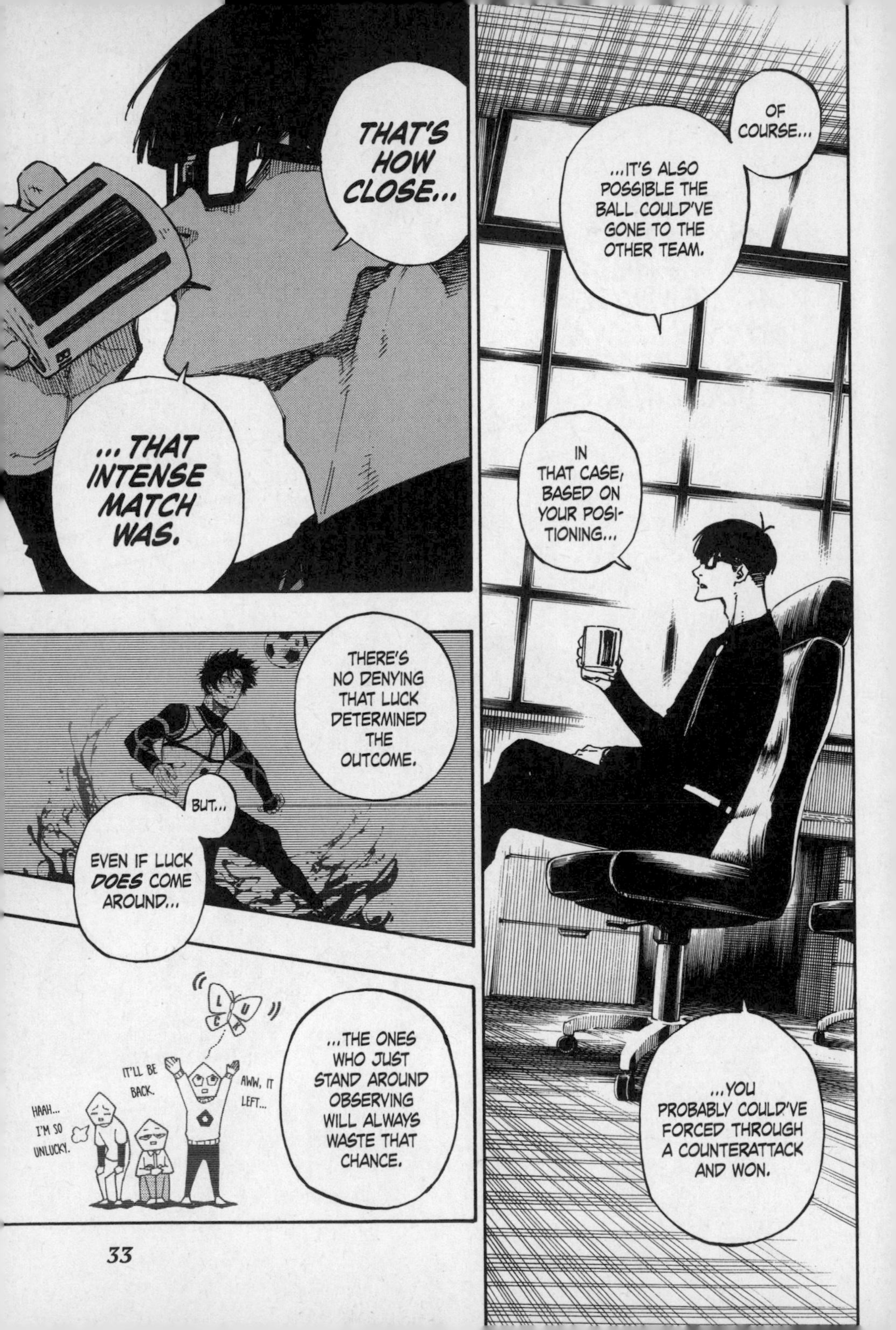

OF COURSE...
...IT'S ALSO POSSIBLE THE BALL COULD'VE GONE TO THE OTHER TEAM.
IN THAT CASE, BASED ON YOUR POSITIONING...
...YOU PROBABLY COULD'VE FORCED THROUGH A COUNTERATTACK AND WON.
THAT'S HOW CLOSE...
...THAT INTENSE MATCH WAS.
THERE'S NO DENYING THAT LUCK DETERMINED THE OUTCOME.
BUT...
EVEN IF LUCK DOES COME AROUND...
...THE ONES WHO JUST STAND AROUND OBSERVING WILL ALWAYS WASTE THAT CHANCE.
LUCK
AWW, IT LEFT...
IT'LL BE BACK.
HAAH... I'M SO UNLUCKY.

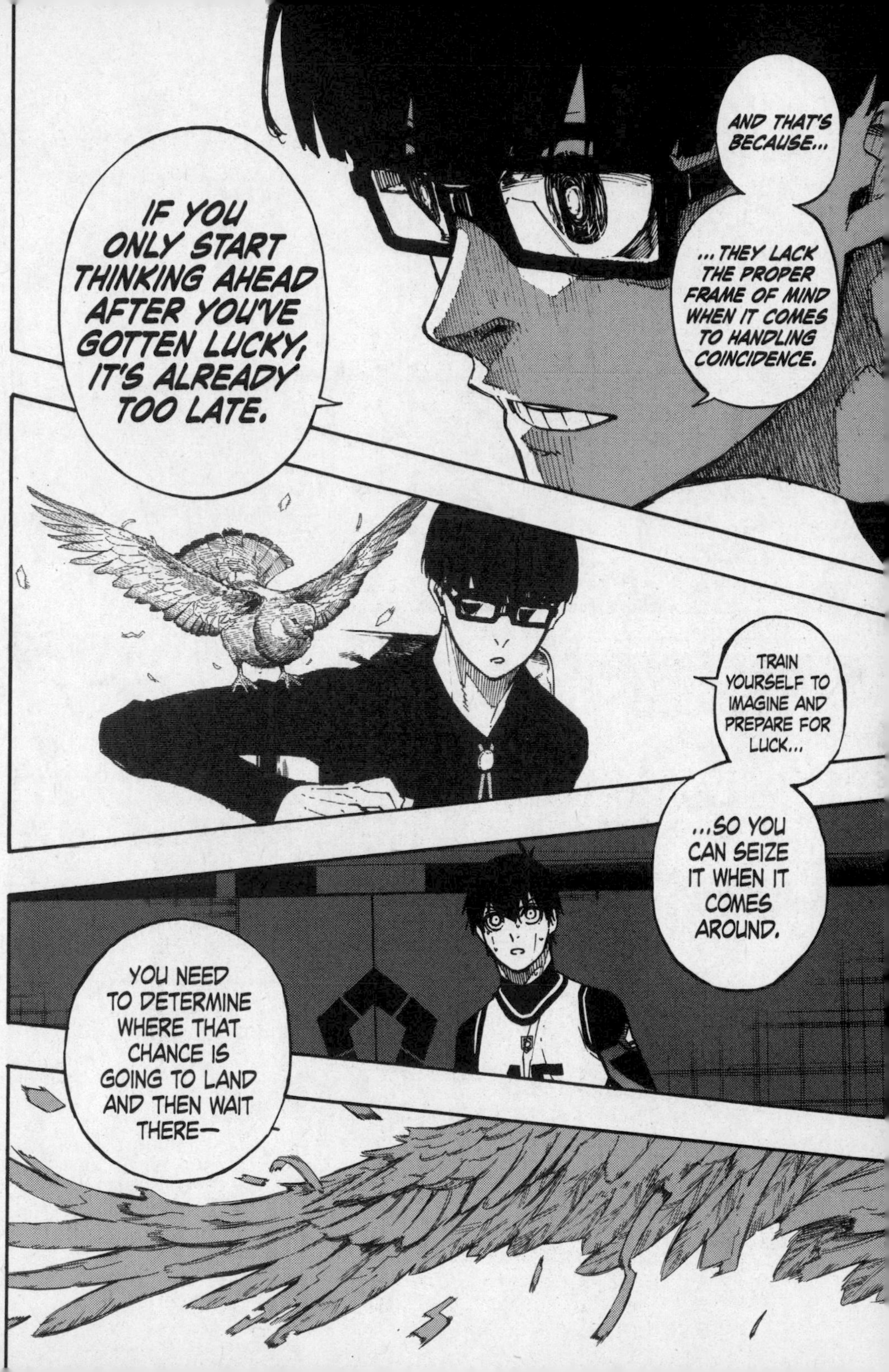
AND THAT'S BECAUSE...
...THEY LACK THE PROPER FRAME OF MIND WHEN IT COMES TO HANDLING COINCIDENCE.
IF YOU ONLY START THINKING AHEAD AFTER YOU'VE GOTTEN LUCKY, IT'S ALREADY TOO LATE.
TRAIN YOURSELF TO IMAGINE AND PREPARE FOR LUCK...
...SO YOU CAN SEIZE IT WHEN IT COMES AROUND.
YOU NEED TO DETERMINE WHERE THAT CHANCE IS GOING TO LAND AND THEN WAIT THERE—

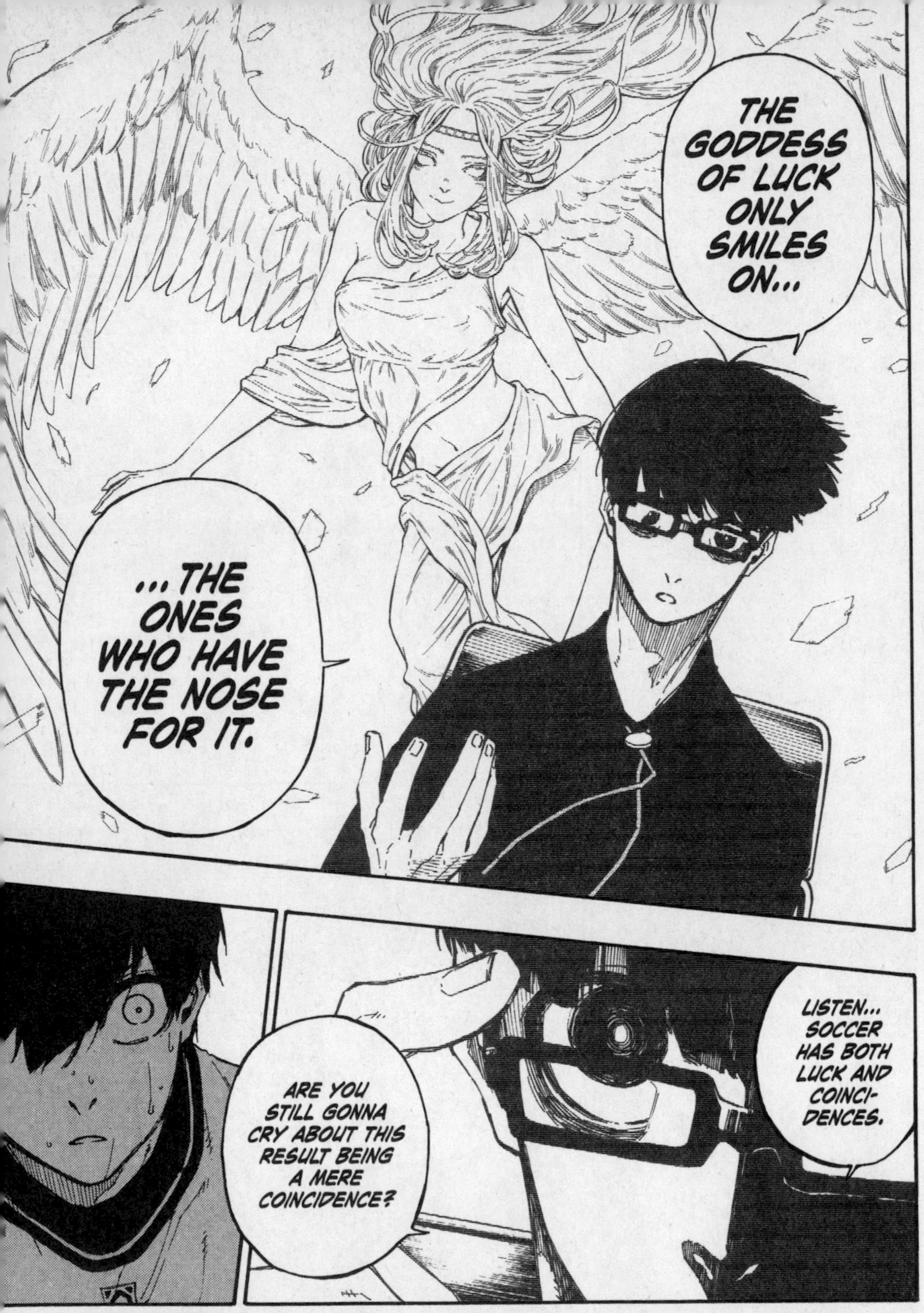
THE GODDESS OF LUCK ONLY SMILES ON...
...THE ONES WHO HAVE THE NOSE FOR IT.
LISTEN... SOCCER HAS BOTH LUCK AND COINCI-DENCES.
ARE YOU STILL GONNA CRY ABOUT THIS RESULT BEING A MERE COINCIDENCE?
YOU'RE STILL JUST SECOND-RATE AS LONG AS YOU'RE AT THE MERCY OF LUCK...

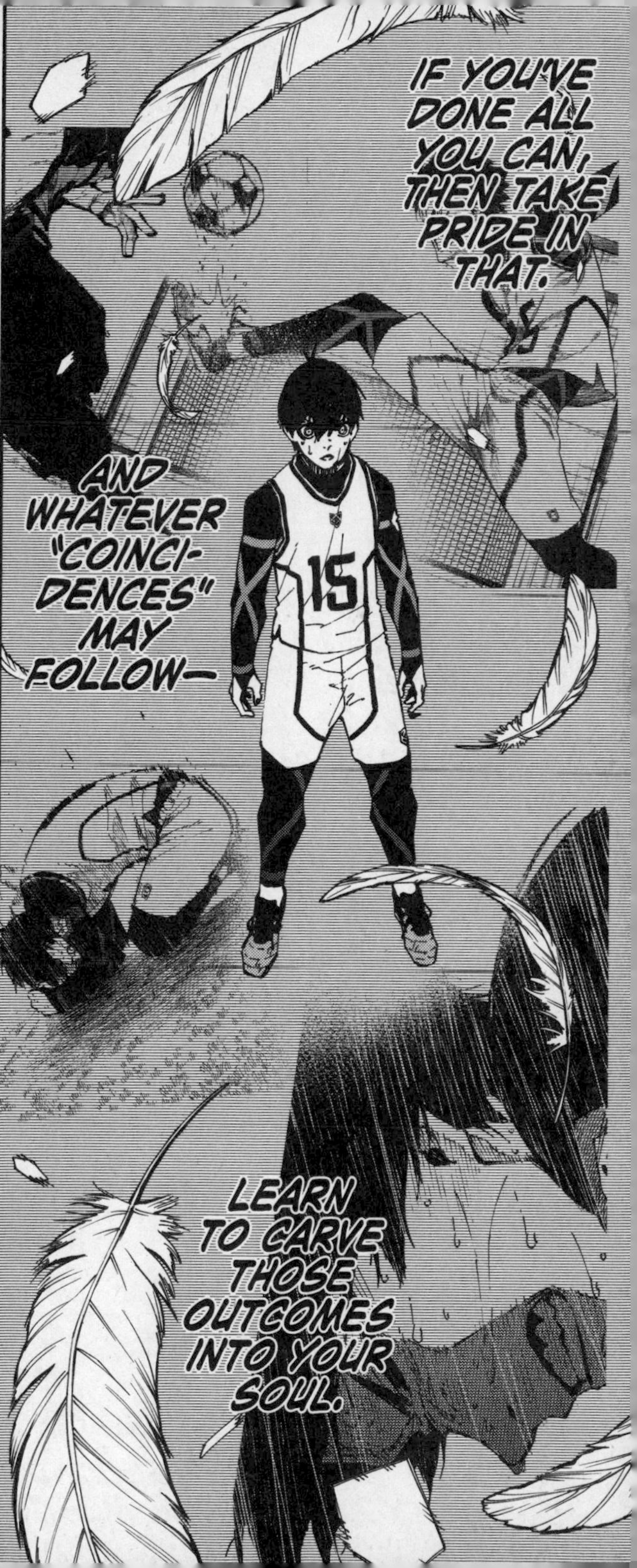
IF YOU'VE DONE ALL YOU CAN, THEN TAKE PRIDE IN THAT.
AND WHATEVER "COINCIDENCES" MAY FOLLOW—
LEARN TO CARVE THOSE OUTCOMES INTO YOUR SOUL.
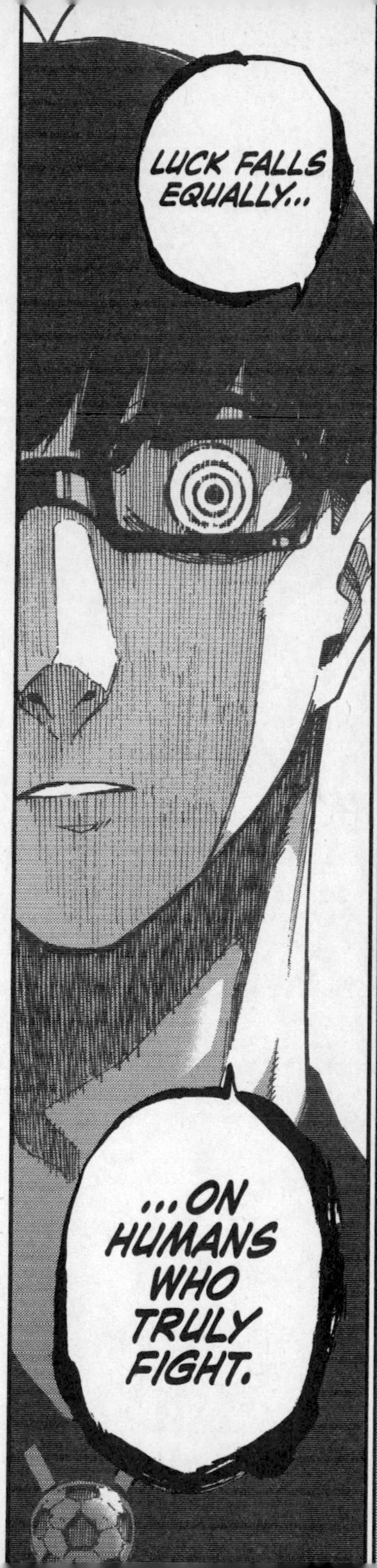
LUCK FALLS EQUALLY...
...ON HUMANS WHO TRULY FIGHT.

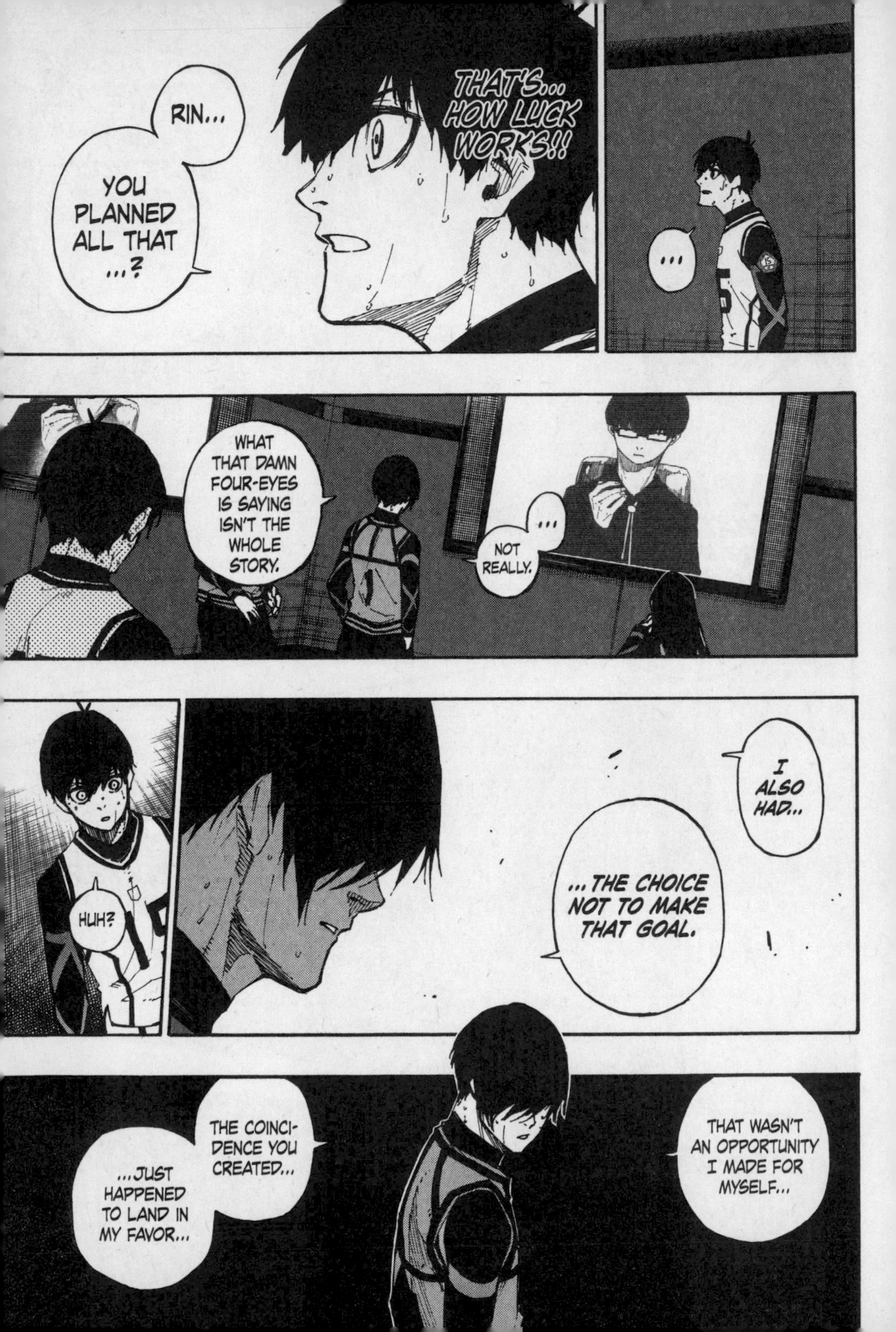
...
THAT'S... HOW LUCK WORKS!!
RIN...
YOU PLANNED ALL THAT ...?
...
NOT REALLY.
WHAT THAT DAMN FOUR-EYES IS SAYING ISN'T THE WHOLE STORY.
I ALSO HAD...
...THE CHOICE NOT TO MAKE THAT GOAL.
HUH?
THAT WASN'T AN OPPORTUNITY I MADE FOR MYSELF...
THE COINCI-DENCE YOU CREATED...
...JUST HAPPENED TO LAND IN MY FAVOR...

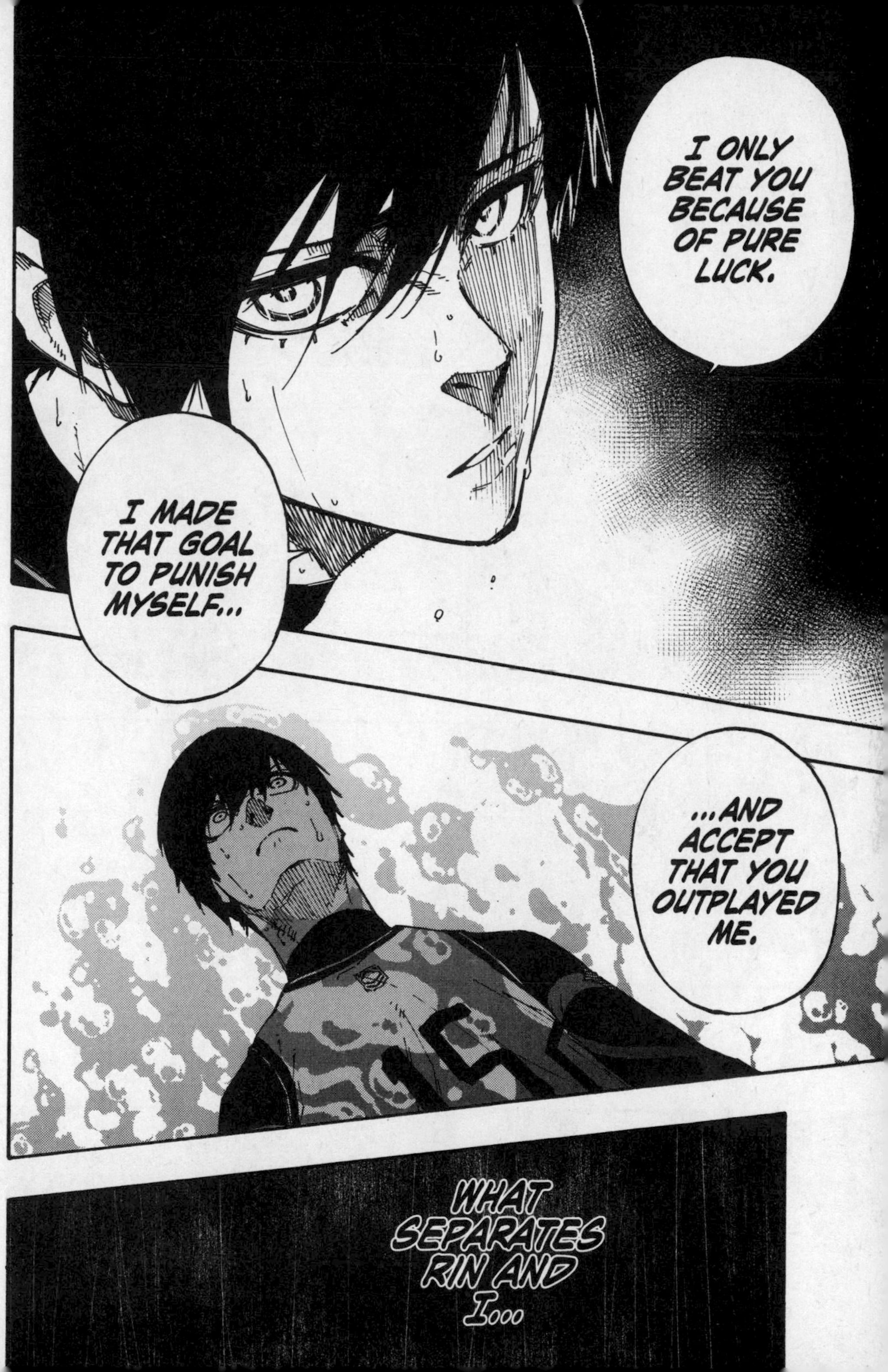
I ONLY BEAT YOU BECAUSE OF PURE LUCK.
I MADE THAT GOAL TO PUNISH MYSELF...
...AND ACCEPT THAT YOU OUTPLAYED ME.
WHAT SEPARATES RIN AND I...

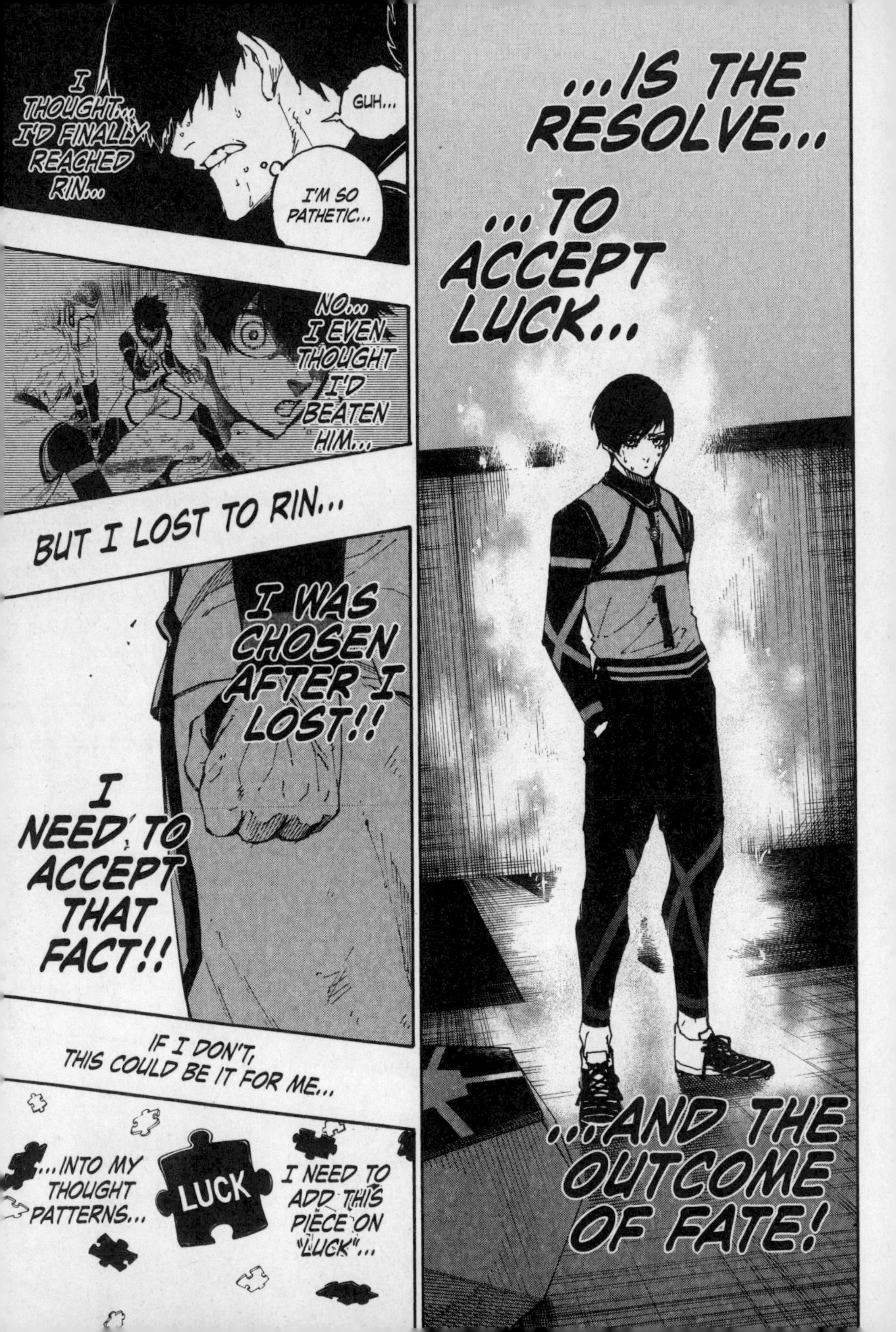
...IS THE RESOLVE...
...TO ACCEPT LUCK...
...AND THE OUTCOME OF FATE!
GUH...
I'M SO PATHETIC...
I THOUGHT... I'D FINALLY REACHED RIN...
NO... I EVEN THOUGHT I'D BEATEN HIM...
BUT I LOST TO RIN...
I WAS CHOSEN AFTER I LOST!!
I NEED TO ACCEPT THAT FACT!!
IF I DON'T, THIS COULD BE IT FOR ME...
I NEED TO ADD THIS PIECE ON "LUCK"...
LUCK
...INTO MY THOUGHT PATTERNS...

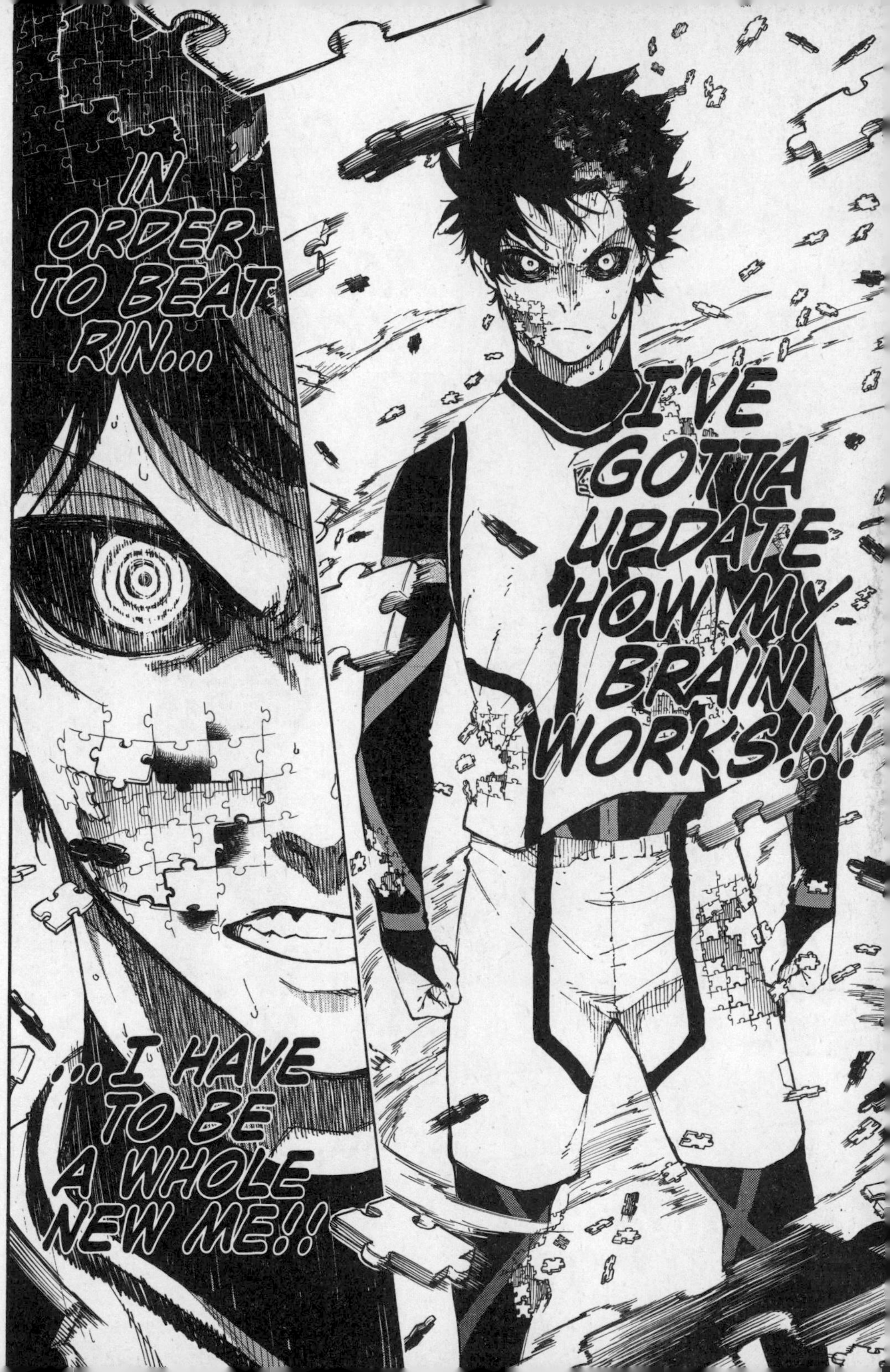
I'VE GOTTA UPDATE HOW MY BRAIN WORKS!!!
IN ORDER TO BEAT RIN...
...I HAVE TO BE A WHOLE NEW ME!!

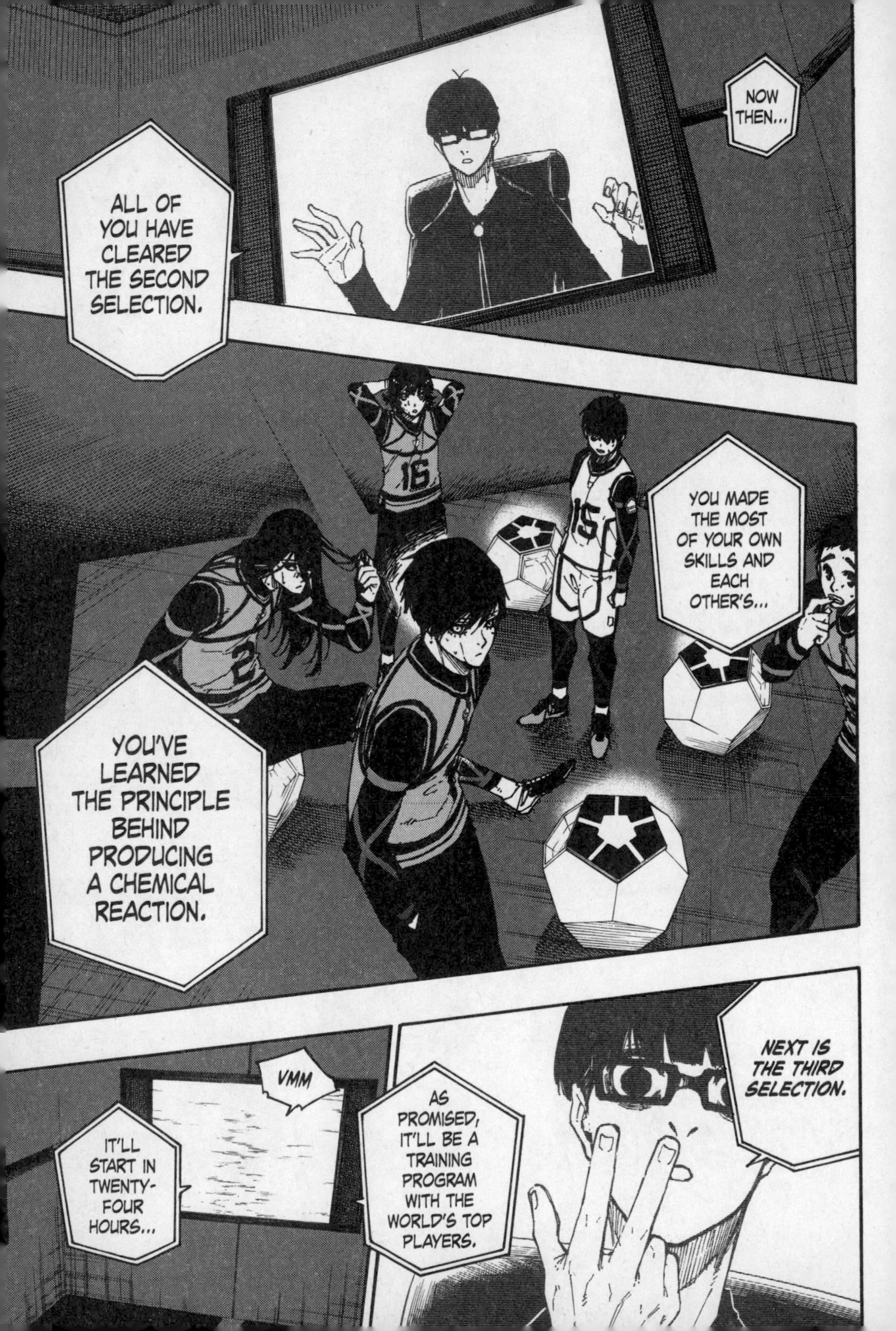
NOW THEN...
ALL OF YOU HAVE CLEARED THE SECOND SELECTION.
YOU MADE THE MOST OF YOUR OWN SKILLS AND EACH OTHER'S...
YOU'VE LEARNED THE PRINCIPLE BEHIND PRODUCING A CHEMICAL REACTION.
NEXT IS THE THIRD SELECTION.
AS PROMISED, IT'LL BE A TRAINING PROGRAM WITH THE WORLD'S TOP PLAYERS.
VMM
IT'LL START IN TWENTY-FOUR HOURS...

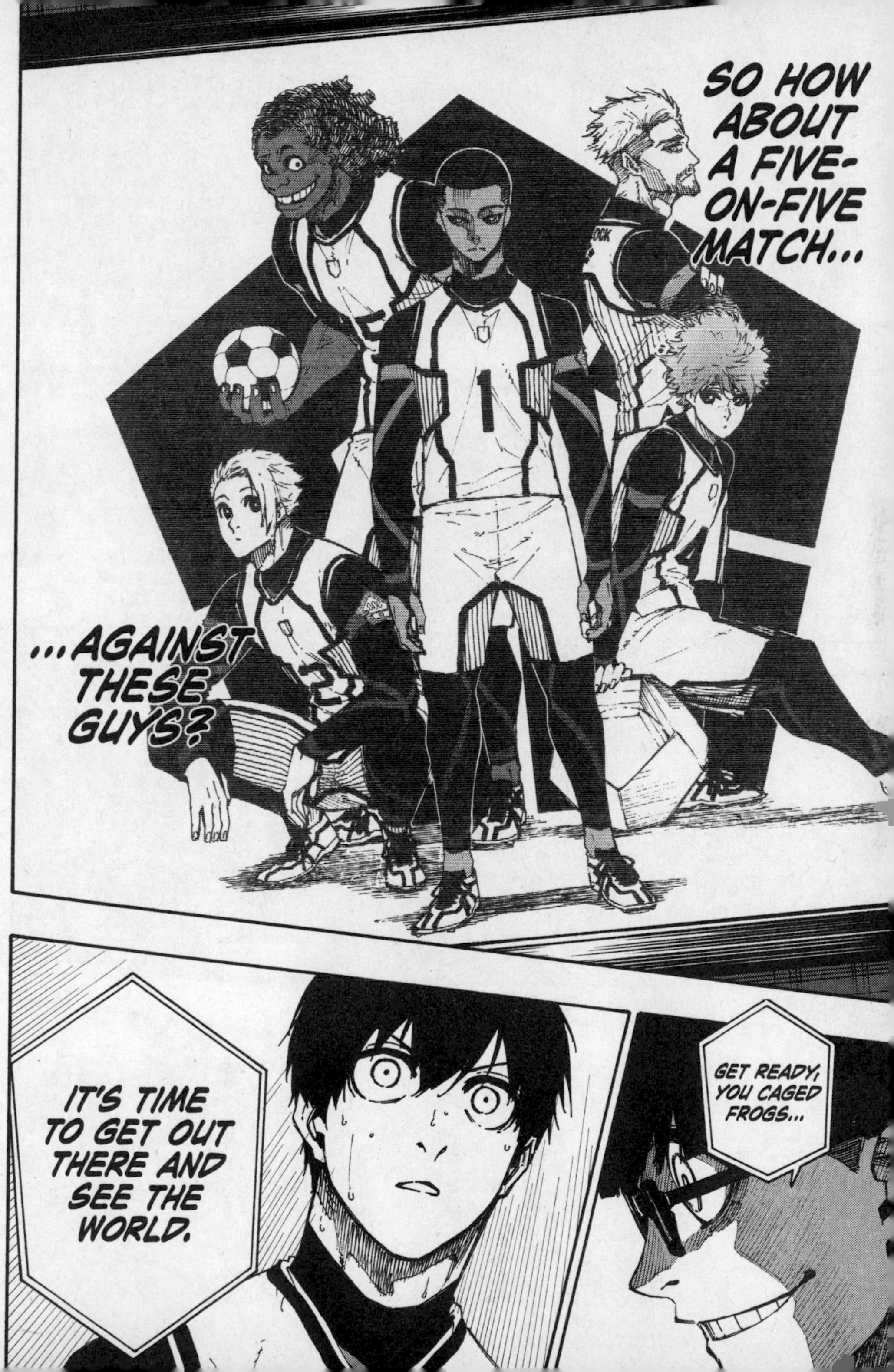
SO HOW ABOUT A FIVE-ON-FIVE MATCH...
...AGAINST THESE GUYS?
GET READY, YOU CAGED FROGS...
IT'S TIME TO GET OUT THERE AND SEE THE WORLD.

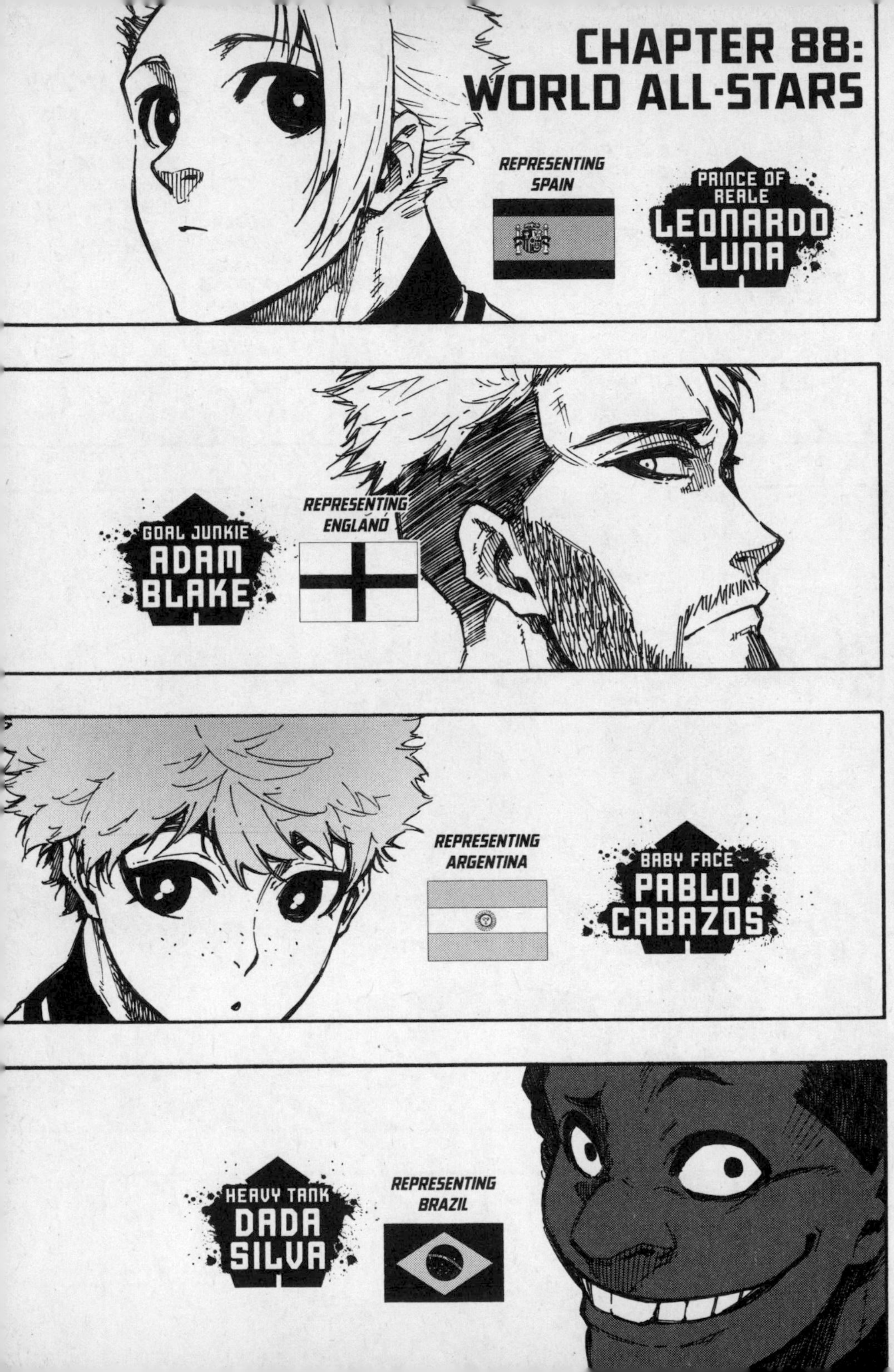
CHAPTER 88: WORLD ALL-STARS
PRINCE OF REALE LEONARDO LUNA
REPRESENTING SPAIN
REPRESENTING ENGLAND
GOAL JUNKIE ADAM BLAKE
BABY FACE PABLO CABAZOS
REPRESENTING ARGENTINA
REPRESENTING BRAZIL
HEAVY TANK DADA SILVA

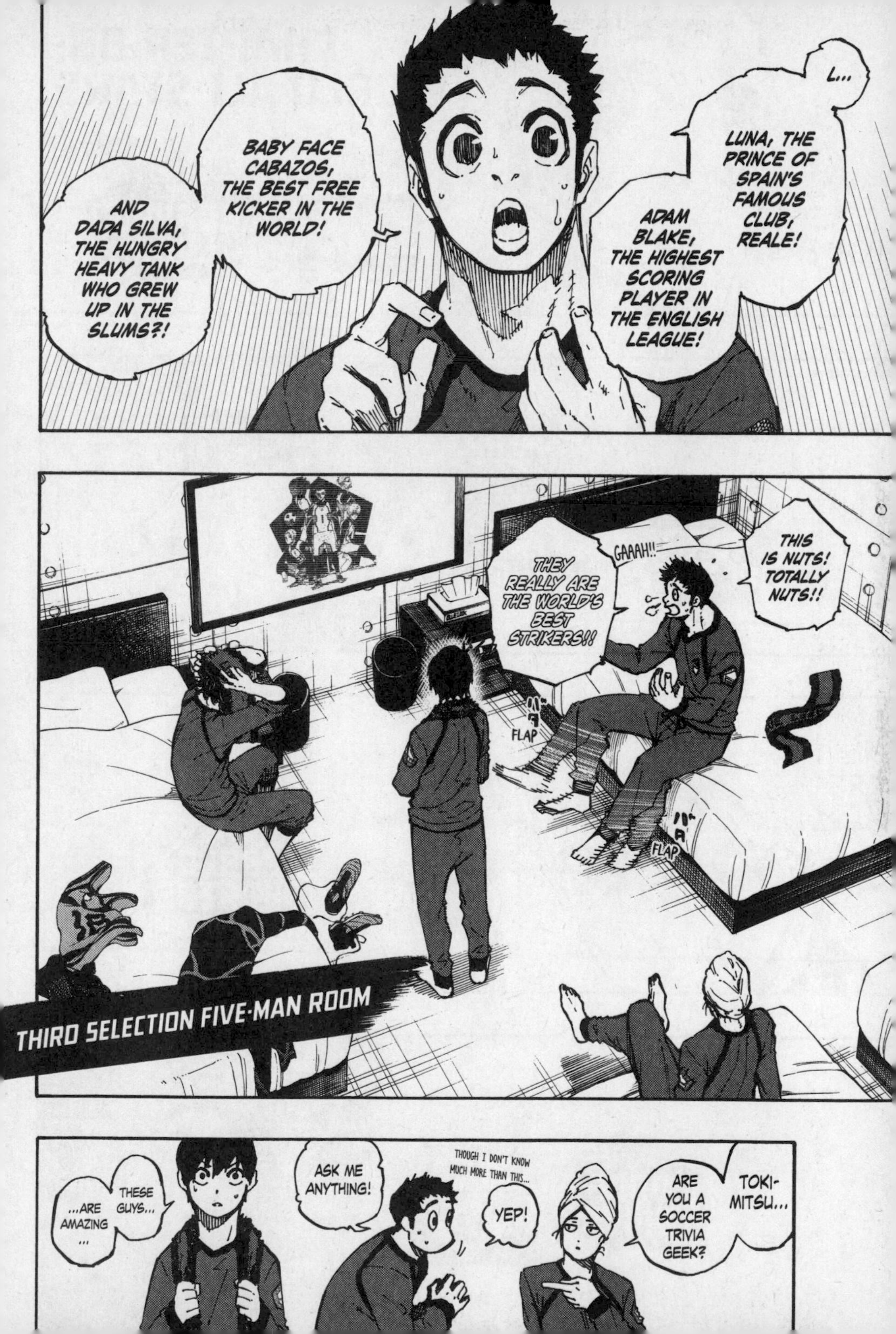
L...
LUNA, THE PRINCE OF SPAIN'S FAMOUS CLUB, REALE!
ADAM BLAKE, THE HIGHEST SCORING PLAYER IN THE ENGLISH LEAGUE!
BABY FACE CABAZOS, THE BEST FREE KICKER IN THE WORLD!
AND DADA SILVA, THE HUNGRY HEAVY TANK WHO GREW UP IN THE SLUMS?!
THIS IS NUTS! TOTALLY NUTS!!
GAAAH!!
THEY REALLY ARE THE WORLD'S BEST STRIKERS!!
FLAP
FLAP
THIRD SELECTION FIVE-MAN ROOM
TOKI-MITSU...
ARE YOU A SOCCER TRIVIA GEEK?
YEP!
THOUGH I DON'T KNOW MUCH MORE THAN THIS...
ASK ME ANYTHING!
THESE GUYS...
...ARE AMAZING ...

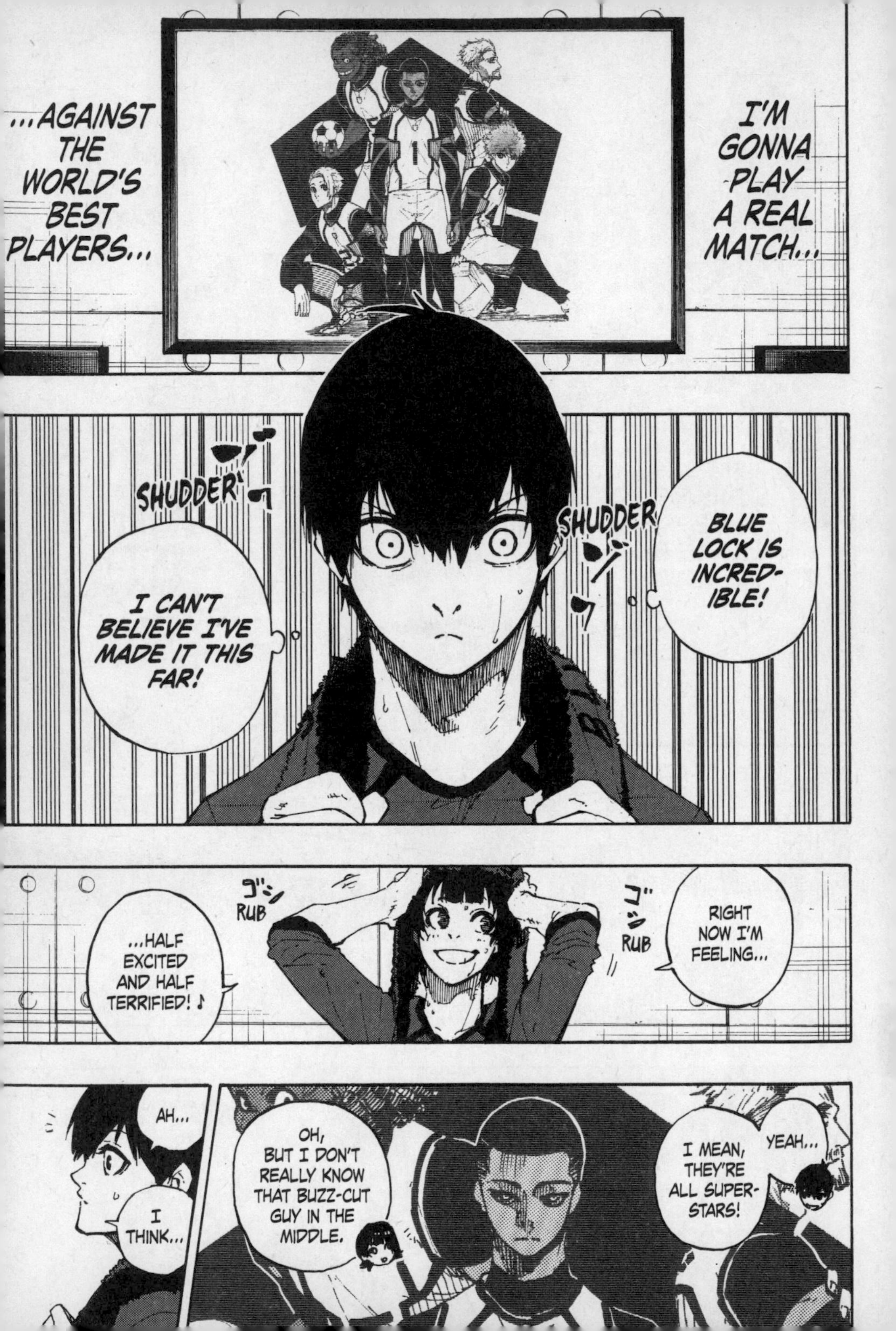

I'M GONNA PLAY A REAL MATCH...
...AGAINST THE WORLD'S BEST PLAYERS...
SHUDDER
BLUE LOCK IS INCREDIBLE!
SHUDDER
I CAN'T BELIEVE I'VE MADE IT THIS FAR!
RIGHT NOW I'M FEELING...
ゴシ RUB
ゴシ RUB
...HALF EXCITED AND HALF TERRIFIED! ♪
YEAH...
I MEAN, THEY'RE ALL SUPER-STARS!
OH, BUT I DON'T REALLY KNOW THAT BUZZ-CUT GUY IN THE MIDDLE.
AH...
I THINK...

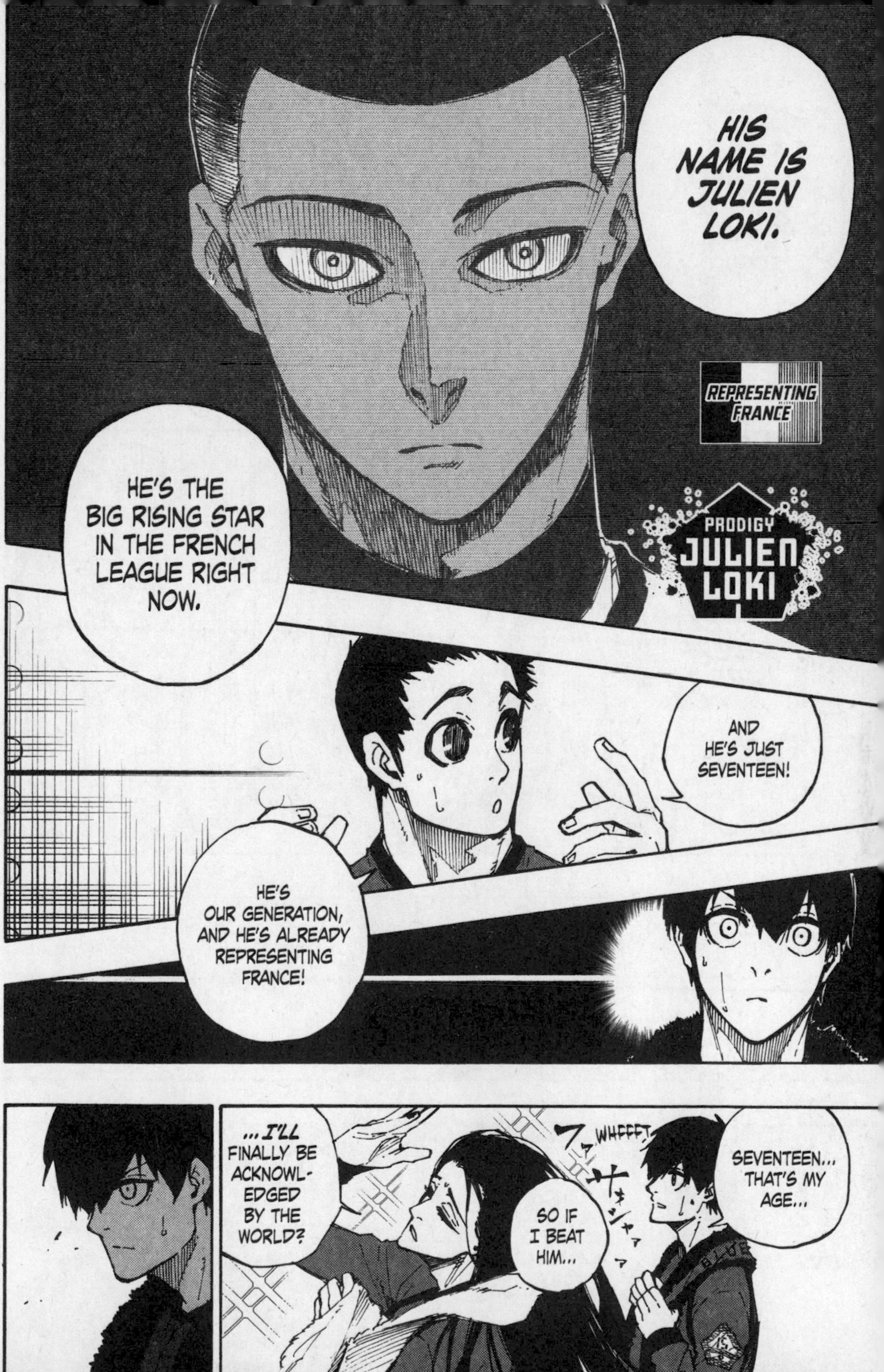
HIS NAME IS JULIEN LOKI.
REPRESENTING FRANCE
PRODIGY JULIEN LOKI
HE'S THE BIG RISING STAR IN THE FRENCH LEAGUE RIGHT NOW.
AND HE'S JUST SEVENTEEN!
HE'S OUR GENERATION, AND HE'S ALREADY REPRESENTING FRANCE!
SEVENTEEN... THAT'S MY AGE...
WHFFFT
SO IF I BEAT HIM...
...I'LL FINALLY BE ACKNOWL-EDGED BY THE WORLD?

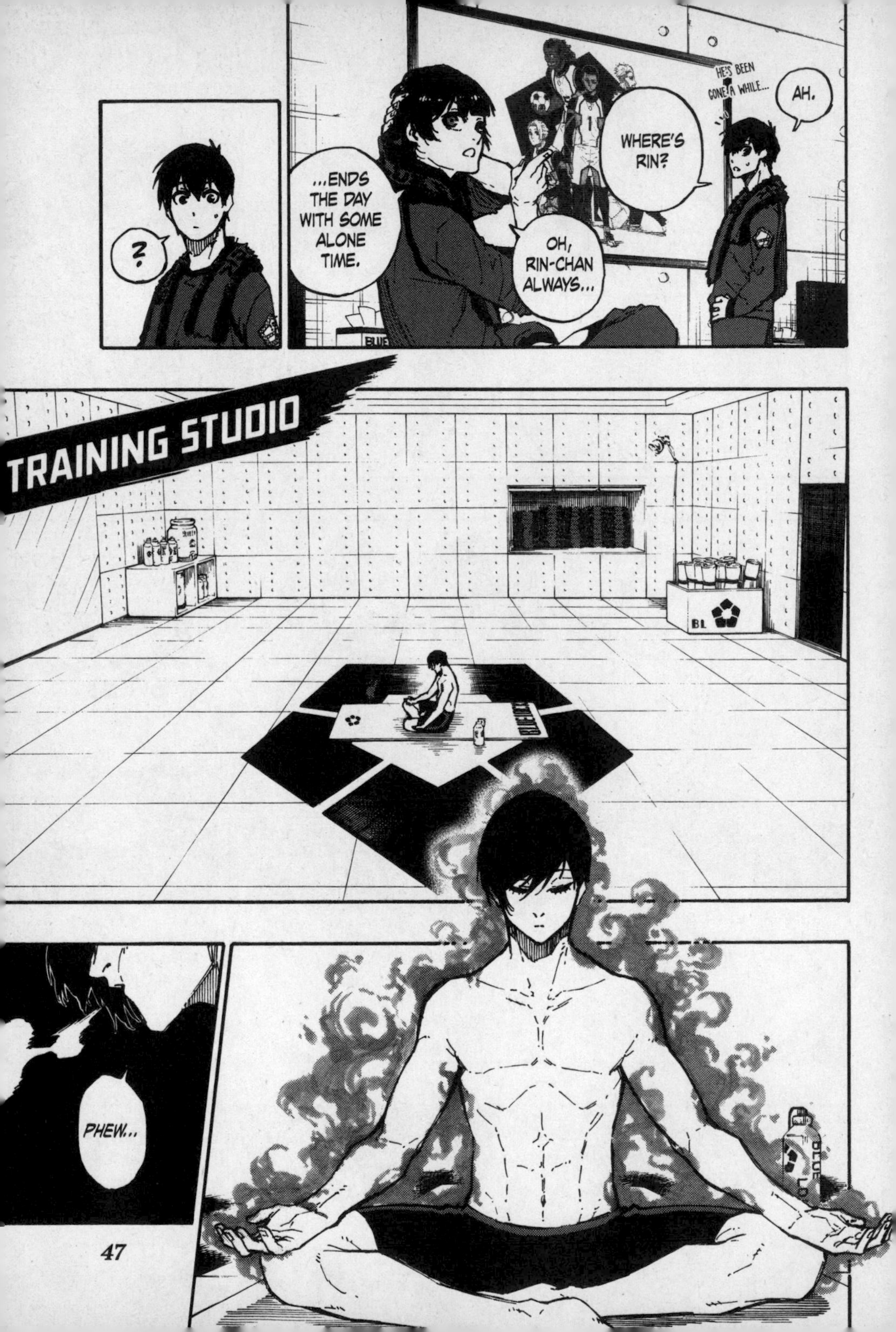
AH.
HE'S BEEN GONE A WHILE...
WHERE'S RIN?
OH, RIN-CHAN ALWAYS...
...ENDS THE DAY WITH SOME ALONE TIME.
?
TRAINING STUDIO
PHEW...

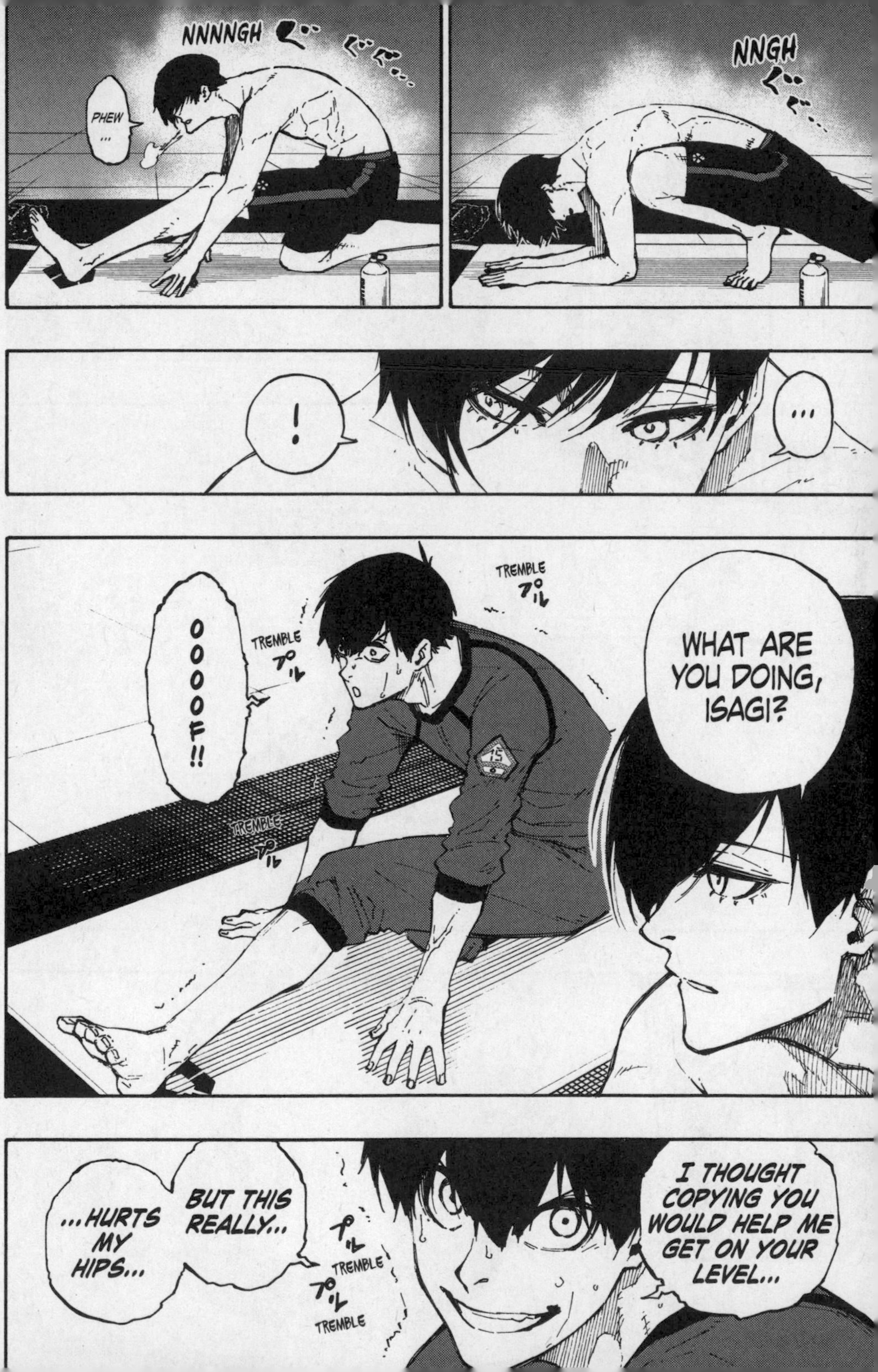
NNGH
NNNNGH
PHEW ...
...
!
WHAT ARE YOU DOING, ISAGI?
TREMBLE
OOOOF!!
TREMBLE
TREMBLE
I THOUGHT COPYING YOU WOULD HELP ME GET ON YOUR LEVEL...
TREMBLE
TREMBLE
BUT THIS REALLY...
...HURTS MY HIPS...

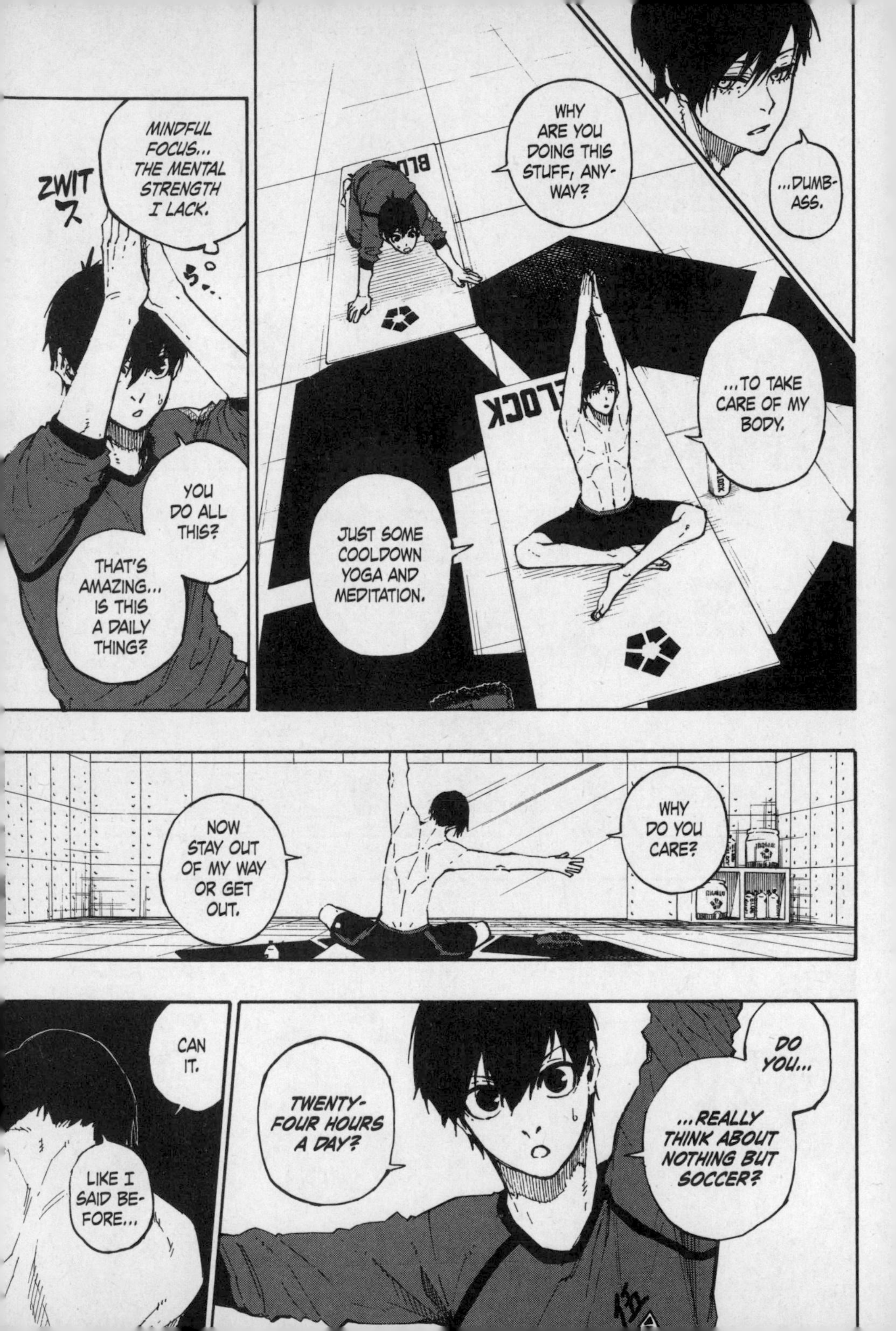
...DUMB-ASS.
WHY ARE YOU DOING THIS STUFF, ANYWAY?
...TO TAKE CARE OF MY BODY.
JUST SOME COOLDOWN YOGA AND MEDITATION.
MINDFUL FOCUS... THE MENTAL STRENGTH I LACK.
ZWIT
YOU DO ALL THIS?
THAT'S AMAZING... IS THIS A DAILY THING?
WHY DO YOU CARE?
NOW STAY OUT OF MY WAY OR GET OUT.
DO YOU...
...REALLY THINK ABOUT NOTHING BUT SOCCER?
TWENTY-FOUR HOURS A DAY?
CAN IT.
LIKE I SAID BEFORE...

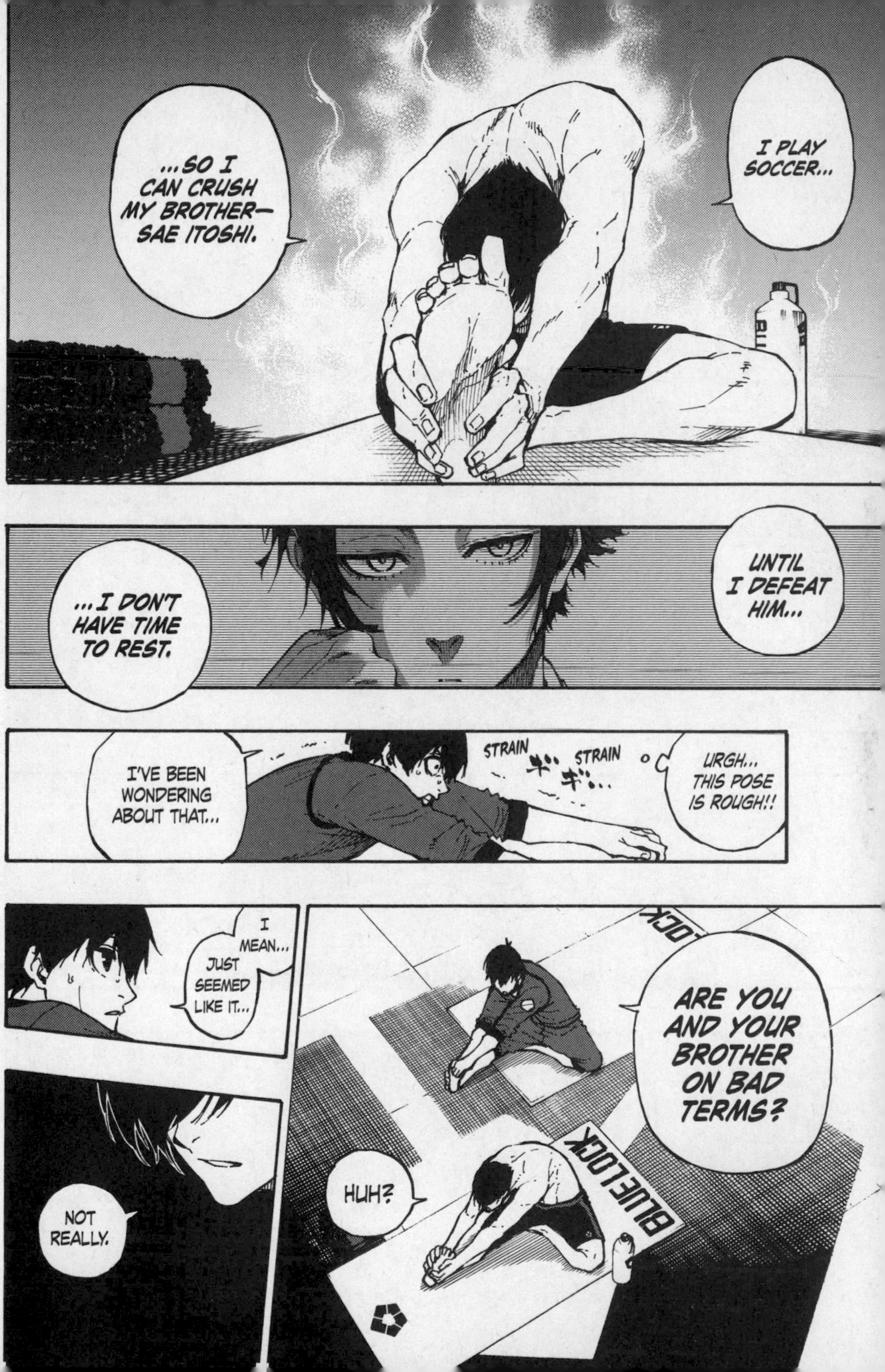
I PLAY SOCCER...
...SO I CAN CRUSH MY BROTHER—SAE ITOSHI.
UNTIL I DEFEAT HIM...
...I DON'T HAVE TIME TO REST.
URGH... THIS POSE IS ROUGH!!
STRAIN
STRAIN
I'VE BEEN WONDERING ABOUT THAT...
ARE YOU AND YOUR BROTHER ON BAD TERMS?
HUH?
BLUELOCK
I MEAN... JUST SEEMED LIKE IT...
NOT REALLY.

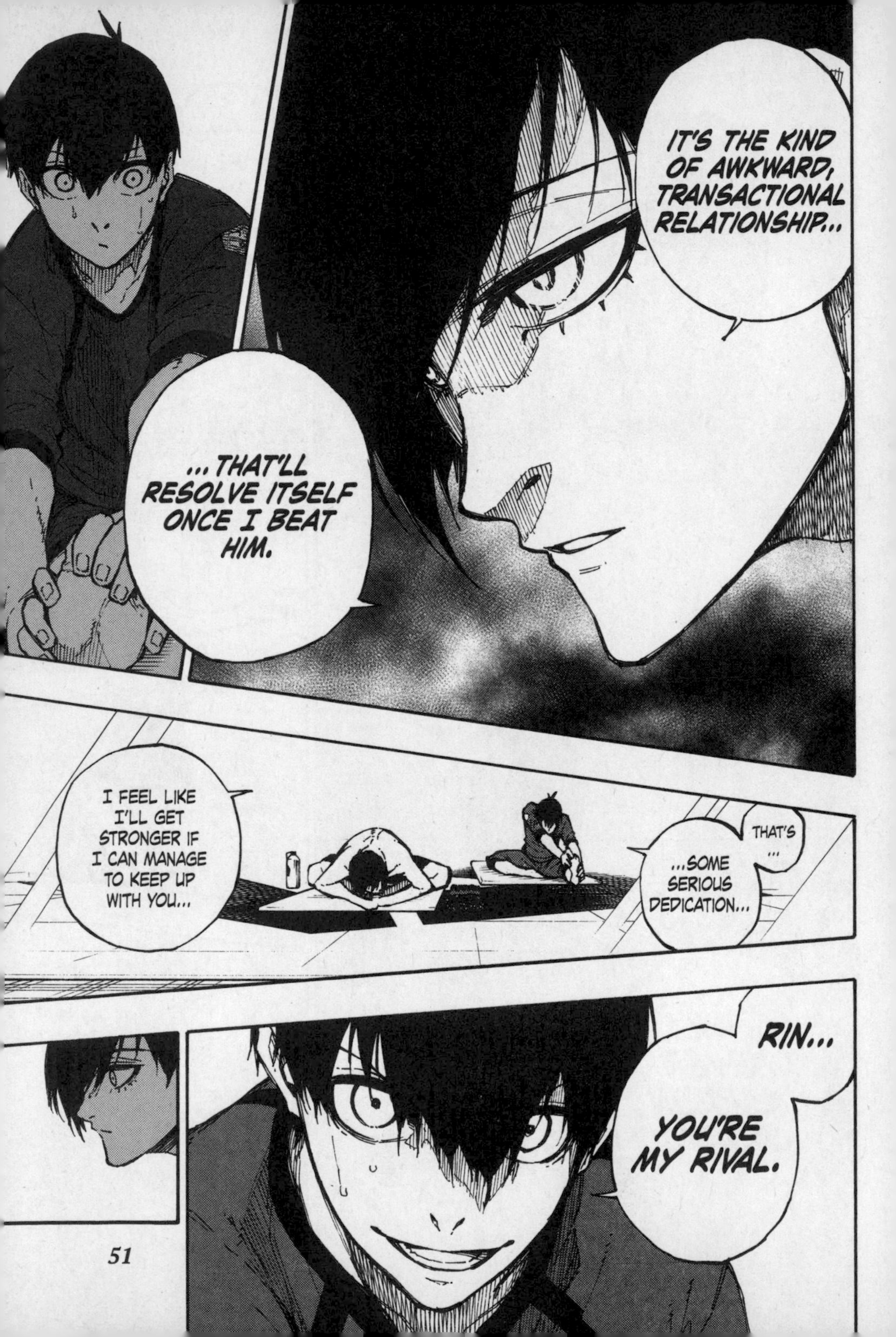
IT'S THE KIND OF AWKWARD, TRANSACTIONAL RELATIONSHIP...
...THAT'LL RESOLVE ITSELF ONCE I BEAT HIM.
THAT'S...
...SOME SERIOUS DEDICATION...
I FEEL LIKE I'LL GET STRONGER IF I CAN MANAGE TO KEEP UP WITH YOU...
RIN...
YOU'RE MY RIVAL.

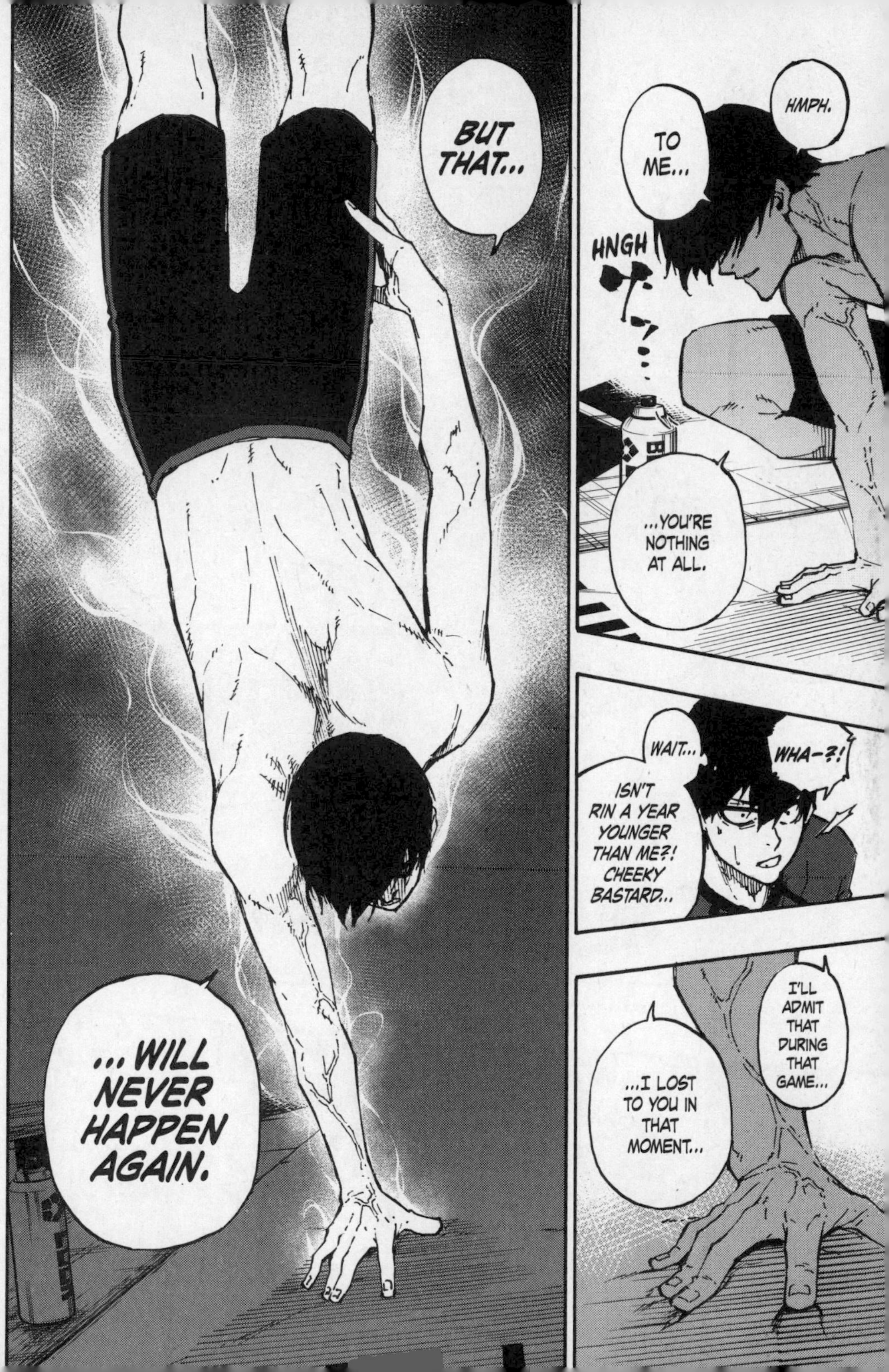
HMPH.
TO ME...
HNGH
...YOU'RE NOTHING AT ALL.
WHA-?!
WAIT...
ISN'T RIN A YEAR YOUNGER THAN ME?! CHEEKY BASTARD...
I'LL ADMIT THAT DURING THAT GAME...
...I LOST TO YOU IN THAT MOMENT...
BUT THAT...
...WILL NEVER HAPPEN AGAIN.

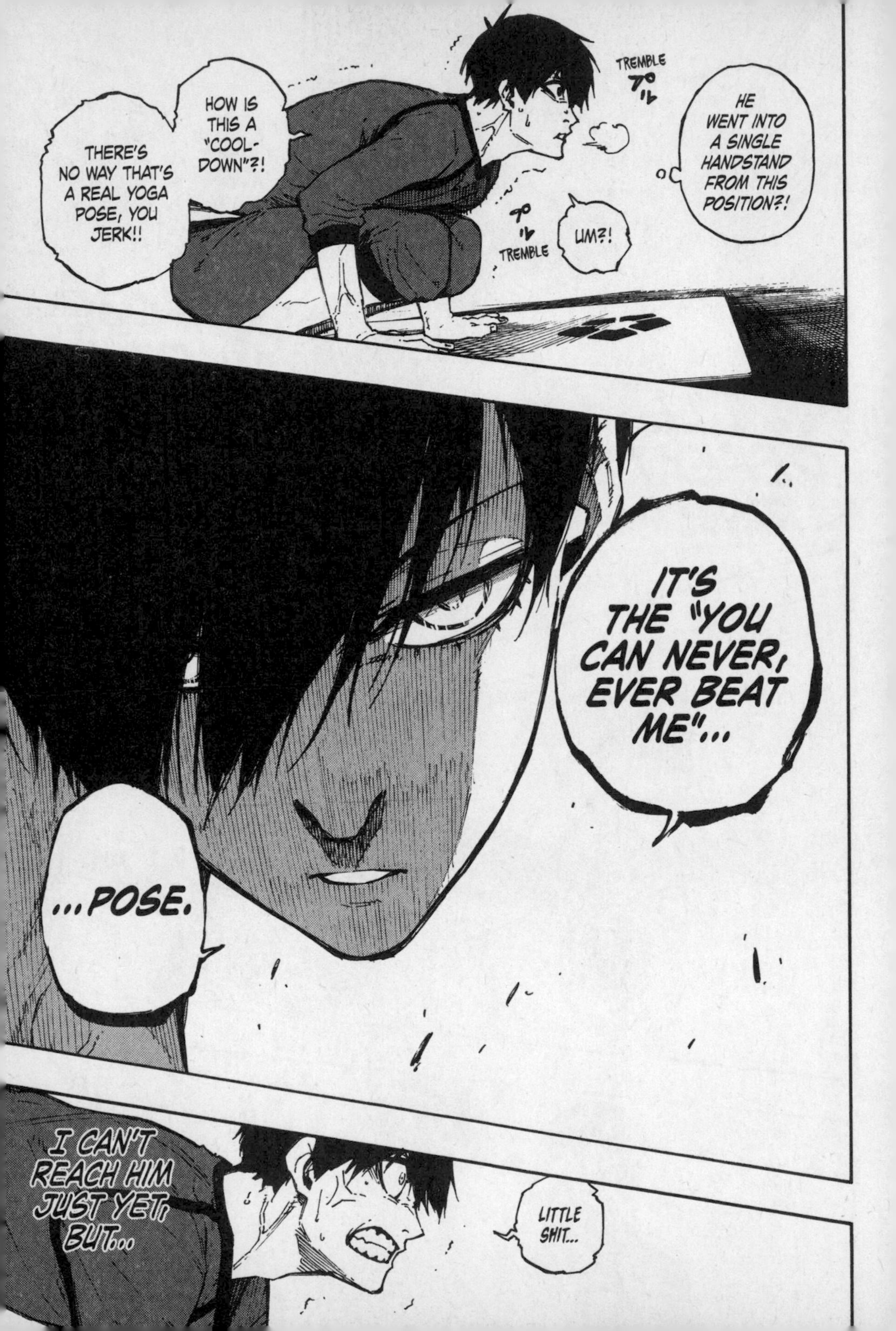
TREMBLE
HE WENT INTO A SINGLE HANDSTAND FROM THIS POSITION?!
UM?!
TREMBLE
HOW IS THIS A "COOL-DOWN"?!
THERE'S NO WAY THAT'S A REAL YOGA POSE, YOU JERK!!
IT'S THE "YOU CAN NEVER, EVER BEAT ME"...
...POSE.
LITTLE SHIT...
I CAN'T REACH HIM JUST YET, BUT...

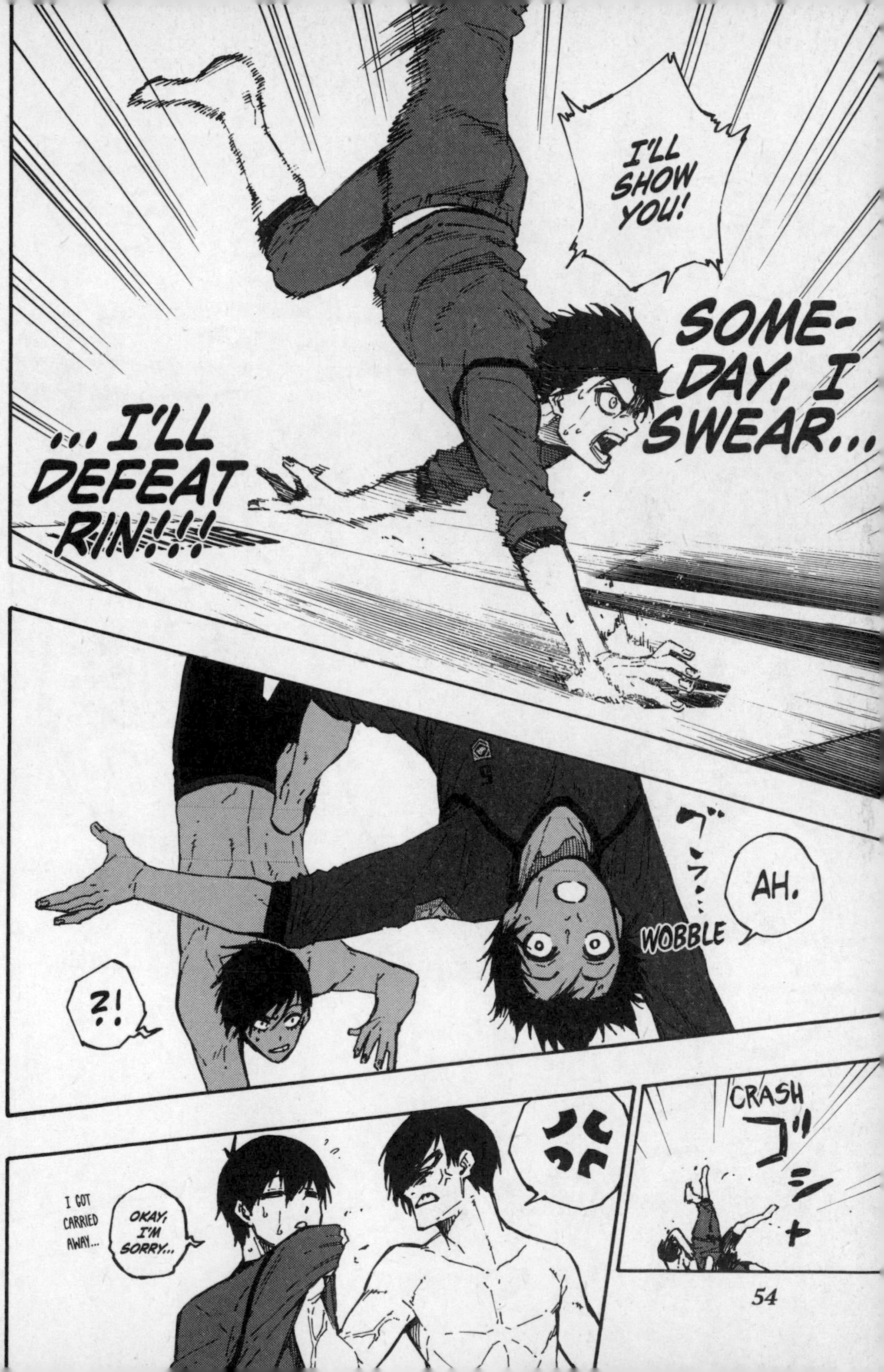

I'LL SHOW YOU!
SOME-DAY, I SWEAR...
...I'LL DEFEAT RIN!!!
WOBBLE
AH.
?!
CRASH
OKAY, I'M SORRY...
I GOT CARRIED AWAY...

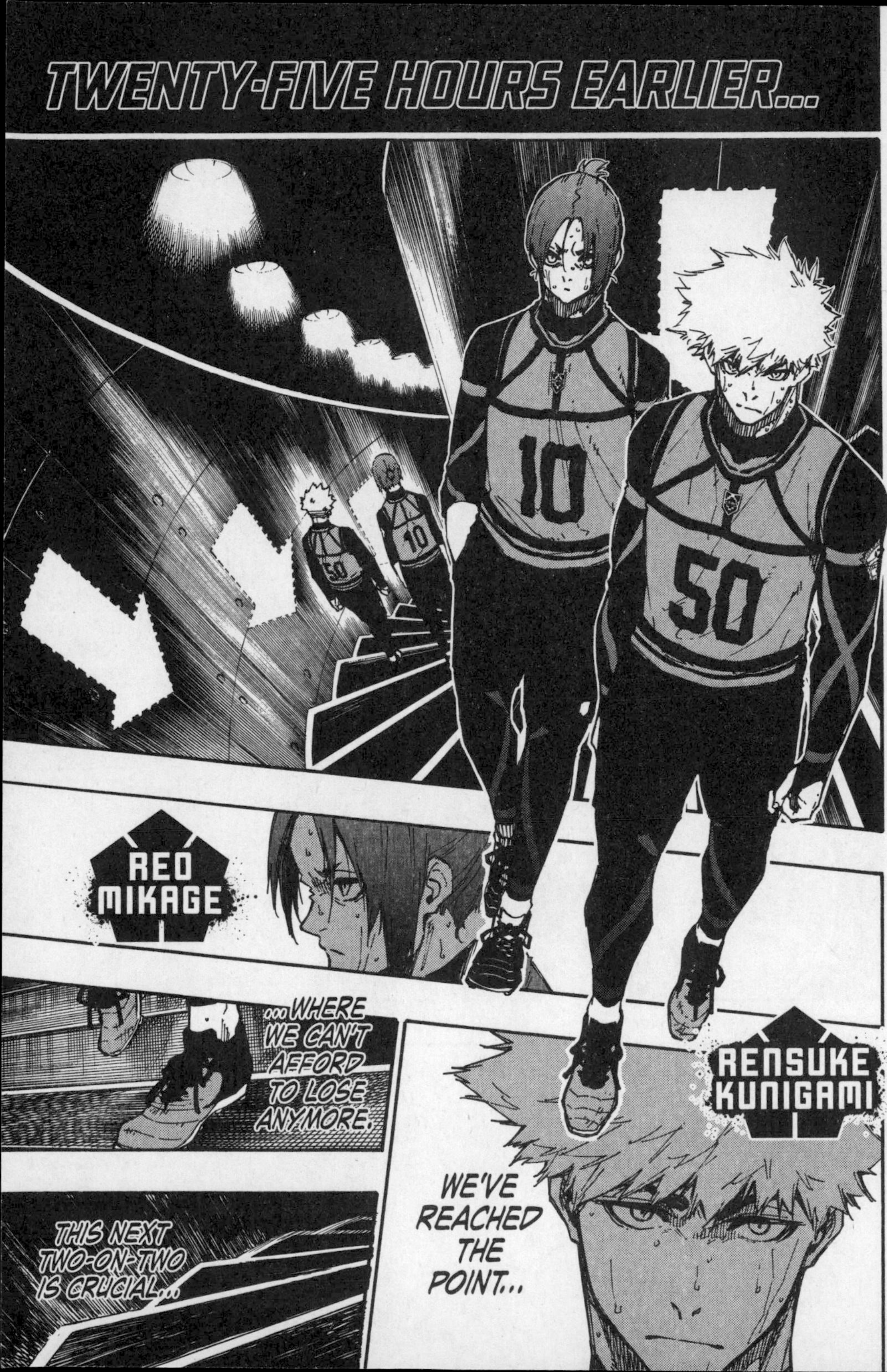
TWENTY-FIVE HOURS EARLIER...
REO MIKAGE
RENSUKE KUNIGAMI
WE'VE REACHED THE POINT...
...WHERE WE CAN'T AFFORD TO LOSE ANYMORE.
THIS NEXT TWO-ON-TWO IS CRUCIAL...

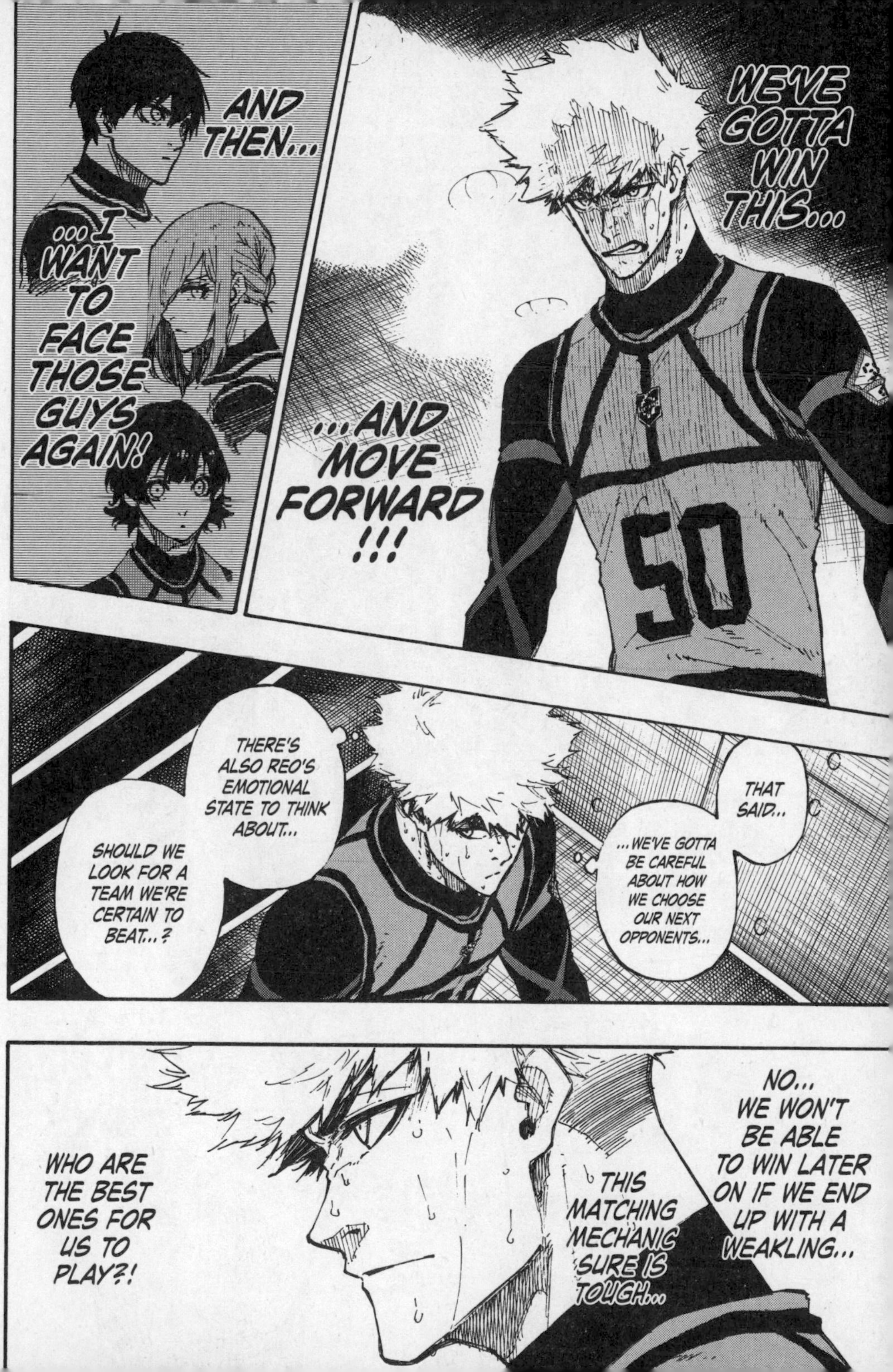
WE'VE GOTTA WIN THIS...
...AND MOVE FORWARD!!!
AND THEN...
...I WANT TO FACE THOSE GUYS AGAIN!
THAT SAID...
...WE'VE GOTTA BE CAREFUL ABOUT HOW WE CHOOSE OUR NEXT OPPONENTS...
THERE'S ALSO REO'S EMOTIONAL STATE TO THINK ABOUT...
SHOULD WE LOOK FOR A TEAM WE'RE CERTAIN TO BEAT...?
NO... WE WON'T BE ABLE TO WIN LATER ON IF WE END UP WITH A WEAKLING...
THIS MATCHING MECHANIC SURE IS TOUGH...
WHO ARE THE BEST ONES FOR US TO PLAY?!

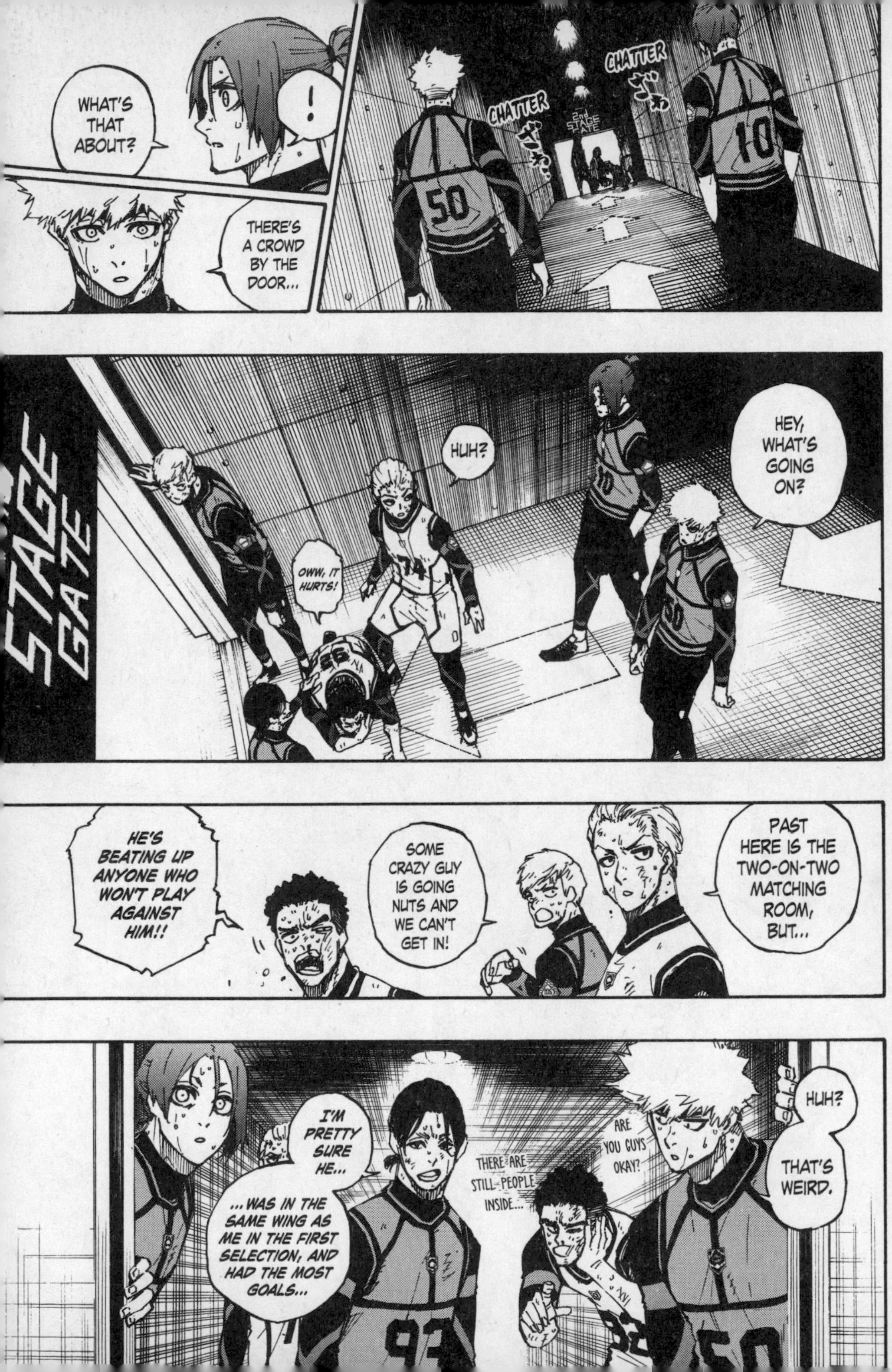
CHATTER
CHATTER
2nd STAGE GATE
WHAT'S THAT ABOUT?
!
THERE'S A CROWD BY THE DOOR...
STAGE GATE
HEY, WHAT'S GOING ON?
HUH?
OWW, IT HURTS!
PAST HERE IS THE TWO-ON-TWO MATCHING ROOM, BUT...
SOME CRAZY GUY IS GOING NUTS AND WE CAN'T GET IN!
HE'S BEATING UP ANYONE WHO WON'T PLAY AGAINST HIM!!
HUH?
THAT'S WEIRD.
ARE YOU GUYS OKAY?
THERE ARE STILL PEOPLE INSIDE...
I'M PRETTY SURE HE...
...WAS IN THE SAME WING AS ME IN THE FIRST SELECTION, AND HAD THE MOST GOALS...

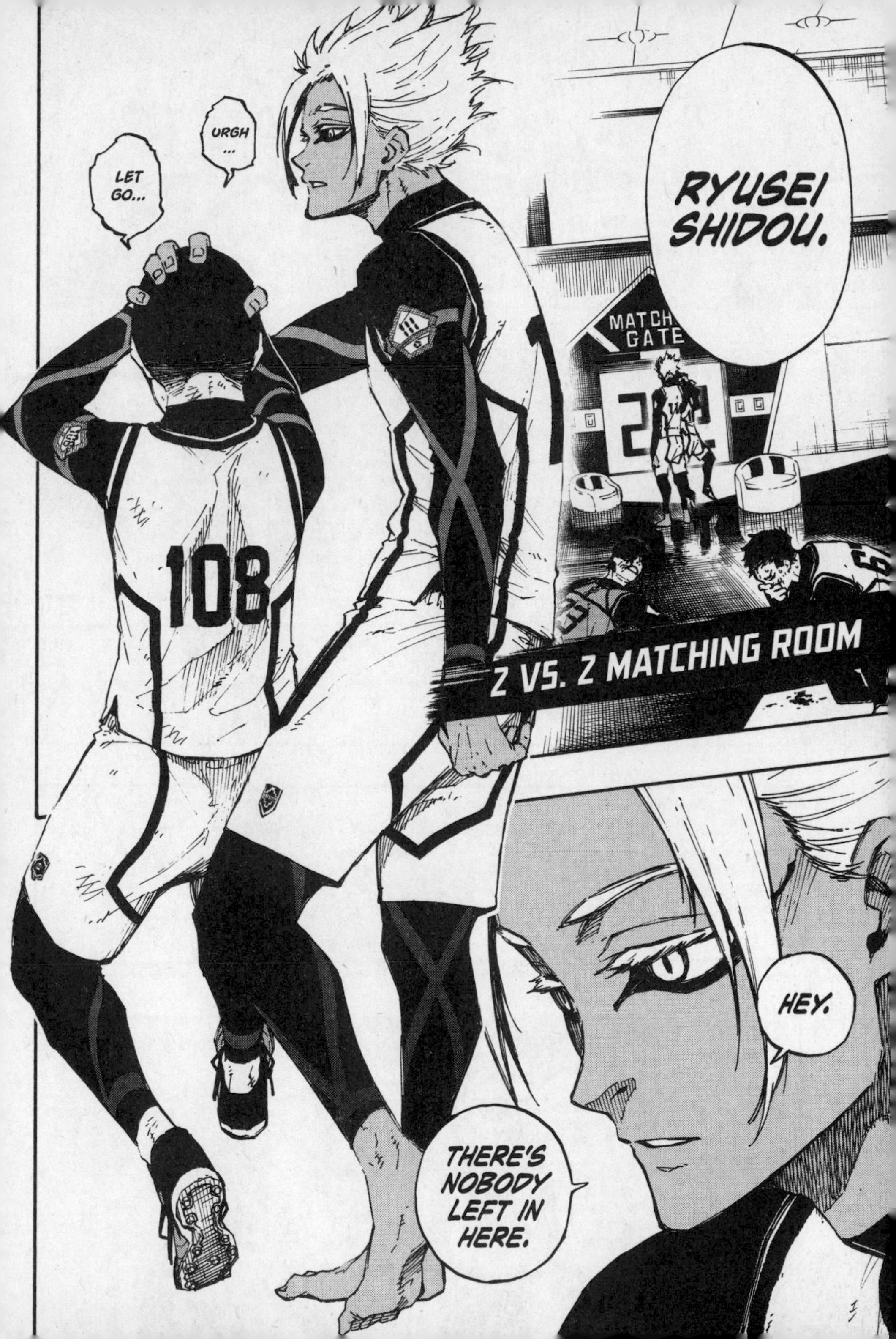
RYUSEI SHIDOU.
MATCH GATE
2 VS. 2 MATCHING ROOM
HEY.
THERE'S NOBODY LEFT IN HERE.
URGH...
LET GO...
108

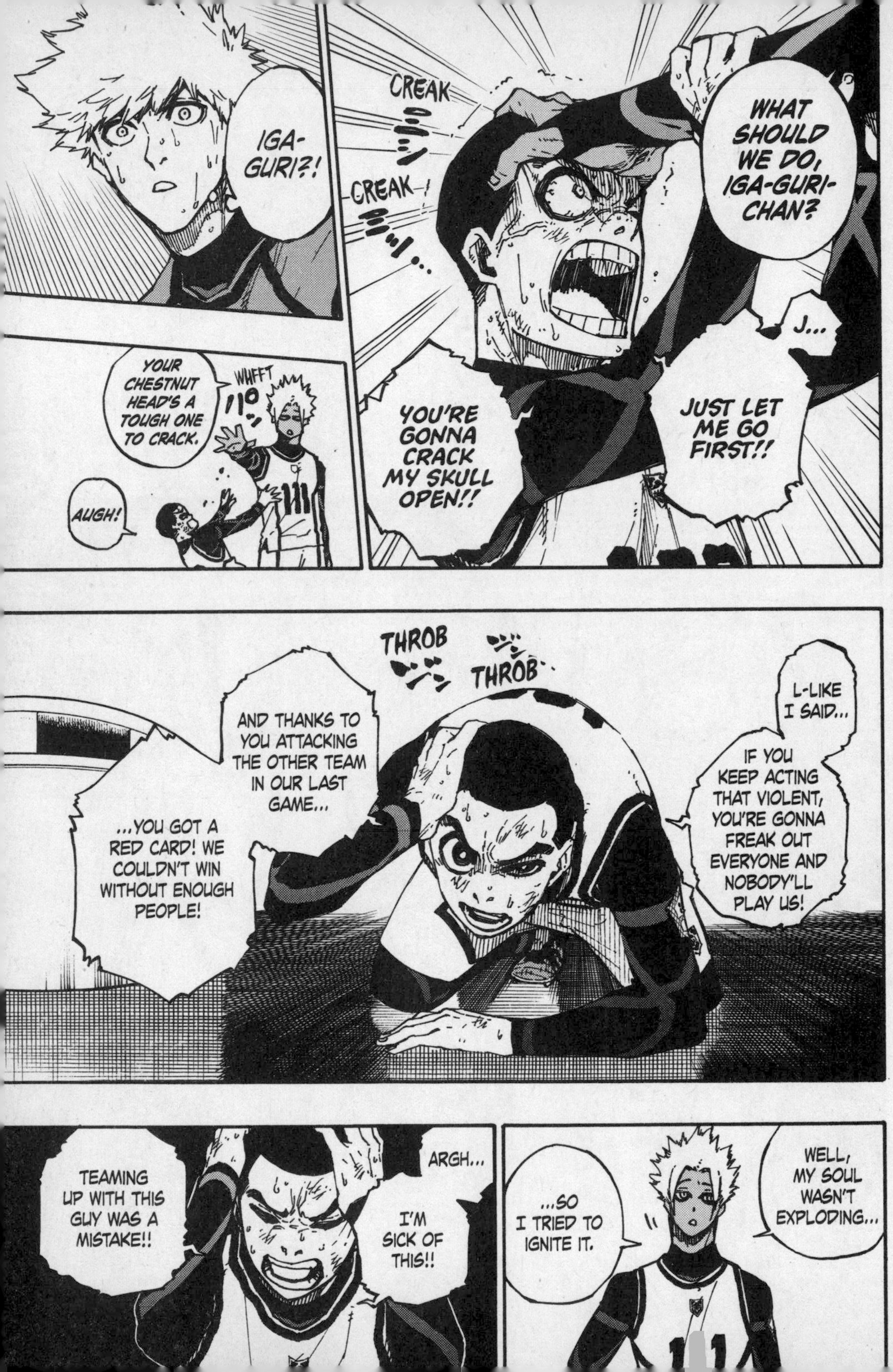
WHAT SHOULD WE DO, IGA-GURI-CHAN?
CREAK
CREAK
J...
JUST LET ME GO FIRST!!
YOU'RE GONNA CRACK MY SKULL OPEN!!
IGA-GURI?!
YOUR CHESTNUT HEAD'S A TOUGH ONE TO CRACK.
WHFFT
AUGH!
THROB
THROB
L-LIKE I SAID...
IF YOU KEEP ACTING THAT VIOLENT, YOU'RE GONNA FREAK OUT EVERYONE AND NOBODY'LL PLAY US!
AND THANKS TO YOU ATTACKING THE OTHER TEAM IN OUR LAST GAME...
...YOU GOT A RED CARD! WE COULDN'T WIN WITHOUT ENOUGH PEOPLE!
WELL, MY SOUL WASN'T EXPLODING...
...SO I TRIED TO IGNITE IT.
ARGH...
I'M SICK OF THIS!!
TEAMING UP WITH THIS GUY WAS A MISTAKE!!

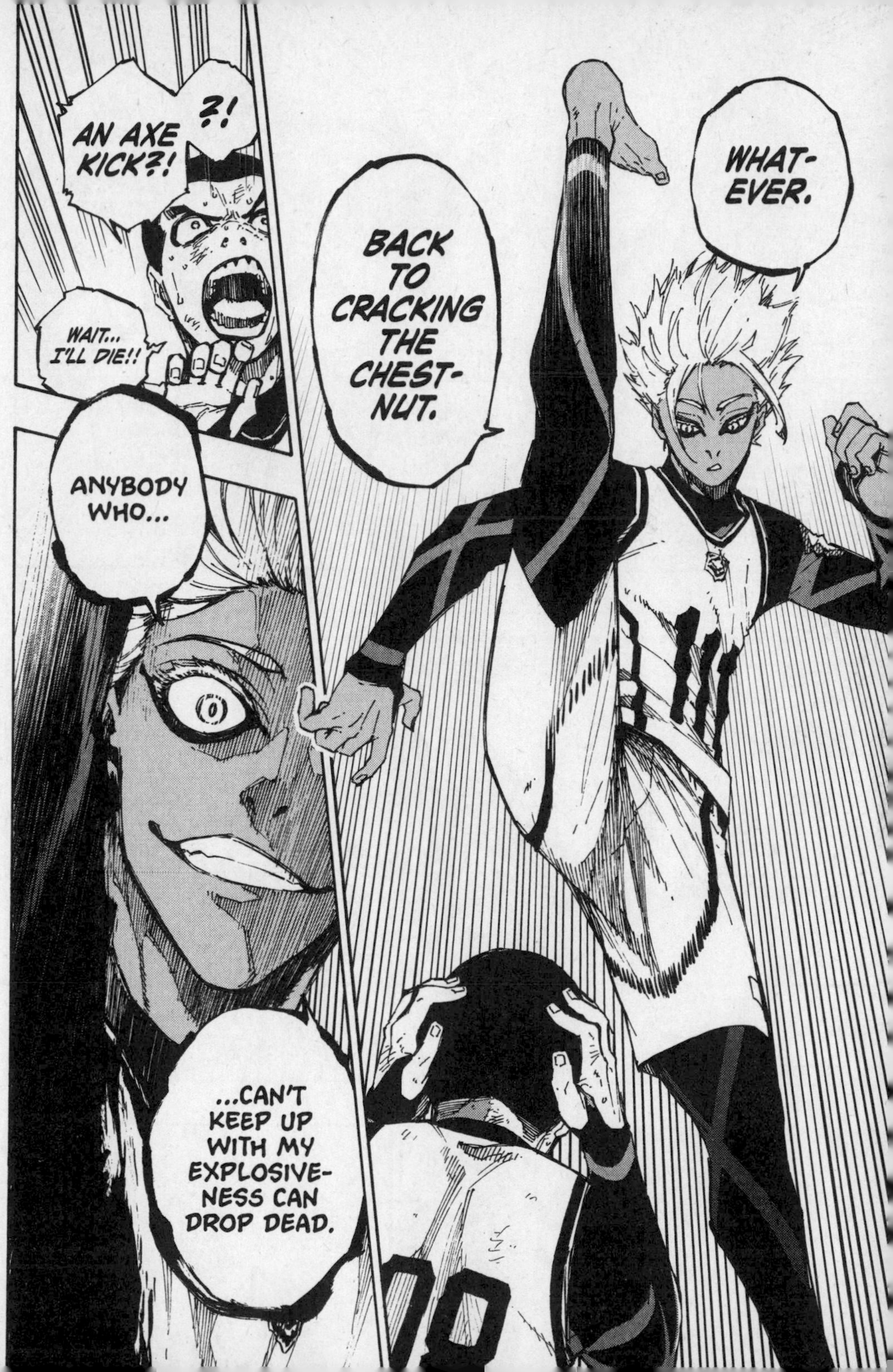
WHAT-EVER.
BACK TO CRACKING THE CHEST-NUT.
?!
AN AXE KICK?!
WAIT... I'LL DIE!!
ANYBODY WHO...
...CAN'T KEEP UP WITH MY EXPLOSIVE-NESS CAN DROP DEAD.

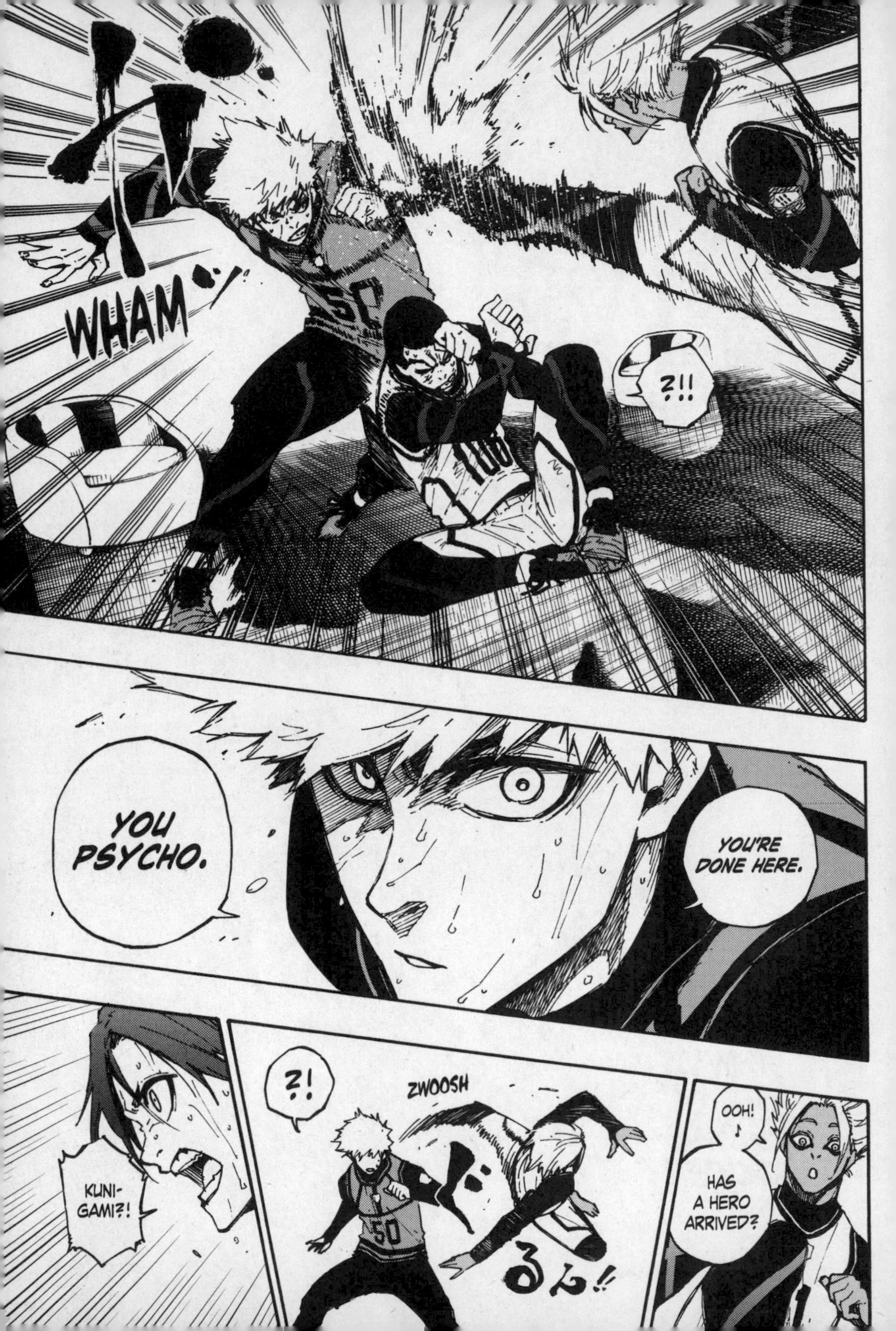
WHAM
?!!
YOU'RE DONE HERE.
YOU PSYCHO.
OOH! ♪
HAS A HERO ARRIVED?
ZWOOSH
?!
るん!!
KUNI-GAMI?!

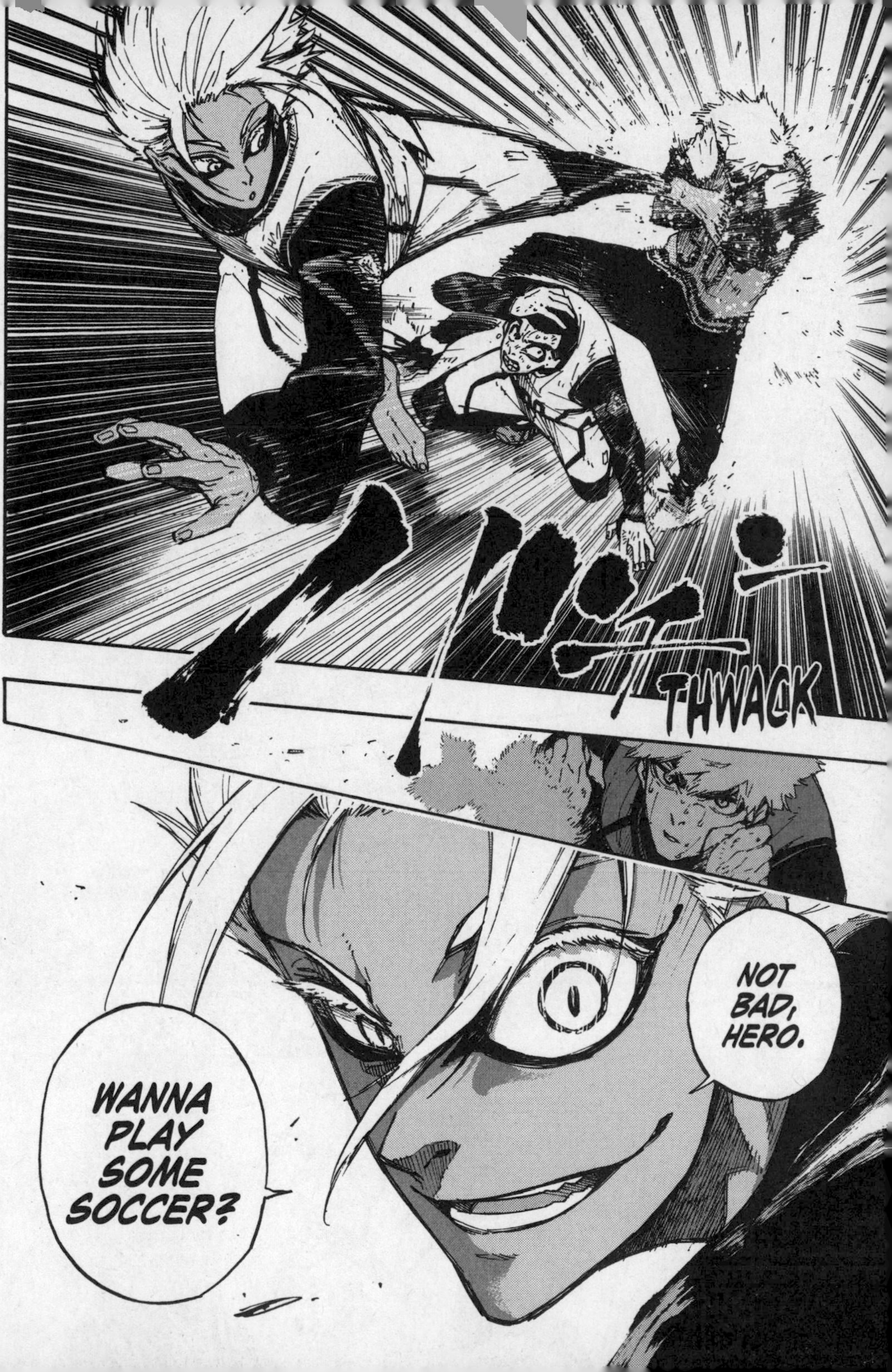
THWACK
NOT BAD, HERO.
WANNA PLAY SOME SOCCER?

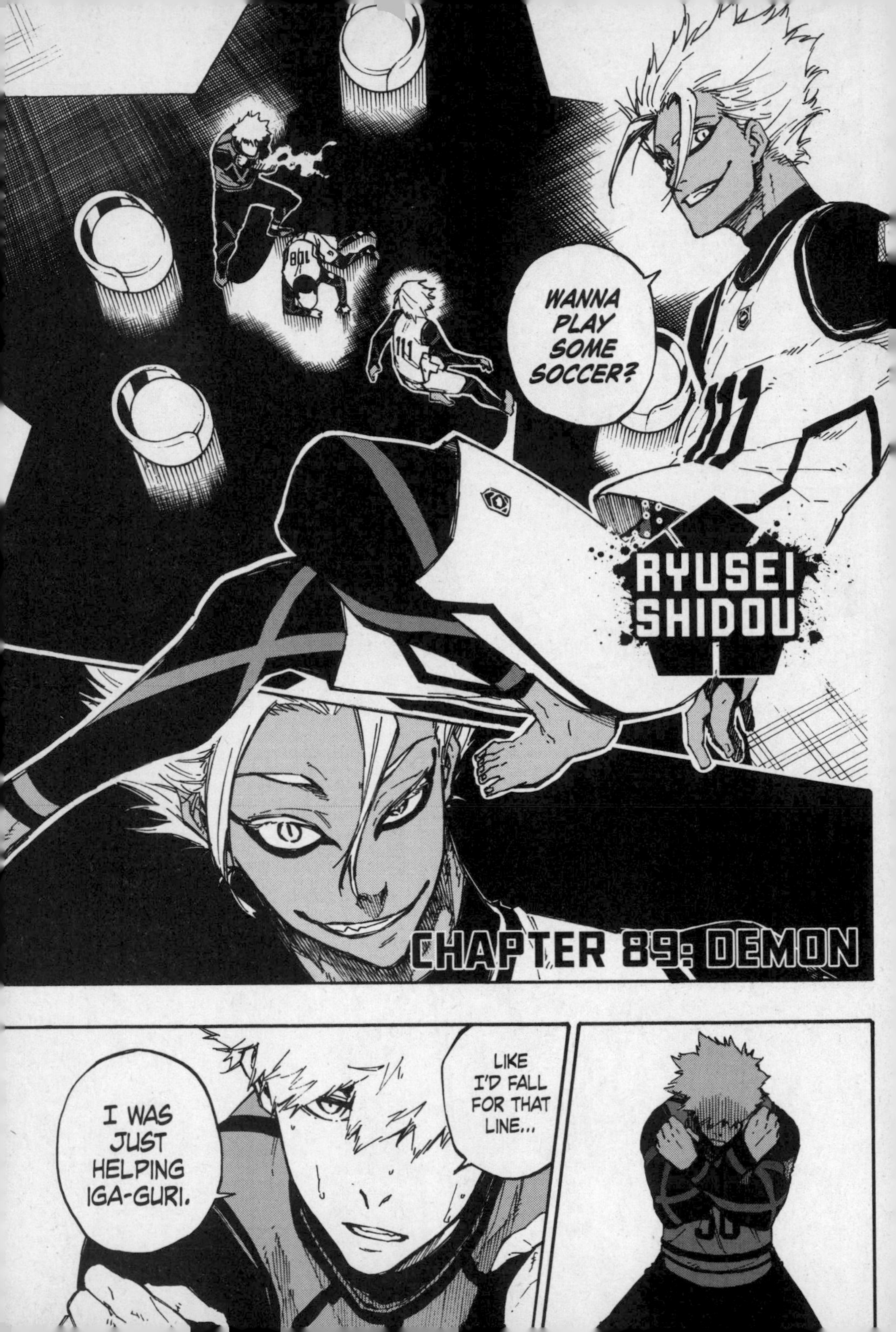
WANNA PLAY SOME SOCCER?
RYUSEI SHIDOU
CHAPTER 89: DEMON
LIKE I'D FALL FOR THAT LINE...
I WAS JUST HELPING IGA-GURI.

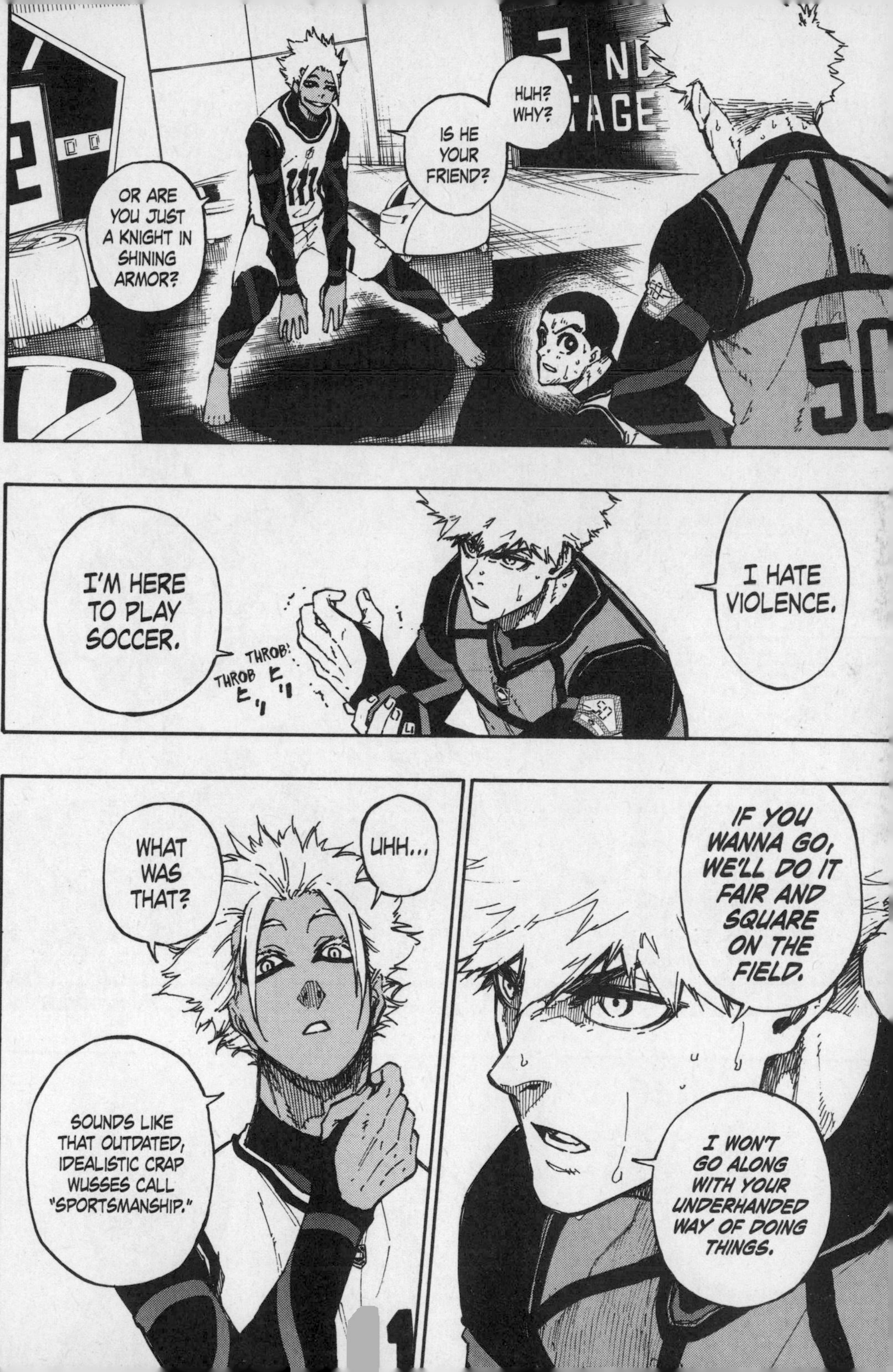
HUH? WHY?
IS HE YOUR FRIEND?
OR ARE YOU JUST A KNIGHT IN SHINING ARMOR?
I HATE VIOLENCE.
THROB THROB
I'M HERE TO PLAY SOCCER.
IF YOU WANNA GO, WE'LL DO IT FAIR AND SQUARE ON THE FIELD.
I WON'T GO ALONG WITH YOUR UNDERHANDED WAY OF DOING THINGS.
UHH...
WHAT WAS THAT?
SOUNDS LIKE THAT OUTDATED, IDEALISTIC CRAP WUSSES CALL "SPORTSMANSHIP."

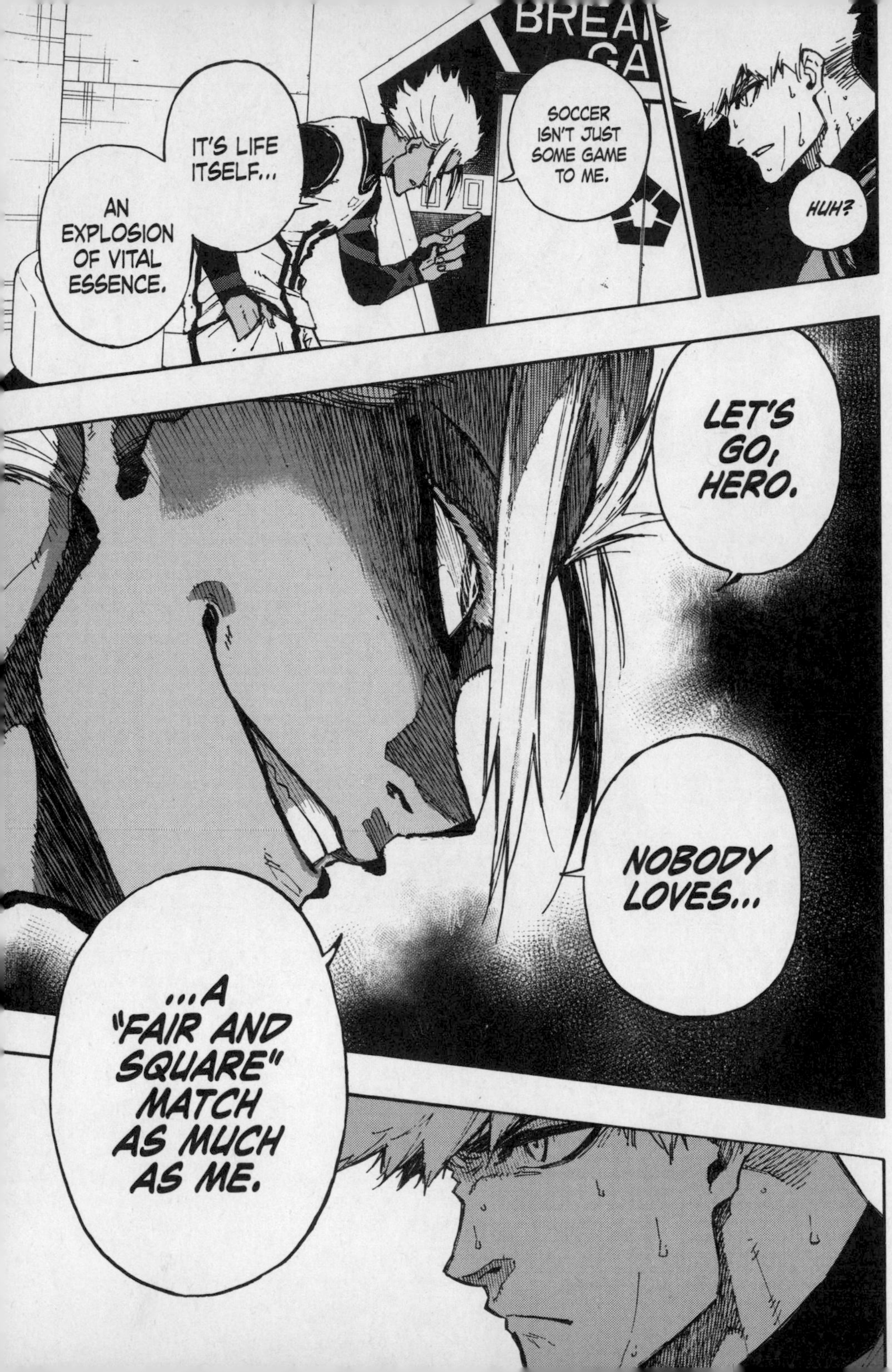
HUH?
SOCCER ISN'T JUST SOME GAME TO ME.
IT'S LIFE ITSELF...
AN EXPLOSION OF VITAL ESSENCE.
LET'S GO, HERO.
NOBODY LOVES...
..."A "FAIR AND SQUARE" MATCH AS MUCH AS ME.

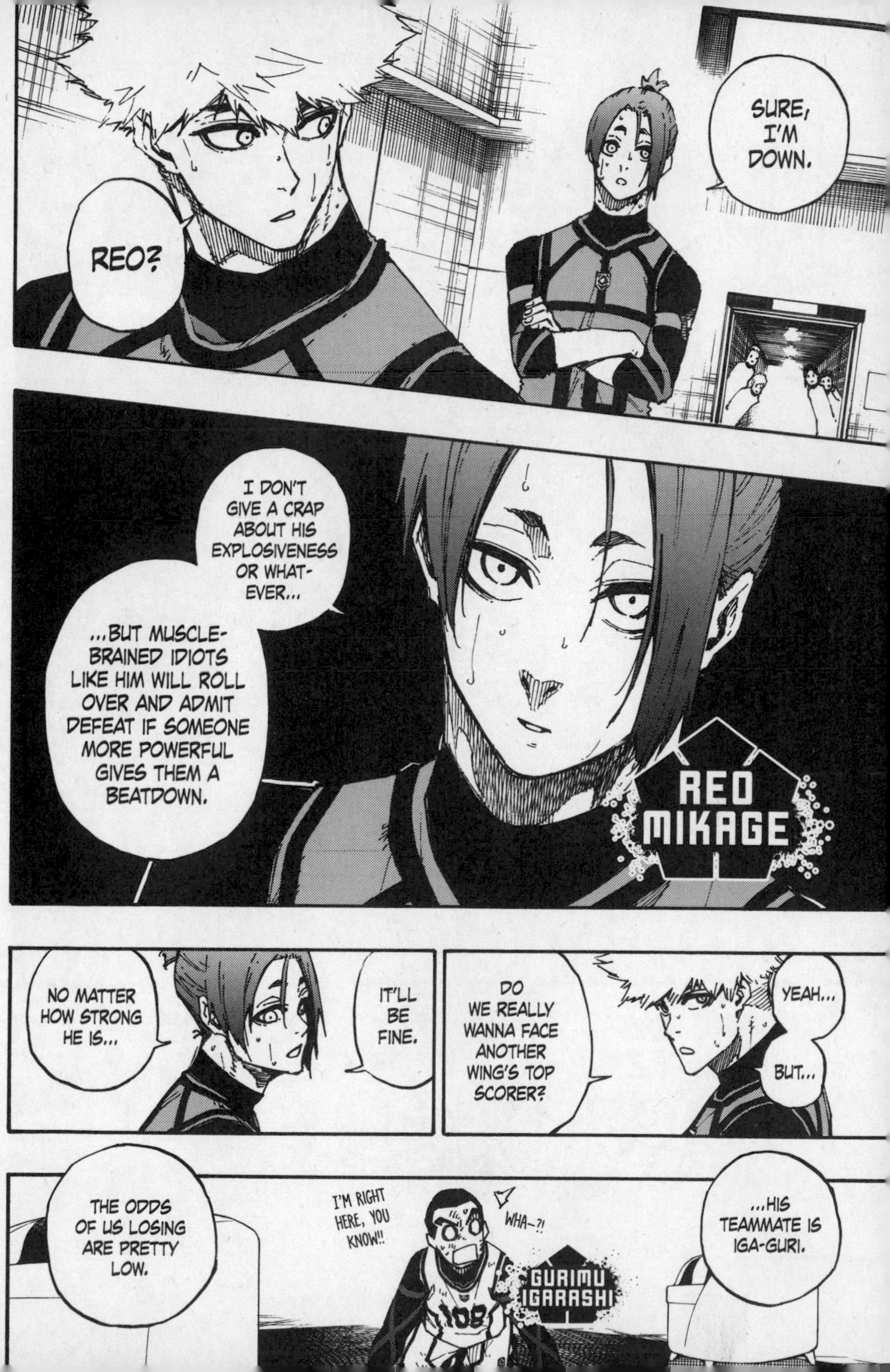
SURE, I'M DOWN.
REO?
I DON'T GIVE A CRAP ABOUT HIS EXPLOSIVENESS OR WHATEVER...
...BUT MUSCLE-BRAINED IDIOTS LIKE HIM WILL ROLL OVER AND ADMIT DEFEAT IF SOMEONE MORE POWERFUL GIVES THEM A BEATDOWN.
REO MIKAGE
YEAH...
BUT...
DO WE REALLY WANNA FACE ANOTHER WING'S TOP SCORER?
IT'LL BE FINE.
NO MATTER HOW STRONG HE IS...
...HIS TEAMMATE IS IGA-GURI.
WHA-?!
I'M RIGHT HERE, YOU KNOW!!
GURIMU IGARASHI
108
THE ODDS OF US LOSING ARE PRETTY LOW.

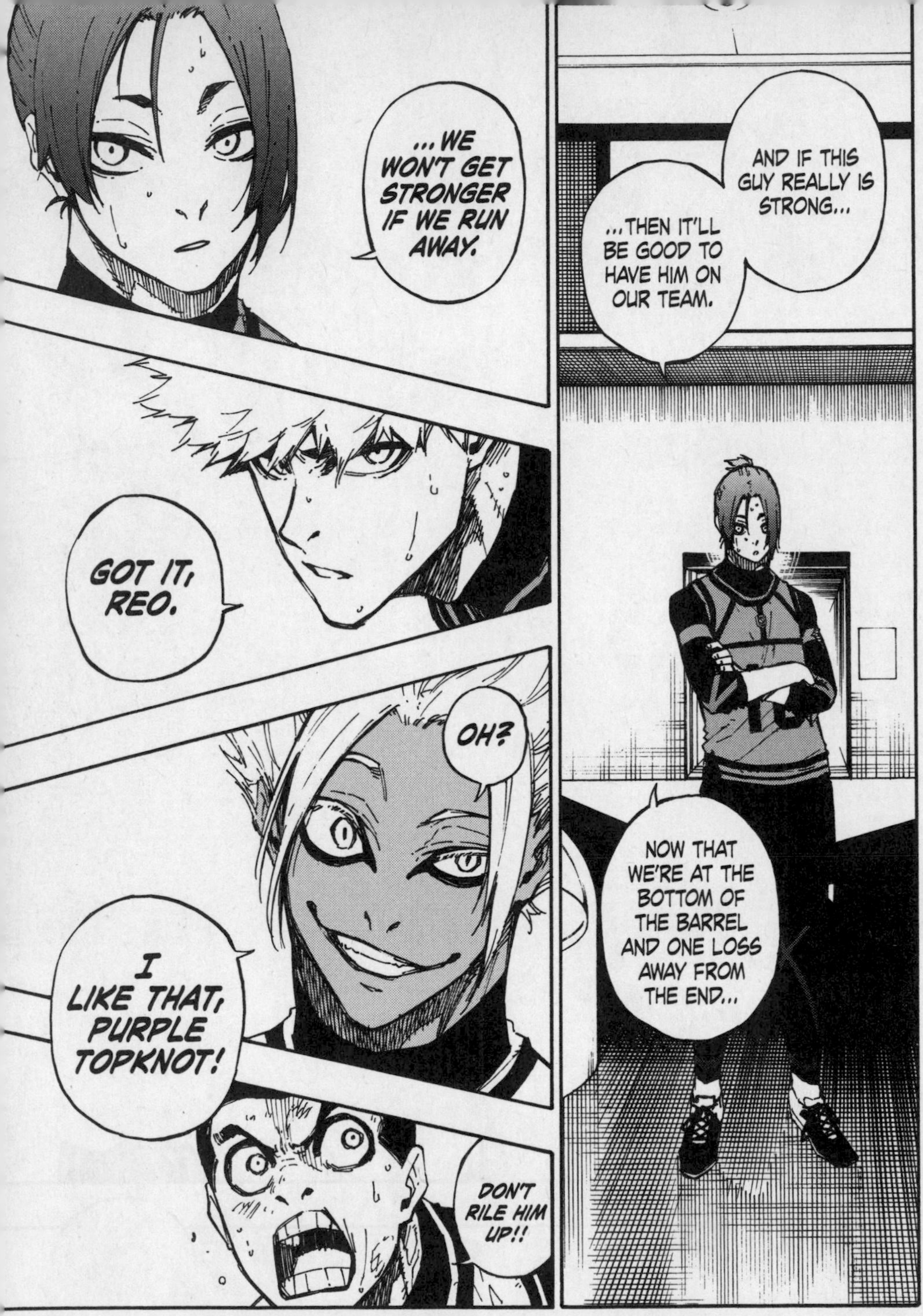
AND IF THIS GUY REALLY IS STRONG...
...THEN IT'LL BE GOOD TO HAVE HIM ON OUR TEAM.
NOW THAT WE'RE AT THE BOTTOM OF THE BARREL AND ONE LOSS AWAY FROM THE END...
...WE WON'T GET STRONGER IF WE RUN AWAY.
GOT IT, REO.
OH?
I LIKE THAT, PURPLE TOPKNOT!
DON'T RILE HIM UP!!

MATCH CONFIRMED!

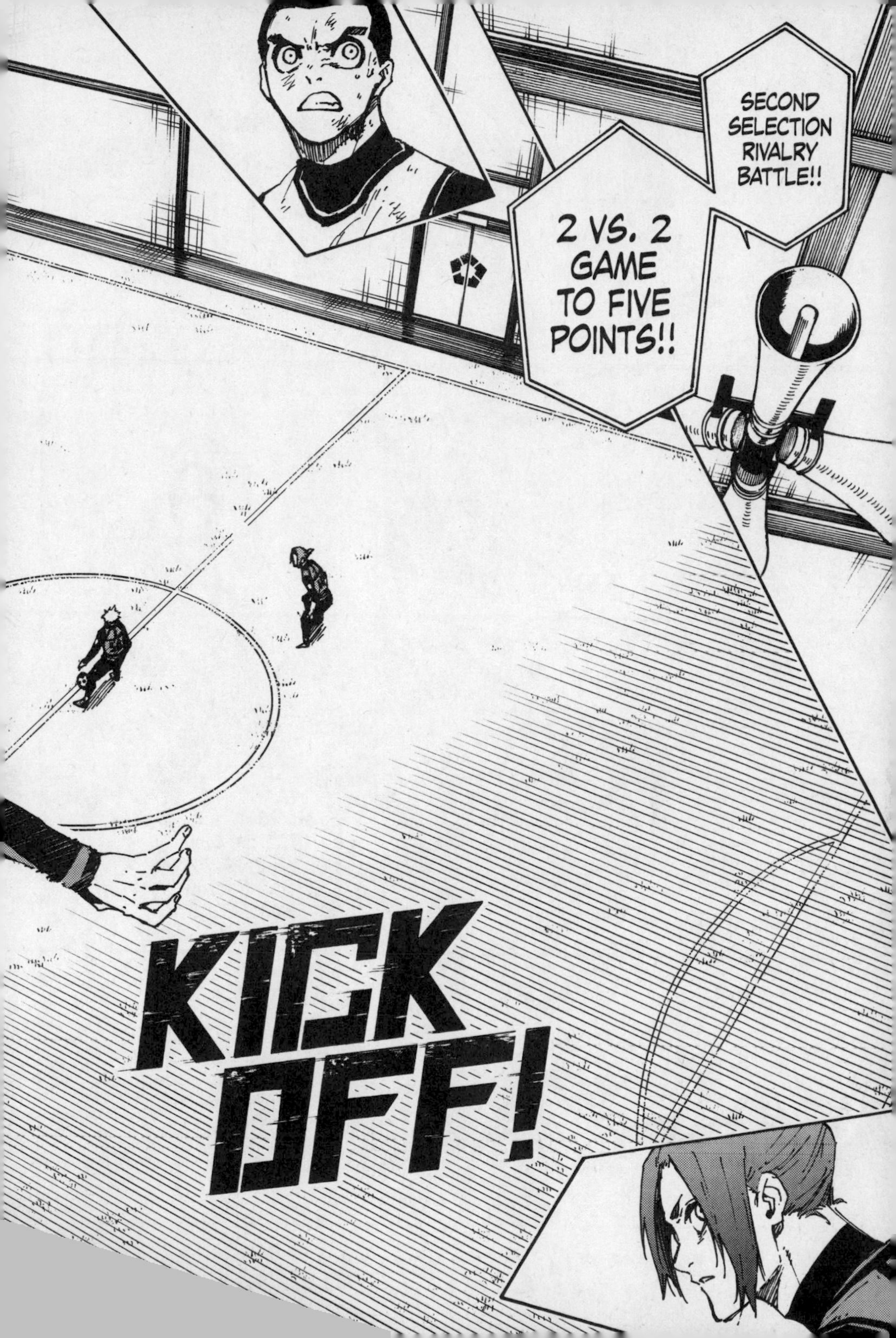
SECOND SELECTION RIVALRY BATTLE!!
2 VS. 2 GAME TO FIVE POINTS!!
KICK OFF!

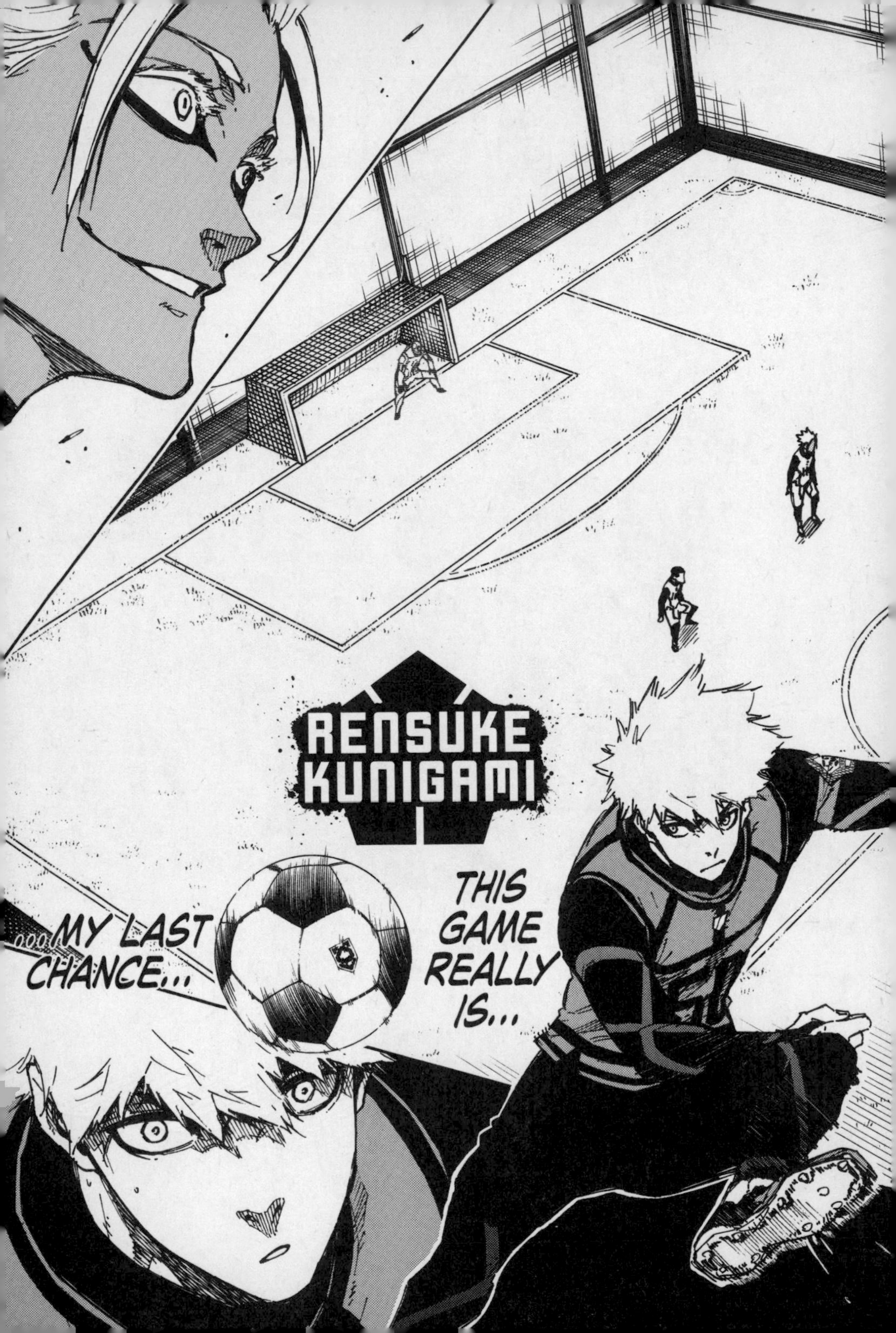
RENSUKE KUNIGAMI
THIS GAME REALLY IS...
...MY LAST CHANCE...

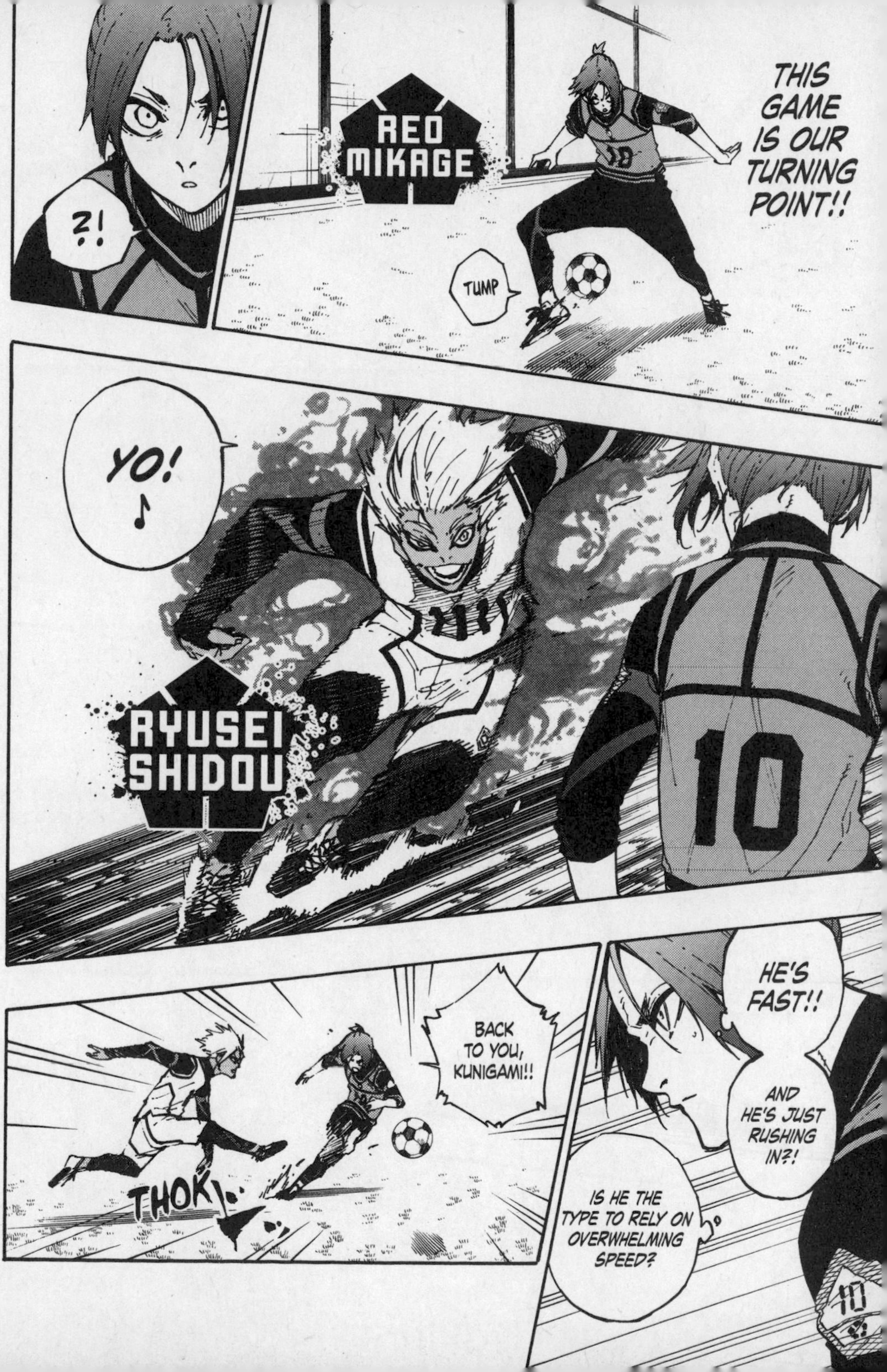
THIS GAME IS OUR TURNING POINT!!
REO MIKAGE
TUMP
?!
YO! ♪
RYUSEI SHIDOU
HE'S FAST!!
AND HE'S JUST RUSHING IN?!
IS HE THE TYPE TO RELY ON OVERWHELMING SPEED?
BACK TO YOU, KUNIGAMI!!
THOK

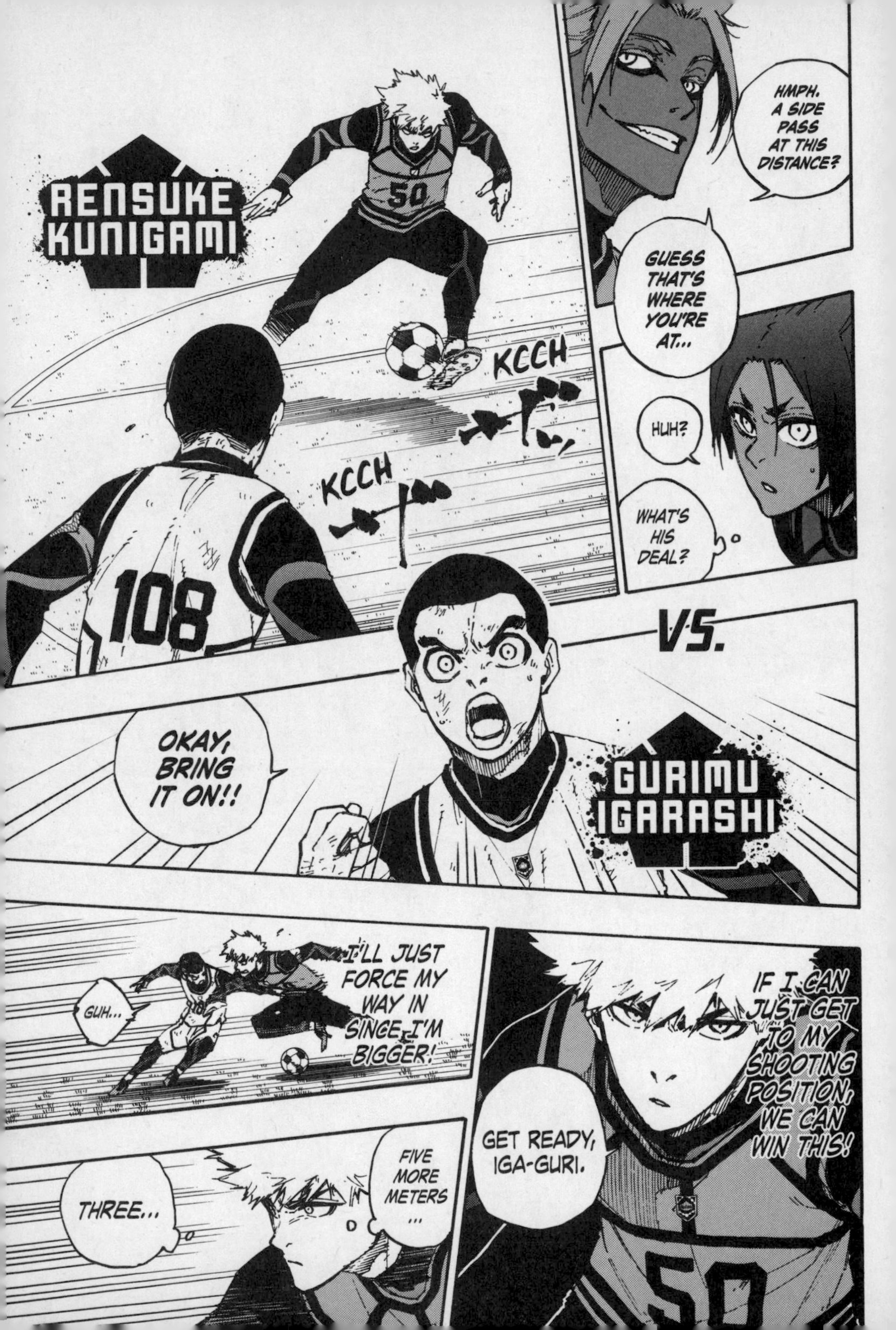
HMPH. A SIDE PASS AT THIS DISTANCE?
GUESS THAT'S WHERE YOU'RE AT...
HUH?
WHAT'S HIS DEAL?
RENSUKE KUNIGAMI
50
KCCH
KCCH
108
V.S.
GURIMU IGARASHI
OKAY, BRING IT ON!!
IF I CAN JUST GET TO MY SHOOTING POSITION, WE CAN WIN THIS!
GET READY, IGA-GURI.
I'LL JUST FORCE MY WAY IN SINCE I'M BIGGER!
GUH...
FIVE MORE METERS...
THREE...
50

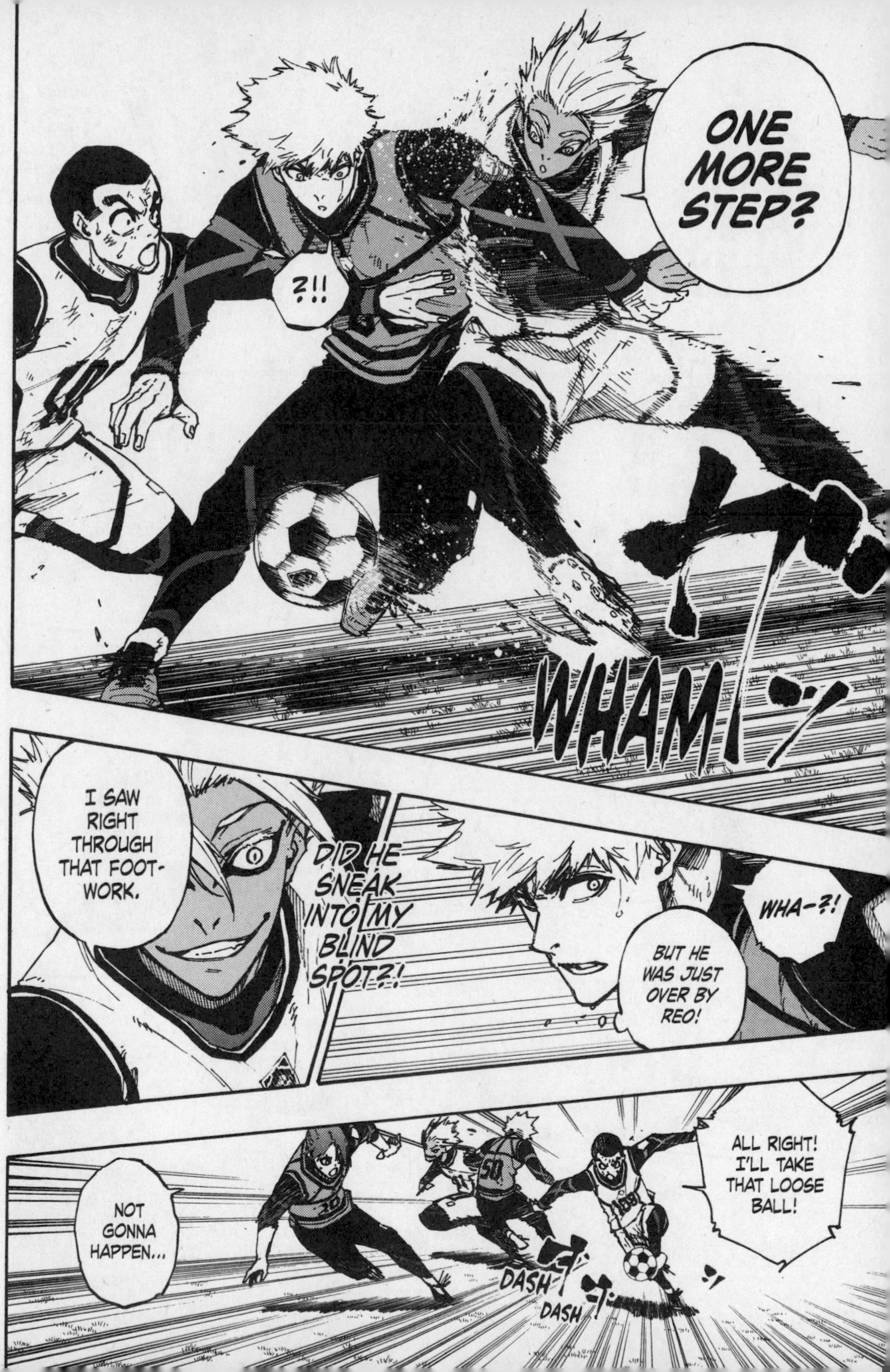
ONE MORE STEP?
?!!
WHAM
WHA-?!
BUT HE WAS JUST OVER BY REO!
DID HE SNEAK INTO MY BLIND SPOT?!
I SAW RIGHT THROUGH THAT FOOT-WORK.
ALL RIGHT! I'LL TAKE THAT LOOSE BALL!
DASH
DASH
NOT GONNA HAPPEN...

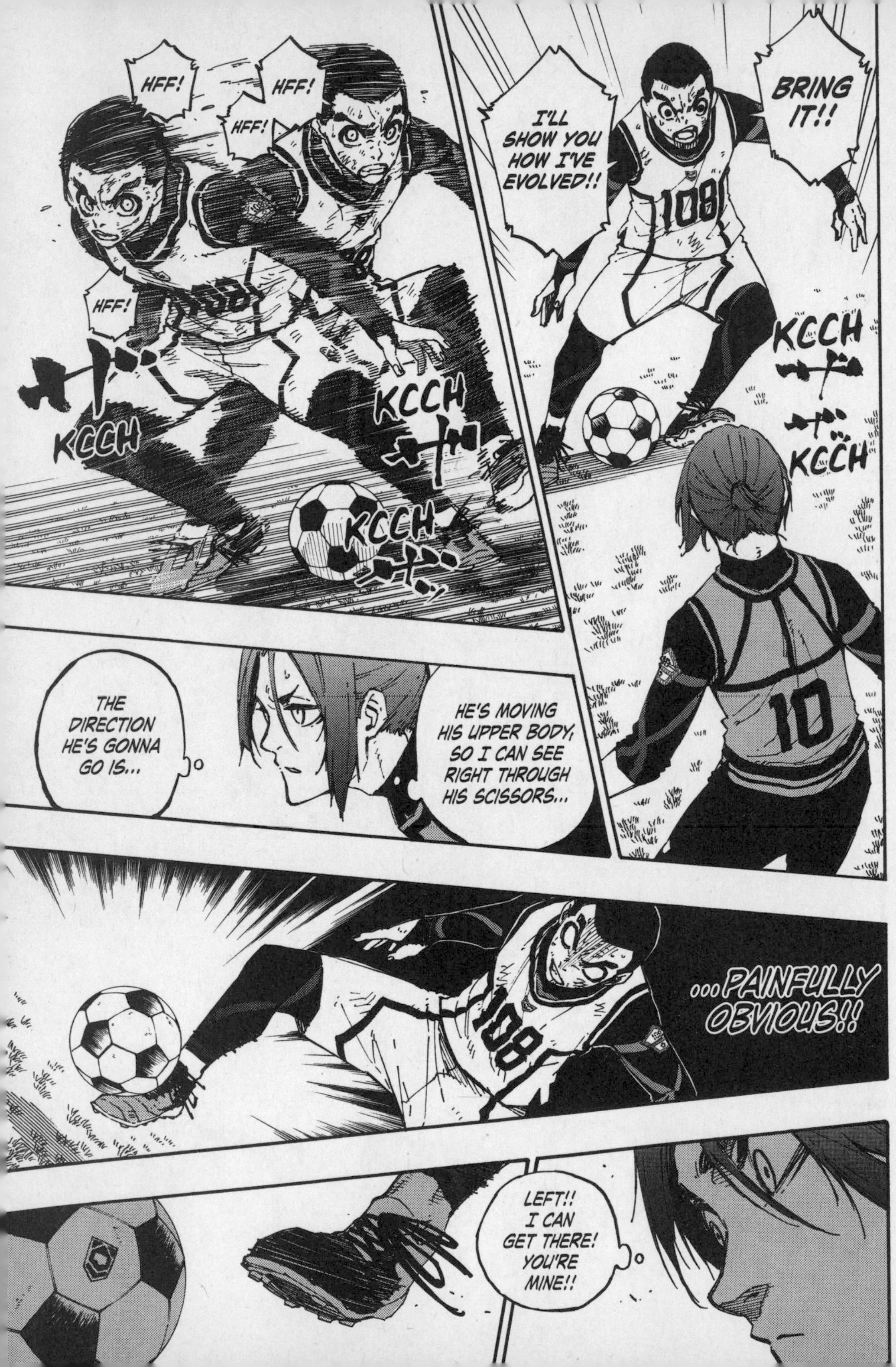
BRING IT!!
I'LL SHOW YOU HOW I'VE EVOLVED!!
KCCH
KCCH
HFF!
HFF!
HFF!
HFF!
KCCH
KCCH
KCCH
HE'S MOVING HIS UPPER BODY, SO I CAN SEE RIGHT THROUGH HIS SCISSORS...
THE DIRECTION HE'S GONNA GO IS...
...PAINFULLY OBVIOUS!!
LEFT!! I CAN GET THERE! YOU'RE MINE!!

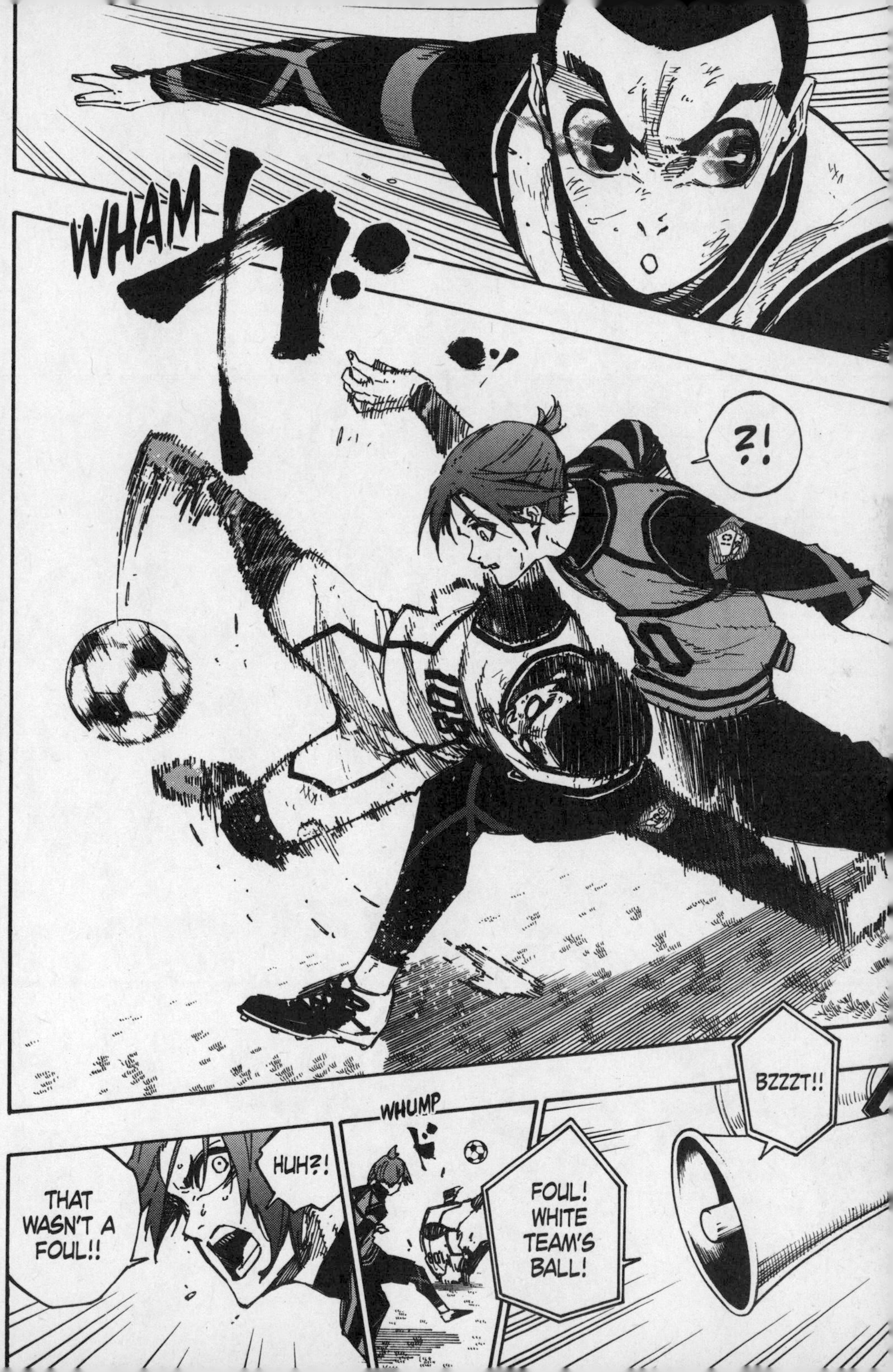
WHAM
?!
BZZZT!!
FOUL! WHITE TEAM'S BALL!
WHUMP
HUH?!
THAT WASN'T A FOUL!!

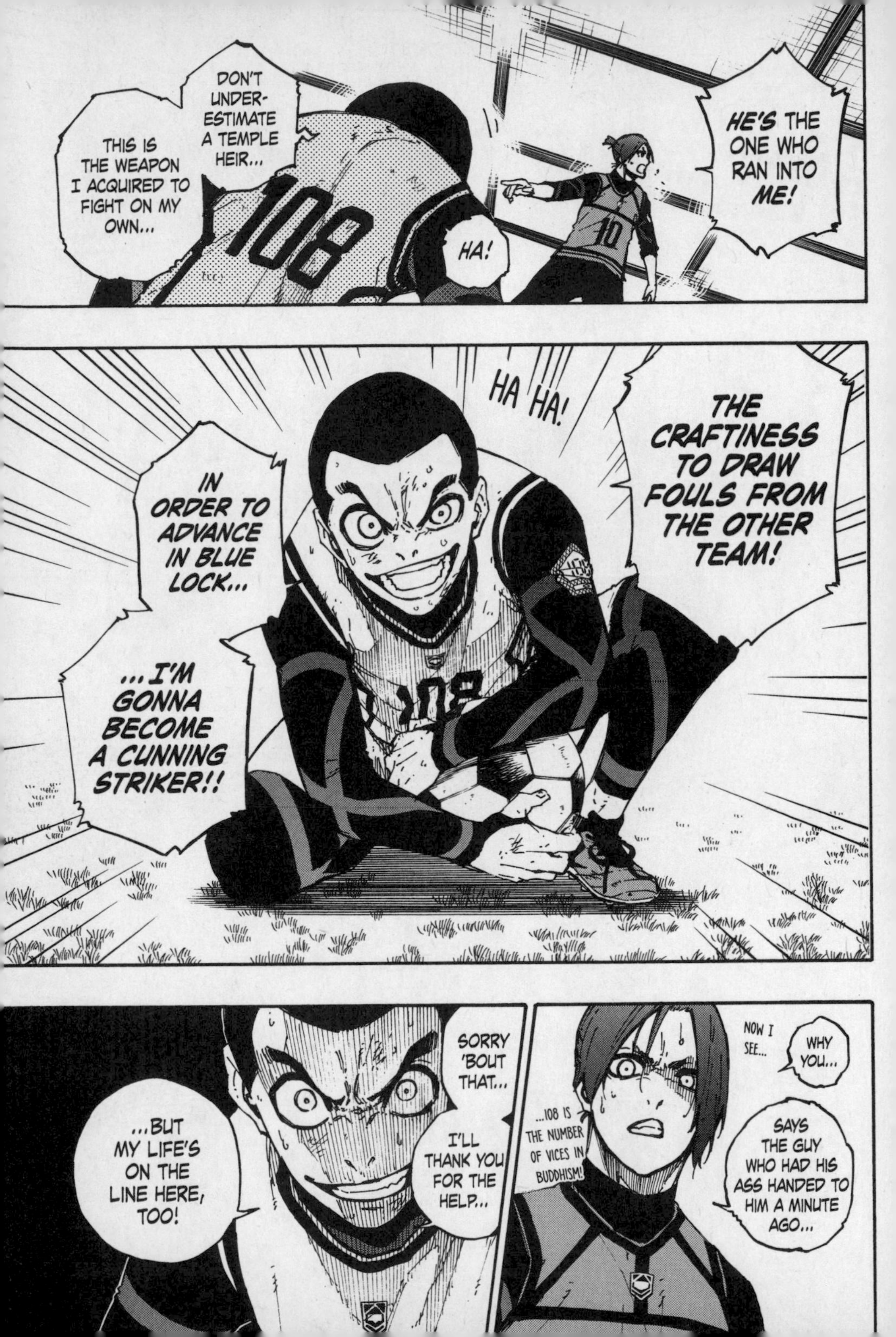
HE'S THE ONE WHO RAN INTO ME!
HA!
DON'T UNDER-ESTIMATE A TEMPLE HEIR...
THIS IS THE WEAPON I ACQUIRED TO FIGHT ON MY OWN...
108
10
HA HA!
THE CRAFTINESS TO DRAW FOULS FROM THE OTHER TEAM!
IN ORDER TO ADVANCE IN BLUE LOCK...
...I'M GONNA BECOME A CUNNING STRIKER!!
WHY YOU...
NOW I SEE...
...108 IS THE NUMBER OF VICES IN BUDDHISM!
SAYS THE GUY WHO HAD HIS ASS HANDED TO HIM A MINUTE AGO...
SORRY 'BOUT THAT...
I'LL THANK YOU FOR THE HELP...
...BUT MY LIFE'S ON THE LINE HERE, TOO!

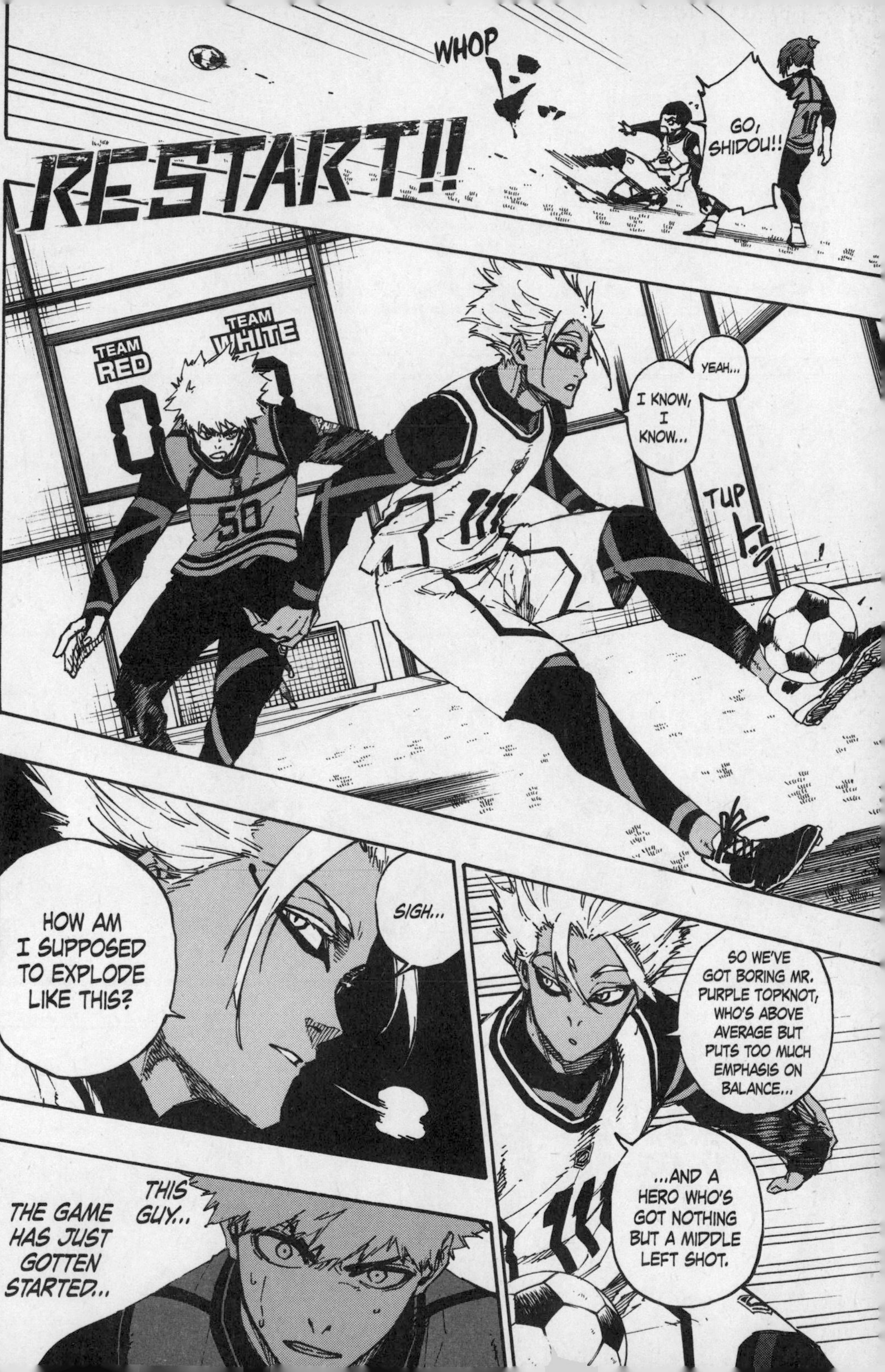
GO, SHIDOU!!
WHOP
RESTART!!
YEAH... I KNOW, I KNOW...
TUP
TEAM WHITE
TEAM RED
SO WE'VE GOT BORING MR. PURPLE TOPKNOT, WHO'S ABOVE AVERAGE BUT PUTS TOO MUCH EMPHASIS ON BALANCE...
...AND A HERO WHO'S GOT NOTHING BUT A MIDDLE LEFT SHOT.
SIGH...
HOW AM I SUPPOSED TO EXPLODE LIKE THIS?
THIS GUY...
THE GAME HAS JUST GOTTEN STARTED...

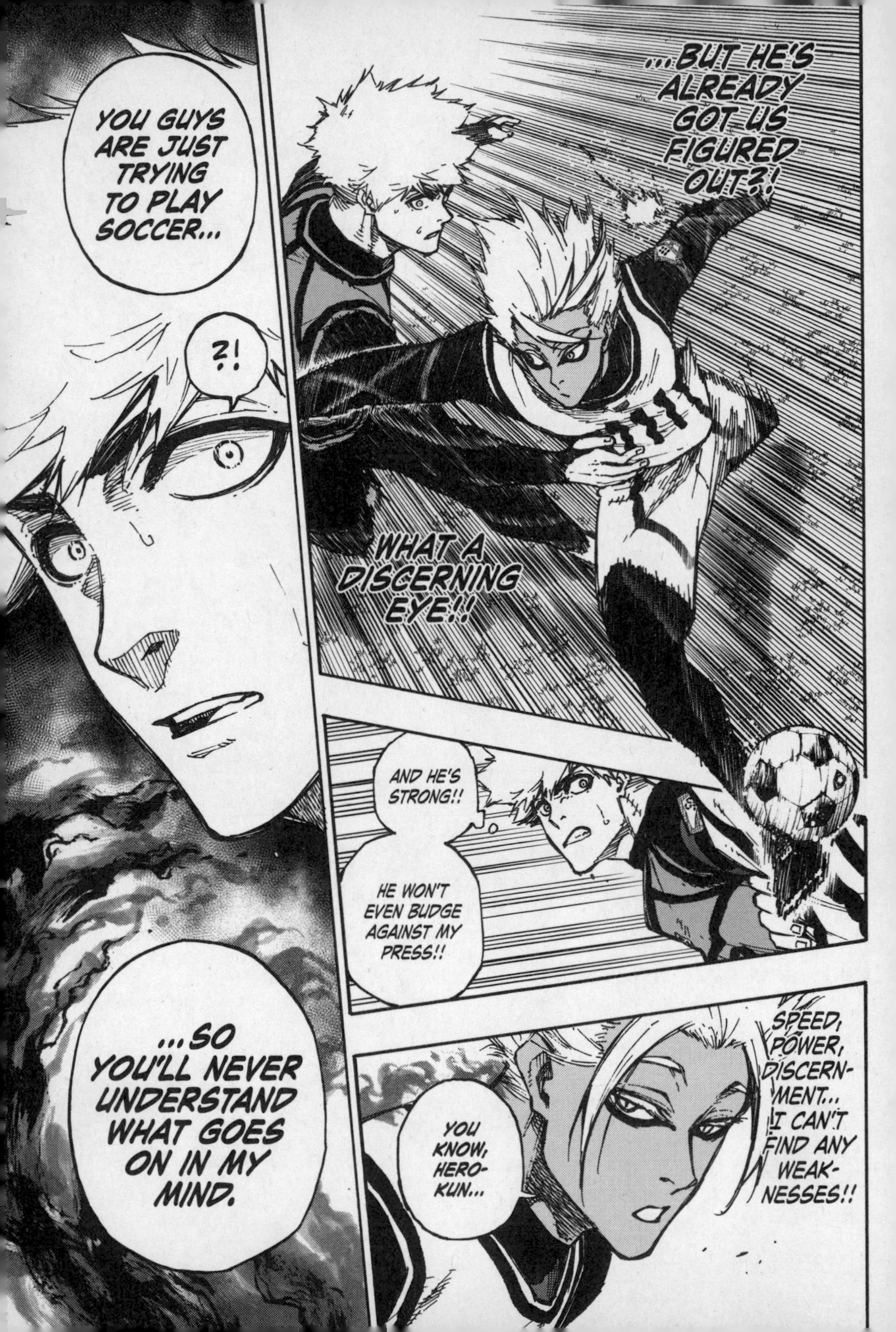
...BUT HE'S ALREADY GOT US FIGURED OUT?!
WHAT A DISCERNING EYE!!
AND HE'S STRONG!!
HE WON'T EVEN BUDGE AGAINST MY PRESS!!
SPEED, POWER, DISCERNMENT... I CAN'T FIND ANY WEAKNESSES!!
YOU KNOW, HERO-KUN...
YOU GUYS ARE JUST TRYING TO PLAY SOCCER...
?!
...SO YOU'LL NEVER UNDERSTAND WHAT GOES ON IN MY MIND.

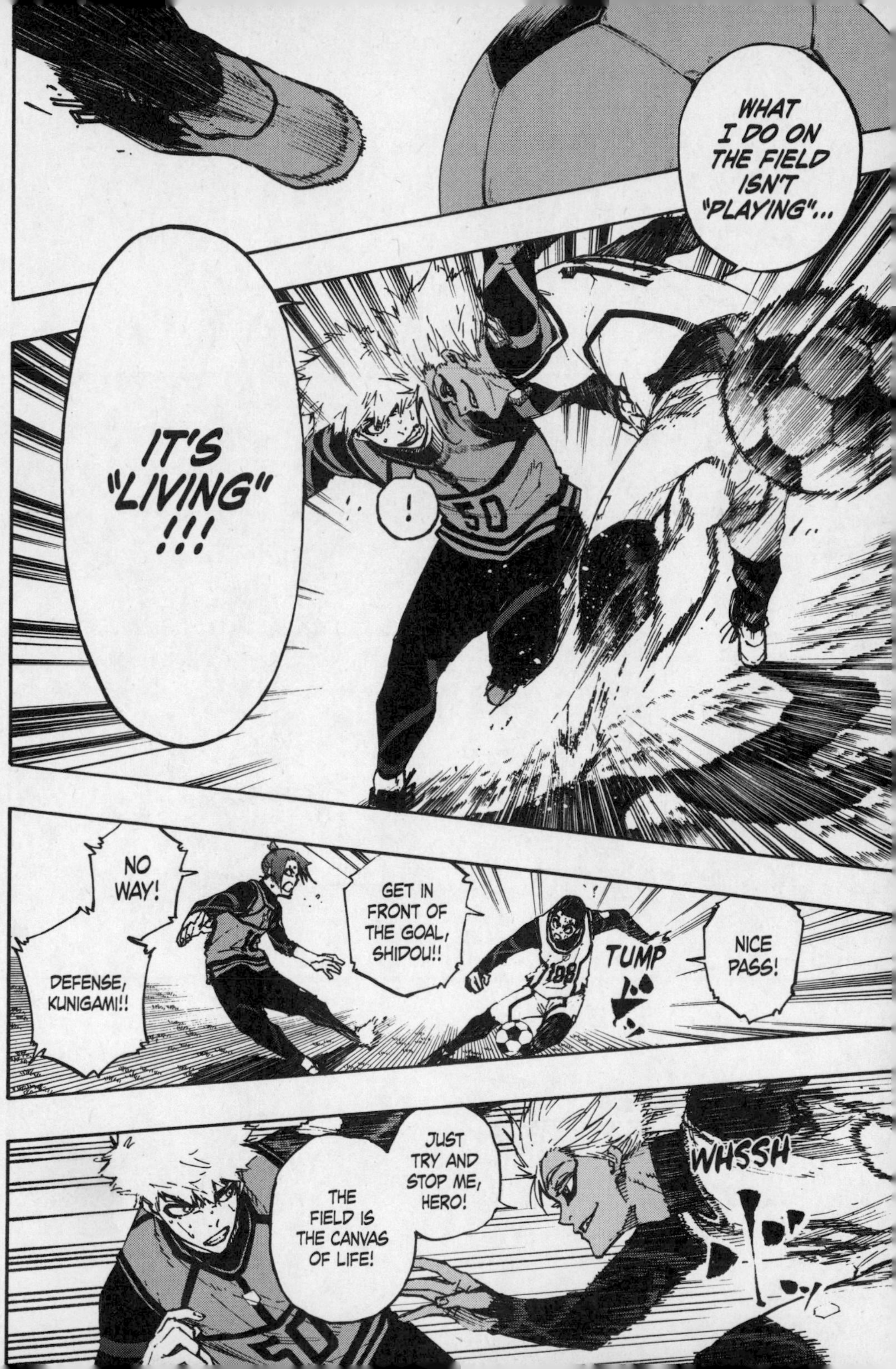
WHAT I DO ON THE FIELD ISN'T "PLAYING"...
IT'S "LIVING" !!!
!
NICE PASS!
TUMP
GET IN FRONT OF THE GOAL, SHIDOU!!
NO WAY!
DEFENSE, KUNIGAMI!!
WHSSH
JUST TRY AND STOP ME, HERO!
THE FIELD IS THE CANVAS OF LIFE!

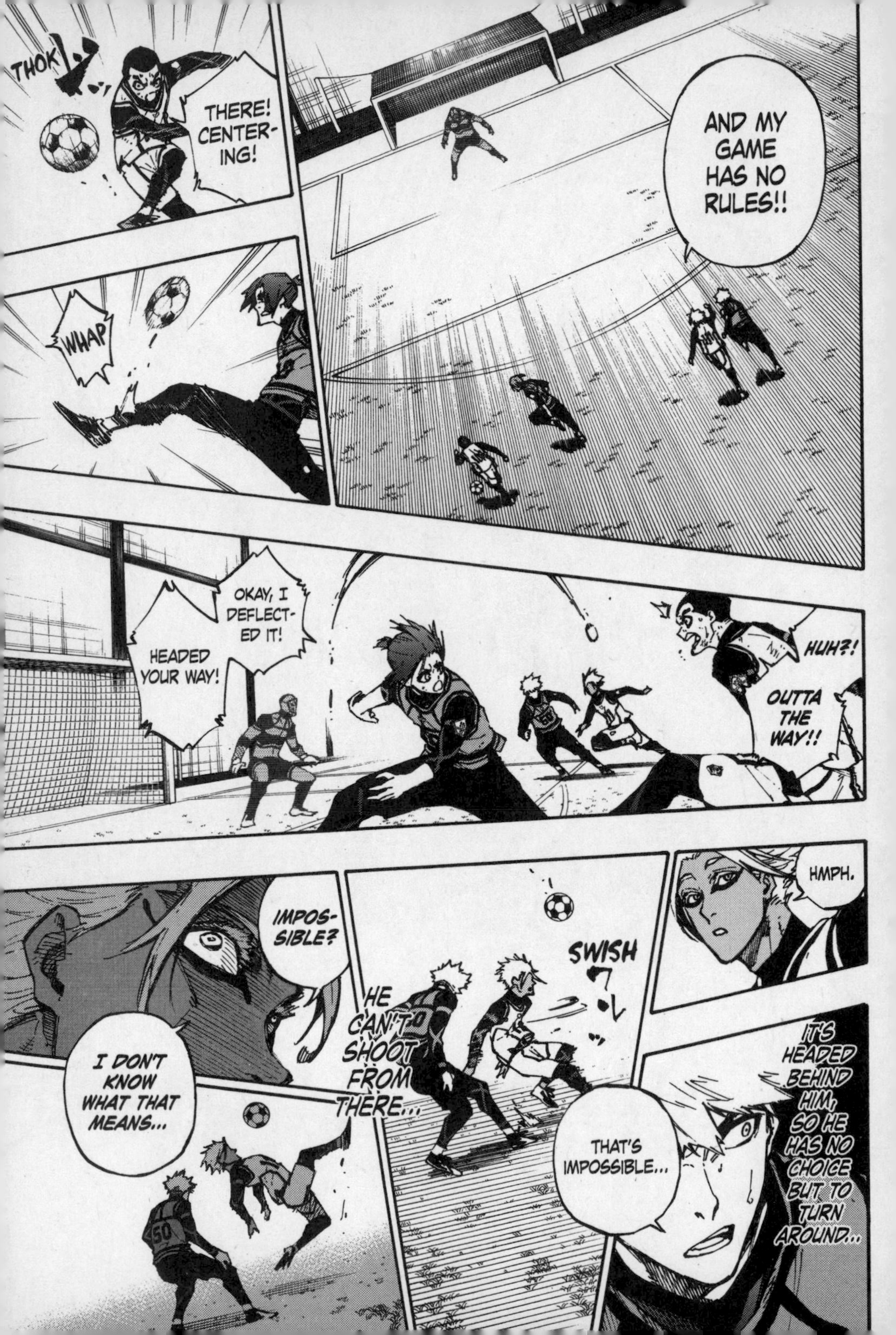
AND MY GAME HAS NO RULES!!
THOK
THERE! CENTERING!
WHAP
HUH?!
OUTTA THE WAY!!
OKAY, I DEFLECTED IT!
HEADED YOUR WAY!
HMPH.
SWISH
HE CAN'T SHOOT FROM THERE...
IT'S HEADED BEHIND HIM, SO HE HAS NO CHOICE BUT TO TURN AROUND...
THAT'S IMPOSSIBLE...
IMPOSSIBLE?
I DON'T KNOW WHAT THAT MEANS...

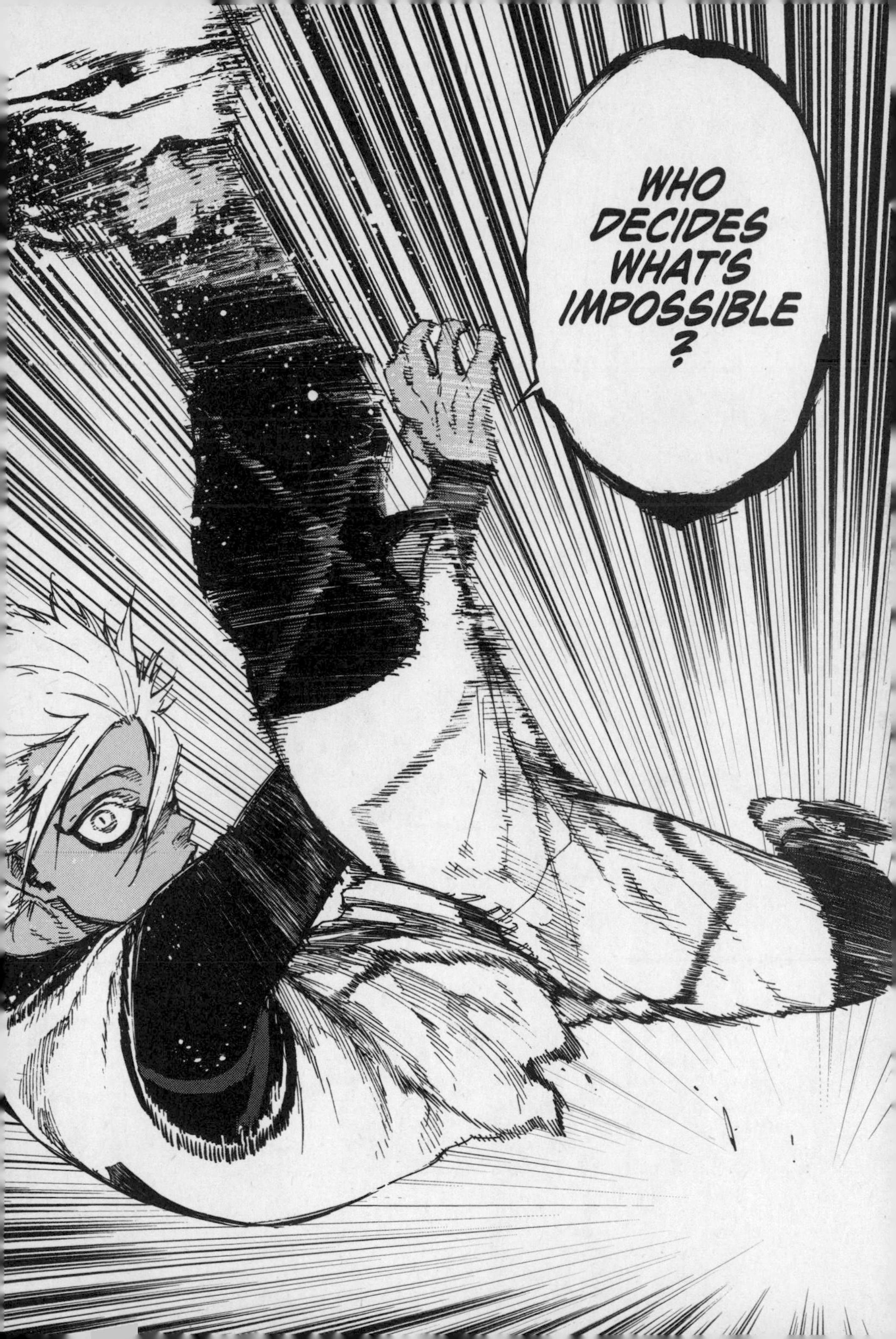
WHO DECIDES WHAT'S IMPOSSIBLE?

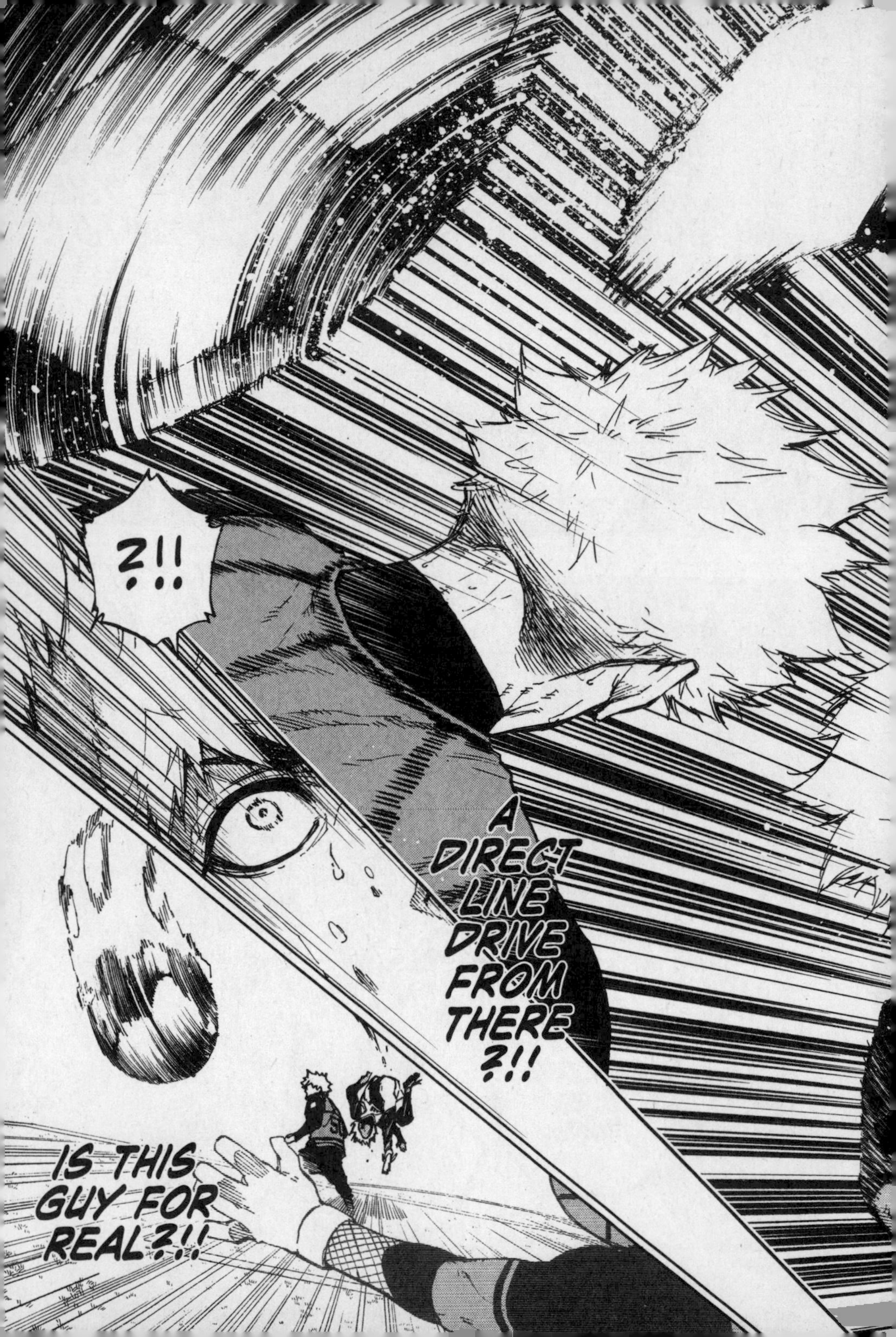
?!!
A DIRECT LINE DRIVE FROM THERE?!!
IS THIS GUY FOR REAL?!!

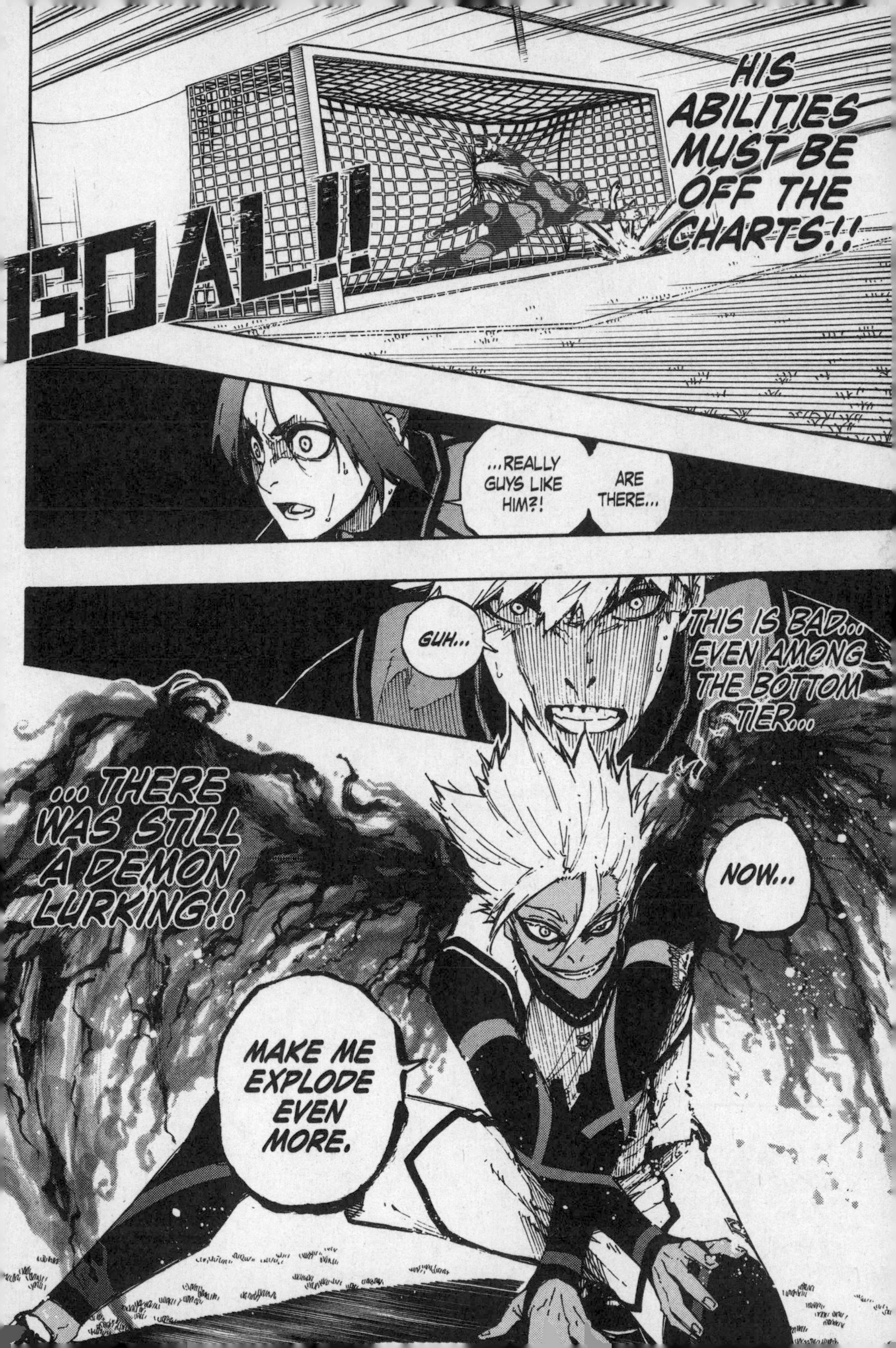
HIS ABILITIES MUST BE OFF THE CHARTS!!
GOAL!!
ARE THERE...
...REALLY GUYS LIKE HIM?!
THIS IS BAD... EVEN AMONG THE BOTTOM TIER...
GUH...
...THERE WAS STILL A DEMON LURKING!!
NOW...
MAKE ME EXPLODE EVEN MORE.

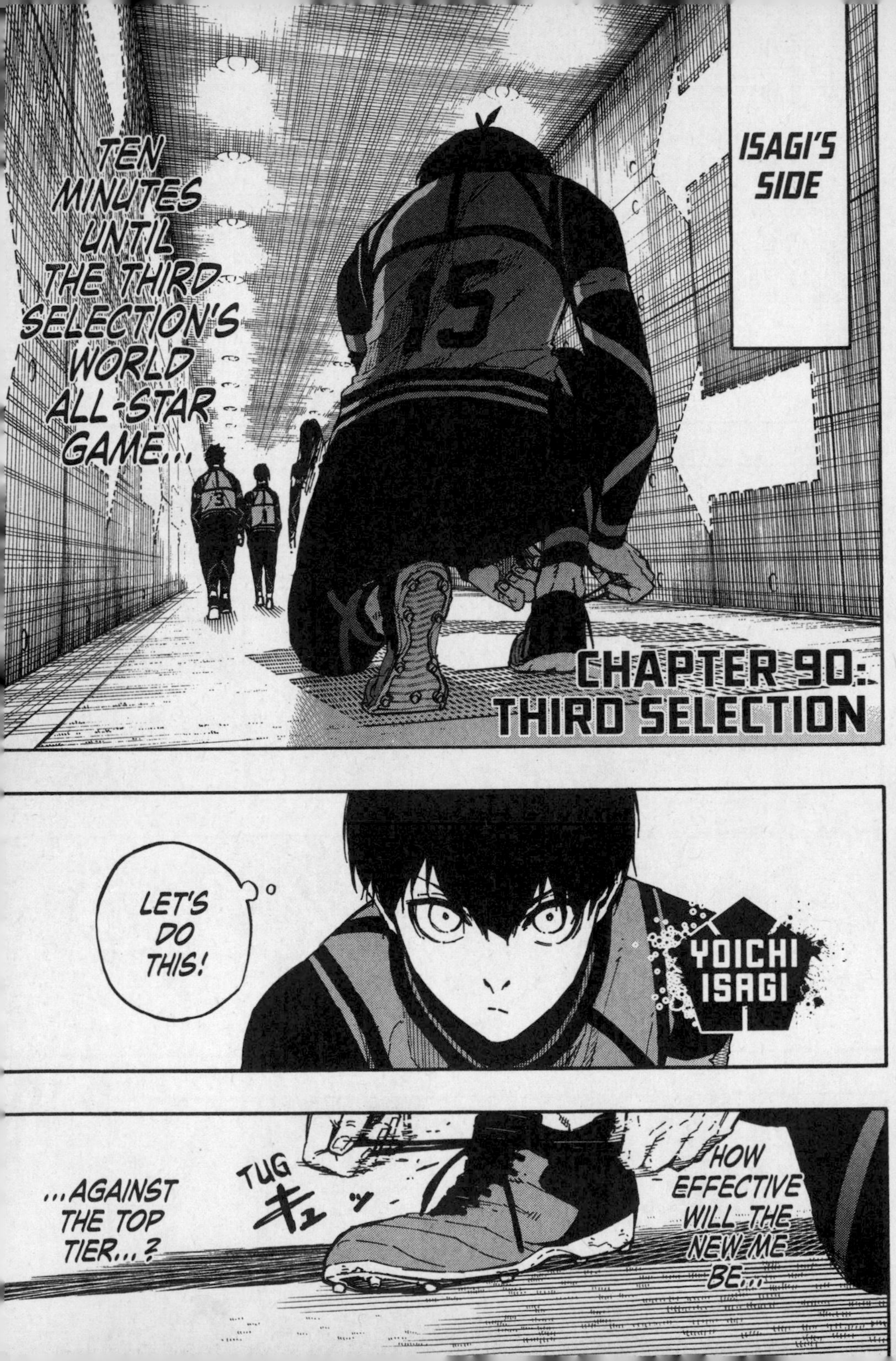
ISAGI'S SIDE
TEN MINUTES UNTIL THE THIRD SELECTION'S WORLD ALL-STAR GAME...
CHAPTER 90: THIRD SELECTION
YOICHI ISAGI
LET'S DO THIS!
HOW EFFECTIVE WILL THE NEW ME BE...
TUG
キュッ
...AGAINST THE TOP TIER...?

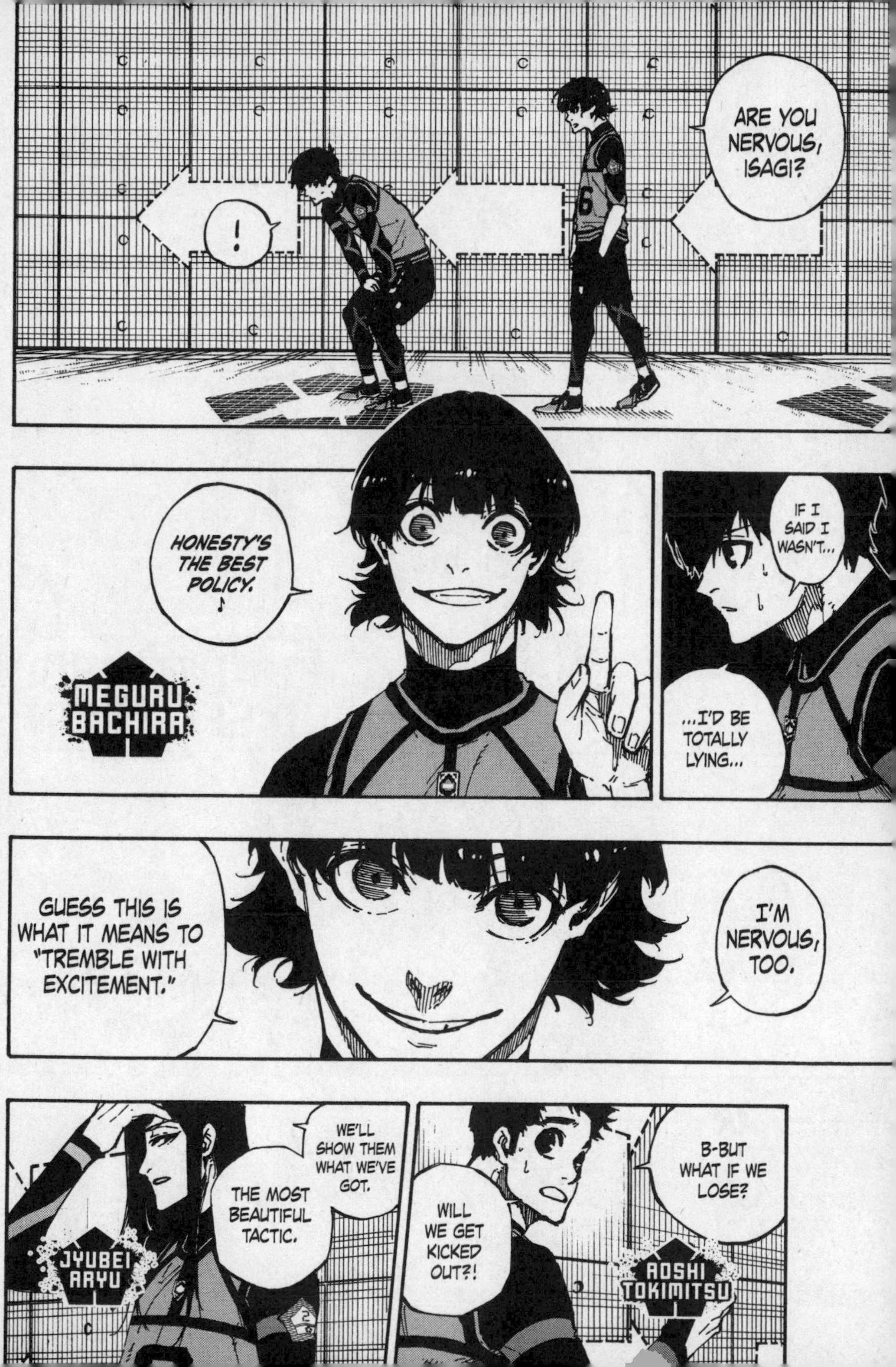
ARE YOU NERVOUS, ISAGI?
!
IF I SAID I WASN'T...
...I'D BE TOTALLY LYING...
HONESTY'S THE BEST POLICY. ♪
MEGURU BACHIRA
I'M NERVOUS, TOO.
GUESS THIS IS WHAT IT MEANS TO "TREMBLE WITH EXCITEMENT."
B-BUT WHAT IF WE LOSE?
WILL WE GET KICKED OUT?!
AOSHI TOKIMITSU
WE'LL SHOW THEM WHAT WE'VE GOT.
THE MOST BEAUTIFUL TACTIC.
JYUBEI ARYU

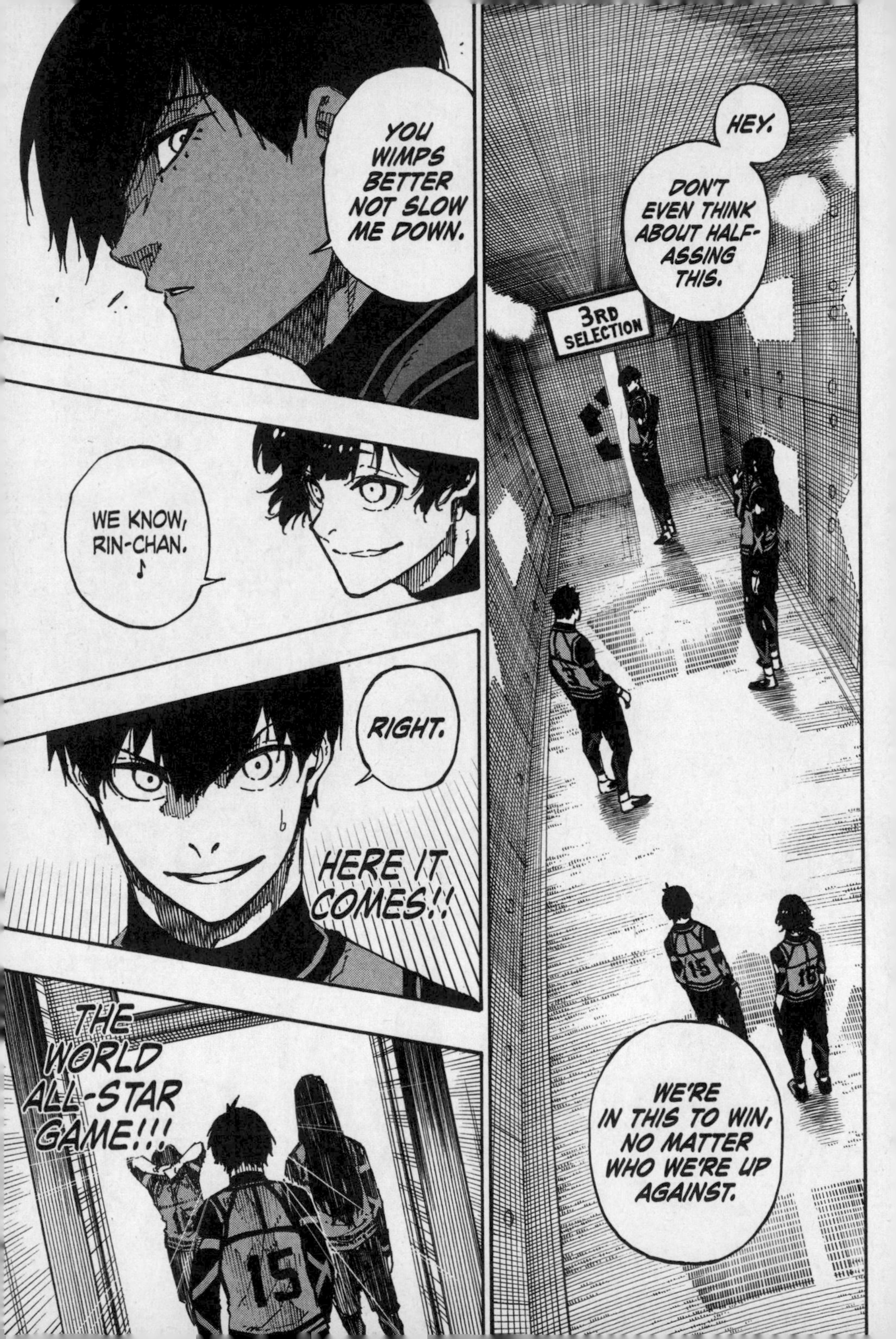
HEY.
DON'T EVEN THINK ABOUT HALF-ASSING THIS.
3RD SELECTION
WE'RE IN THIS TO WIN, NO MATTER WHO WE'RE UP AGAINST.
YOU WIMPS BETTER NOT SLOW ME DOWN.
WE KNOW, RIN-CHAN. ♪
RIGHT.
HERE IT COMES!!
THE WORLD ALL-STAR GAME!!!

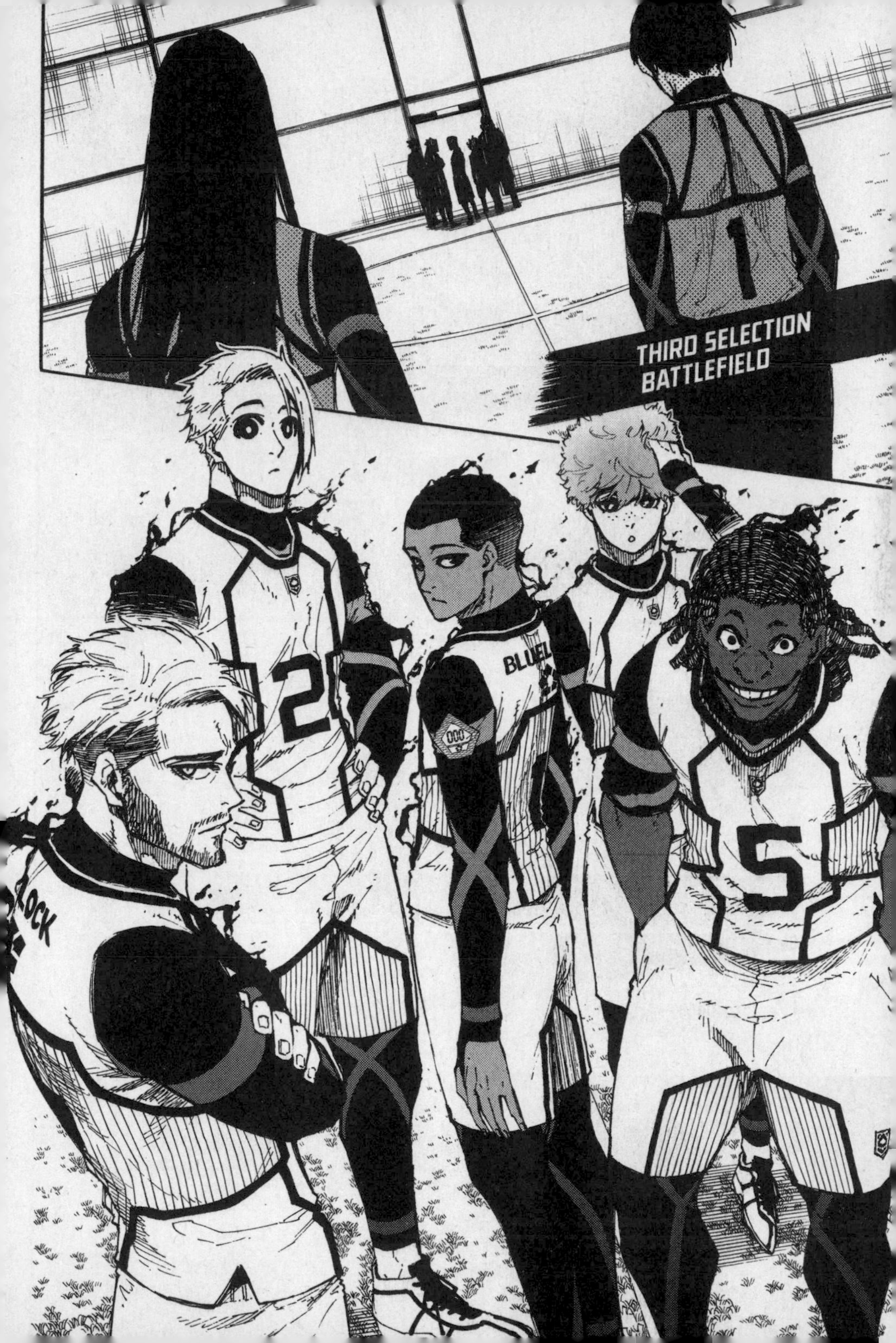
THIRD SELECTION BATTLEFIELD
1
2
BLUEL
5
LOCK

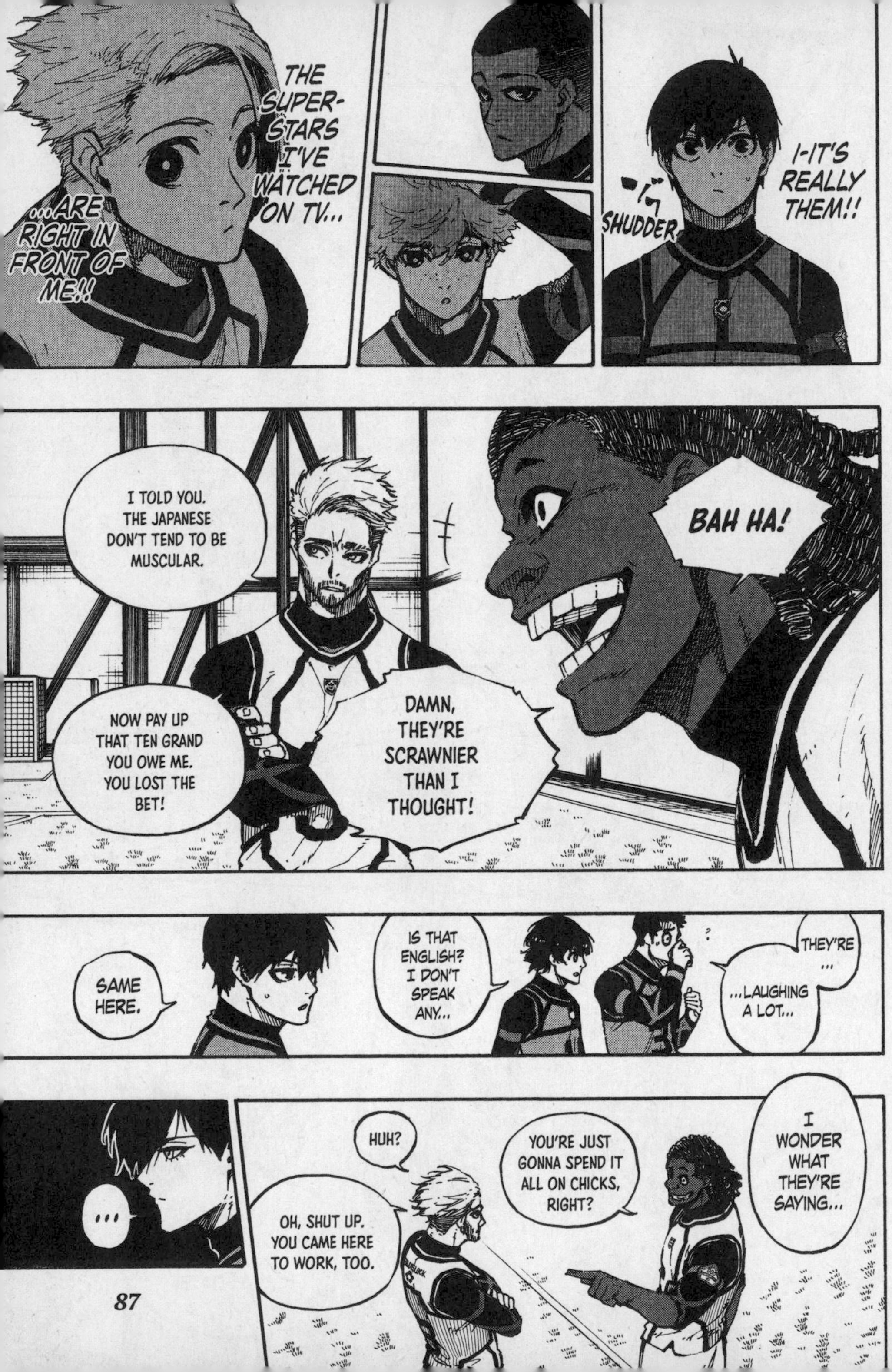
I-IT'S REALLY THEM!!
SHUDDER
THE SUPER-STARS I'VE WÄTCHED ON TV...
...ARE RIGHT IN FRONT OF ME!!
BAH HA!
DAMN, THEY'RE SCRAWNIER THAN I THOUGHT!
I TOLD YOU. THE JAPANESE DON'T TEND TO BE MUSCULAR.
NOW PAY UP THAT TEN GRAND YOU OWE ME. YOU LOST THE BET!
THEY'RE ... ...LAUGHING A LOT...
IS THAT ENGLISH? I DON'T SPEAK ANY...
SAME HERE.
I WONDER WHAT THEY'RE SAYING...
YOU'RE JUST GONNA SPEND IT ALL ON CHICKS, RIGHT?
HUH?
OH, SHUT UP. YOU CAME HERE TO WORK, TOO.
...

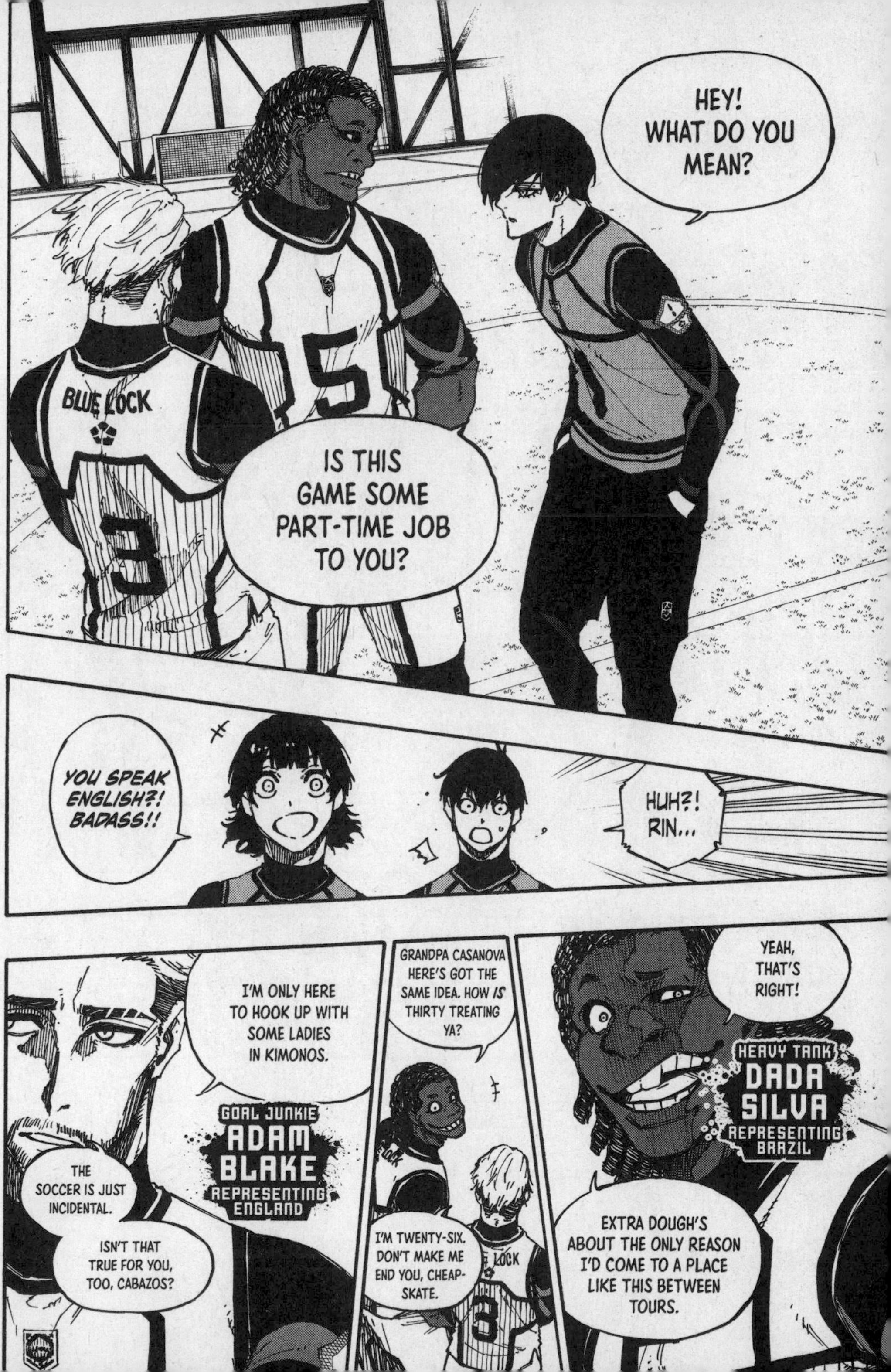

HEY! WHAT DO YOU MEAN?
IS THIS GAME SOME PART-TIME JOB TO YOU?
HUH?! RIN...
YOU SPEAK ENGLISH?! BADASS!!
YEAH, THAT'S RIGHT!
HEAVY TANK DADA SILVA REPRESENTING BRAZIL
EXTRA DOUGH'S ABOUT THE ONLY REASON I'D COME TO A PLACE LIKE THIS BETWEEN TOURS.
GRANDPA CASANOVA HERE'S GOT THE SAME IDEA. HOW *IS* THIRTY TREATING YA?
I'M TWENTY-SIX. DON'T MAKE ME END YOU, CHEAP-SKATE.
I'M ONLY HERE TO HOOK UP WITH SOME LADIES IN KIMONOS.
GOAL JUNKIE ADAM BLAKE REPRESENTING ENGLAND
THE SOCCER IS JUST INCIDENTAL.
ISN'T THAT TRUE FOR YOU, TOO, CABAZOS?

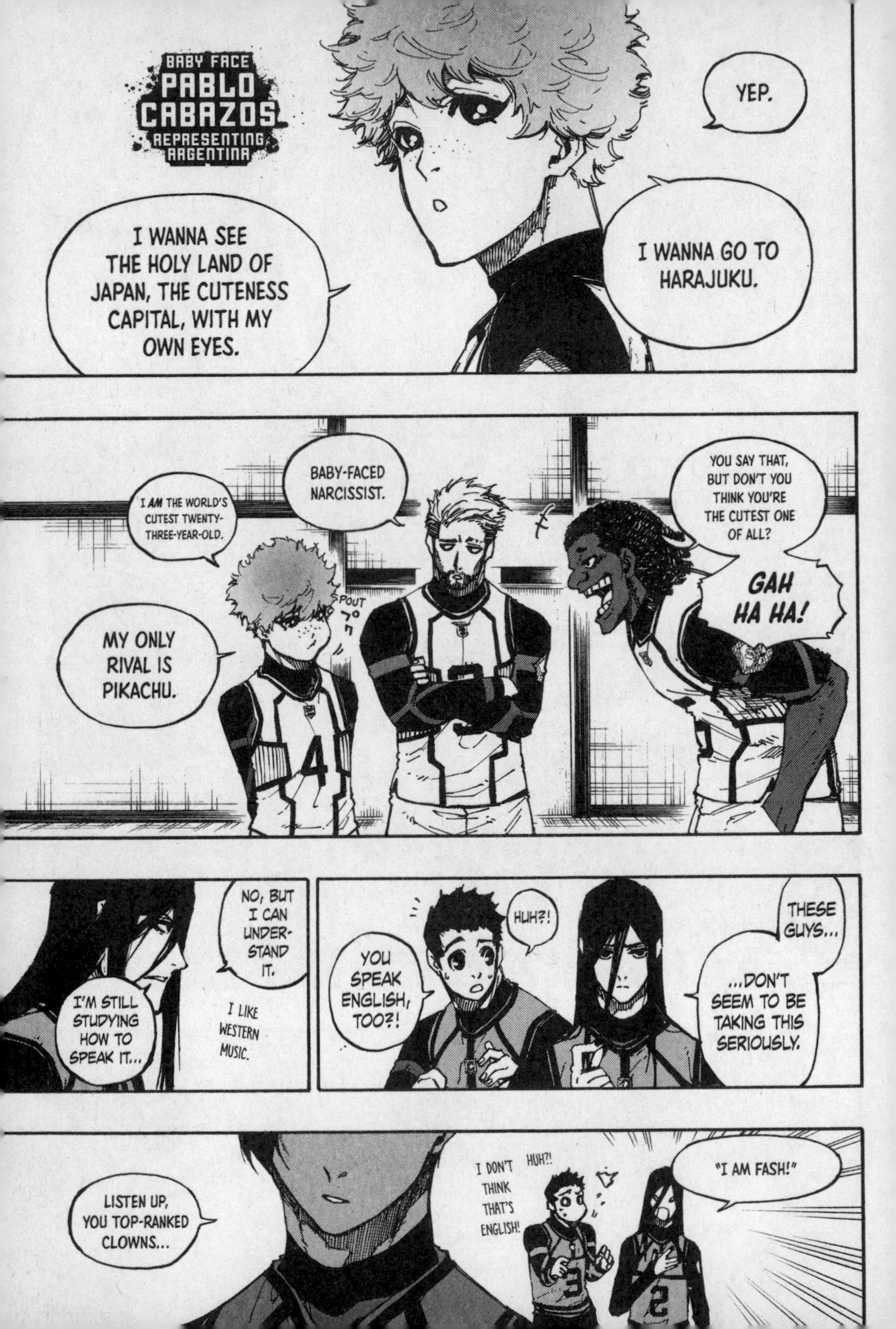
YEP.
I WANNA GO TO HARAJUKU.
BABY FACE PABLO CABAZOS REPRESENTING ARGENTINA
I WANNA SEE THE HOLY LAND OF JAPAN, THE CUTENESS CAPITAL, WITH MY OWN EYES.
YOU SAY THAT, BUT DON'T YOU THINK YOU'RE THE CUTEST ONE OF ALL?
GAH HA HA!
BABY-FACED NARCISSIST.
I AM THE WORLD'S CUTEST TWENTY-THREE-YEAR-OLD.
POUT
MY ONLY RIVAL IS PIKACHU.
THESE GUYS...
...DON'T SEEM TO BE TAKING THIS SERIOUSLY.
HUH?!
YOU SPEAK ENGLISH, TOO?!
NO, BUT I CAN UNDER-STAND IT.
I LIKE WESTERN MUSIC.
I'M STILL STUDYING HOW TO SPEAK IT...
"I AM FASH!"
HUH?!
I DON'T THINK THAT'S ENGLISH!
LISTEN UP, YOU TOP-RANKED CLOWNS...

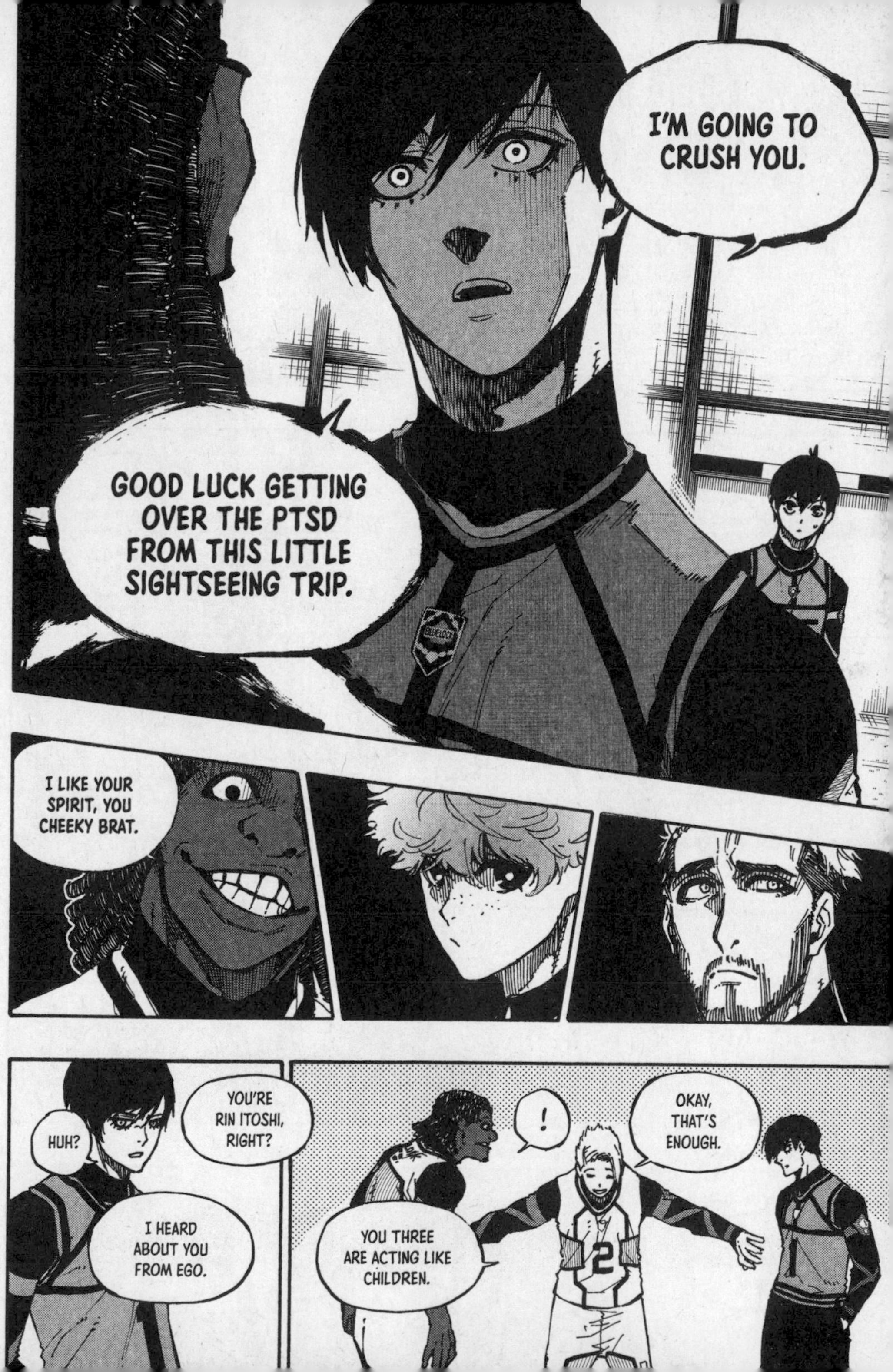
I'M GOING TO CRUSH YOU.
GOOD LUCK GETTING OVER THE PTSD FROM THIS LITTLE SIGHTSEEING TRIP.
I LIKE YOUR SPIRIT, YOU CHEEKY BRAT.
OKAY, THAT'S ENOUGH.
!
YOU THREE ARE ACTING LIKE CHILDREN.
YOU'RE RIN ITOSHI, RIGHT?
HUH?
I HEARD ABOUT YOU FROM EGO.

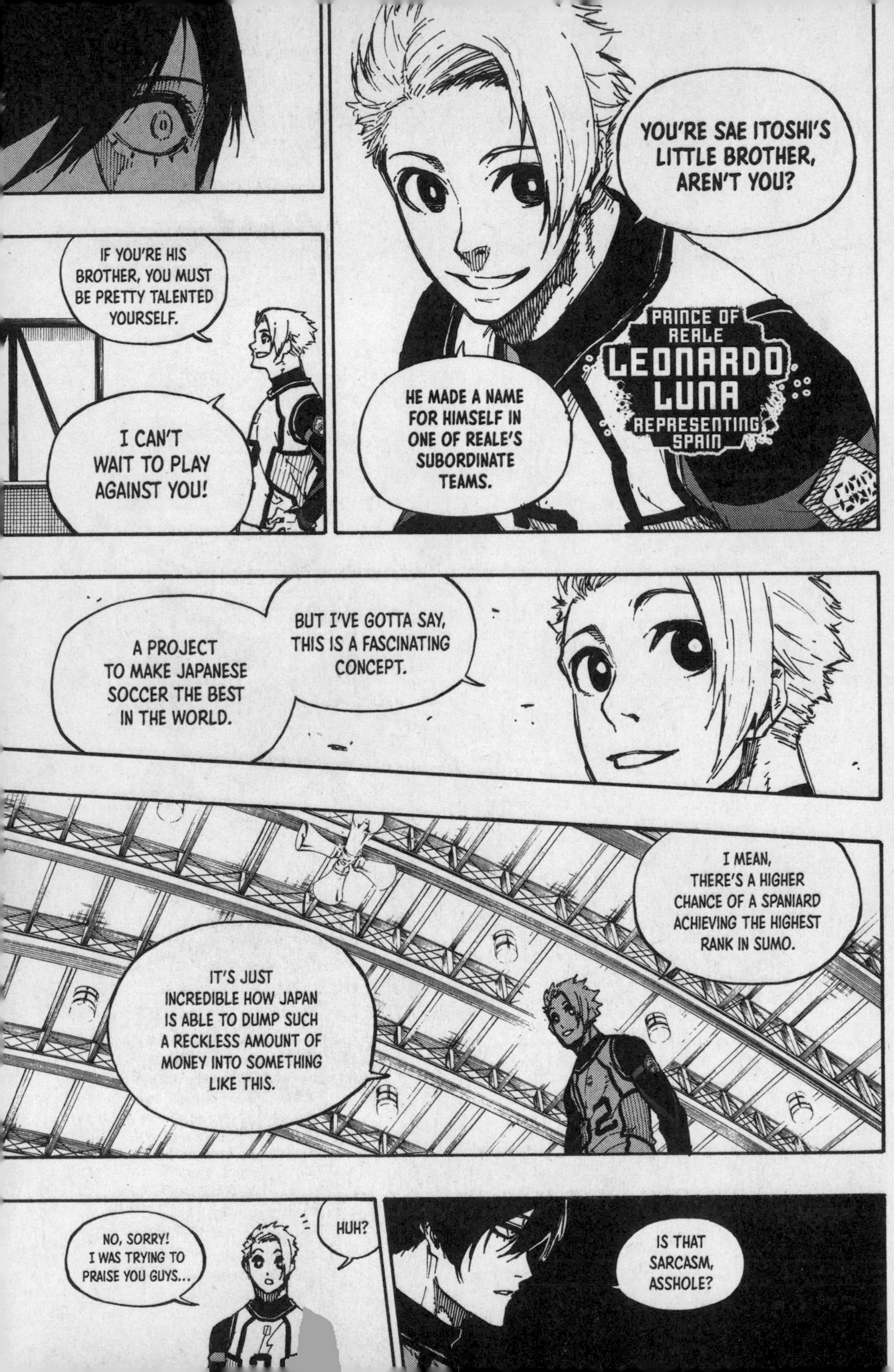
YOU'RE SAE ITOSHI'S LITTLE BROTHER, AREN'T YOU?
PRINCE OF REALE
LEONARDO LUNA
REPRESENTING SPAIN
HE MADE A NAME FOR HIMSELF IN ONE OF REALE'S SUBORDINATE TEAMS.
IF YOU'RE HIS BROTHER, YOU MUST BE PRETTY TALENTED YOURSELF.
I CAN'T WAIT TO PLAY AGAINST YOU!
BUT I'VE GOTTA SAY, THIS IS A FASCINATING CONCEPT.
A PROJECT TO MAKE JAPANESE SOCCER THE BEST IN THE WORLD.
I MEAN, THERE'S A HIGHER CHANCE OF A SPANIARD ACHIEVING THE HIGHEST RANK IN SUMO.
IT'S JUST INCREDIBLE HOW JAPAN IS ABLE TO DUMP SUCH A RECKLESS AMOUNT OF MONEY INTO SOMETHING LIKE THIS.
IS THAT SARCASM, ASSHOLE?
HUH?
NO, SORRY! I WAS TRYING TO PRAISE YOU GUYS...

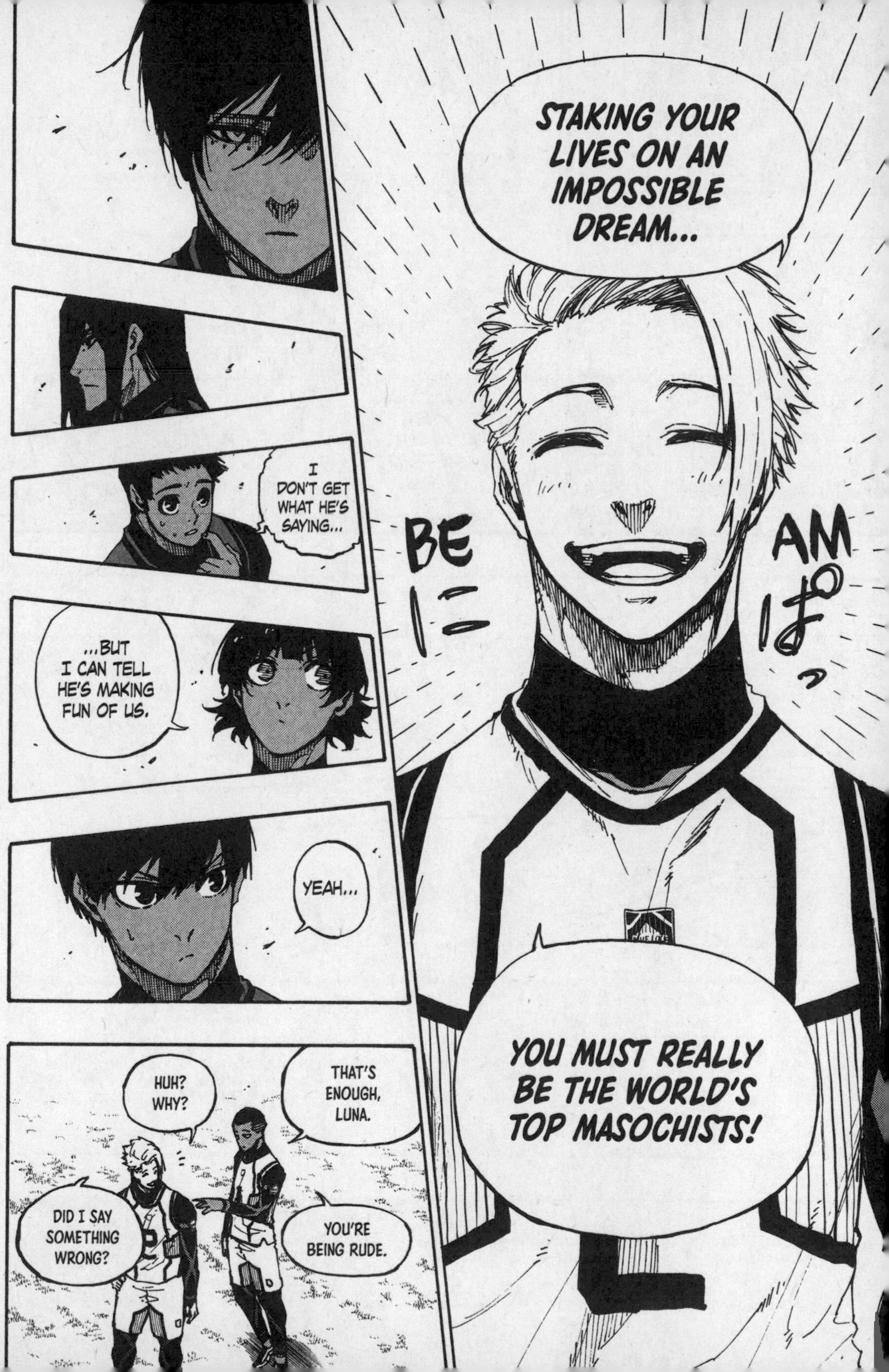
STAKING YOUR LIVES ON AN IMPOSSIBLE DREAM...
BE
AM
ぱっ
YOU MUST REALLY BE THE WORLD'S TOP MASOCHISTS!
I DON'T GET WHAT HE'S SAYING...
...BUT I CAN TELL HE'S MAKING FUN OF US.
YEAH...
THAT'S ENOUGH, LUNA.
HUH? WHY?
YOU'RE BEING RUDE.
DID I SAY SOMETHING WRONG?

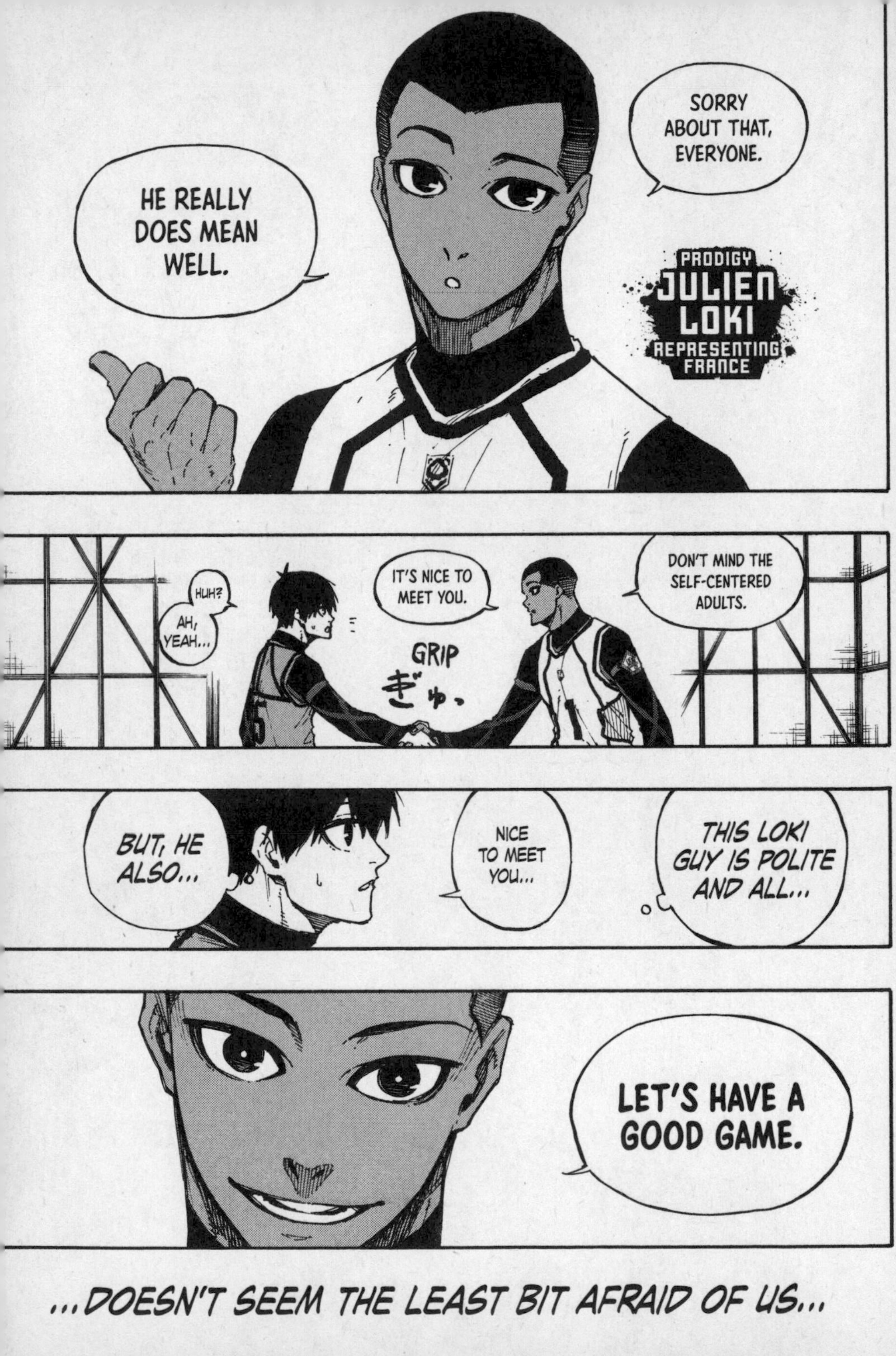
SORRY ABOUT THAT, EVERYONE.
PRODIGY JULIEN LOKI REPRESENTING FRANCE
HE REALLY DOES MEAN WELL.
DON'T MIND THE SELF-CENTERED ADULTS.
IT'S NICE TO MEET YOU.
GRIP
ぎゅっ
HUH?
AH, YEAH...
THIS LOKI GUY IS POLITE AND ALL...
NICE TO MEET YOU...
BUT, HE ALSO...
LET'S HAVE A GOOD GAME.
...DOESN'T SEEM THE LEAST BIT AFRAID OF US...

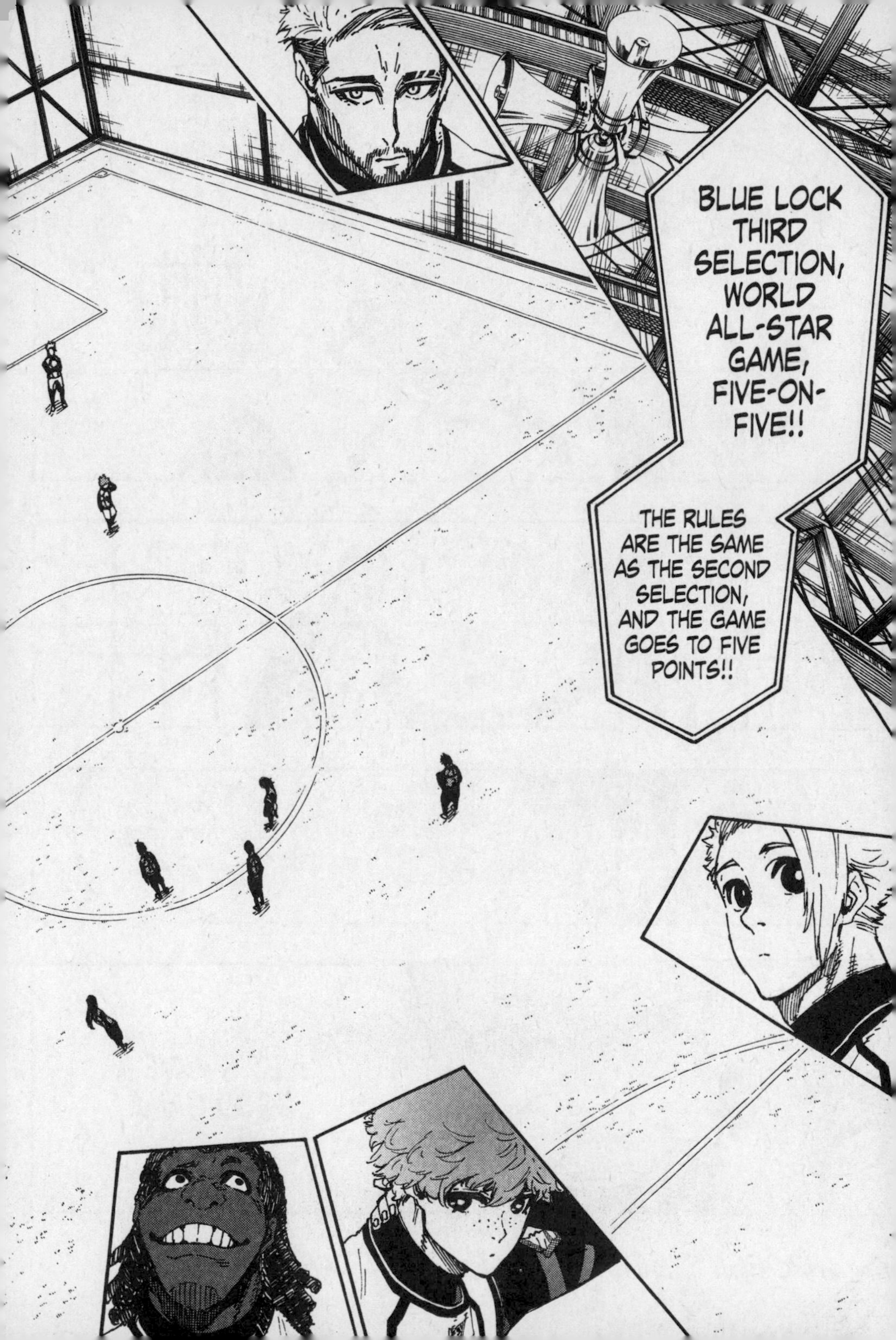
BLUE LOCK THIRD SELECTION, WORLD ALL-STAR GAME, FIVE-ON-FIVE!!
THE RULES ARE THE SAME AS THE SECOND SELECTION, AND THE GAME GOES TO FIVE POINTS!!

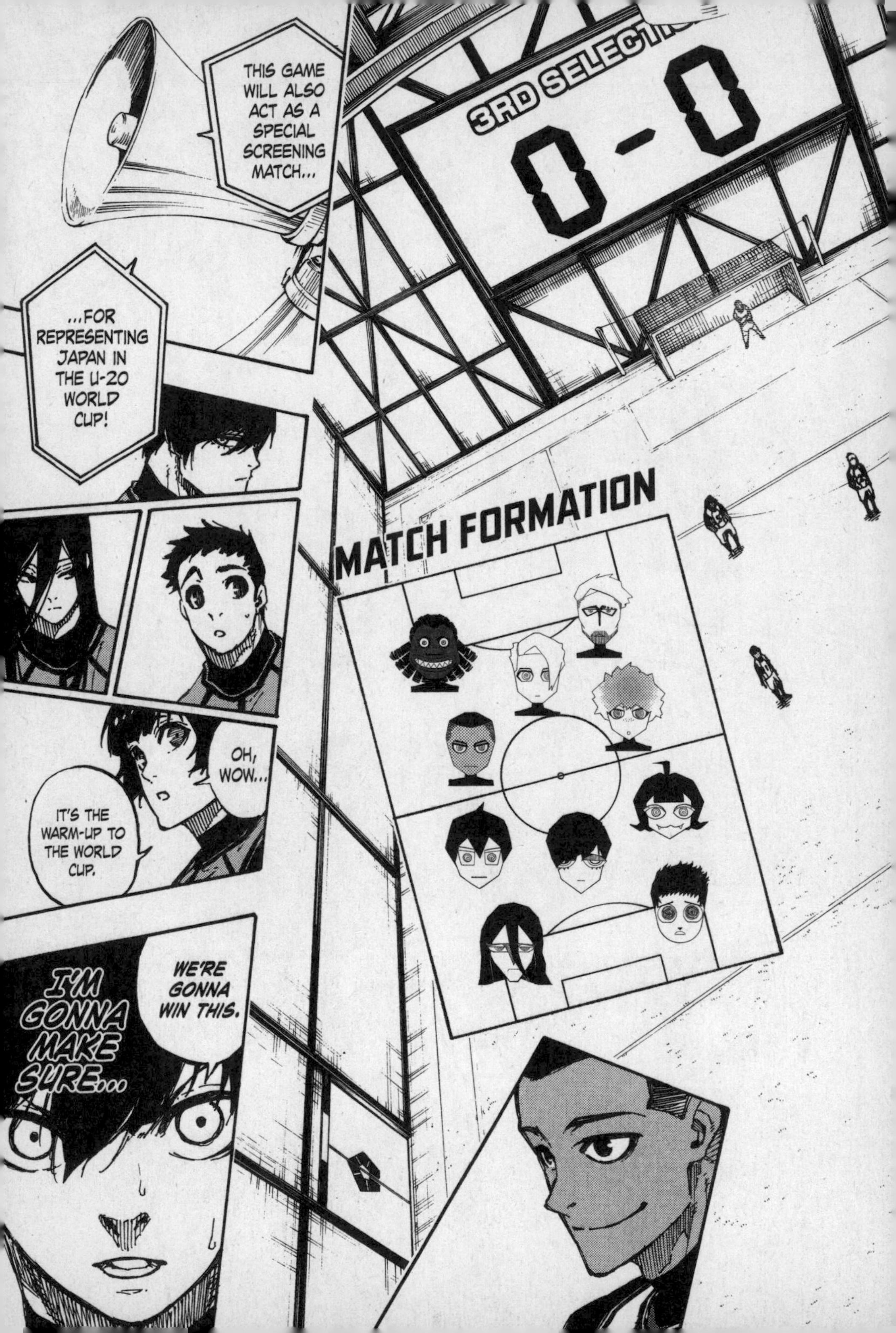
0 - 0
MATCH FORMATION
THIS GAME WILL ALSO ACT AS A SPECIAL SCREENING MATCH...
...FOR REPRESENTING JAPAN IN THE U-20 WORLD CUP!
OH, WOW...
IT'S THE WARM-UP TO THE WORLD CUP.
WE'RE GONNA WIN THIS.
I'M GONNA MAKE SURE...

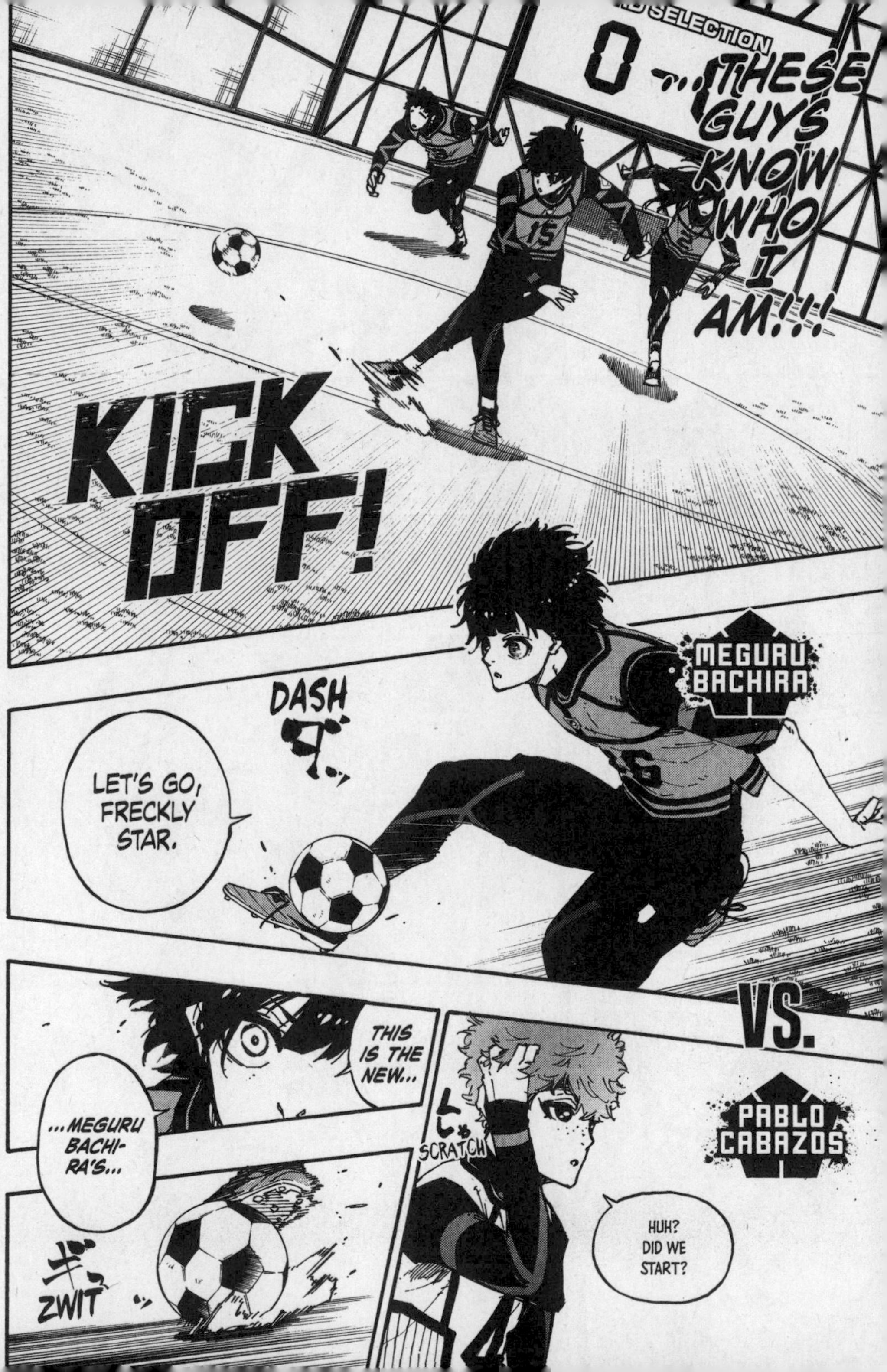
SELECTION
0
...THESE GUYS KNOW WHO I AM!!!
KICK OFF!
MEGURU BACHIRA
DASH
LET'S GO, FRECKLY STAR.
VS.
PABLO CABAZOS
SCRATCH
HUH? DID WE START?
THIS IS THE NEW...
...MEGURU BACHIRA'S...
ZWIT

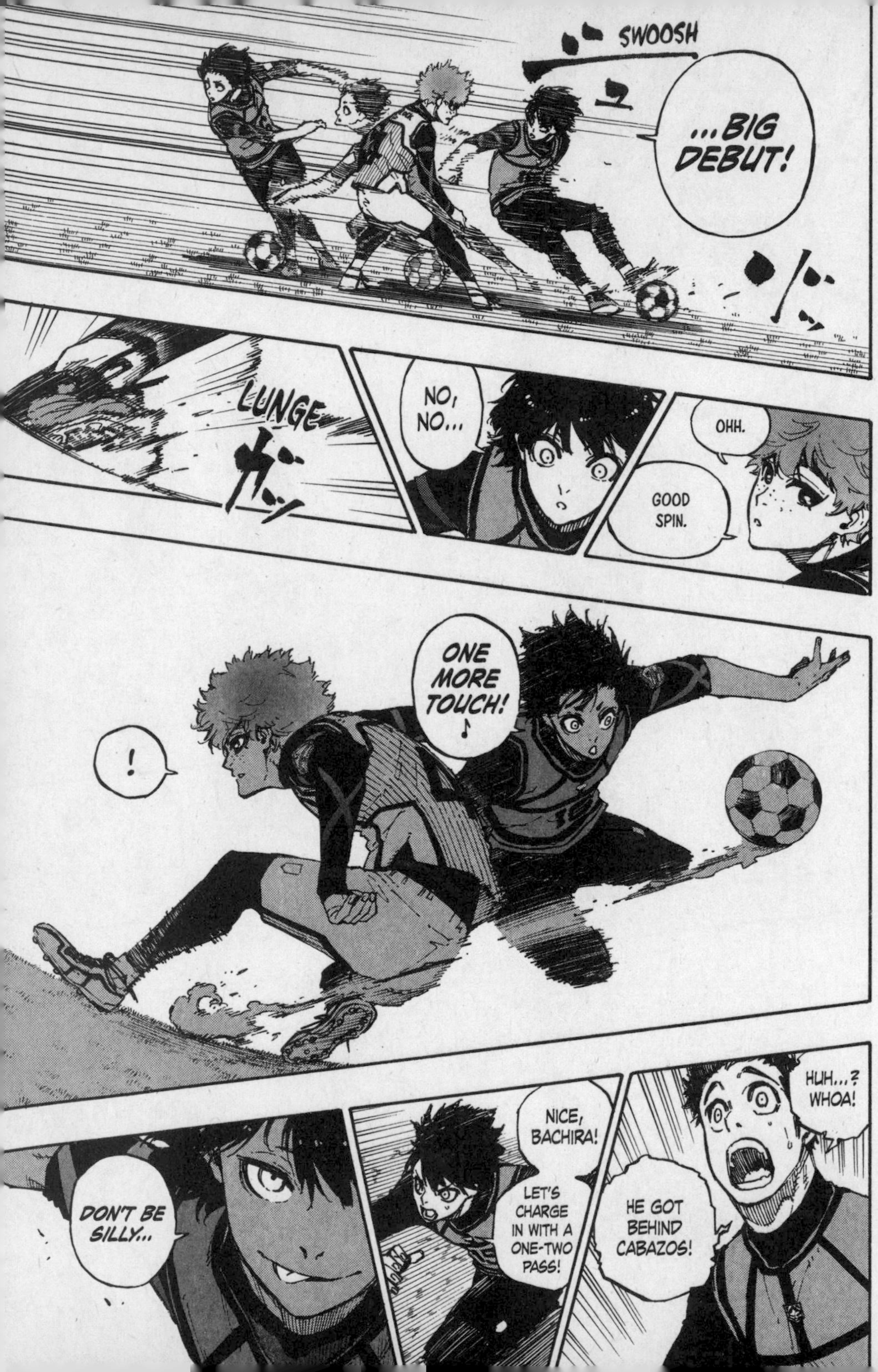
SWOOSH
...BIG DEBUT!
OHH.
GOOD SPIN.
NO, NO...
LUNGE
ONE MORE TOUCH! ♪
!
HUH...? WHOA!
HE GOT BEHIND CABAZOS!
NICE, BACHIRA!
LET'S CHARGE IN WITH A ONE-TWO PASS!
DON'T BE SILLY...

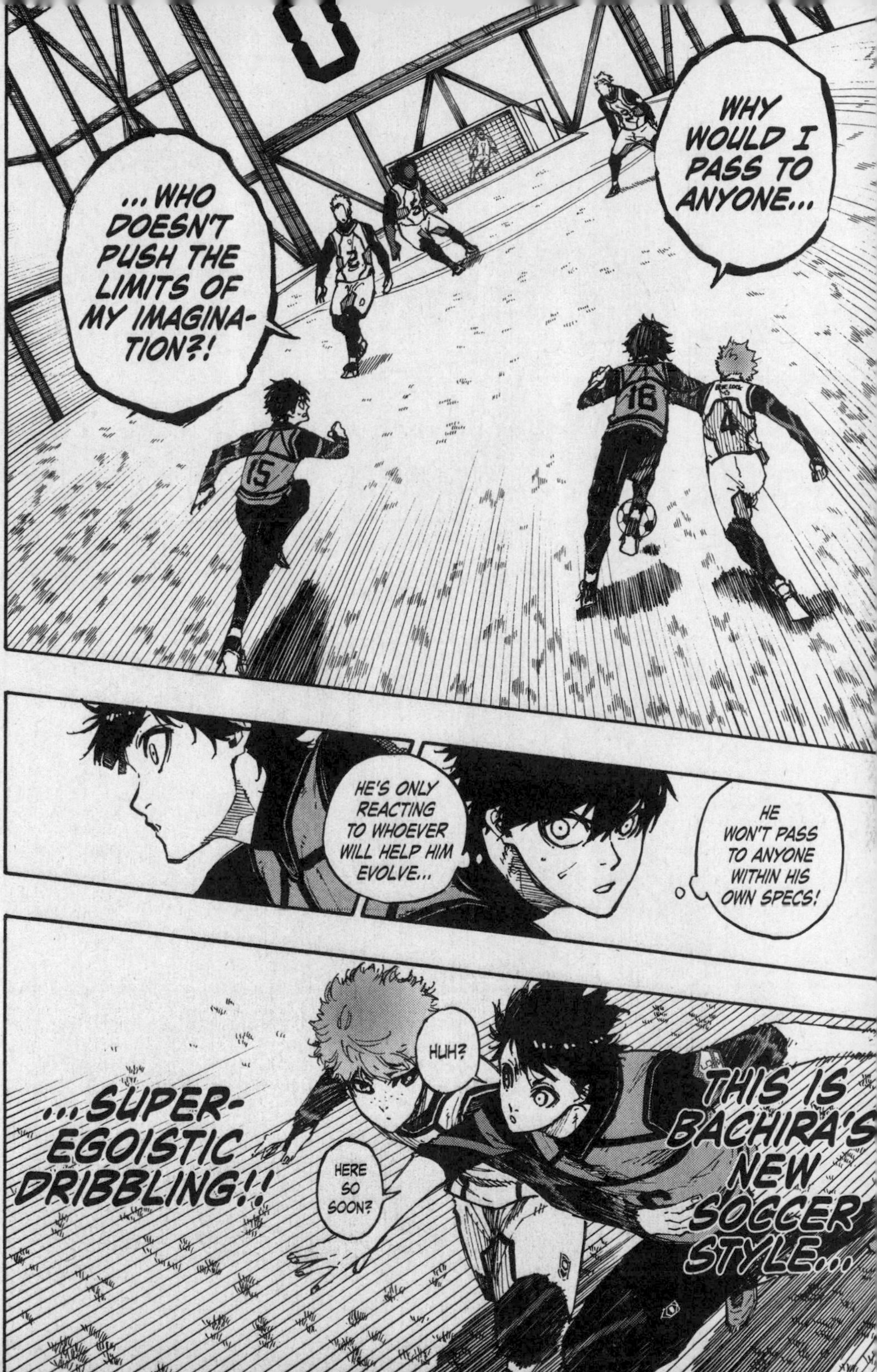
WHY WOULD I PASS TO ANYONE...
...WHO DOESN'T PUSH THE LIMITS OF MY IMAGINATION?!
HE WON'T PASS TO ANYONE WITHIN HIS OWN SPECS!
HE'S ONLY REACTING TO WHOEVER WILL HELP HIM EVOLVE...
THIS IS BACHIRA'S NEW SOCCER STYLE...
HUH?
HERE SO SOON?
...SUPER-EGOISTIC DRIBBLING!!

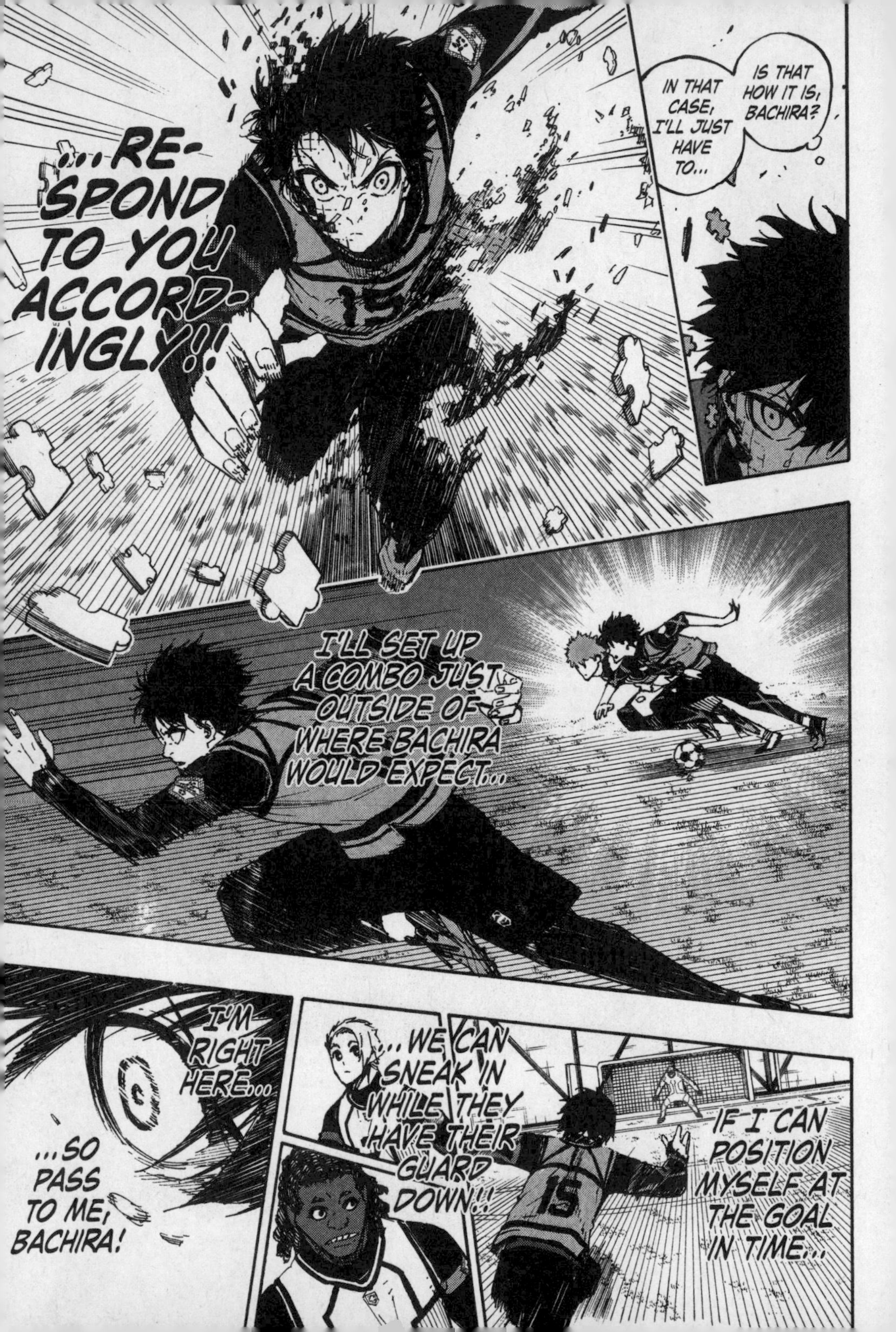
IS THAT HOW IT IS, BACHIRA?
IN THAT CASE, I'LL JUST HAVE TO...
...RE-SPOND TO YOU ACCORD-INGLY!!
I'LL SET UP A COMBO JUST OUTSIDE OF WHERE BACHIRA WOULD EXPECT...
IF I CAN POSITION MYSELF AT THE GOAL IN TIME...
...WE CAN SNEAK IN WHILE THEY HAVE THEIR GUARD DOWN!!
I'M RIGHT HERE...
...SO PASS TO ME, BACHIRA!

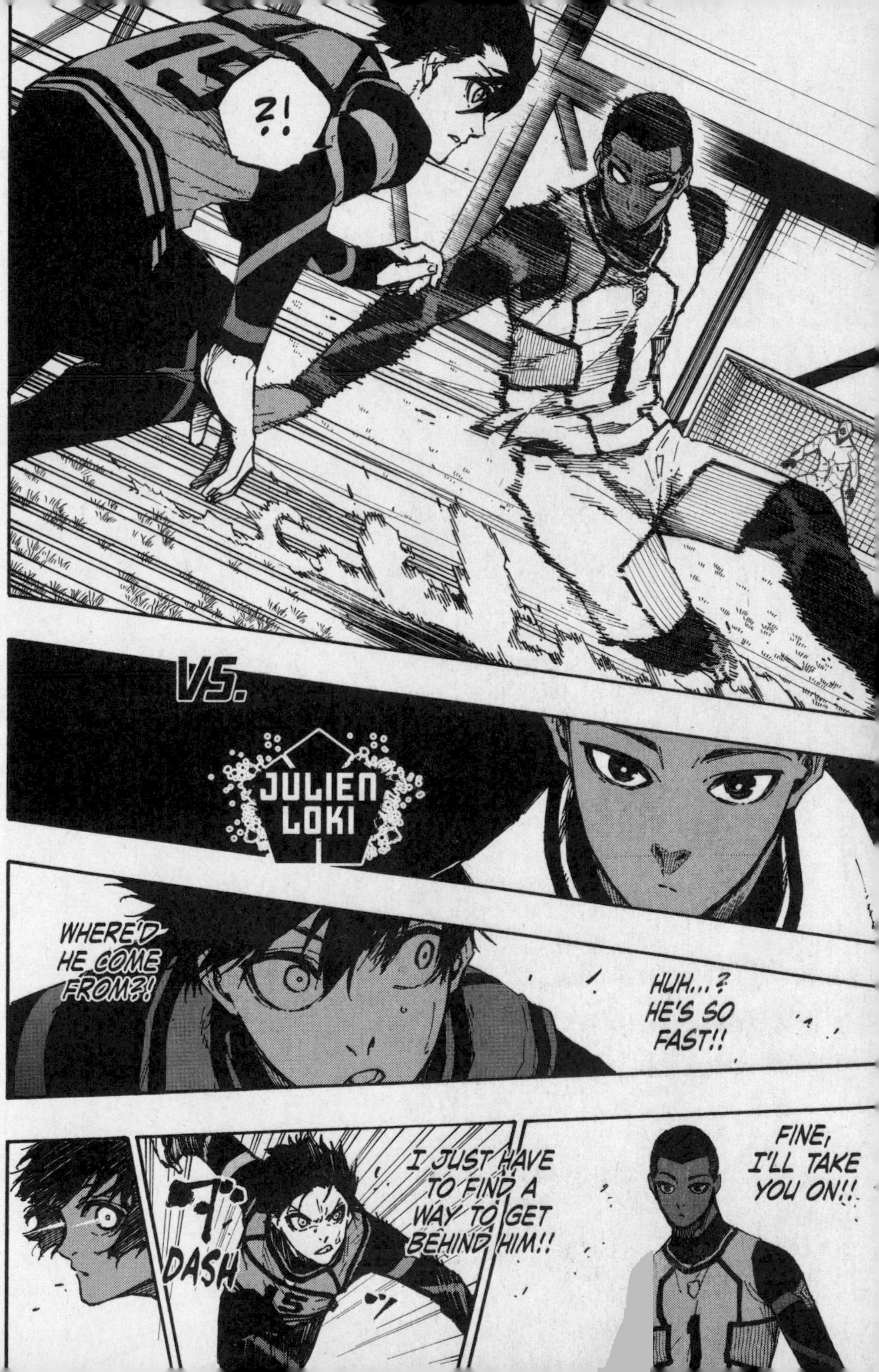
?!
VS.
JULIEN LOKI
HUH...? HE'S SO FAST!!
WHERE'D HE COME FROM?!
FINE, I'LL TAKE YOU ON!!
I JUST HAVE TO FIND A WAY TO GET BEHIND HIM!!
DASH

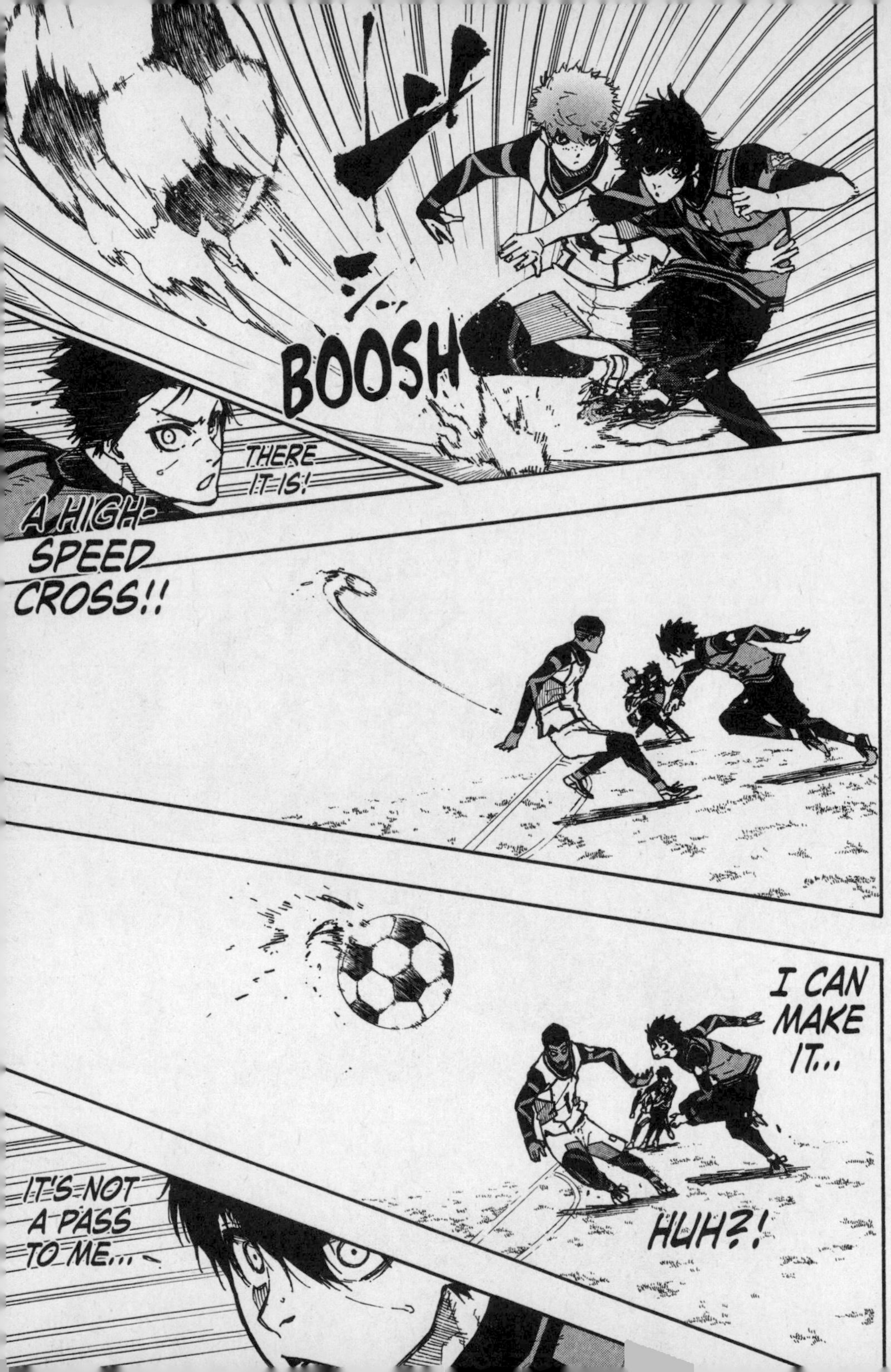
BOOSH
THERE IT IS!
A HIGH-SPEED CROSS!!
I CAN MAKE IT...
HUH?!
IT'S NOT A PASS TO ME...

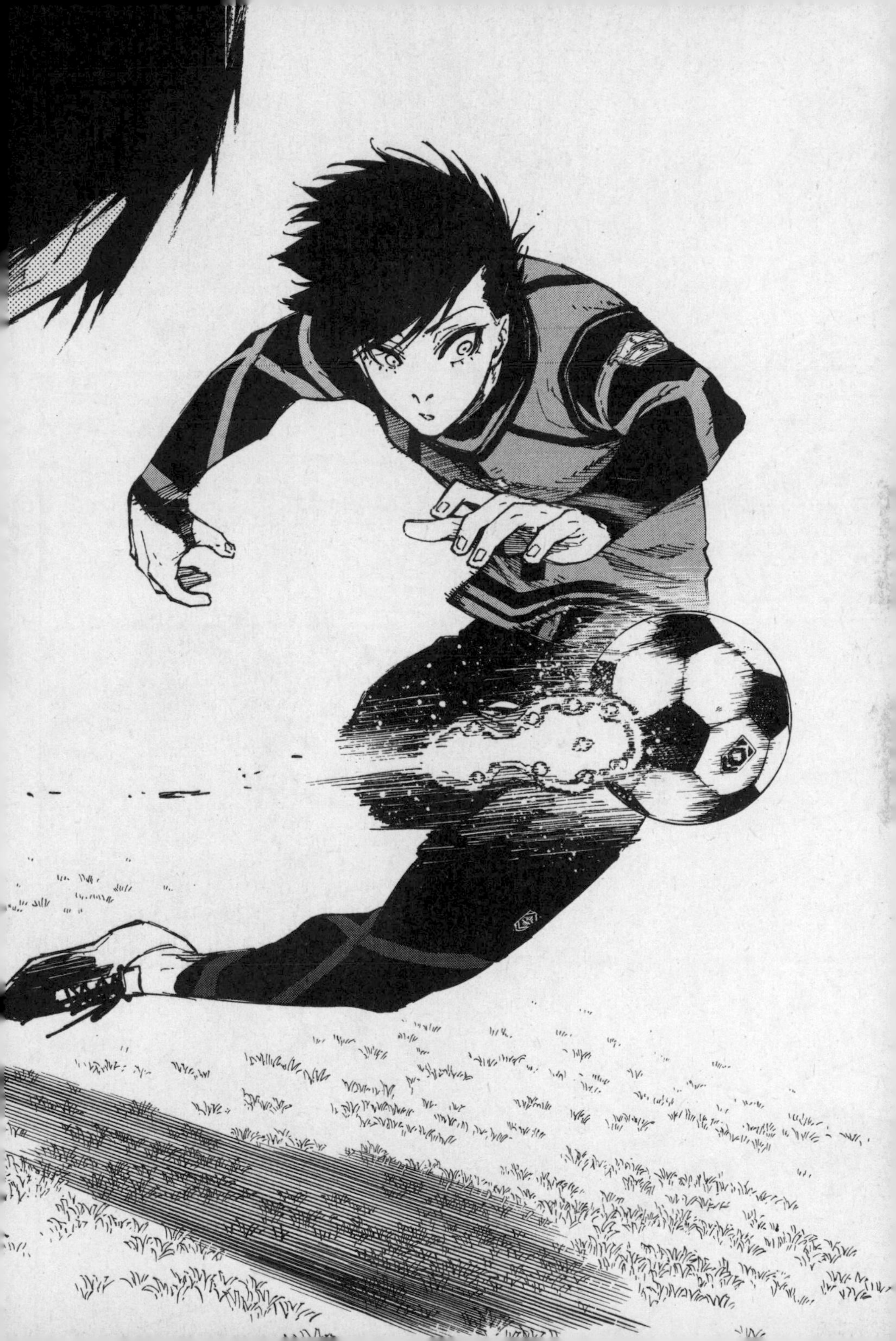

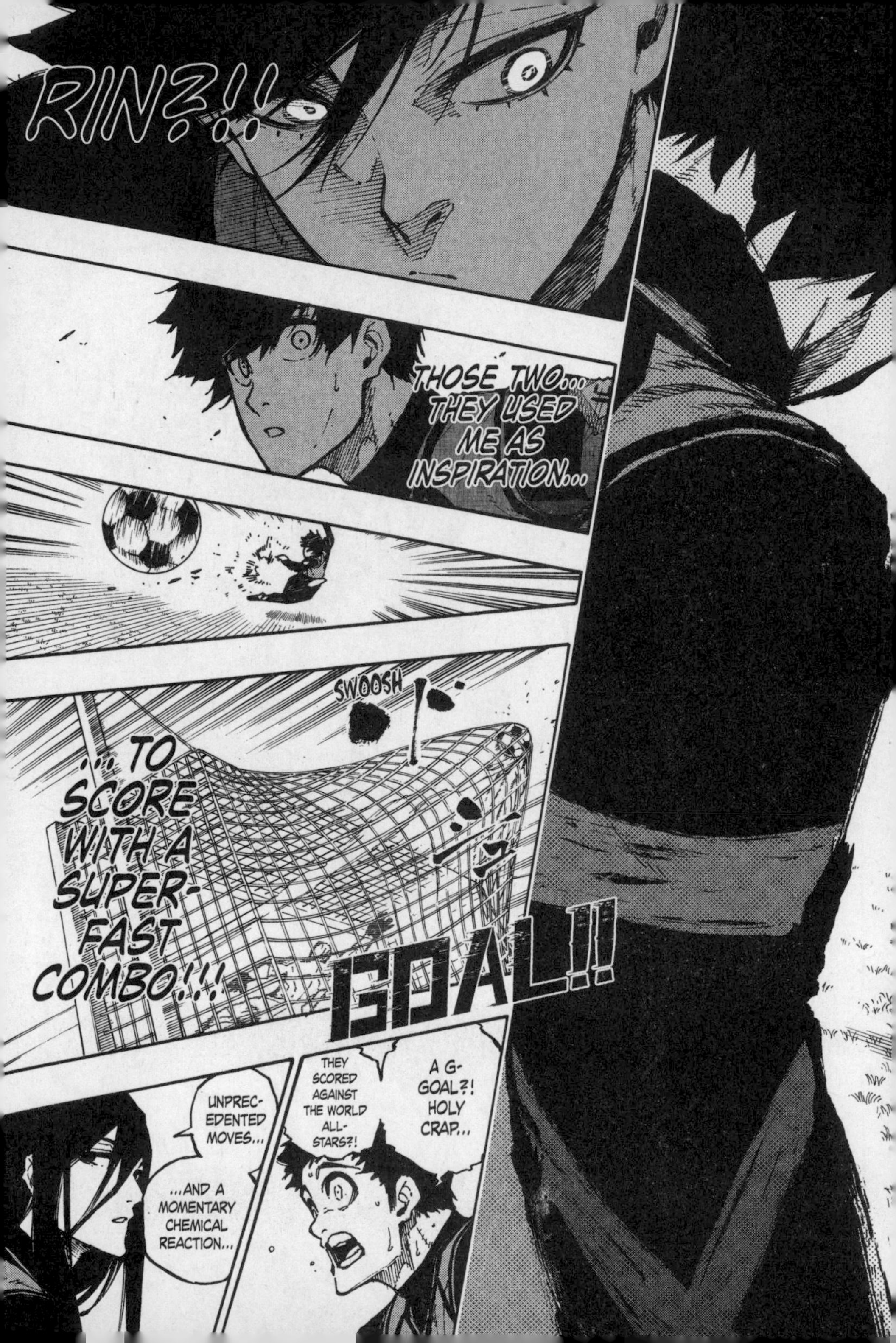
RIN?!!
THOSE TWO... THEY USED ME AS INSPIRATION...
SWOOSH
...TO SCORE WITH A SUPER-FAST COMBO!!!
GOAL!!
A G-GOAL?! HOLY CRAP...
THEY SCORED AGAINST THE WORLD ALL-STARS?!
UNPREC-EDENTED MOVES...
...AND A MOMENTARY CHEMICAL REACTION...

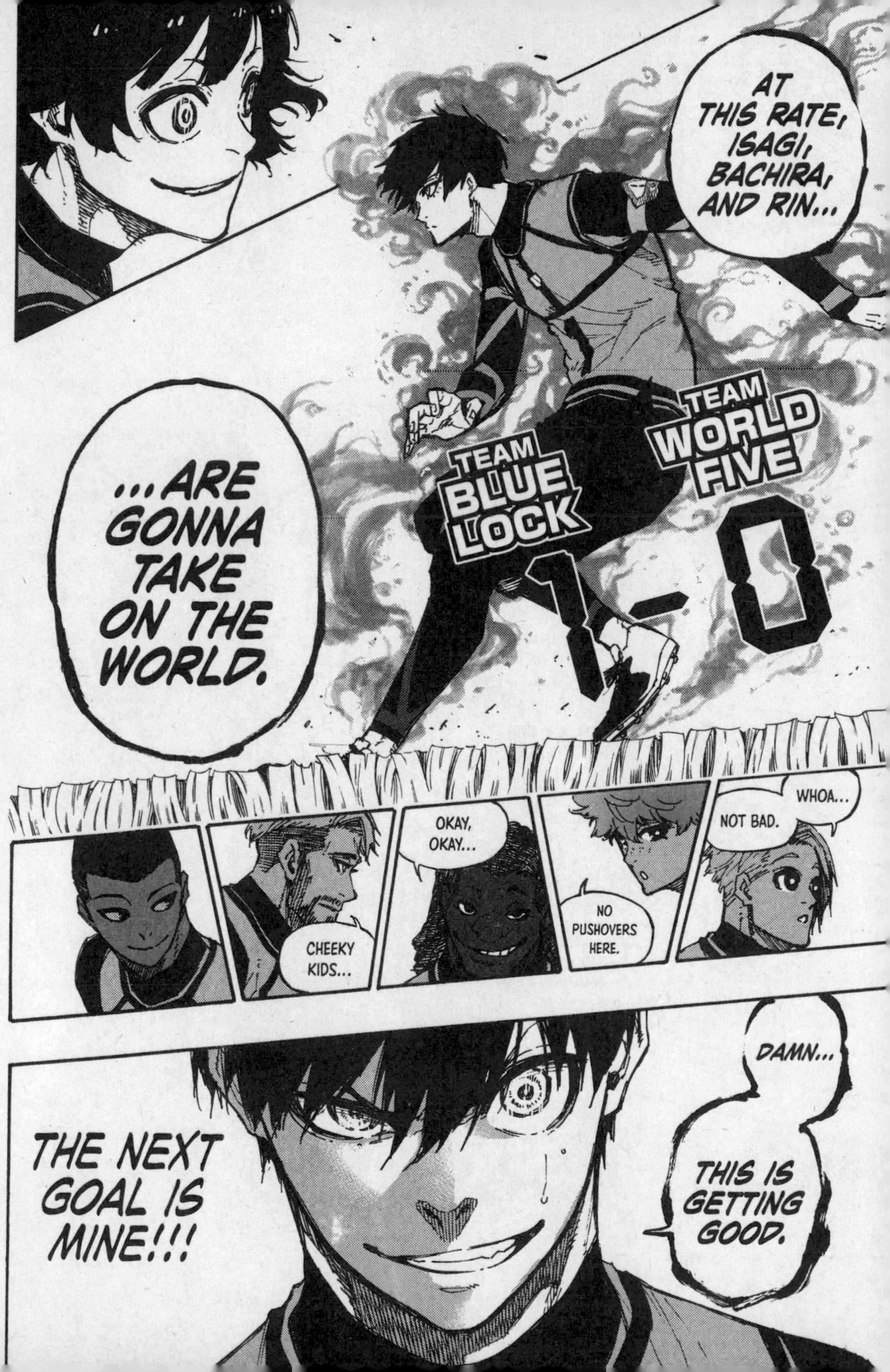
AT THIS RATE, ISAGI, BACHIRA, AND RIN...
...ARE GONNA TAKE ON THE WORLD.
TEAM BLUE LOCK
TEAM WORLD FIVE
1-0
WHOA...
NOT BAD.
NO PUSHOVERS HERE.
OKAY, OKAY...
CHEEKY KIDS...
DAMN...
THIS IS GETTING GOOD.
THE NEXT GOAL IS MINE!!!

CHAPTER 91: DIVINE SPEED

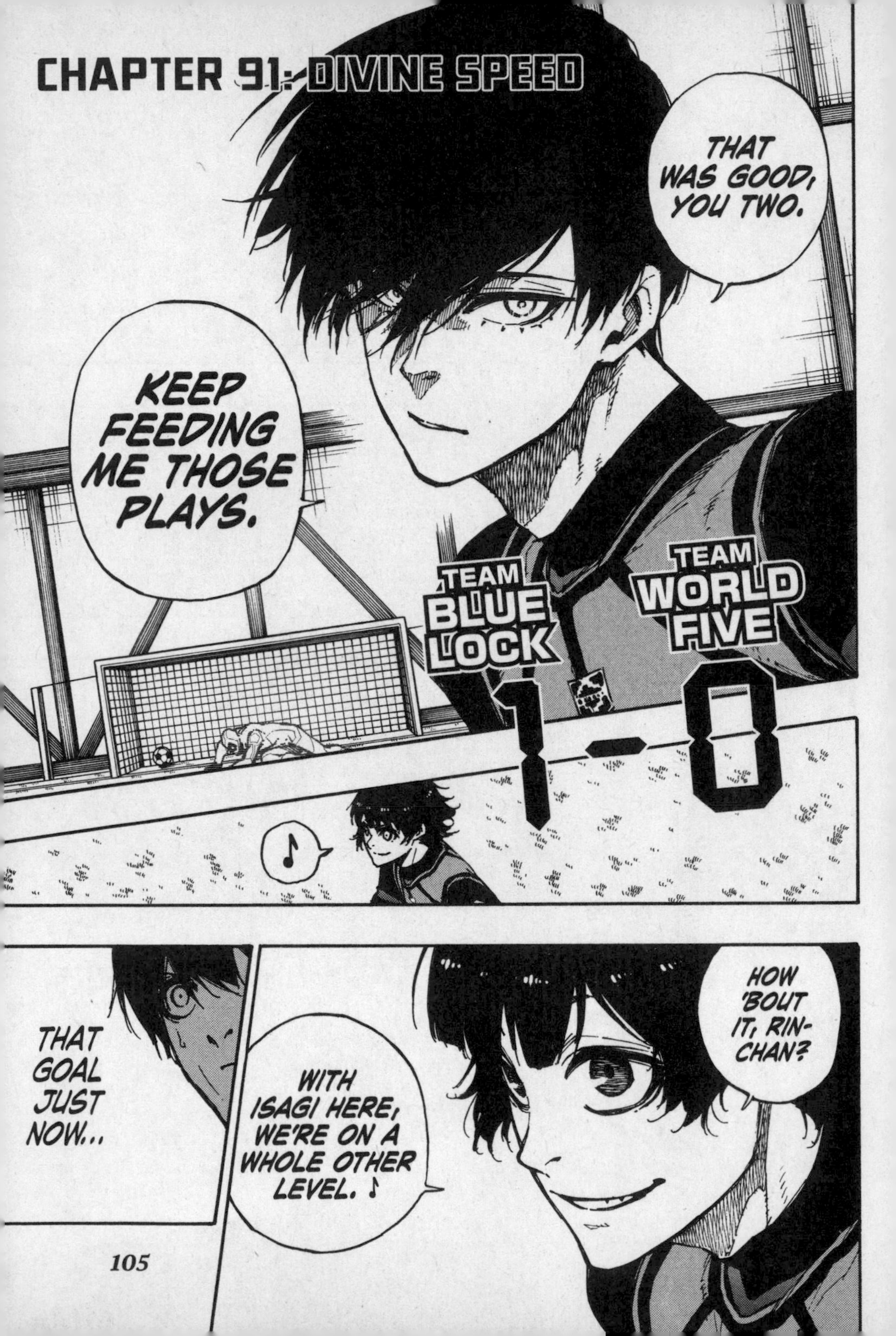

THAT WAS GOOD, YOU TWO.
KEEP FEEDING ME THOSE PLAYS.
TEAM BLUE LOCK
TEAM WORLD FIVE
1-0
♪
HOW 'BOUT IT, RIN-CHAN?
WITH ISAGI HERE, WE'RE ON A WHOLE OTHER LEVEL. ♪
THAT GOAL JUST NOW...

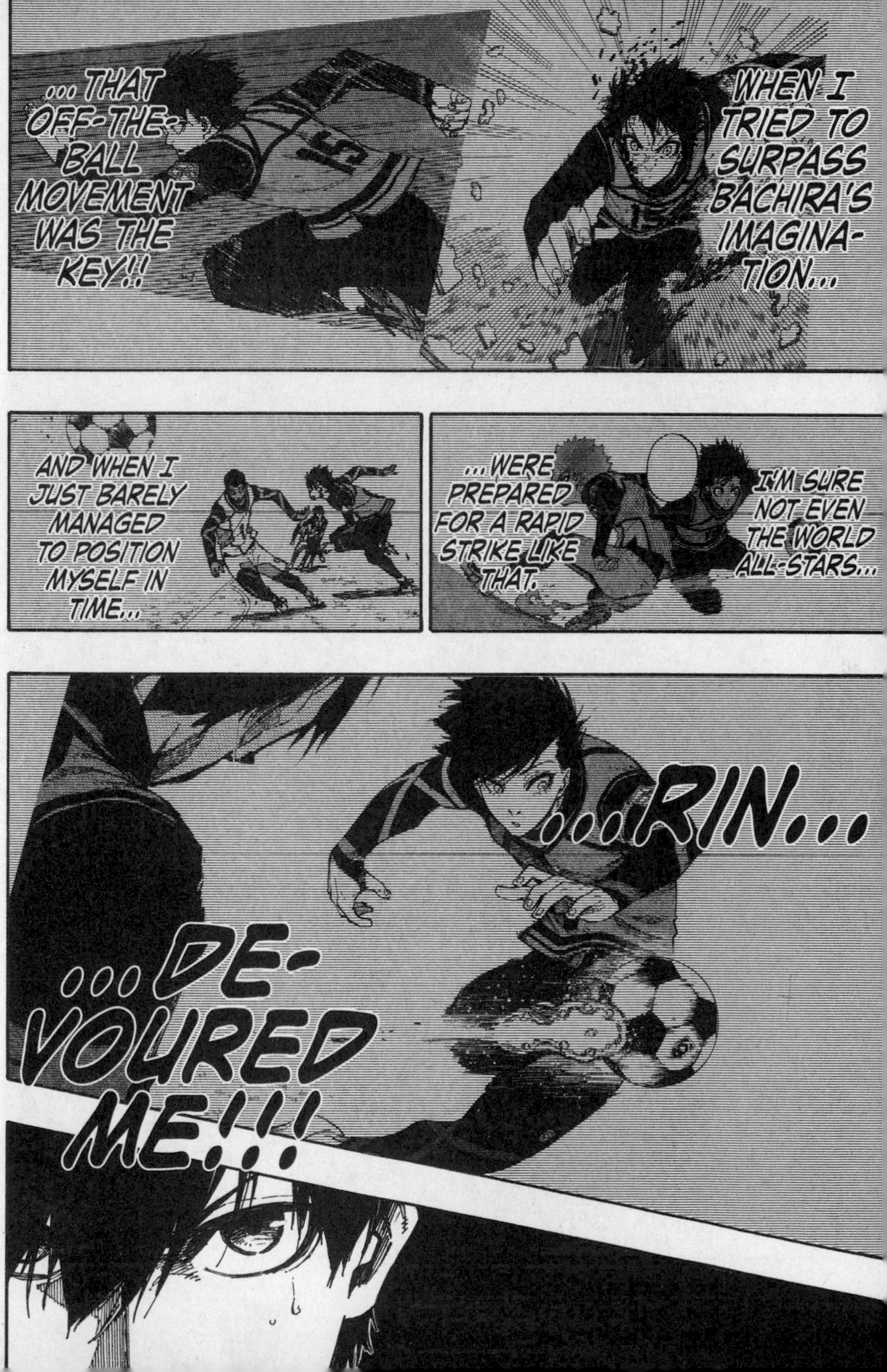
WHEN I TRIED TO SURPASS BACHIRA'S IMAGINA-TION...
...THAT OFF-THE-BALL MOVEMENT WAS THE KEY!!
I'M SURE NOT EVEN THE WORLD ALL-STARS...
...WERE PREPARED FOR A RAPID STRIKE LIKE THAT.
AND WHEN I JUST BARELY MANAGED TO POSITION MYSELF IN TIME...
...RIN...
...DE-VOURED ME!!!

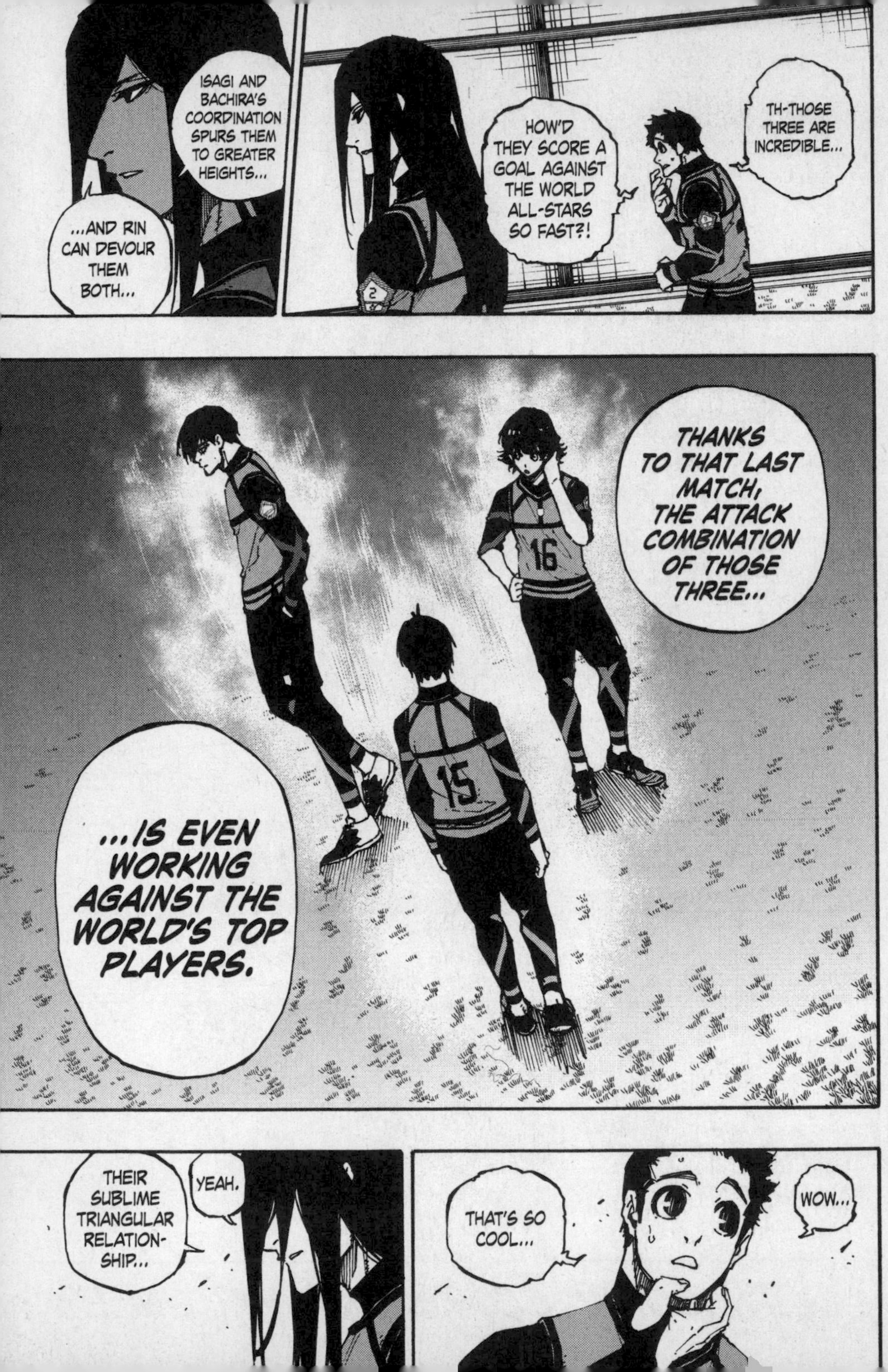
TH-THOSE THREE ARE INCREDIBLE...
HOW'D THEY SCORE A GOAL AGAINST THE WORLD ALL-STARS SO FAST?!
ISAGI AND BACHIRA'S COORDINATION SPURS THEM TO GREATER HEIGHTS...
...AND RIN CAN DEVOUR THEM BOTH...
THANKS TO THAT LAST MATCH, THE ATTACK COMBINATION OF THOSE THREE...
...IS EVEN WORKING AGAINST THE WORLD'S TOP PLAYERS.
WOW...
THAT'S SO COOL...
YEAH.
THEIR SUBLIME TRIANGULAR RELATION-SHIP...

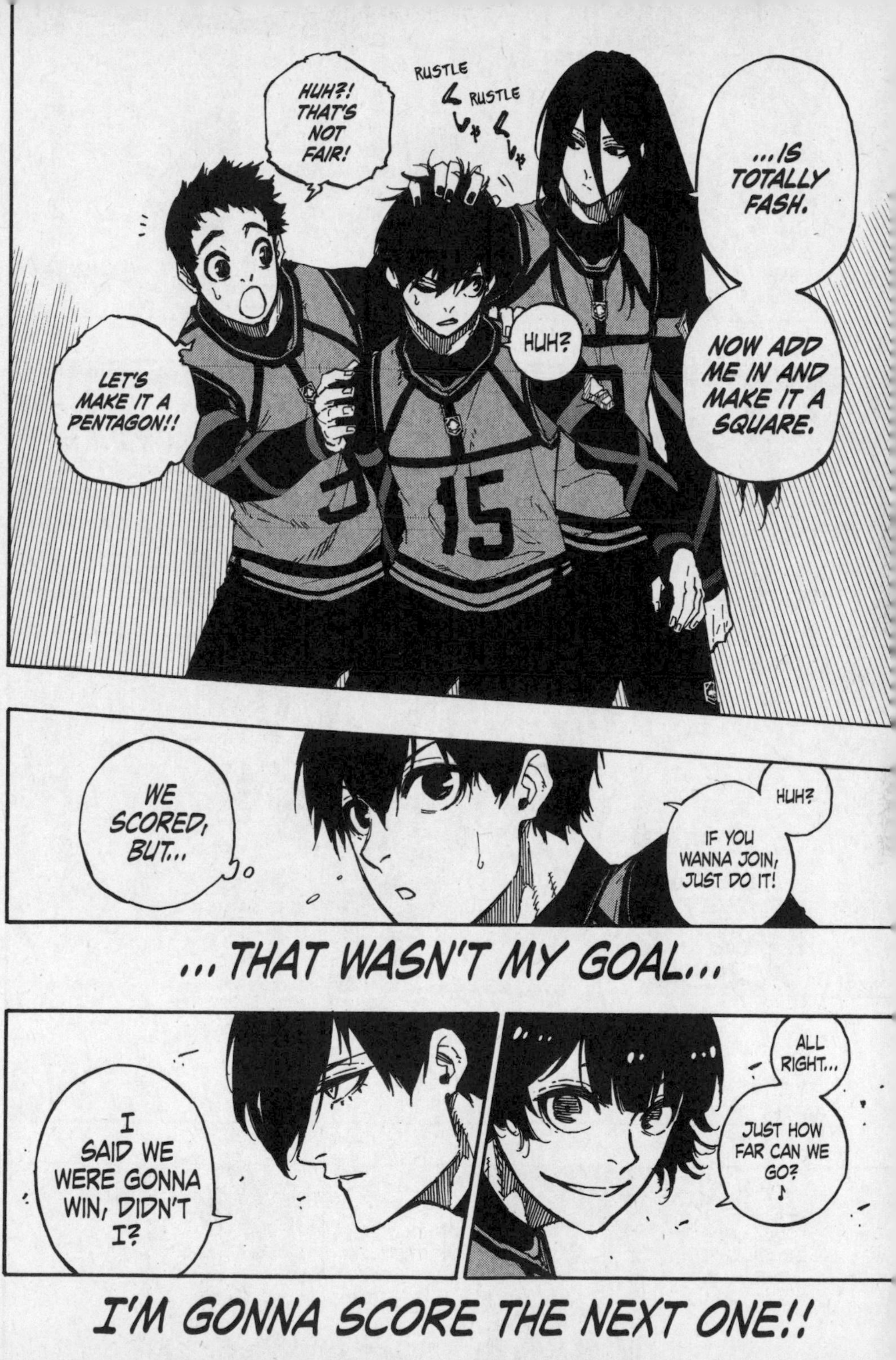
...IS TOTALLY FASH.
NOW ADD ME IN AND MAKE IT A SQUARE.
RUSTLE RUSTLE
HUH?
HUH?! THAT'S NOT FAIR!
LET'S MAKE IT A PENTAGON!!
HUH? IF YOU WANNA JOIN, JUST DO IT!
WE SCORED, BUT...
...THAT WASN'T MY GOAL...
ALL RIGHT... JUST HOW FAR CAN WE GO? ♪
I SAID WE WERE GONNA WIN, DIDN'T I?
I'M GONNA SCORE THE NEXT ONE!!

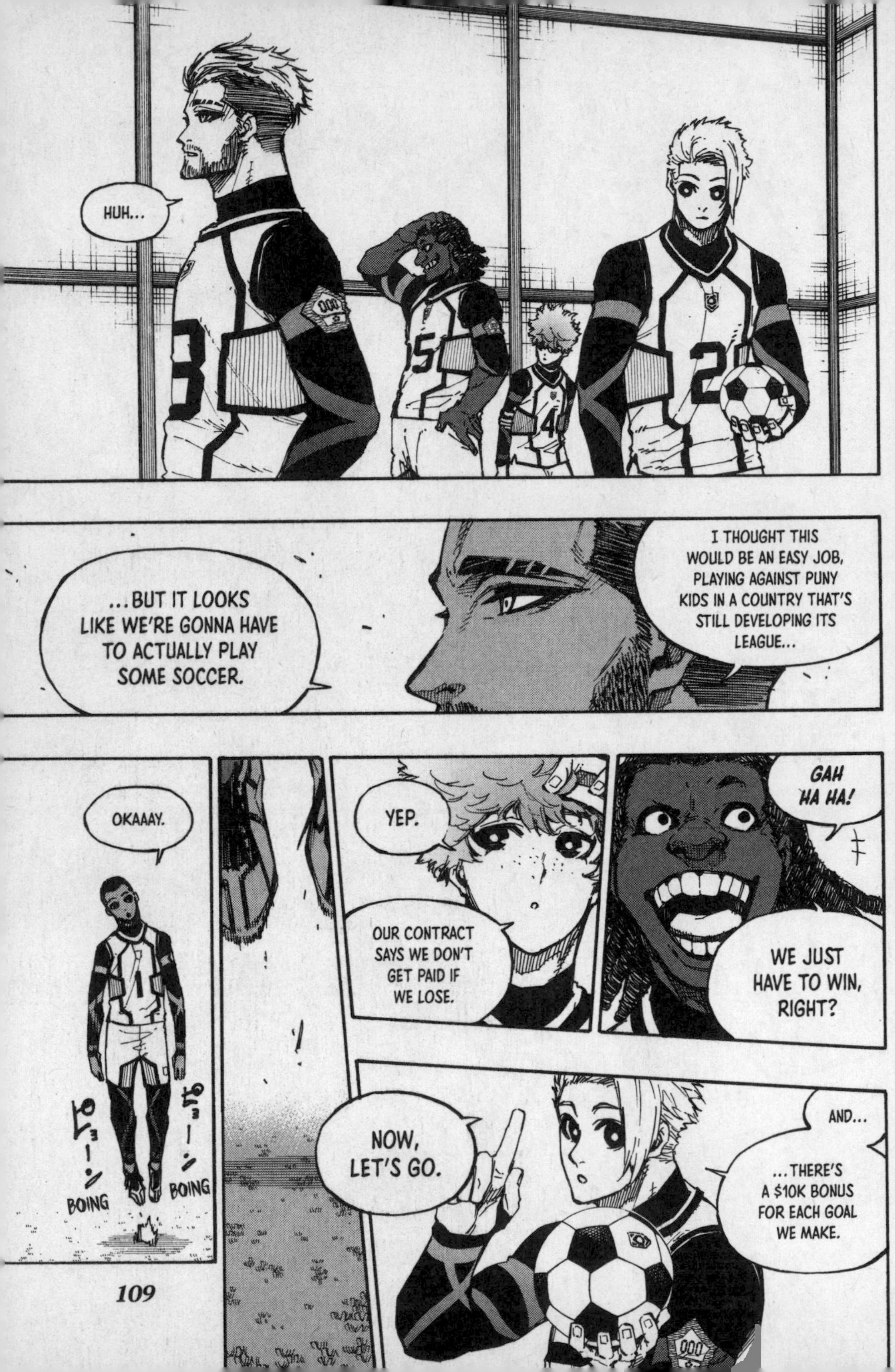
HUH...
I THOUGHT THIS WOULD BE AN EASY JOB, PLAYING AGAINST PUNY KIDS IN A COUNTRY THAT'S STILL DEVELOPING ITS LEAGUE...
...BUT IT LOOKS LIKE WE'RE GONNA HAVE TO ACTUALLY PLAY SOME SOCCER.
GAH HA HA!
WE JUST HAVE TO WIN, RIGHT?
YEP.
OUR CONTRACT SAYS WE DON'T GET PAID IF WE LOSE.
AND...
...THERE'S A $10K BONUS FOR EACH GOAL WE MAKE.
NOW, LET'S GO.
OKAAAY.
BOING
BOING

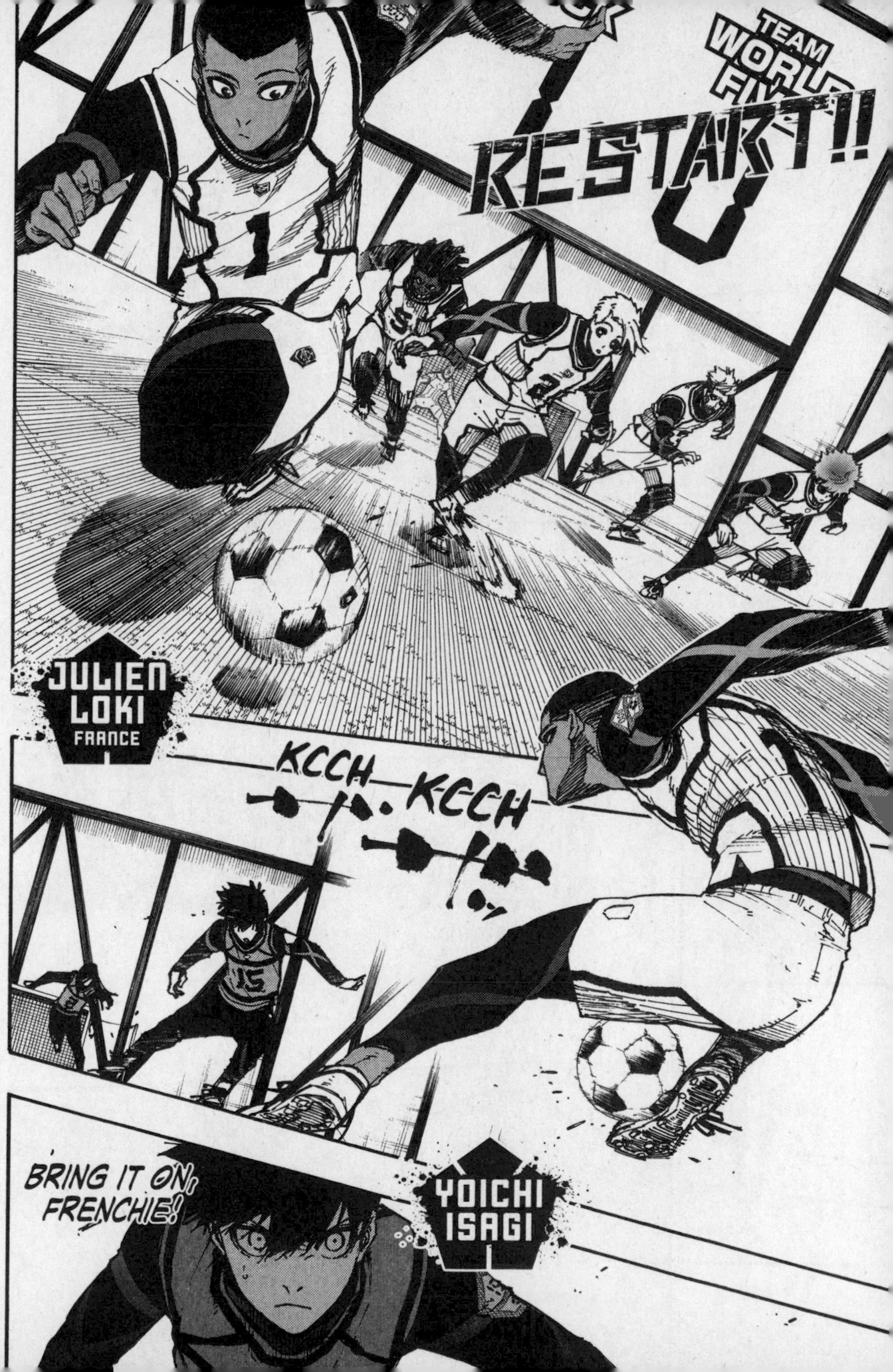
TEAM
RESTART!!
JULIEN LOKI
FRANCE
KCCH KCCH
YOICHI ISAGI
BRING IT ON, FRENCHIE!

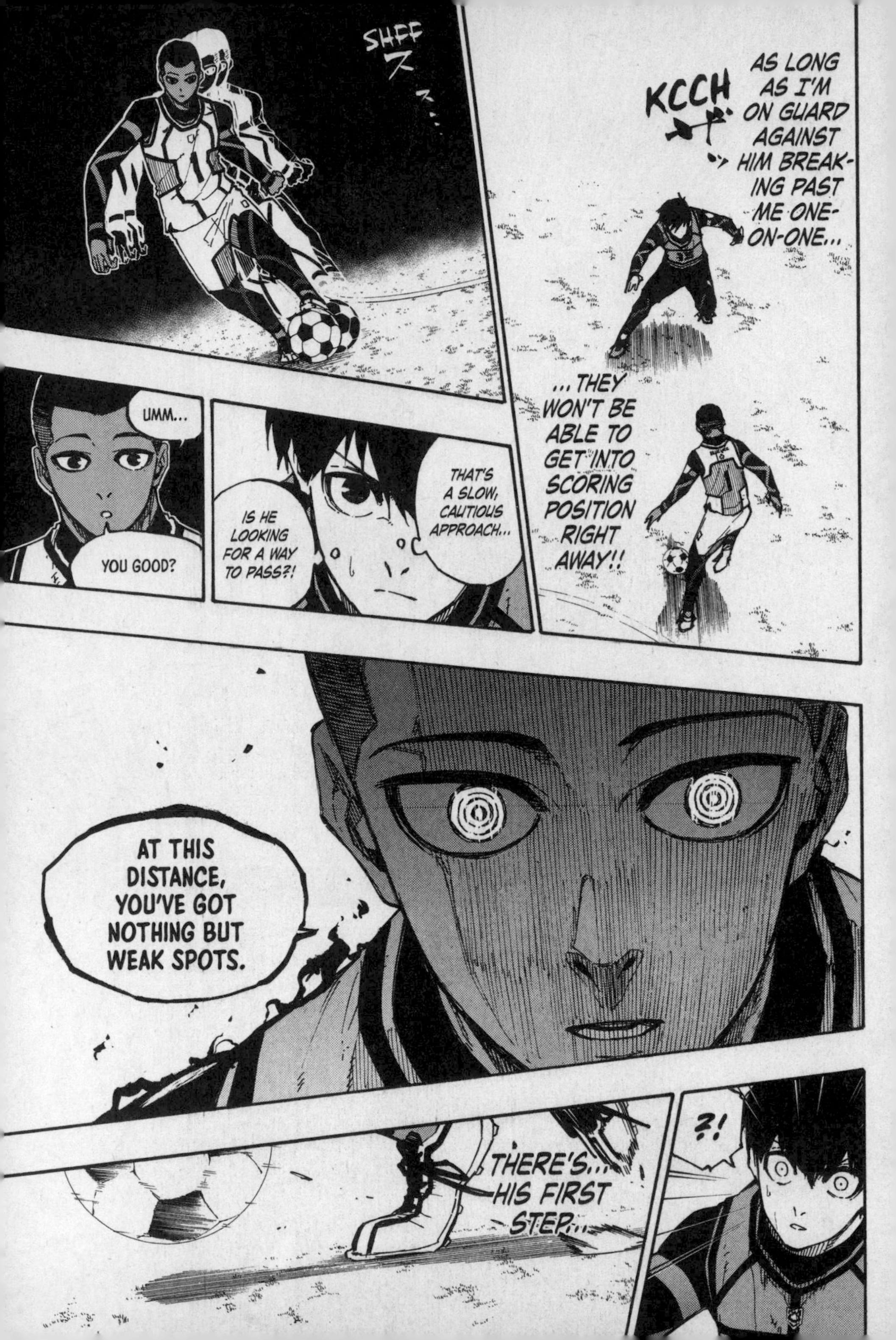
KCCH
AS LONG AS I'M ON GUARD AGAINST HIM BREAKING PAST ME ONE-ON-ONE...
...THEY WON'T BE ABLE TO GET INTO SCORING POSITION RIGHT AWAY!!
SHFF
ス
THAT'S A SLOW, CAUTIOUS APPROACH...
IS HE LOOKING FOR A WAY TO PASS?!
UMM...
YOU GOOD?
AT THIS DISTANCE, YOU'VE GOT NOTHING BUT WEAK SPOTS.
?!
THERE'S... HIS FIRST STEP...

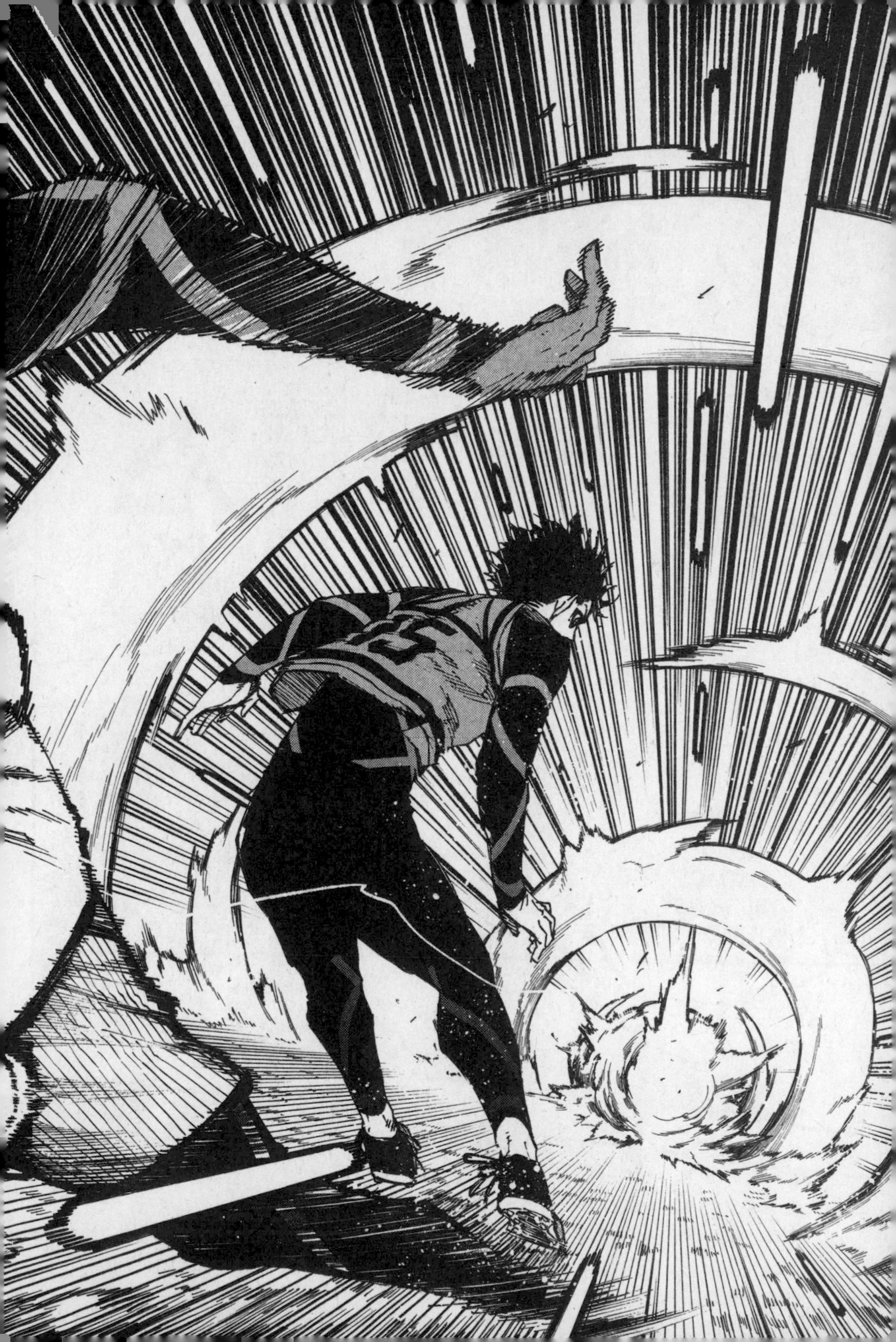

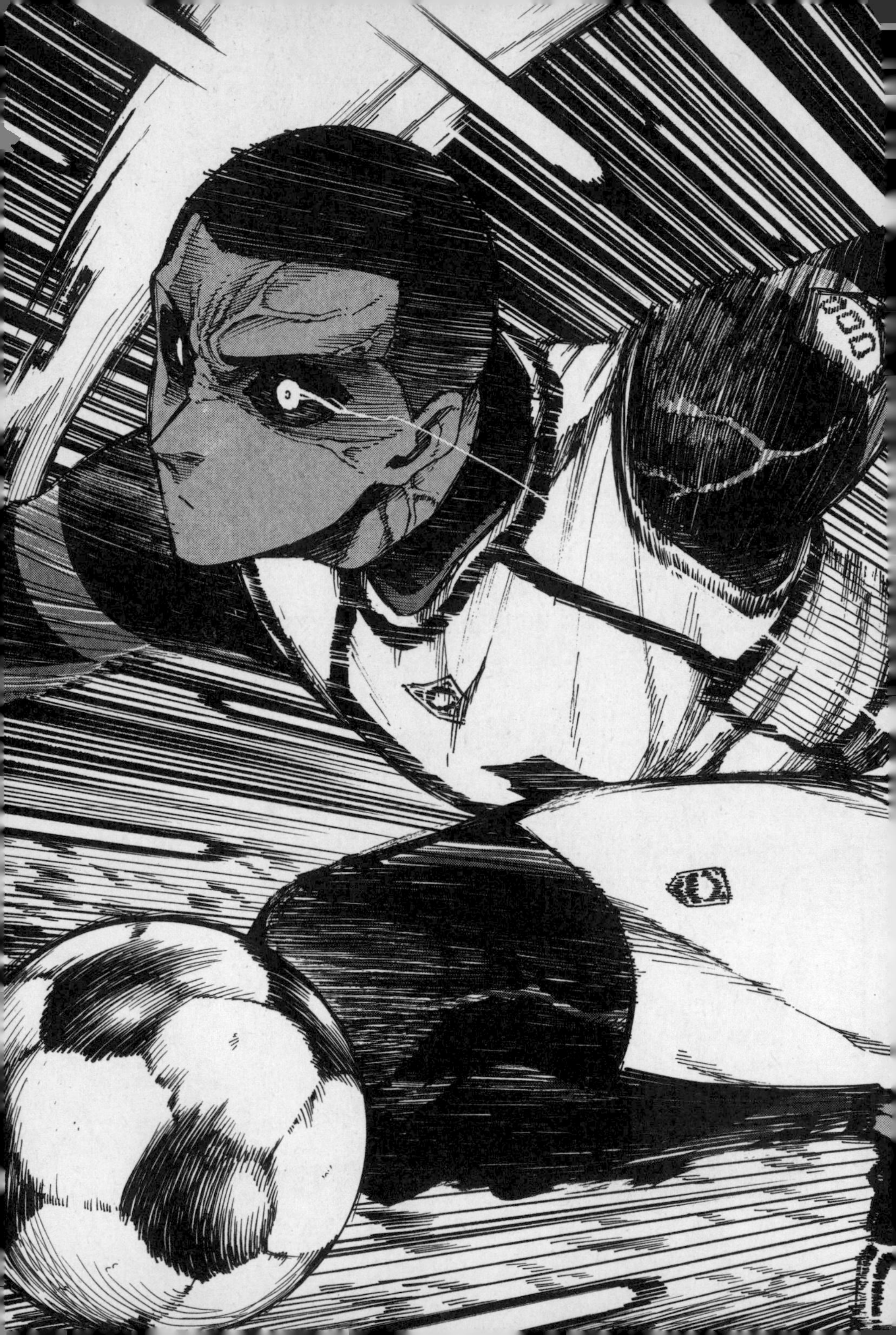

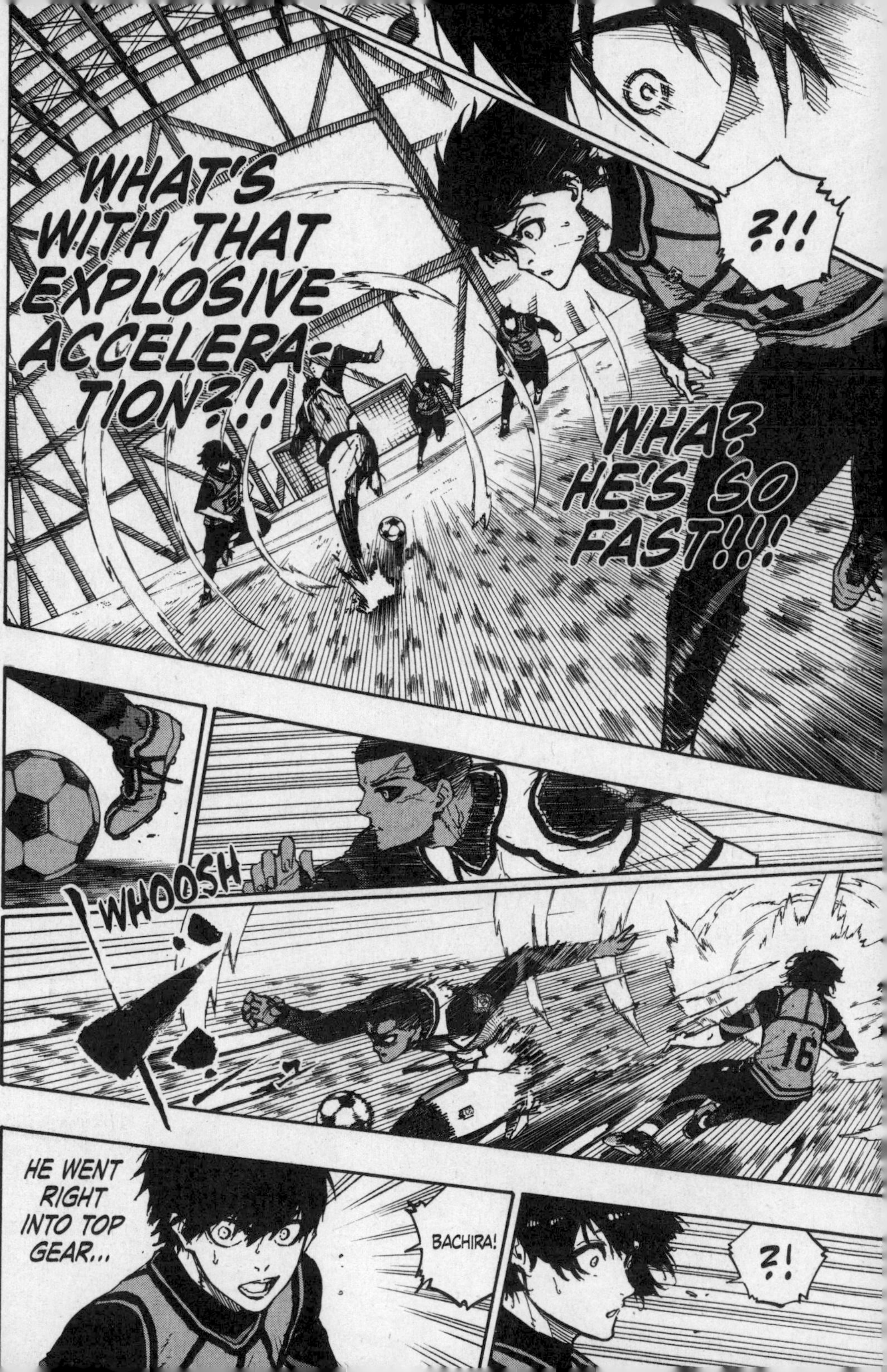
?!!
WHAT'S WITH THAT EXPLOSIVE ACCELERA-TION?!!
WHA? HE'S SO FAST!!!
WHOOSH
BACHIRA!
?!
HE WENT RIGHT INTO TOP GEAR...

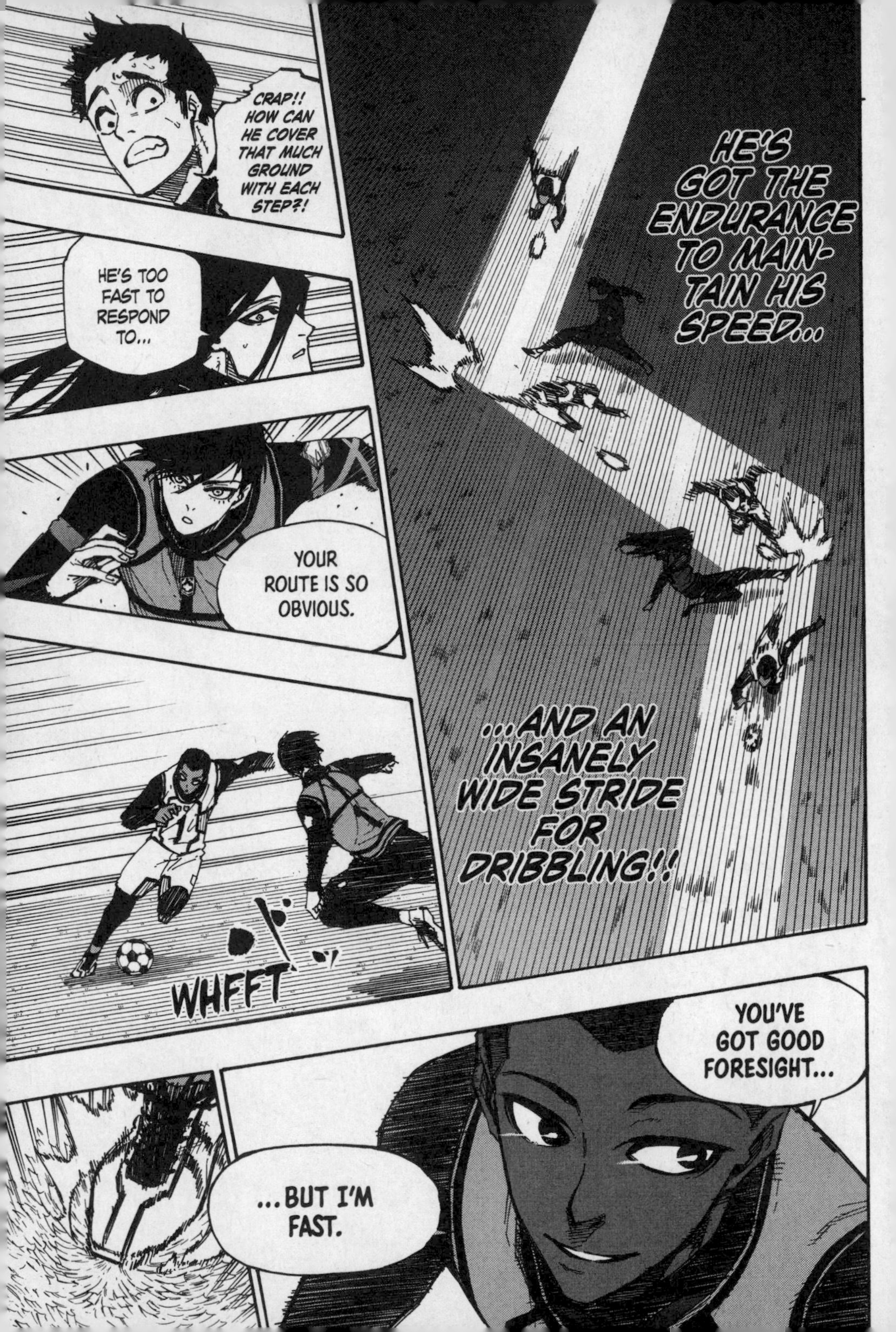
HE'S GOT THE ENDURANCE TO MAIN-TAIN HIS SPEED...
...AND AN INSANELY WIDE STRIDE FOR DRIBBLING!!
CRAP!! HOW CAN HE COVER THAT MUCH GROUND WITH EACH STEP?!
HE'S TOO FAST TO RESPOND TO...
YOUR ROUTE IS SO OBVIOUS.
WHFFT
YOU'VE GOT GOOD FORESIGHT...
...BUT I'M FAST.

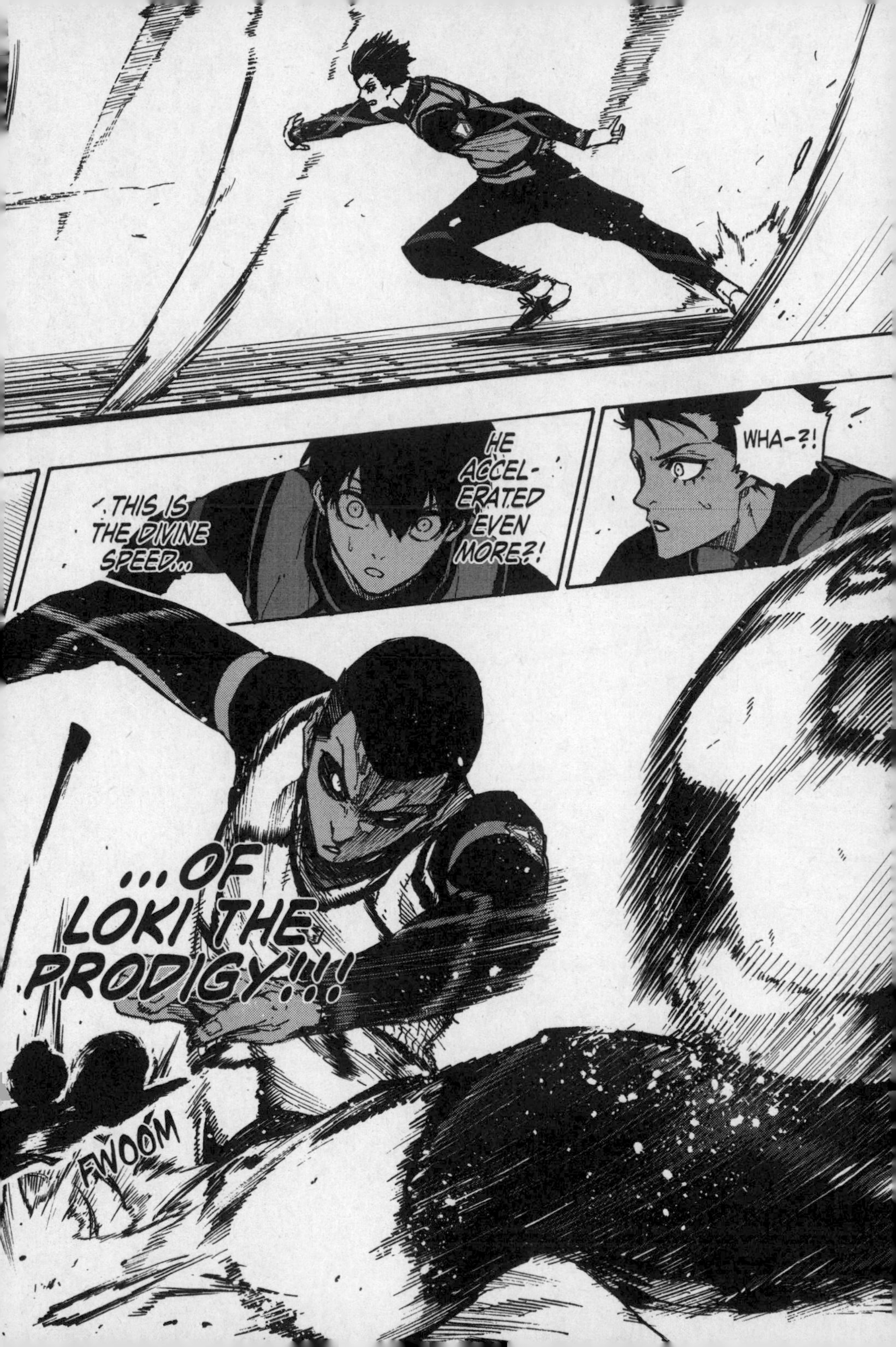
WHA-?!
HE ACCEL-ERATED EVEN MORE?!
THIS IS THE DIVINE SPEED...
...OF LOKI THE PRODIGY!!!
FWOOM

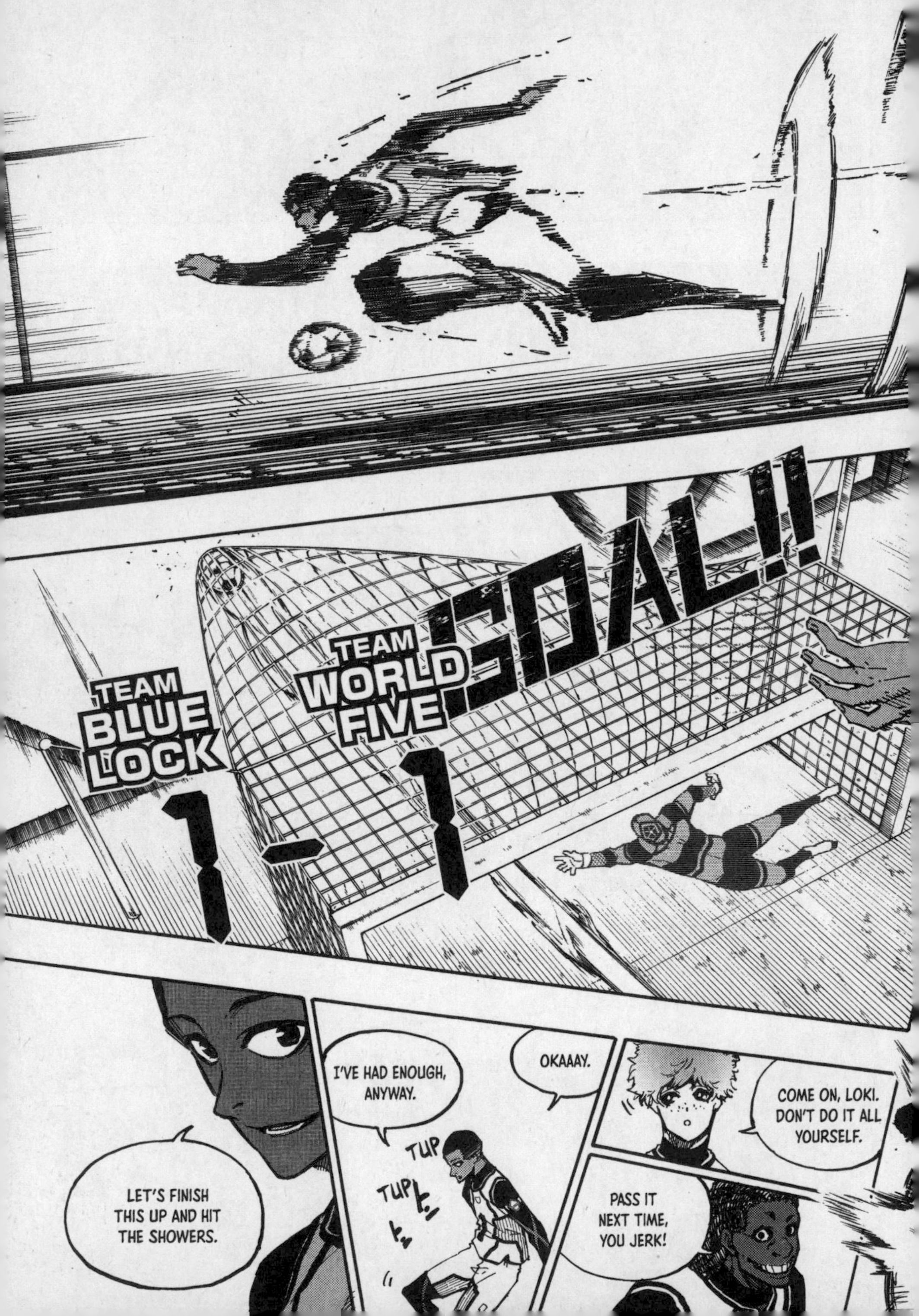
GOAL!!
TEAM BLUE LOCK
1-1
TEAM WORLD FIVE
COME ON, LOKI. DON'T DO IT ALL YOURSELF.
PASS IT NEXT TIME, YOU JERK!
OKAAAY.
I'VE HAD ENOUGH, ANYWAY.
TUP
TUP
LET'S FINISH THIS UP AND HIT THE SHOWERS.

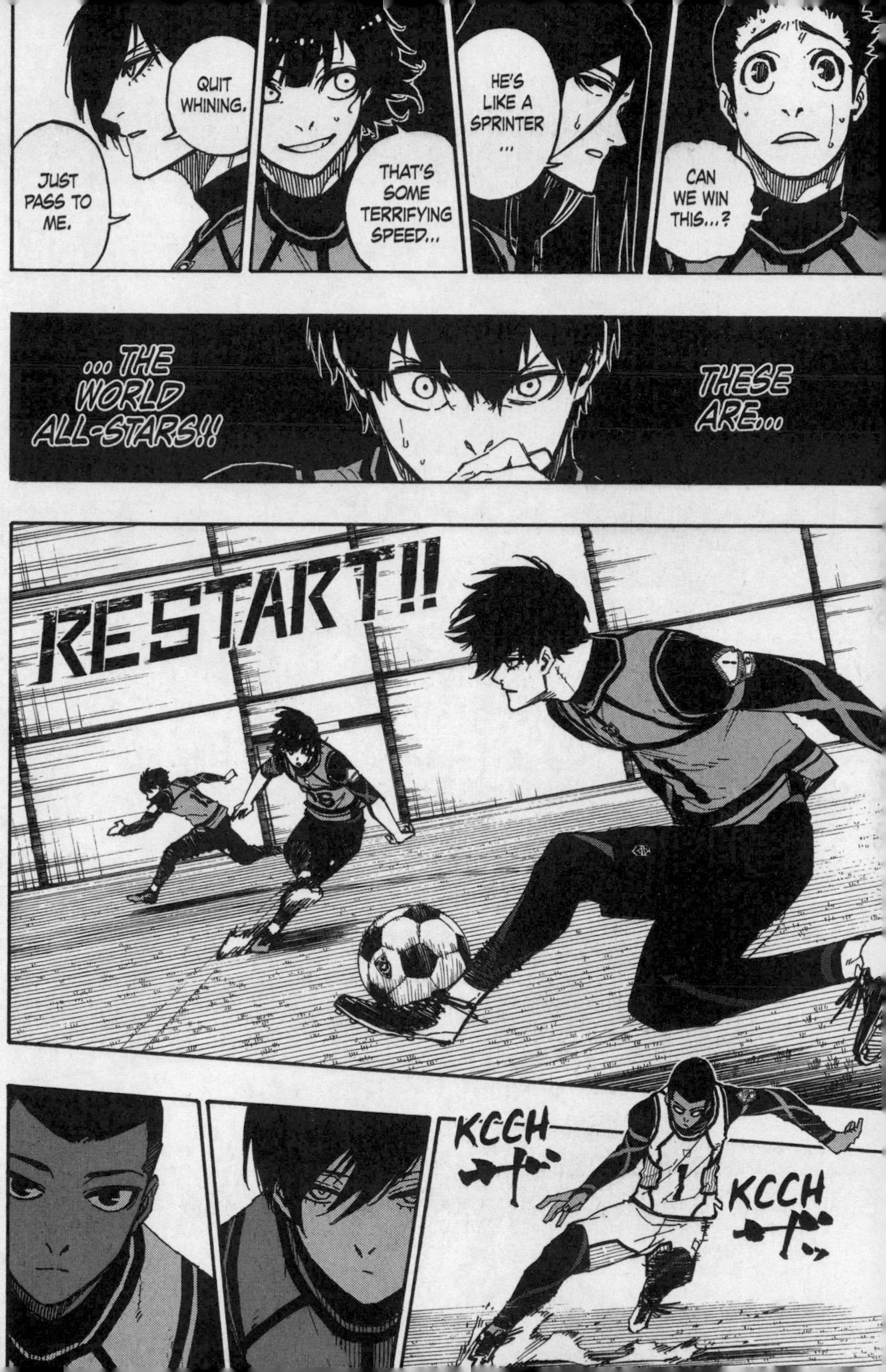
CAN WE WIN THIS...?
HE'S LIKE A SPRINTER...
QUIT WHINING.
THAT'S SOME TERRIFYING SPEED...
JUST PASS TO ME.
THESE ARE...
...THE WORLD ALL-STARS!!
RESTART!!
KCCH
KCCH

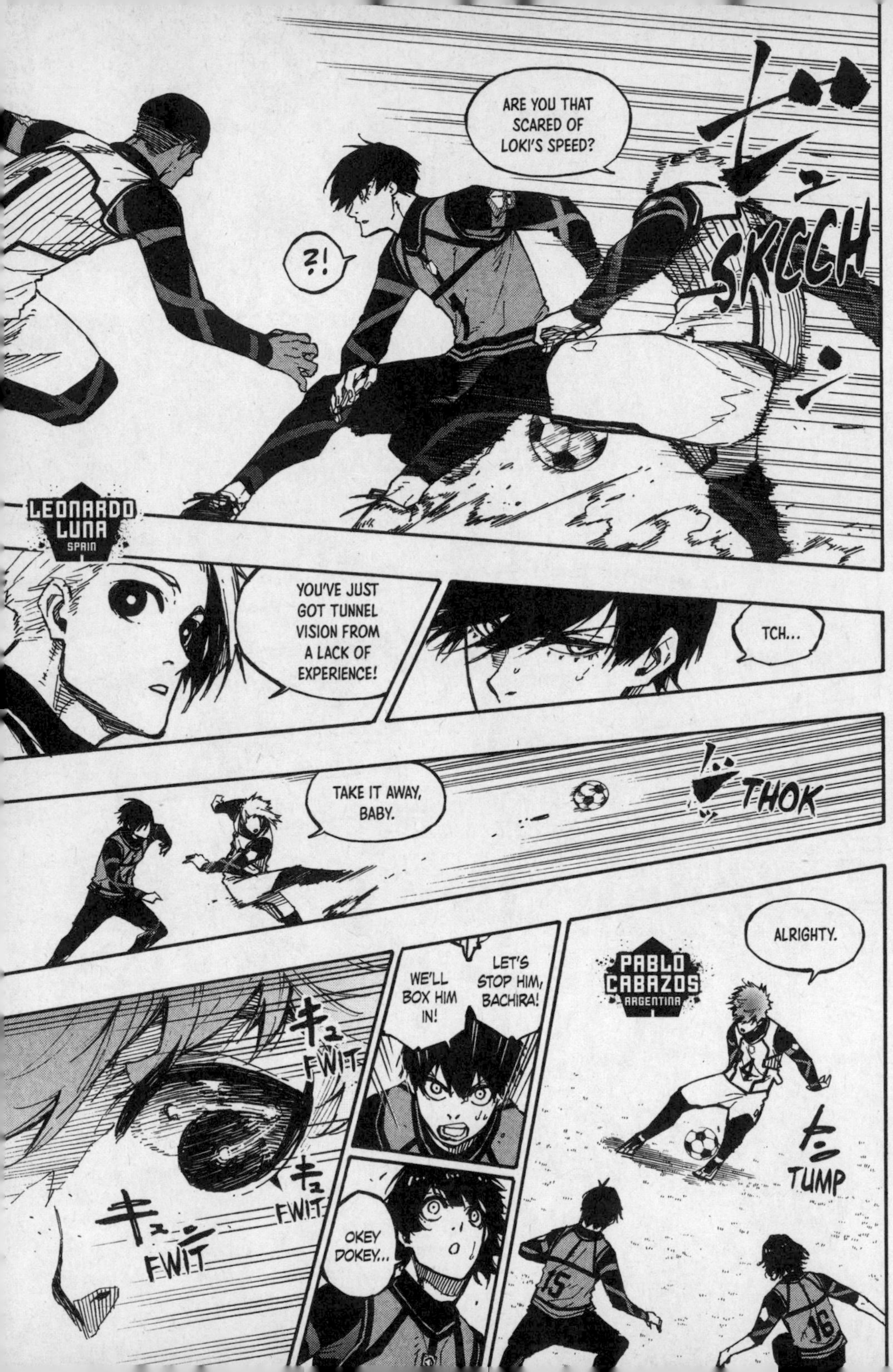
ARE YOU THAT SCARED OF LOKI'S SPEED?
SKCCH
?!
LEONARDO LUNA
SPAIN
TCH...
YOU'VE JUST GOT TUNNEL VISION FROM A LACK OF EXPERIENCE!
THOK
TAKE IT AWAY, BABY.
ALRIGHTY.
PABLO CABAZOS
ARGENTINA
TUMP
LET'S STOP HIM, BACHIRA!
WE'LL BOX HIM IN!
OKEY DOKEY...
FWIT
FWIT
FWIT

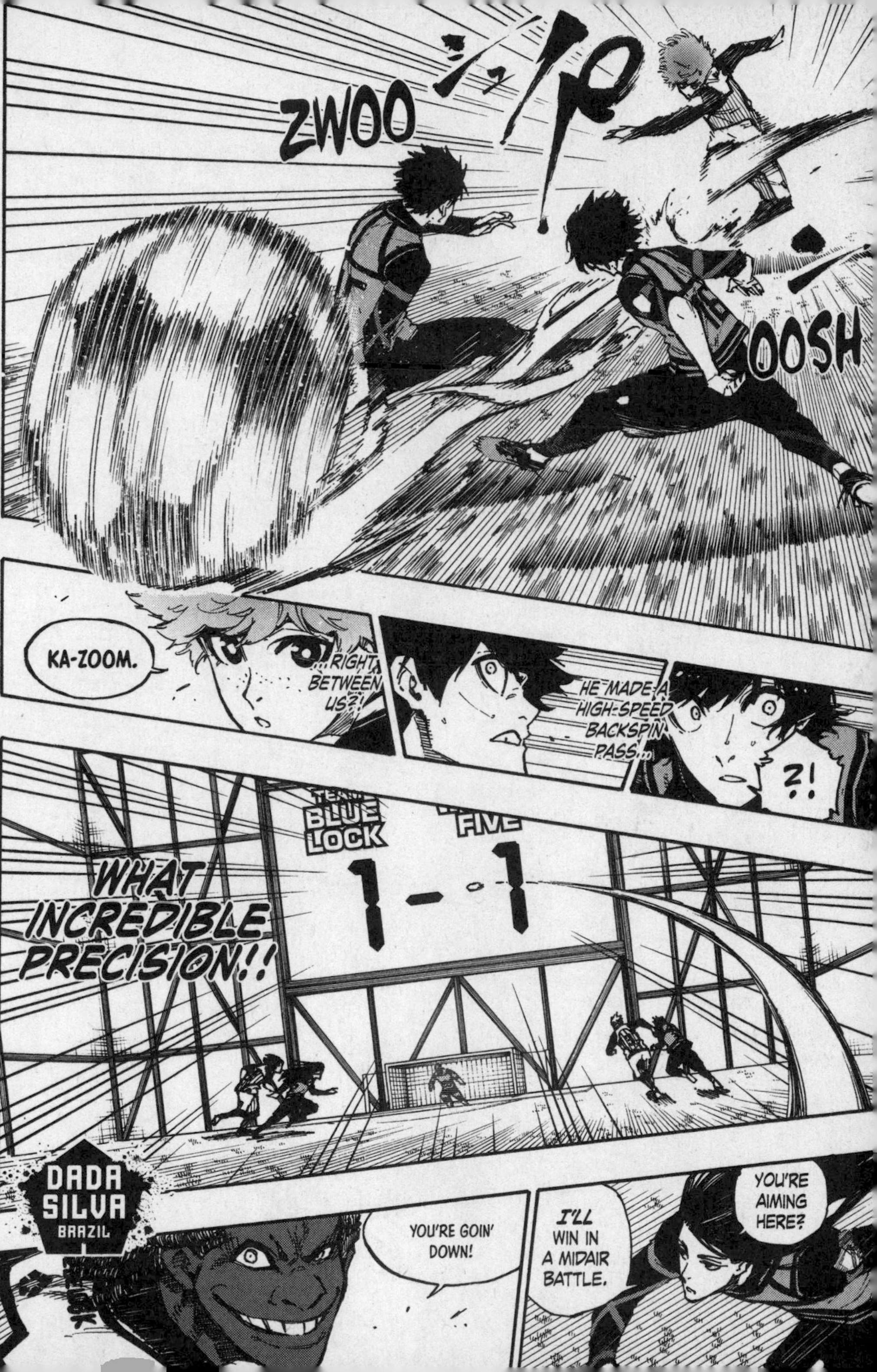
ZWOO
OOSH
HE MADE A HIGH-SPEED BACKSPIN PASS...
?!
...RIGHT BETWEEN US?!
KA-ZOOM.
BLUE LOCK
FIVE
1-1
WHAT INCREDIBLE PRECISION!!
YOU'RE AIMING HERE?
I'LL WIN IN A MIDAIR BATTLE.
DADA SILVA
BRAZIL
YOU'RE GOIN' DOWN!

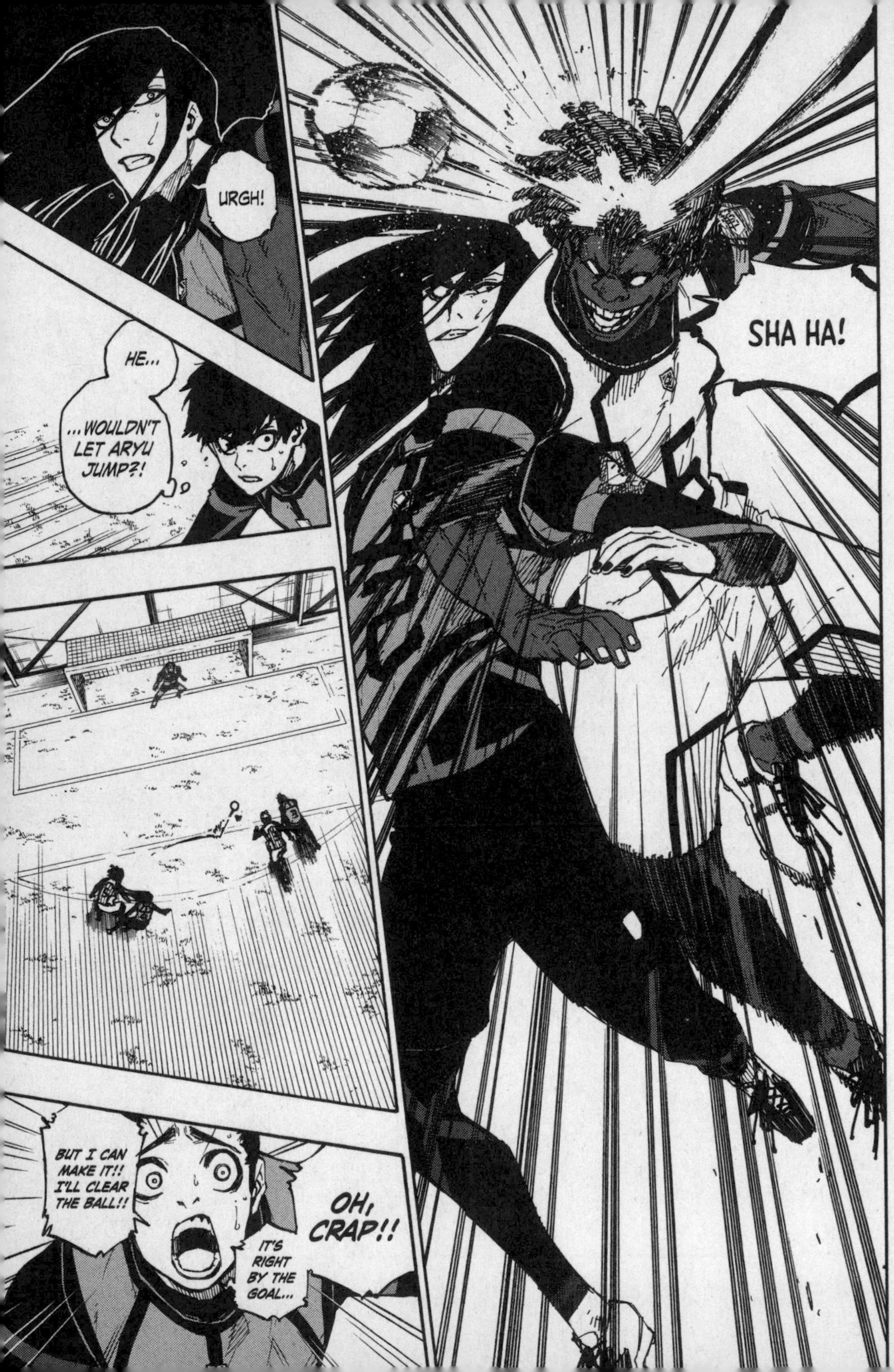
SHA HA!
URGH!
HE...
...WOULDN'T LET ARYU JUMP?!
OH, CRAP!!
IT'S RIGHT BY THE GOAL...
BUT I CAN MAKE IT!! I'LL CLEAR THE BALL!!

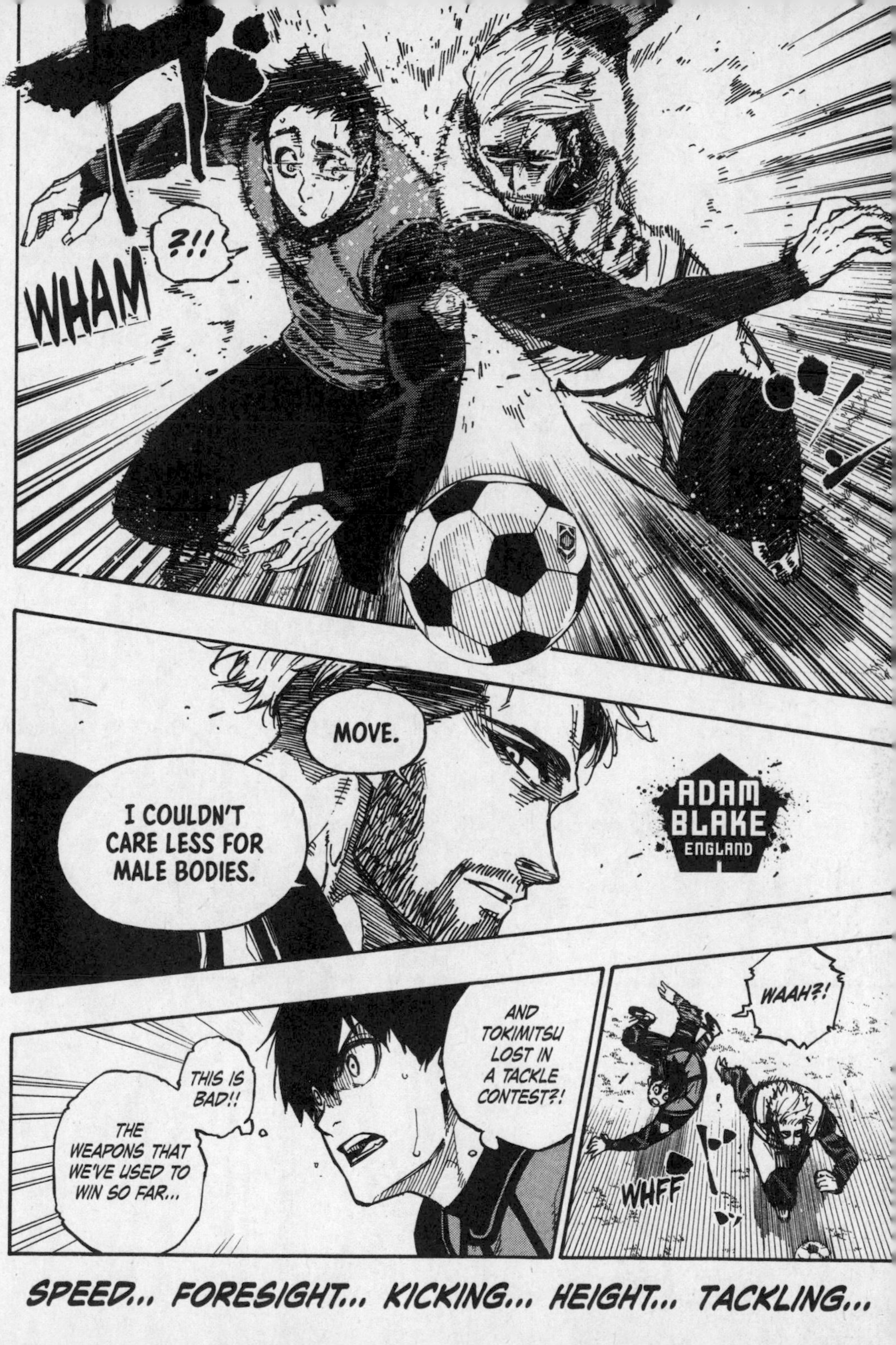
WHAM
?!!
MOVE.
I COULDN'T CARE LESS FOR MALE BODIES.
ADAM BLAKE ENGLAND
WAAH?!
WHFF
AND TOKIMITSU LOST IN A TACKLE CONTEST?!
THIS IS BAD!!
THE WEAPONS THAT WE'VE USED TO WIN SO FAR...
SPEED... FORESIGHT... KICKING... HEIGHT... TACKLING...

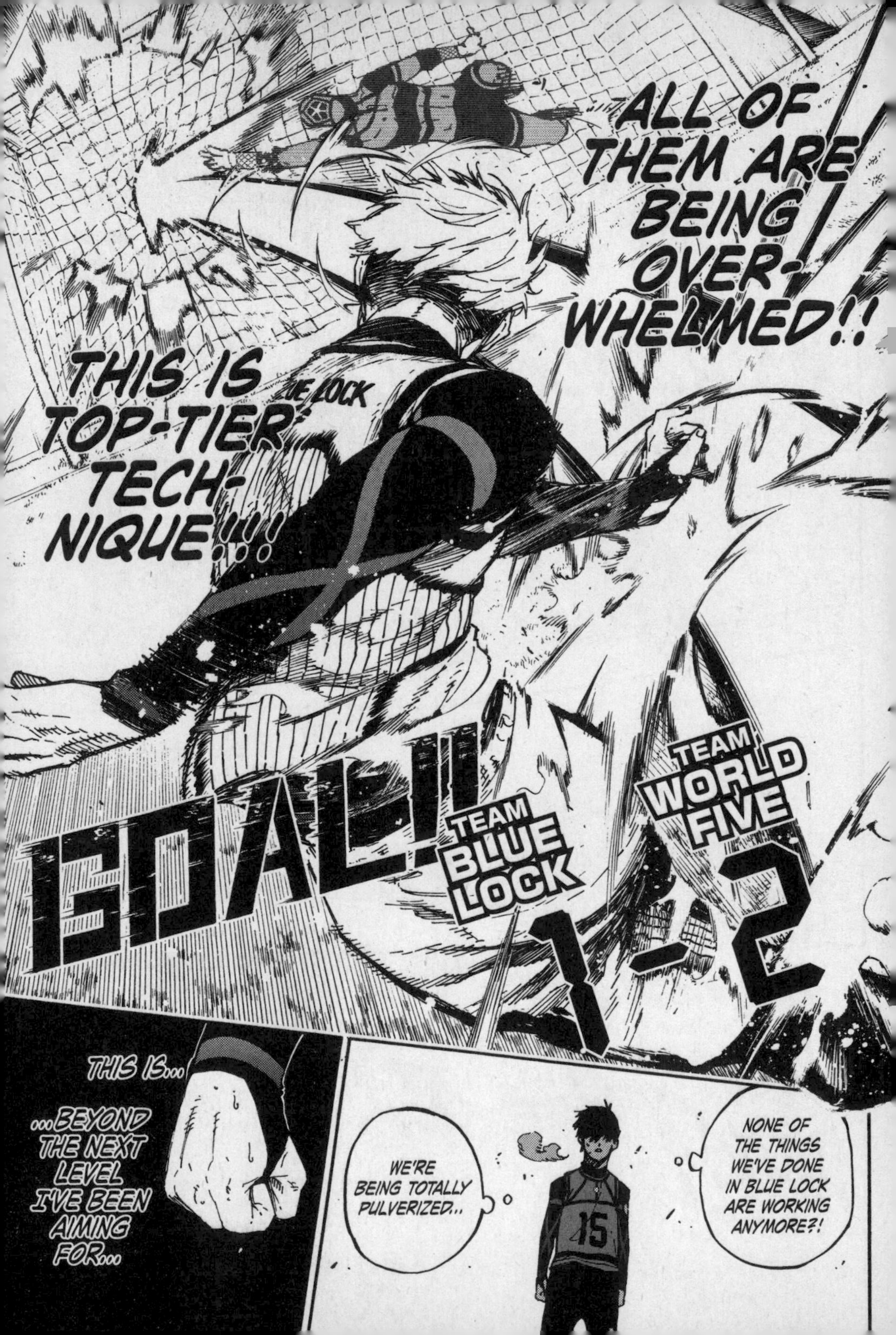
ALL OF THEM ARE BEING OVER-WHELMED!!
THIS IS TOP-TIER TECH-NIQUE!!!
BLUE LOCK
GOAL!!
TEAM BLUE LOCK
TEAM WORLD FIVE
1-2
NONE OF THE THINGS WE'VE DONE IN BLUE LOCK ARE WORKING ANYMORE?!
WE'RE BEING TOTALLY PULVERIZED...
15
THIS IS...
...BEYOND THE NEXT LEVEL I'VE BEEN AIMING FOR...

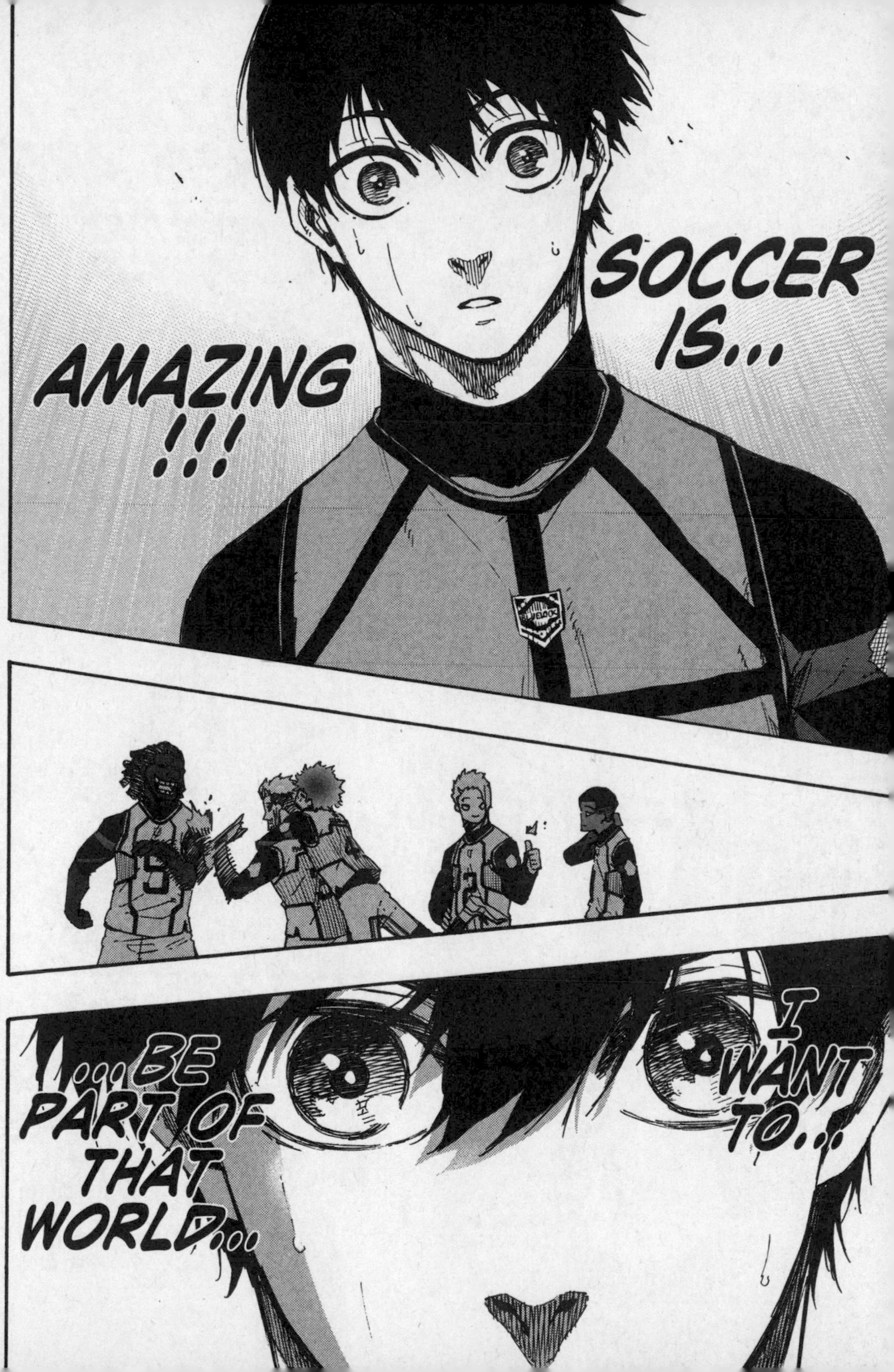
SOCCER IS...
AMAZING!!!
I WANT TO...
...BE PART OF THAT WORLD...

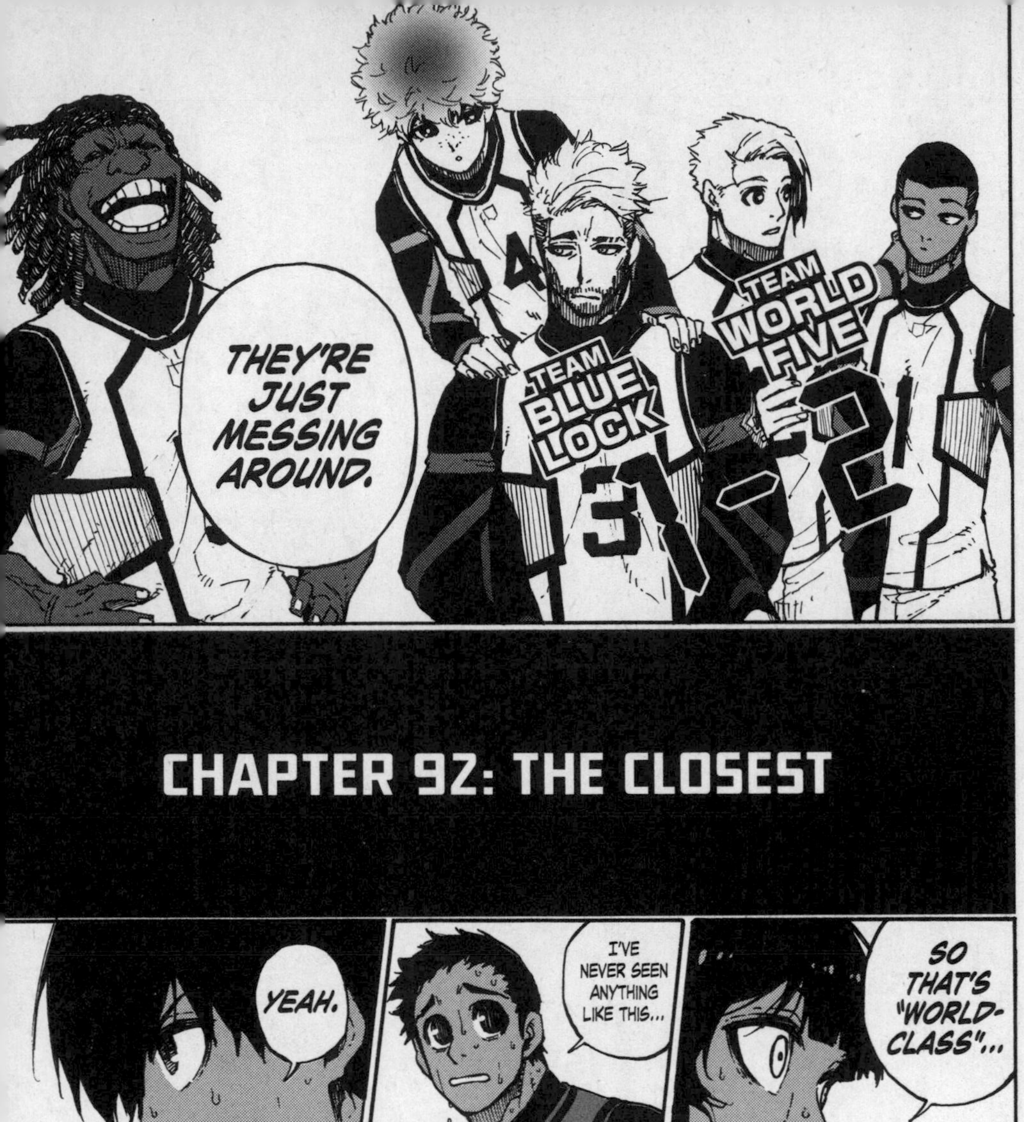
TEAM BLUE LOCK
3 - 2
TEAM WORLD FIVE
THEY'RE JUST MESSING AROUND.

CHAPTER 92: THE CLOSEST

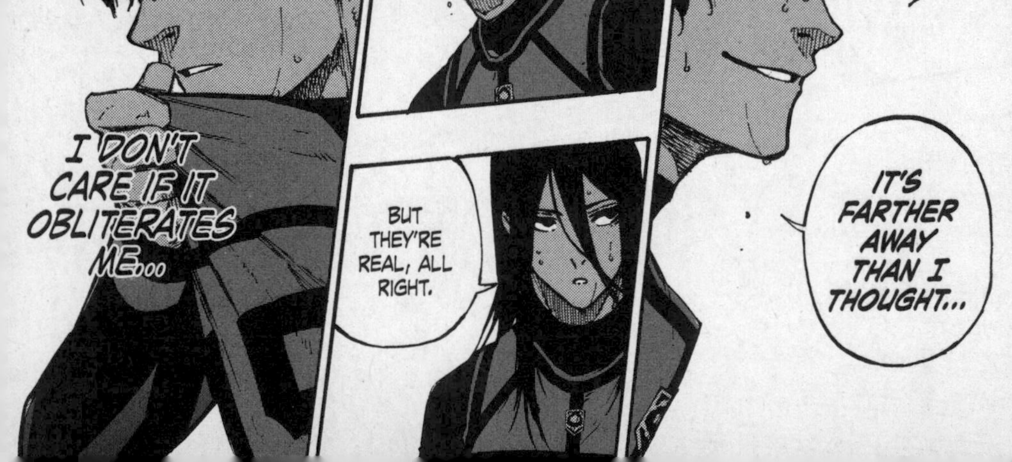
SO THAT'S "WORLD-CLASS"...
IT'S FARTHER AWAY THAN I THOUGHT...
I'VE NEVER SEEN ANYTHING LIKE THIS...
BUT THEY'RE REAL, ALL RIGHT.
YEAH.
I DON'T CARE IF IT OBLITERATES ME...

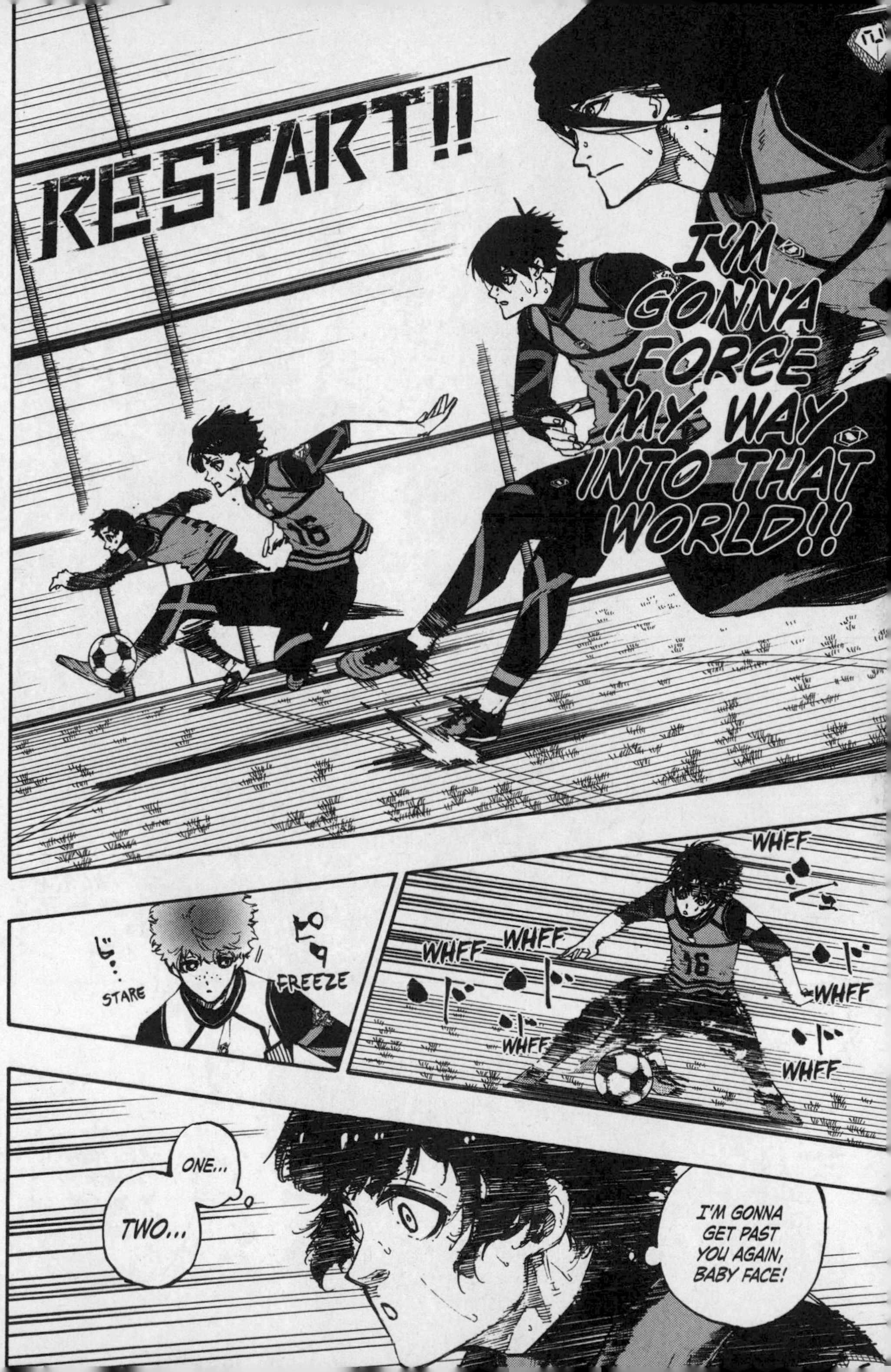
I'M GONNA FORCE MY WAY INTO THAT WORLD!!
RESTART!!
WHFF
WHFF
WHFF
WHFF
WHFF
WHFF
FREEZE
STARE
I'M GONNA GET PAST YOU AGAIN, BABY FACE!
ONE...
TWO...

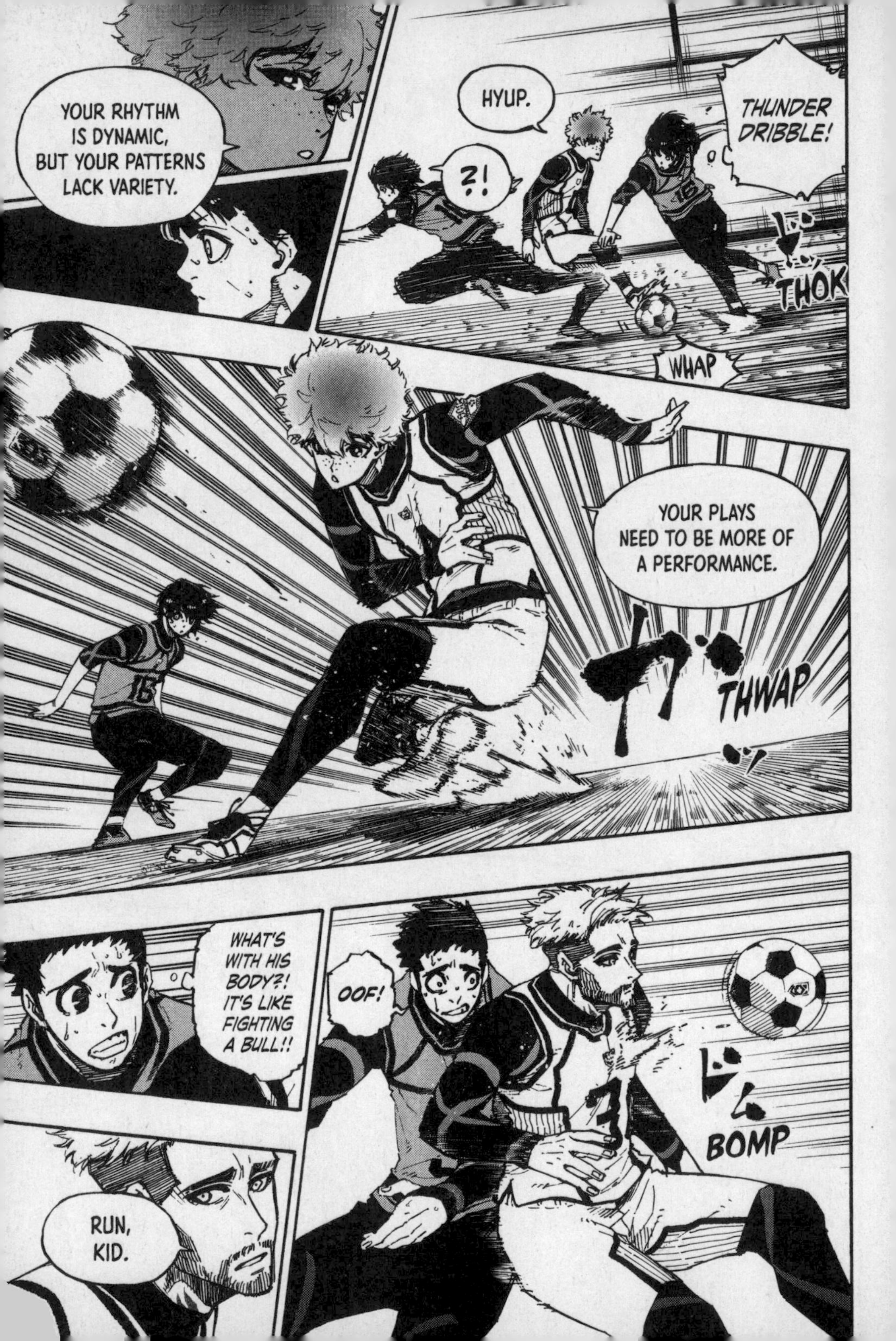
THUNDER DRIBBLE!
HYUP.
?!
THOK
WHAP
YOUR RHYTHM IS DYNAMIC, BUT YOUR PATTERNS LACK VARIETY.
YOUR PLAYS NEED TO BE MORE OF A PERFORMANCE.
THWAP
BOMP
OOF!
WHAT'S WITH HIS BODY?! IT'S LIKE FIGHTING A BULL!!
RUN, KID.

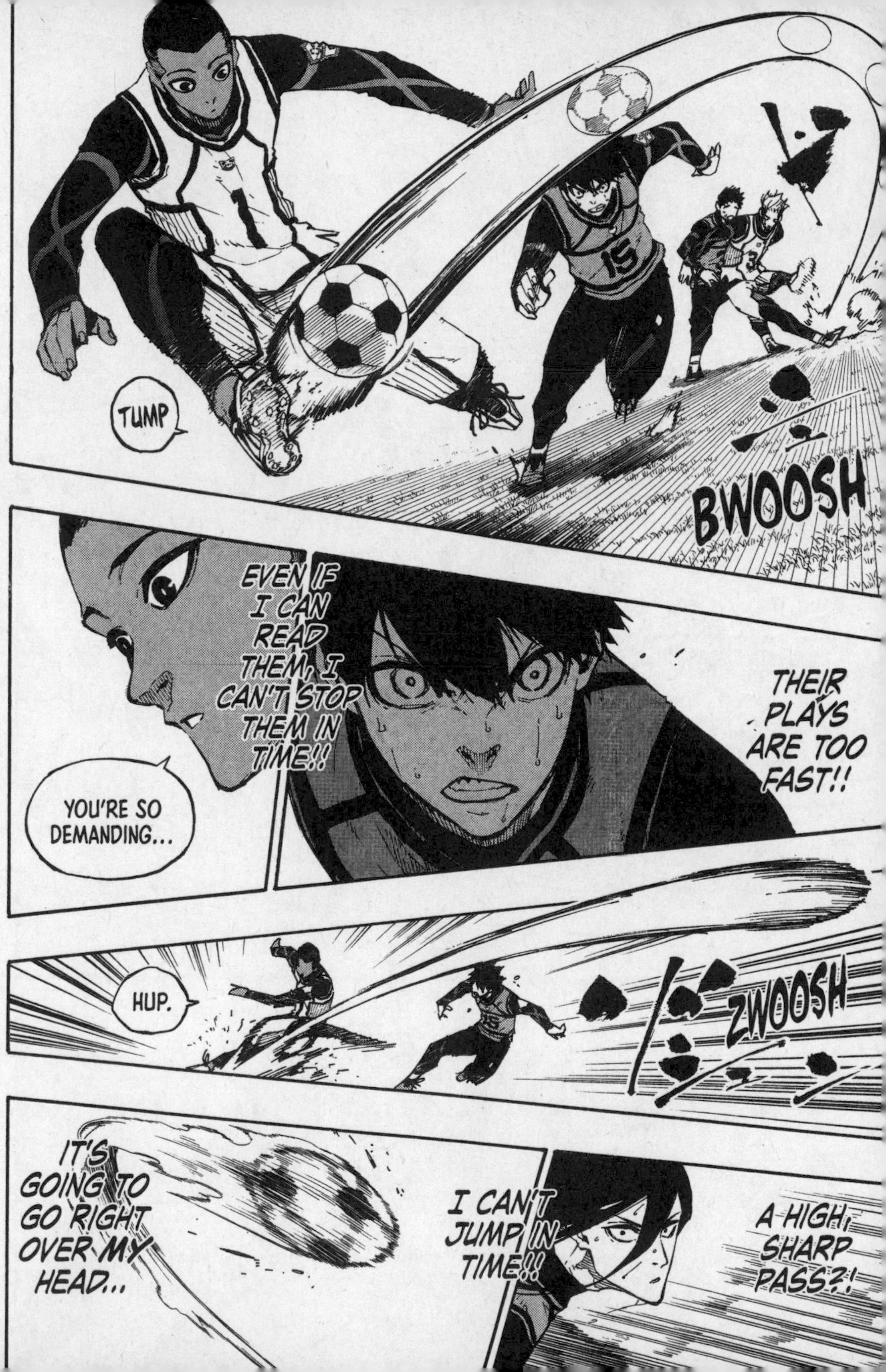
TUMP
BWOOSH
THEIR PLAYS ARE TOO FAST!!
EVEN IF I CAN READ THEM, I CAN'T STOP THEM IN TIME!!
YOU'RE SO DEMANDING...
ZWOOSH
HUP.
A HIGH, SHARP PASS?!
I CAN'T JUMP IN TIME!!
IT'S GOING TO GO RIGHT OVER MY HEAD...

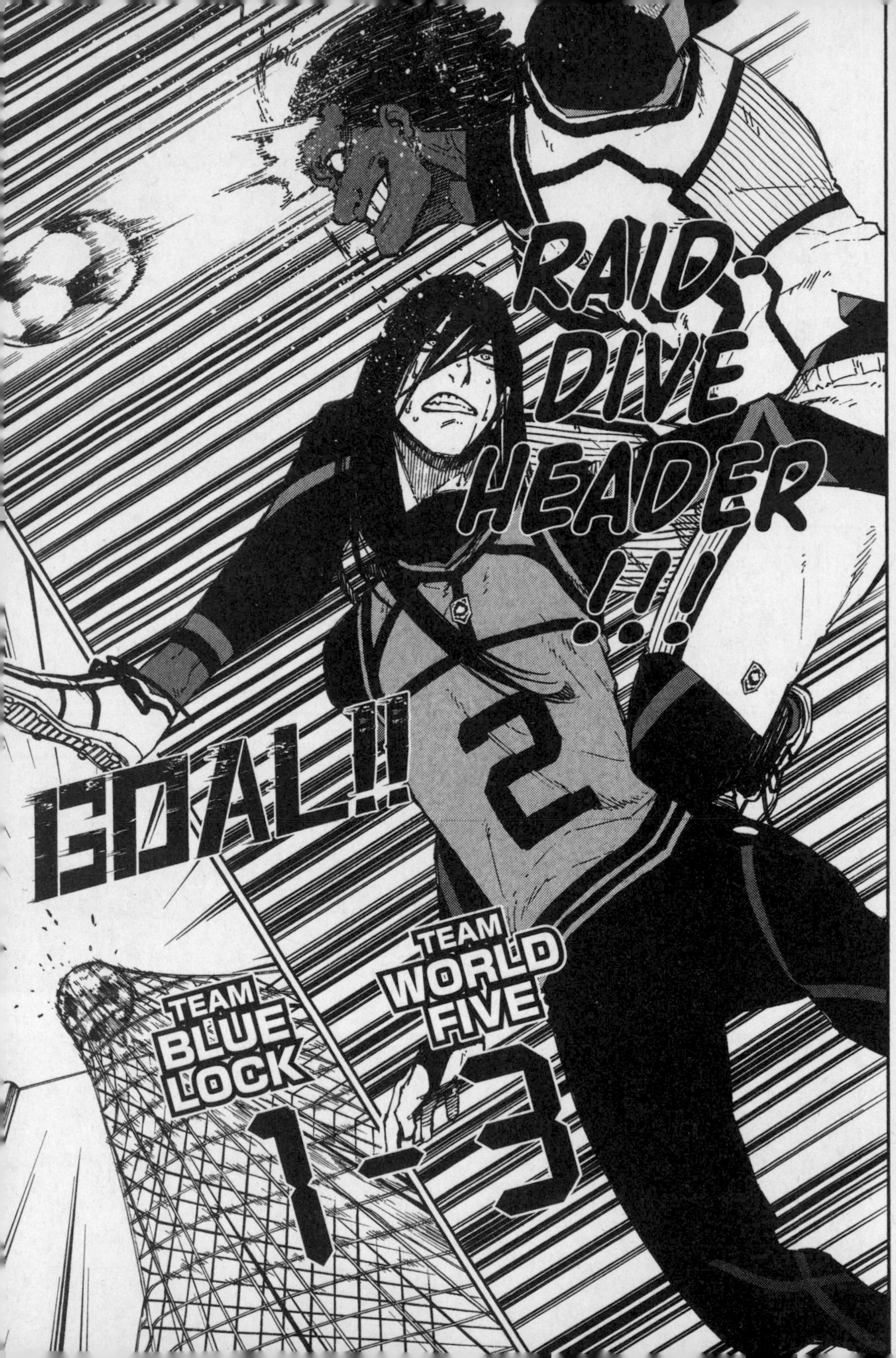
RAID-DIVE HEADER !!!
GOAL!!
TEAM WORLD FIVE
TEAM BLUE LOCK
1-3

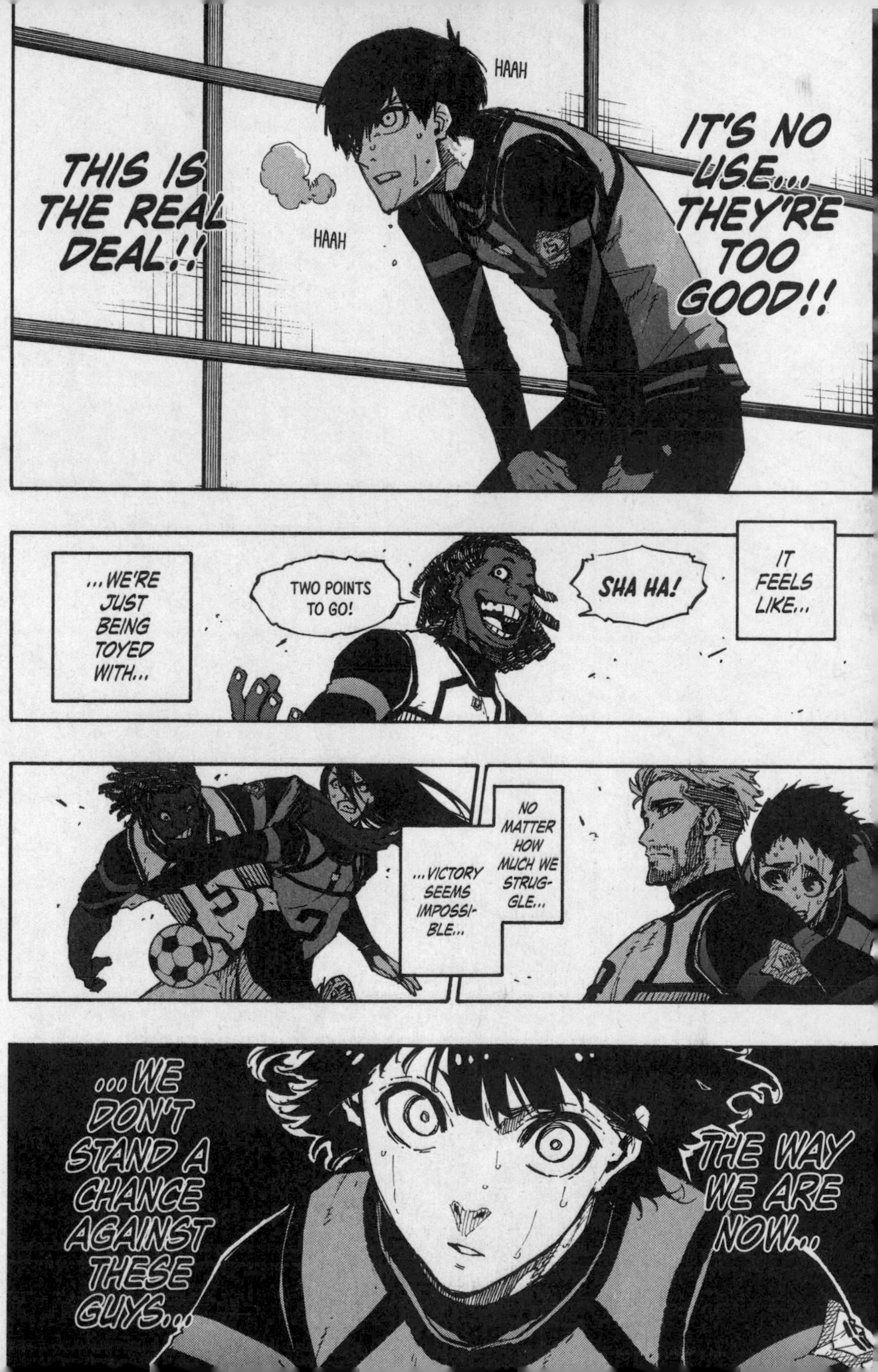
IT'S NO USE... THEY'RE TOO GOOD!!
HAAH
HAAH
THIS IS THE REAL DEAL!!
IT FEELS LIKE...
SHA HA!
TWO POINTS TO GO!
...WE'RE JUST BEING TOYED WITH...
NO MATTER HOW MUCH WE STRUG-GLE...
...VICTORY SEEMS IMPOSSI-BLE...
THE WAY WE ARE NOW...
...WE DON'T STAND A CHANCE AGAINST THESE GUYS...

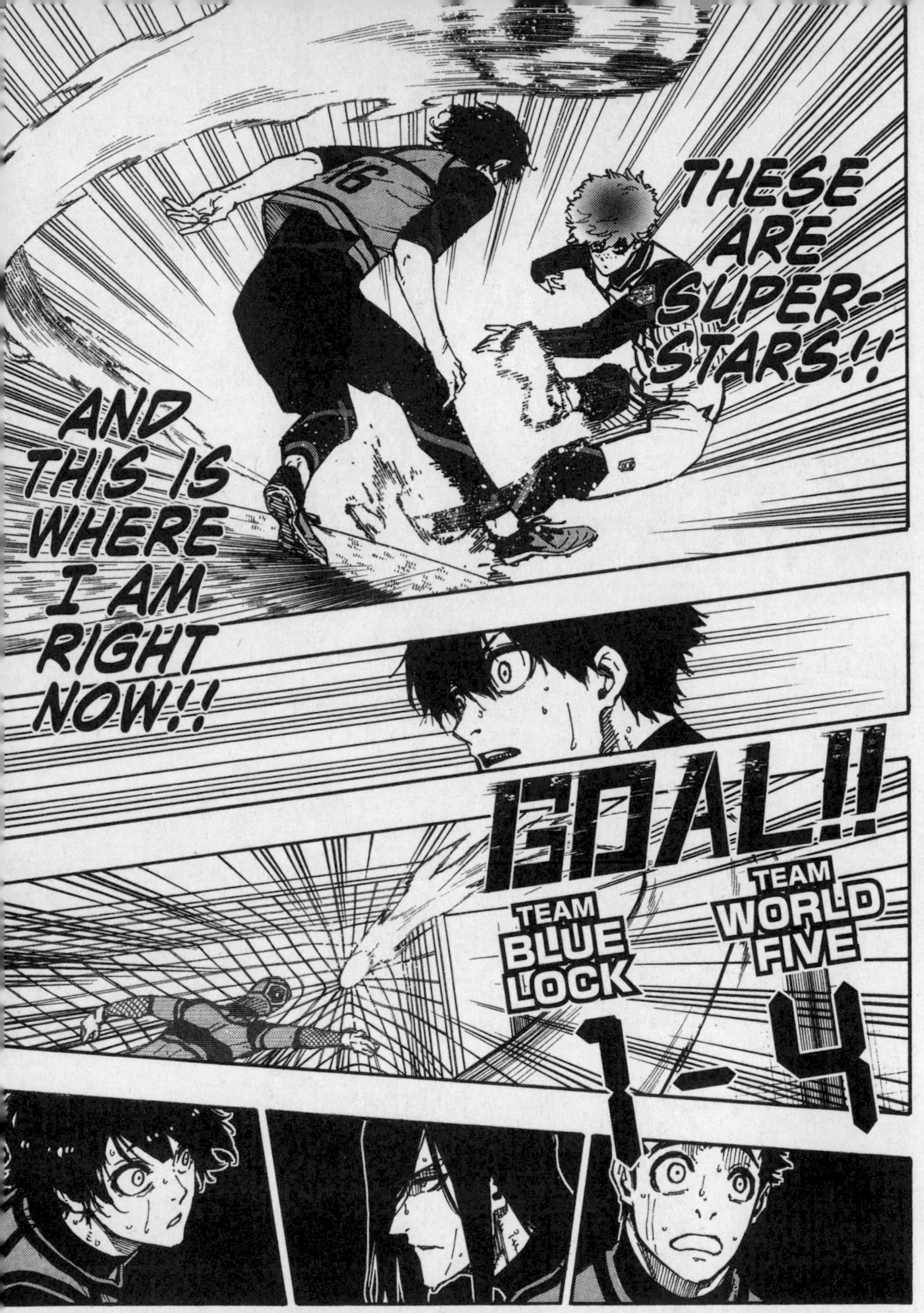
THESE ARE SUPER-STARS!!
AND THIS IS WHERE I AM RIGHT NOW!!
GOAL!!
TEAM BLUE LOCK
TEAM WORLD FIVE
1-4

THIS IS THE DISTANCE TO THE WORLD'S PEAK!!

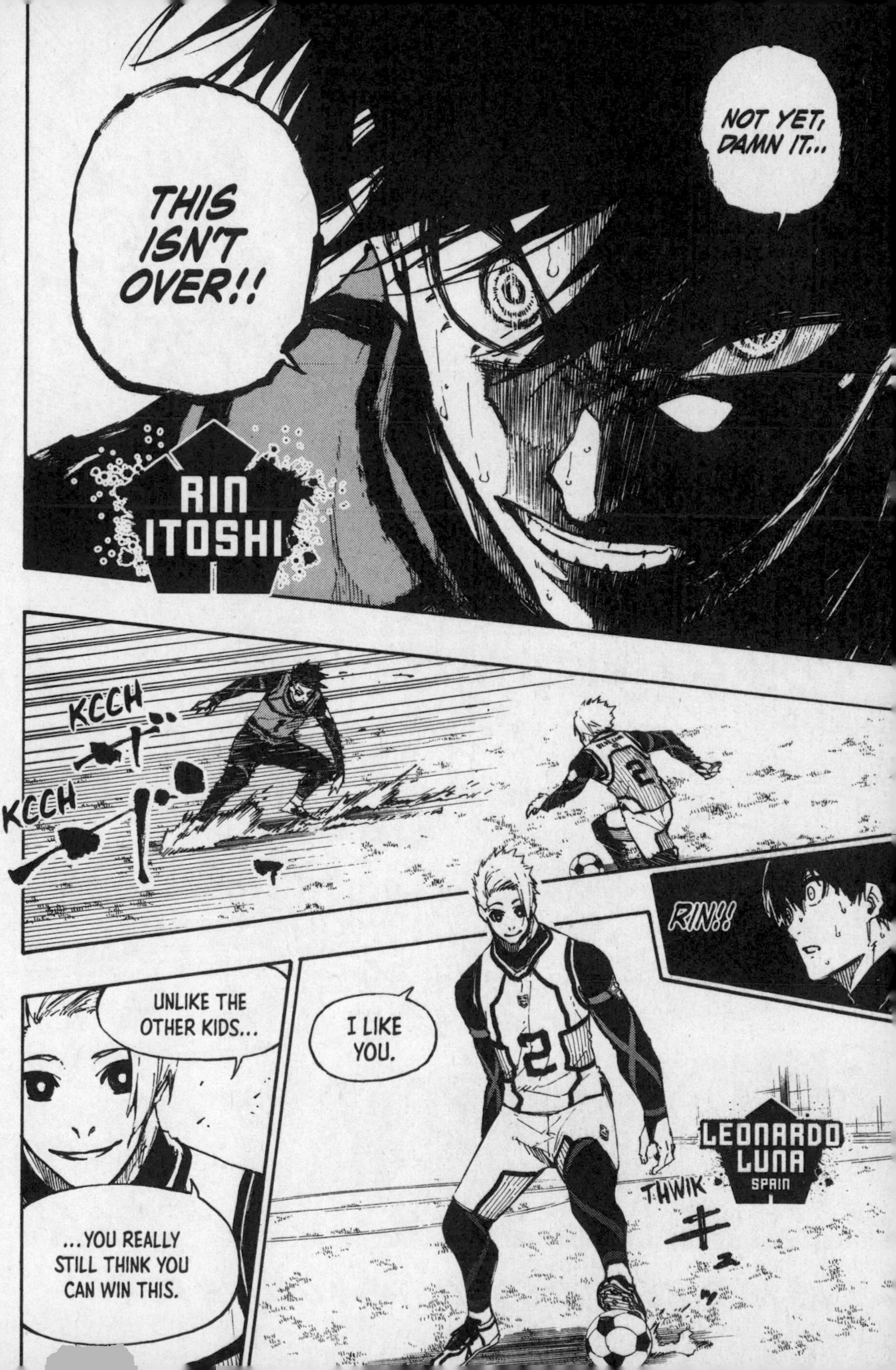
NOT YET, DAMN IT...
THIS ISN'T OVER!!
RIN ITOSHI
KCCH
KCCH
RIN!!
I LIKE YOU.
LEONARDO LUNA
SPAIN
THWIK
UNLIKE THE OTHER KIDS...
...YOU REALLY STILL THINK YOU CAN WIN THIS.

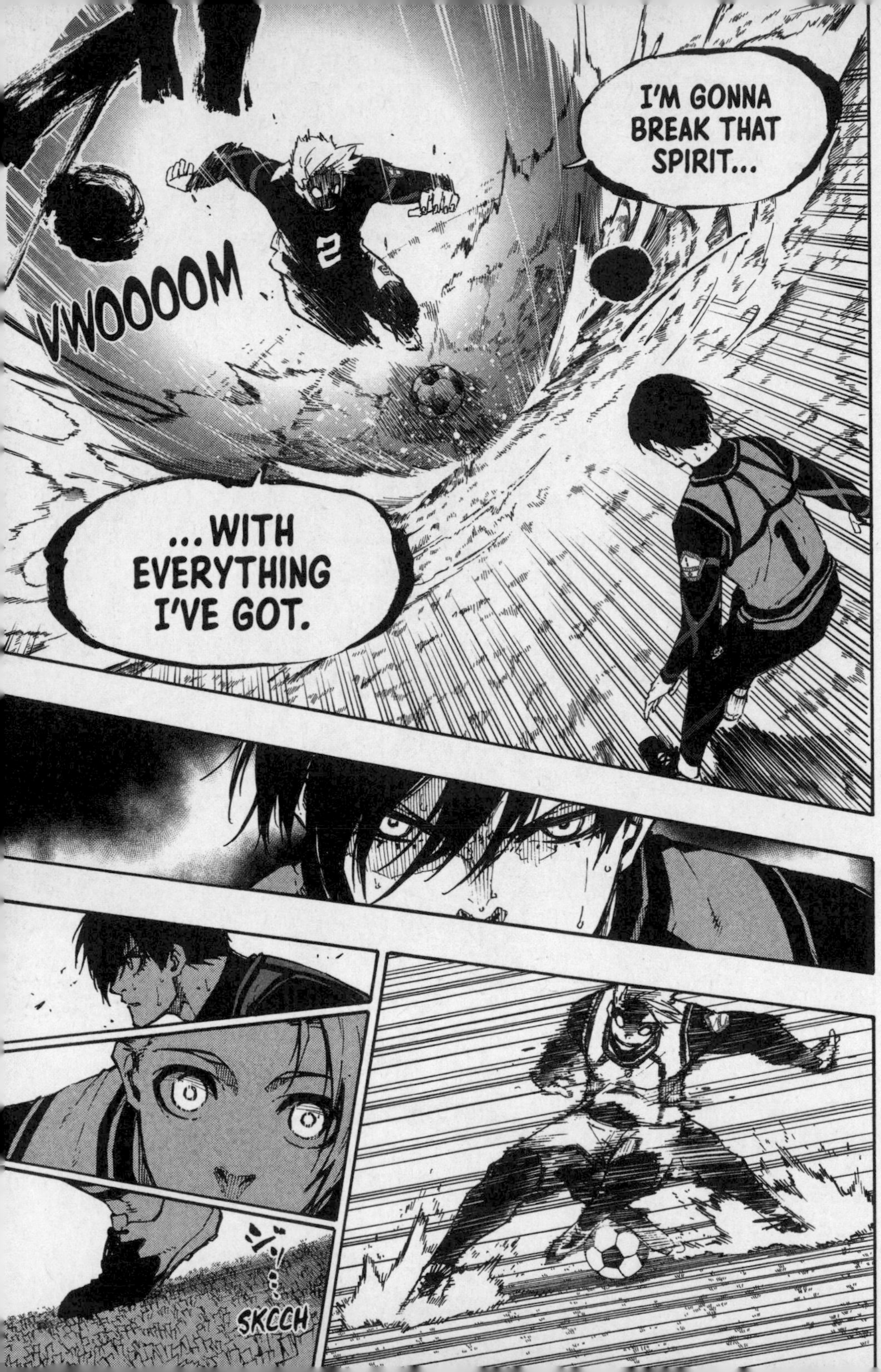
I'M GONNA BREAK THAT SPIRIT...
VWOOOM
...WITH EVERYTHING I'VE GOT.
SKCCH

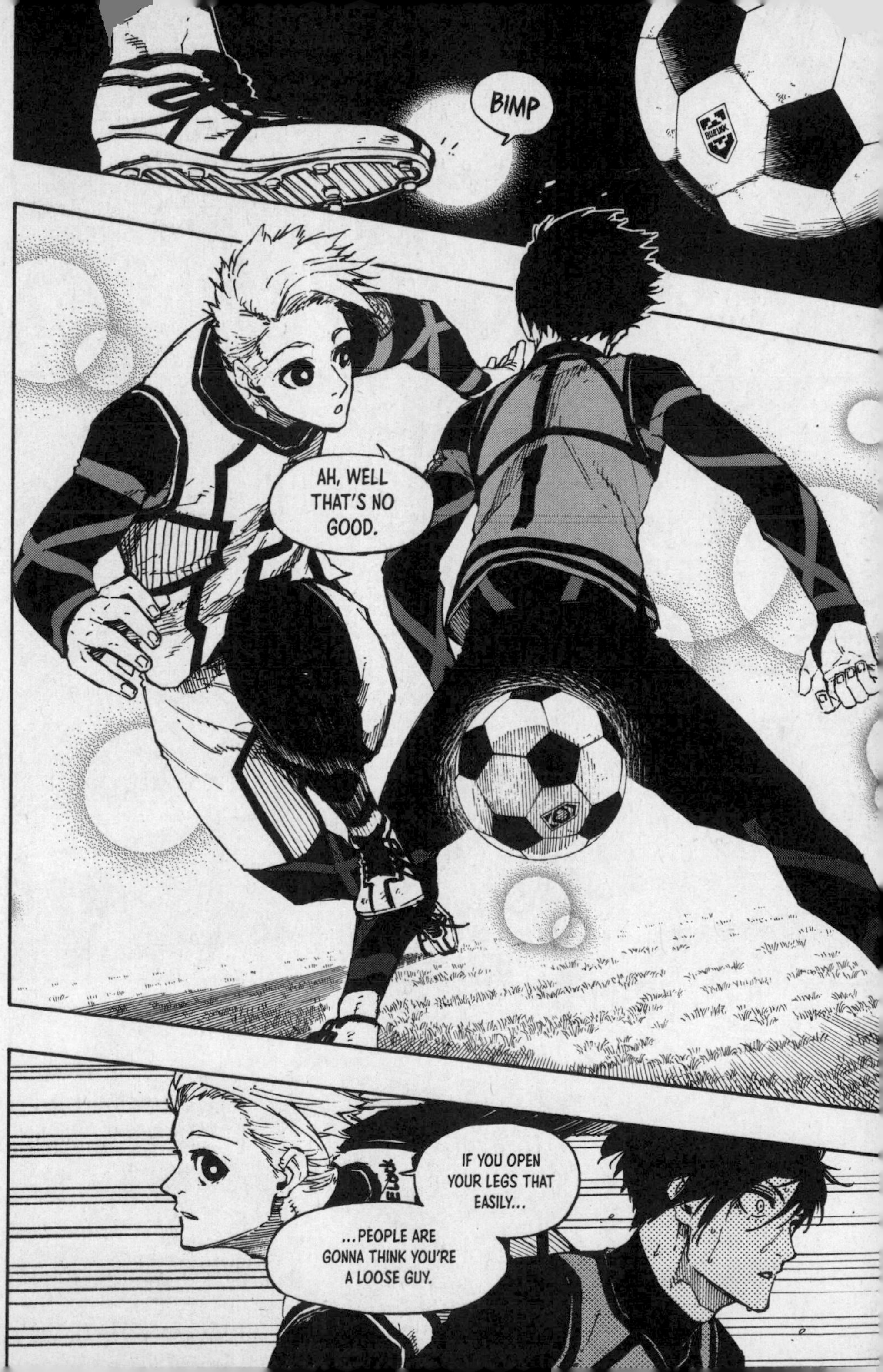
BIMP
AH, WELL THAT'S NO GOOD.
IF YOU OPEN YOUR LEGS THAT EASILY...
...PEOPLE ARE GONNA THINK YOU'RE A LOOSE GUY.

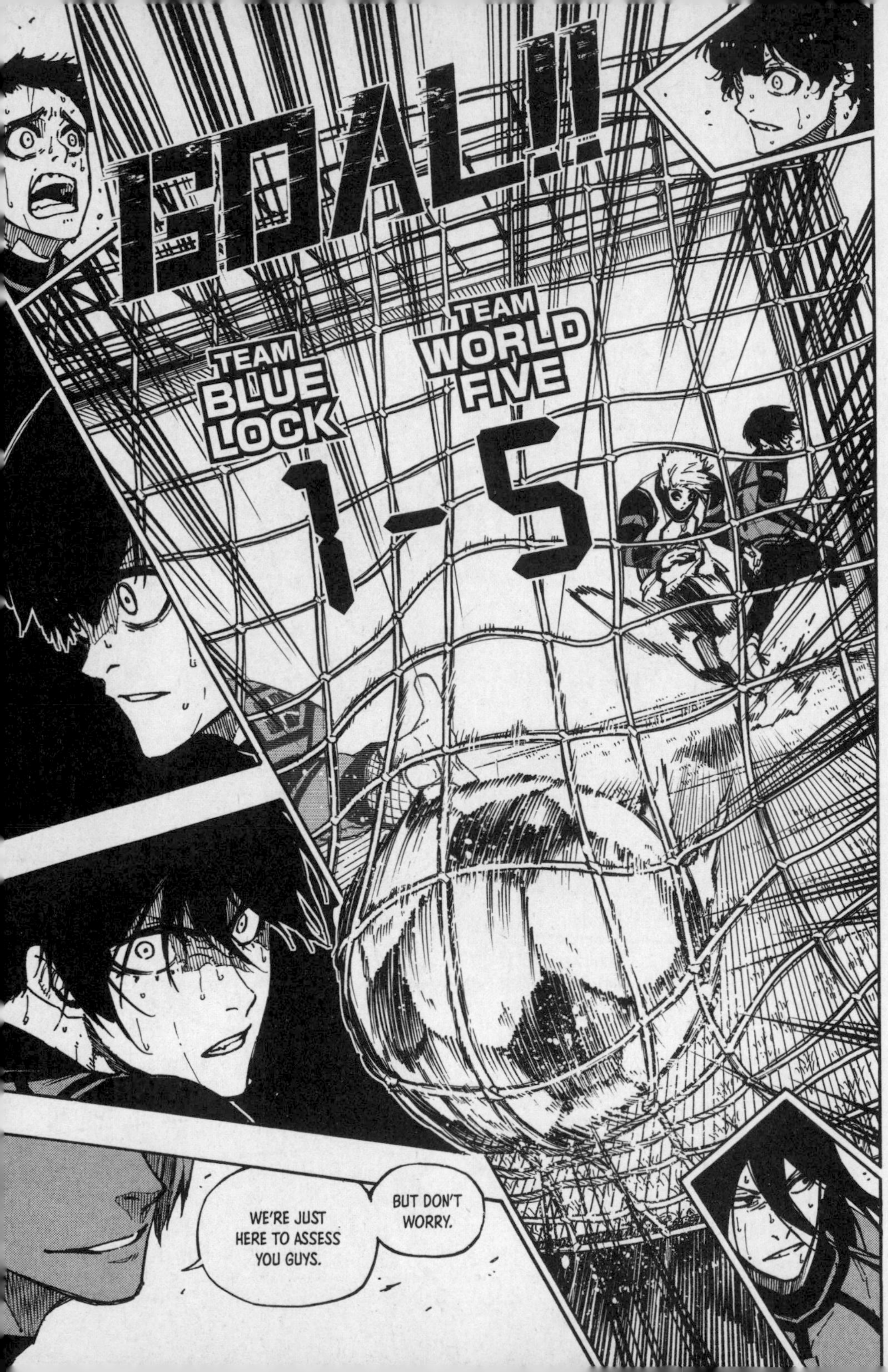
GOAL!!
TEAM BLUE LOCK
TEAM WORLD FIVE
1-5
BUT DON'T WORRY.
WE'RE JUST HERE TO ASSESS YOU GUYS.

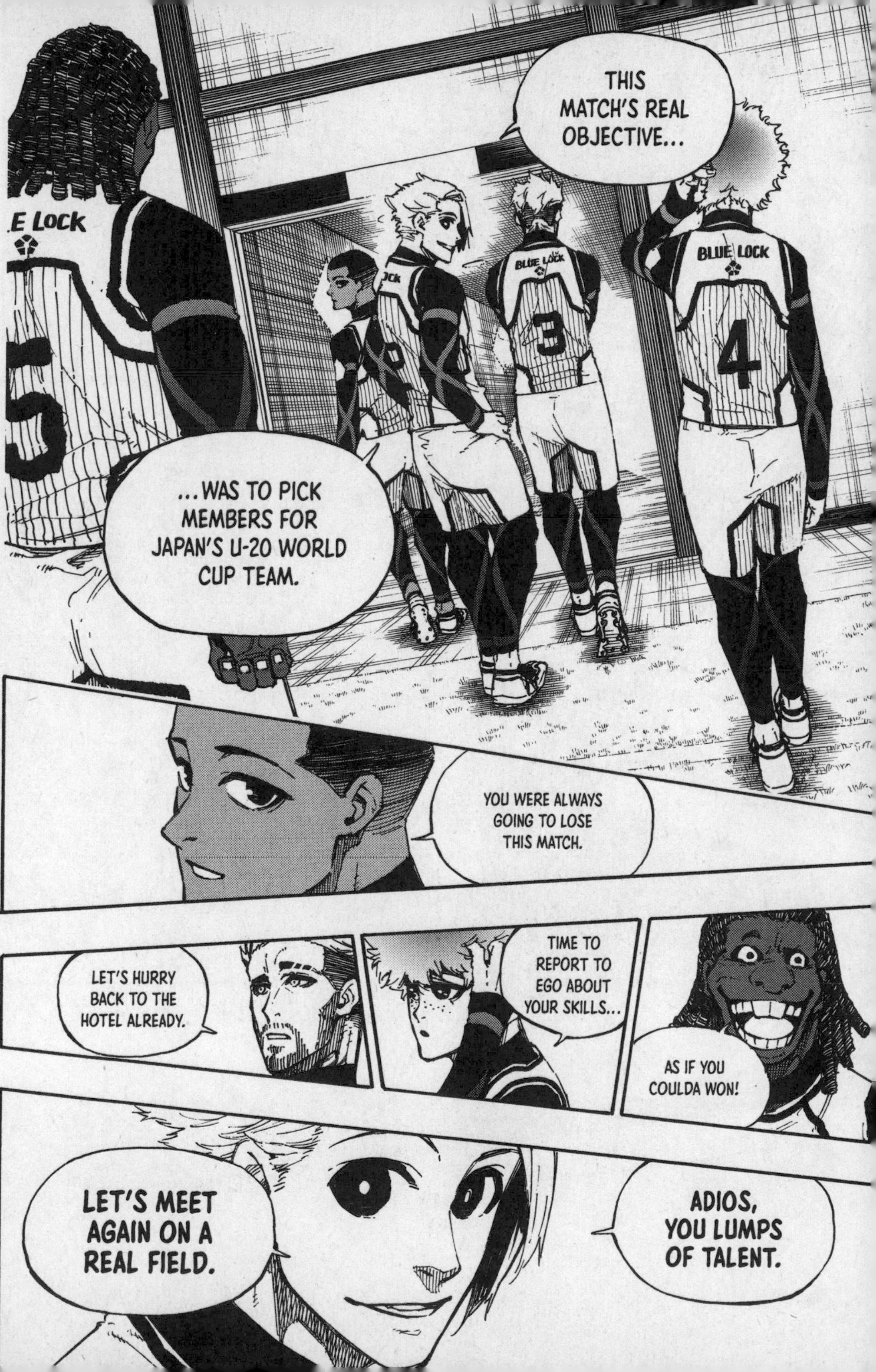
THIS MATCH'S REAL OBJECTIVE...
...WAS TO PICK MEMBERS FOR JAPAN'S U-20 WORLD CUP TEAM.
YOU WERE ALWAYS GOING TO LOSE THIS MATCH.
AS IF YOU COULDA WON!
TIME TO REPORT TO EGO ABOUT YOUR SKILLS...
LET'S HURRY BACK TO THE HOTEL ALREADY.
ADIOS, YOU LUMPS OF TALENT.
LET'S MEET AGAIN ON A REAL FIELD.

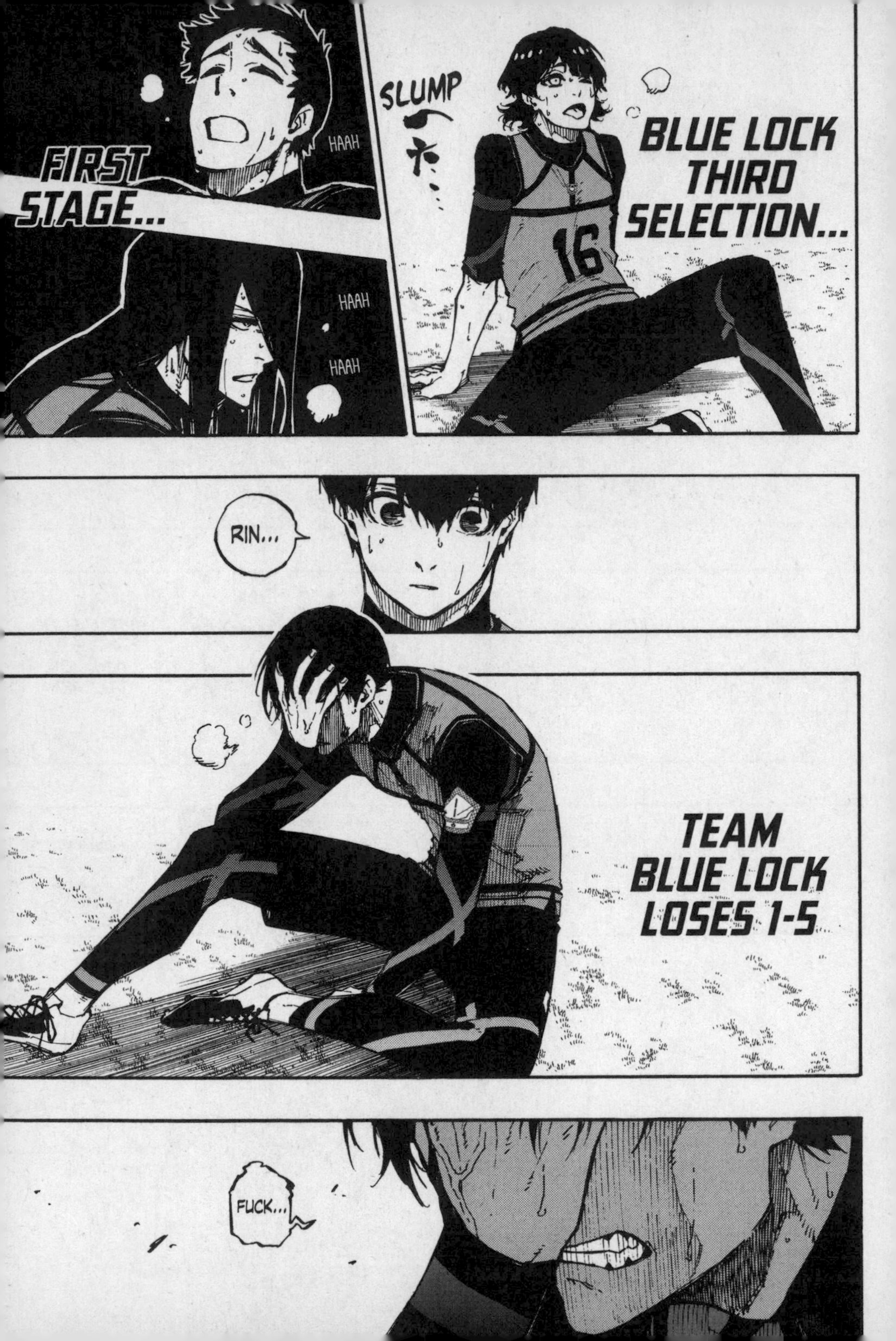
SLUMP
BLUE LOCK THIRD SELECTION...
FIRST STAGE...
HAAH
HAAH
HAAH
RIN...
TEAM BLUE LOCK LOSES 1-5
FUCK...

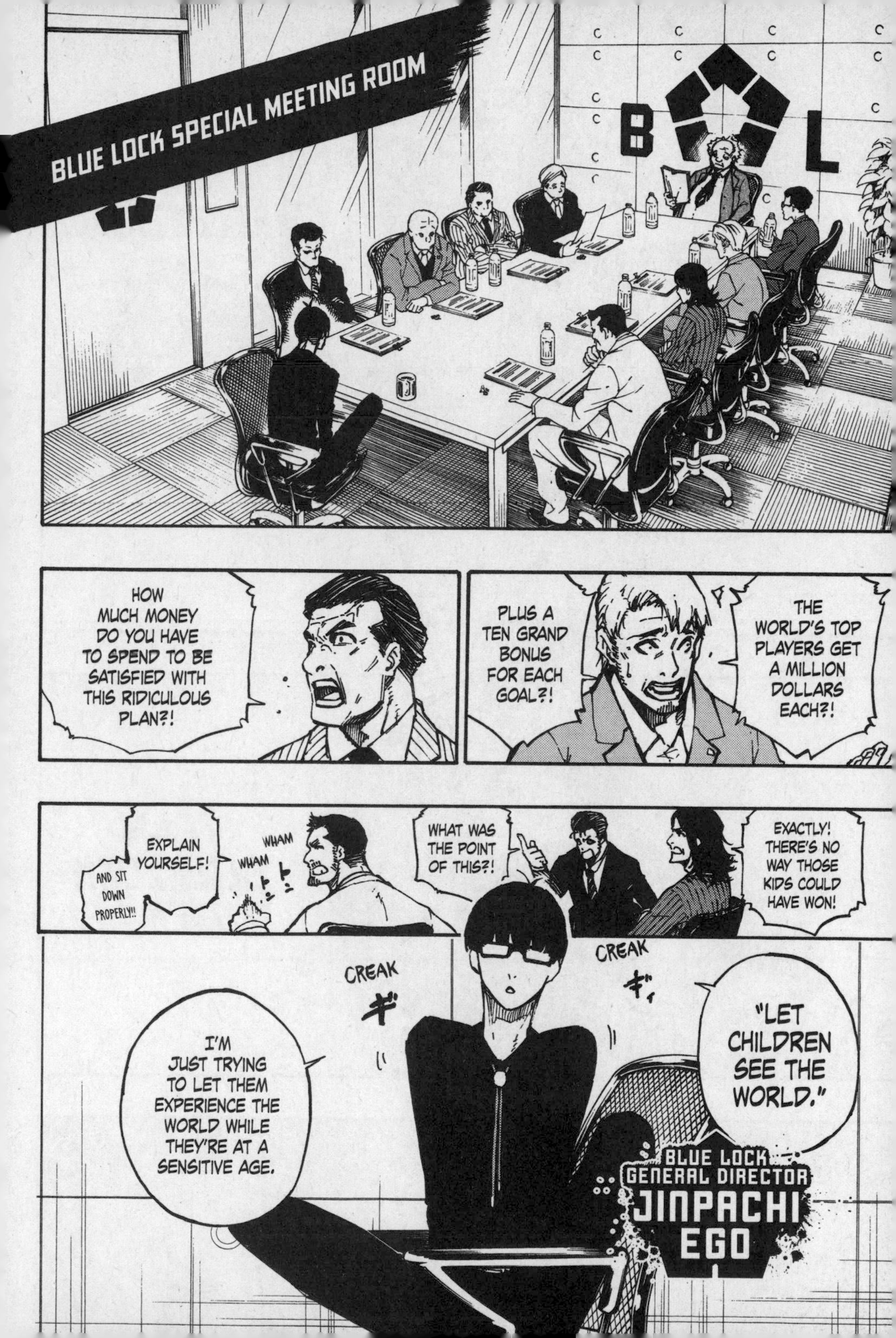
BLUE LOCK SPECIAL MEETING ROOM
THE WORLD'S TOP PLAYERS GET A MILLION DOLLARS EACH?!
PLUS A TEN GRAND BONUS FOR EACH GOAL?!
HOW MUCH MONEY DO YOU HAVE TO SPEND TO BE SATISFIED WITH THIS RIDICULOUS PLAN?!
EXACTLY! THERE'S NO WAY THOSE KIDS COULD HAVE WON!
WHAT WAS THE POINT OF THIS?!
WHAM
WHAM
EXPLAIN YOURSELF!
AND SIT DOWN PROPERLY!!
CREAK
"LET CHILDREN SEE THE WORLD."
CREAK
I'M JUST TRYING TO LET THEM EXPERIENCE THE WORLD WHILE THEY'RE AT A SENSITIVE AGE.
BLUE LOCK GENERAL DIRECTOR
JINPACHI EGO

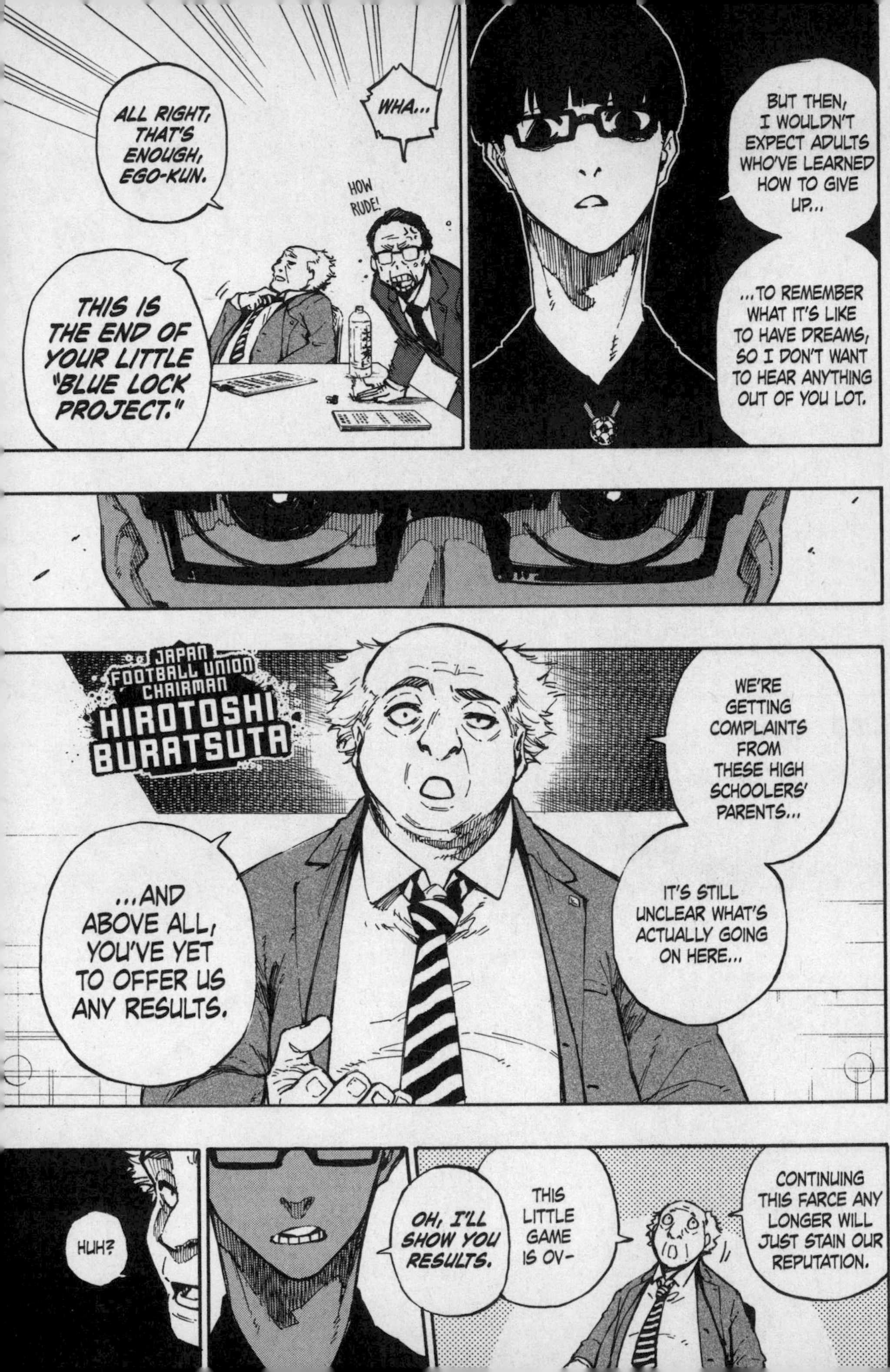
BUT THEN, I WOULDN'T EXPECT ADULTS WHO'VE LEARNED HOW TO GIVE UP...
...TO REMEMBER WHAT IT'S LIKE TO HAVE DREAMS, SO I DON'T WANT TO HEAR ANYTHING OUT OF YOU LOT.
WHA...
HOW RUDE!
ALL RIGHT, THAT'S ENOUGH, EGO-KUN.
THIS IS THE END OF YOUR LITTLE "BLUE LOCK PROJECT."
JAPAN FOOTBALL UNION CHAIRMAN
HIROTOSHI BURATSUTA
WE'RE GETTING COMPLAINTS FROM THESE HIGH SCHOOLERS' PARENTS...
IT'S STILL UNCLEAR WHAT'S ACTUALLY GOING ON HERE...
...AND ABOVE ALL, YOU'VE YET TO OFFER US ANY RESULTS.
CONTINUING THIS FARCE ANY LONGER WILL JUST STAIN OUR REPUTATION.
THIS LITTLE GAME IS OV-
OH, I'LL SHOW YOU RESULTS.
HUH?

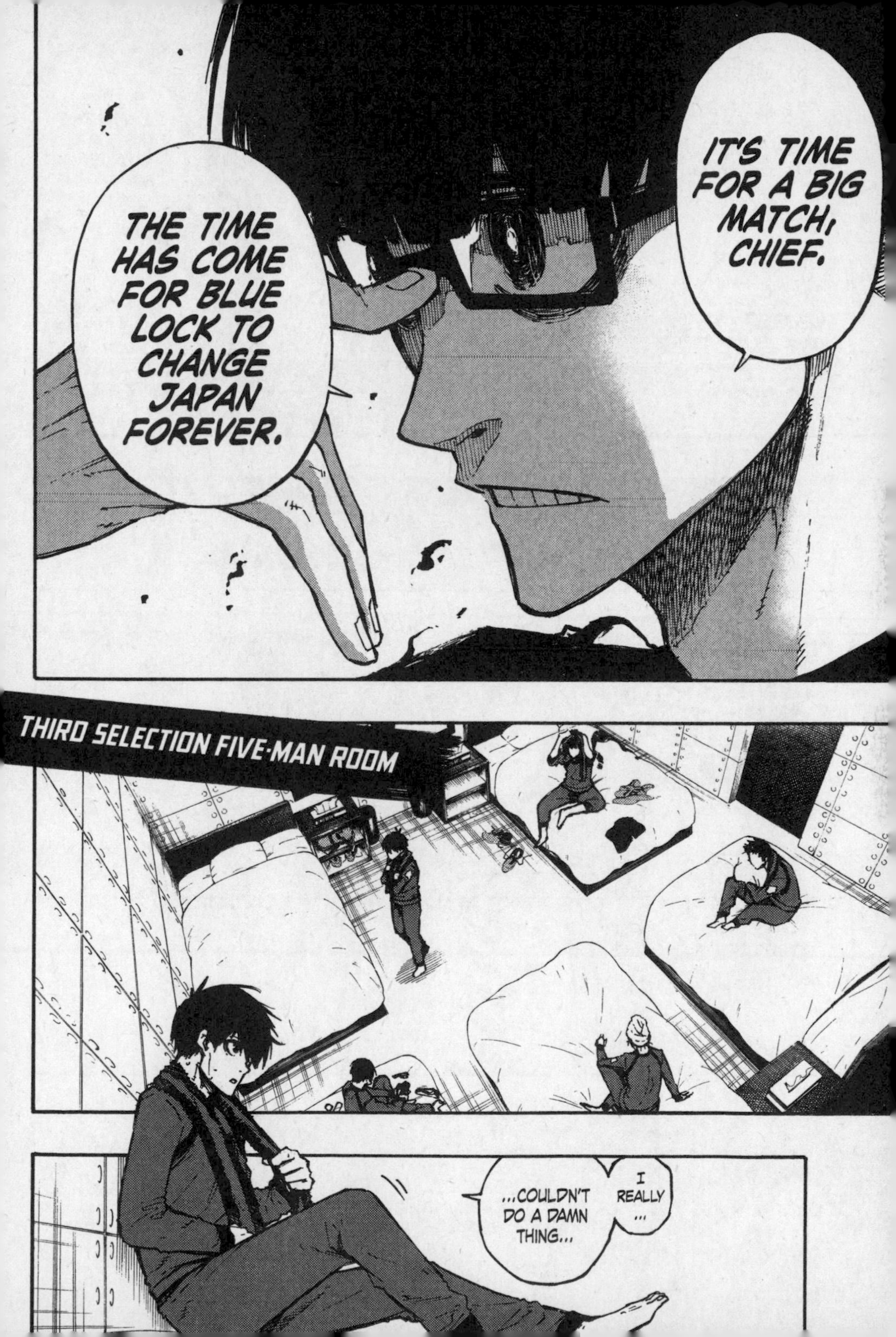
IT'S TIME FOR A BIG MATCH, CHIEF.
THE TIME HAS COME FOR BLUE LOCK TO CHANGE JAPAN FOREVER.
THIRD SELECTION FIVE-MAN ROOM
I REALLY ...
...COULDN'T DO A DAMN THING...

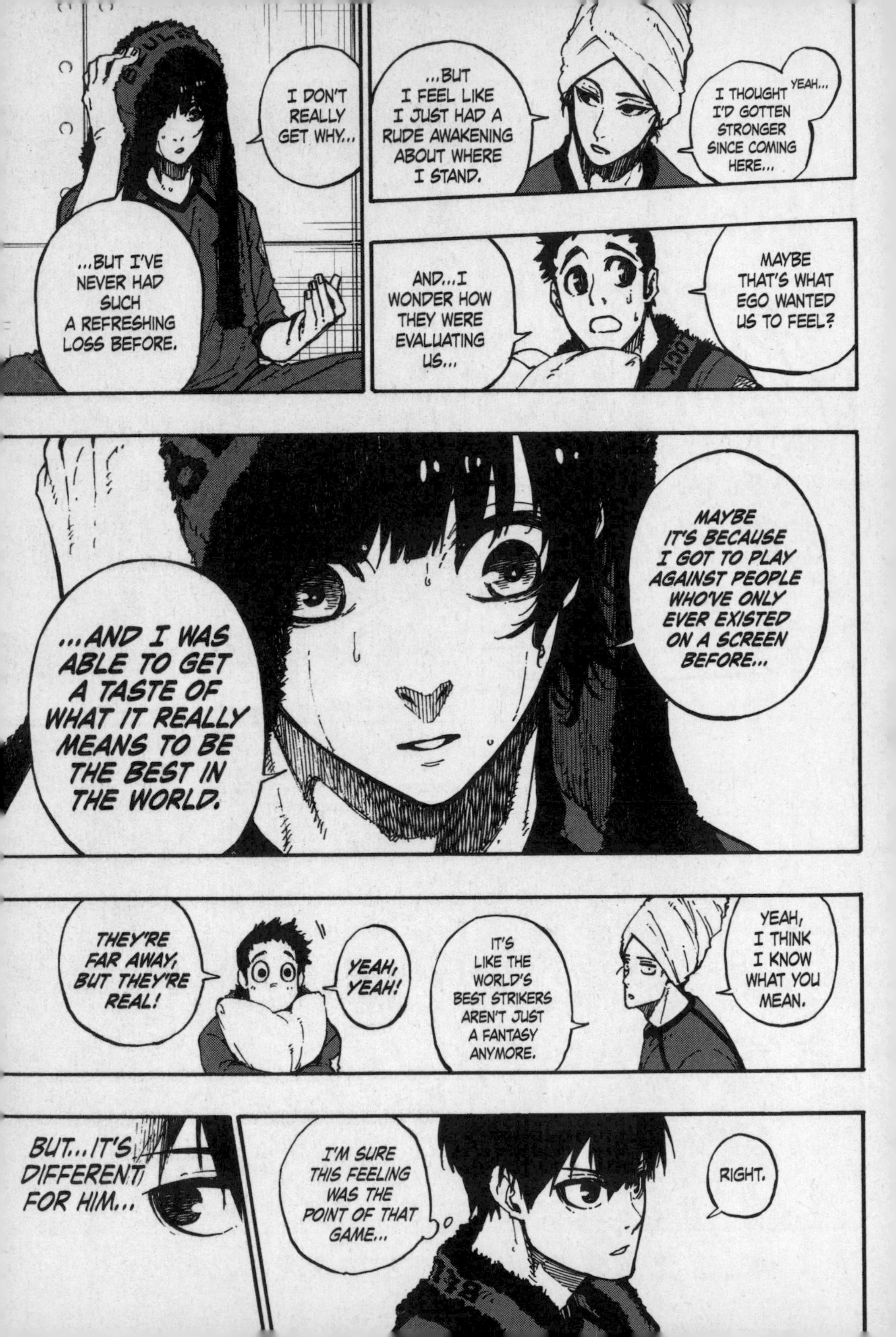
YEAH...
I THOUGHT I'D GOTTEN STRONGER SINCE COMING HERE...
...BUT I FEEL LIKE I JUST HAD A RUDE AWAKENING ABOUT WHERE I STAND.
MAYBE THAT'S WHAT EGO WANTED US TO FEEL?
AND...I WONDER HOW THEY WERE EVALUATING US...
I DON'T REALLY GET WHY...
...BUT I'VE NEVER HAD SUCH A REFRESHING LOSS BEFORE.
MAYBE IT'S BECAUSE I GOT TO PLAY AGAINST PEOPLE WHO'VE ONLY EVER EXISTED ON A SCREEN BEFORE...
...AND I WAS ABLE TO GET A TASTE OF WHAT IT REALLY MEANS TO BE THE BEST IN THE WORLD.
YEAH, I THINK I KNOW WHAT YOU MEAN.
IT'S LIKE THE WORLD'S BEST STRIKERS AREN'T JUST A FANTASY ANYMORE.
YEAH, YEAH!
THEY'RE FAR AWAY, BUT THEY'RE REAL!
RIGHT.
I'M SURE THIS FEELING WAS THE POINT OF THAT GAME...
BUT...IT'S DIFFERENT FOR HIM...

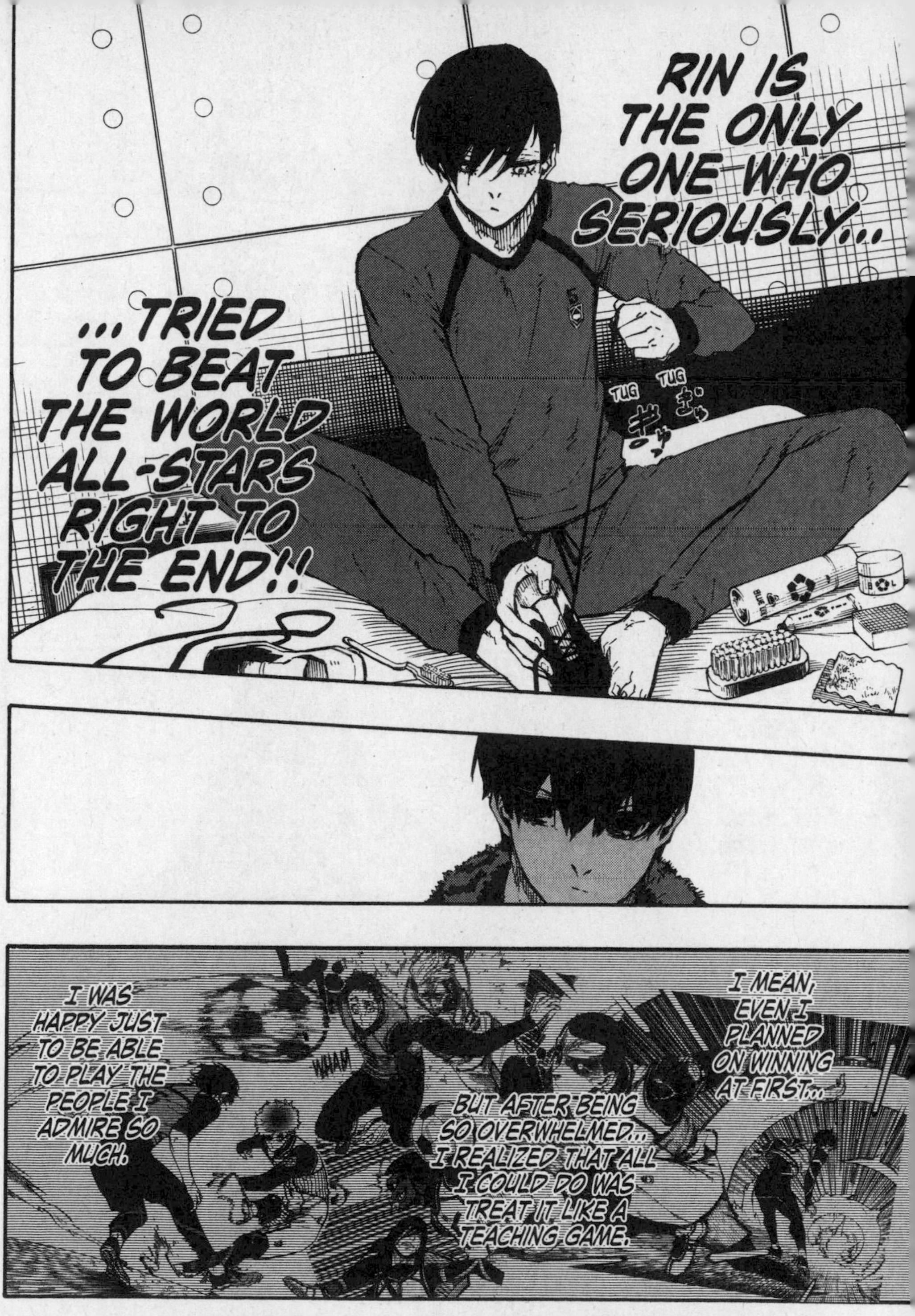
RIN IS THE ONLY ONE WHO SERIOUSLY...
...TRIED TO BEAT THE WORLD ALL-STARS RIGHT TO THE END!!
TUG TUG
I MEAN, EVEN I PLANNED ON WINNING AT FIRST...
BUT AFTER BEING SO OVERWHELMED... I REALIZED THAT ALL I COULD DO WAS TREAT IT LIKE A TEACHING GAME.
I WAS HAPPY JUST TO BE ABLE TO PLAY THE PEOPLE I ADMIRE SO MUCH.

ALL I COULD DO WAS ACCEPT OUR SITUATION...

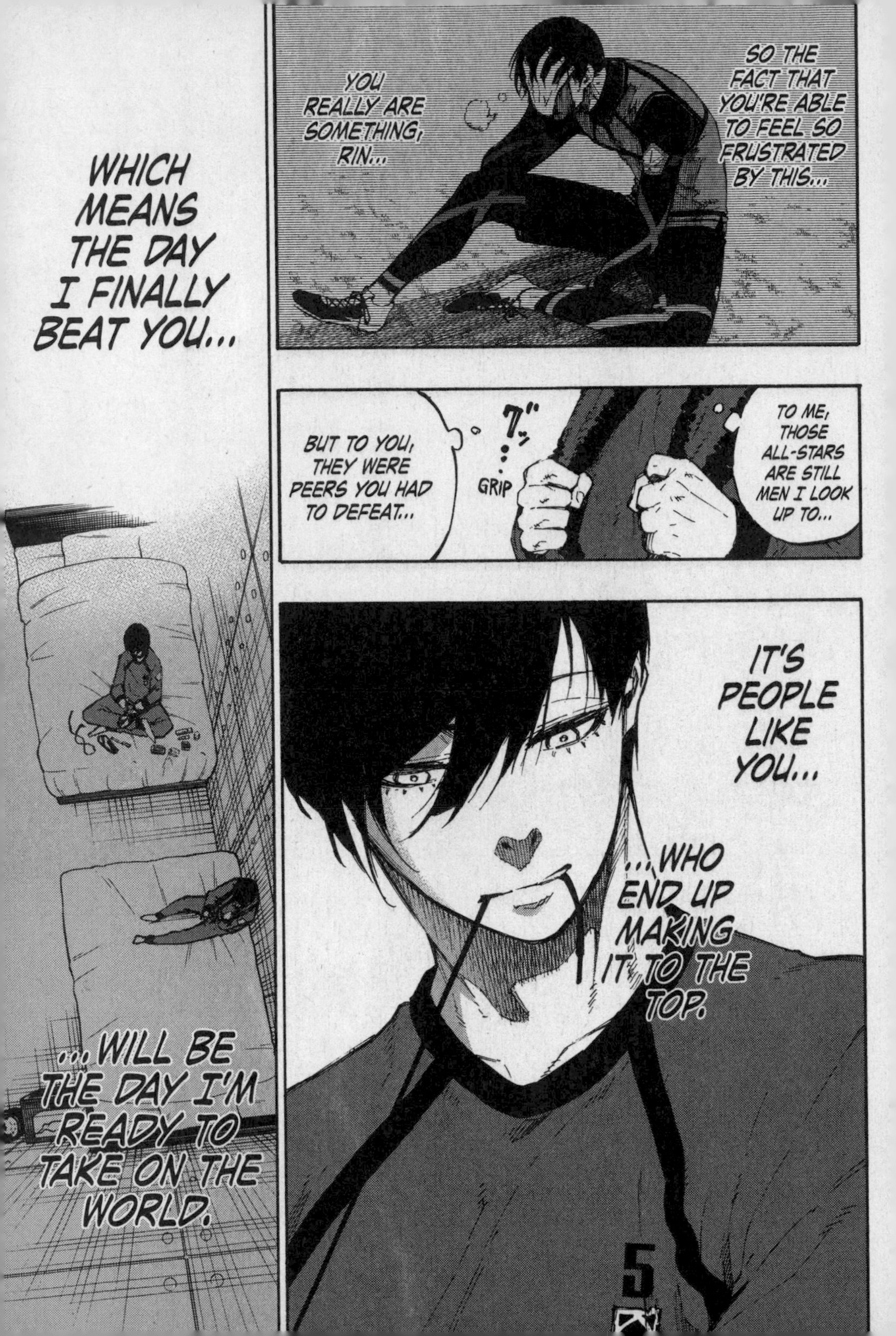
SO THE FACT THAT YOU'RE ABLE TO FEEL SO FRUSTRATED BY THIS...
YOU REALLY ARE SOMETHING, RIN...
TO ME, THOSE ALL-STARS ARE STILL MEN I LOOK UP TO...
GRIP
BUT TO YOU, THEY WERE PEERS YOU HAD TO DEFEAT...
IT'S PEOPLE LIKE YOU...
...WHO END UP MAKING IT TO THE TOP.
WHICH MEANS THE DAY I FINALLY BEAT YOU...
...WILL BE THE DAY I'M READY TO TAKE ON THE WORLD.
5

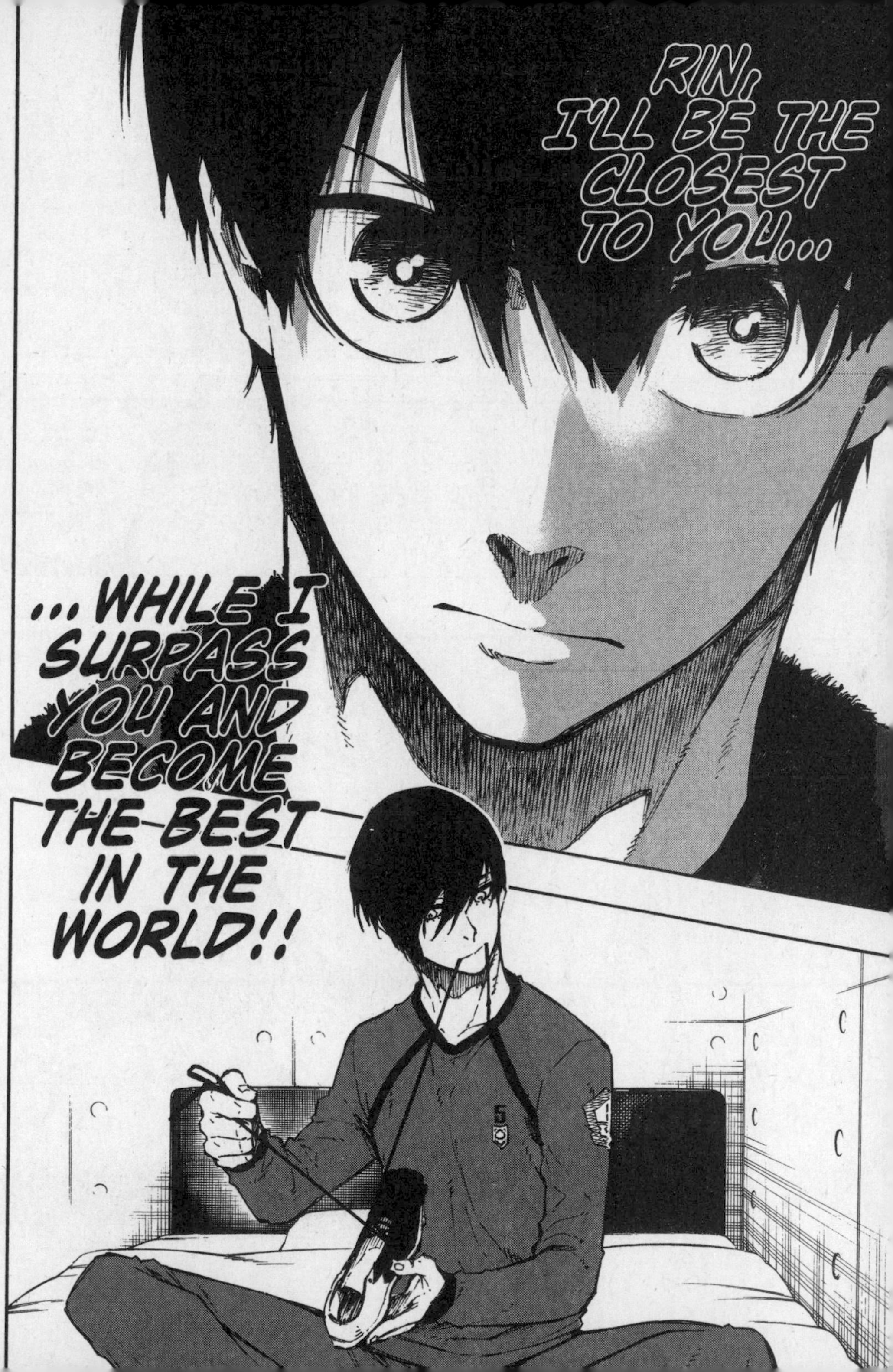
RIN, I'LL BE THE CLOSEST TO YOU...
...WHILE I SURPASS YOU AND BECOME THE BEST IN THE WORLD!!

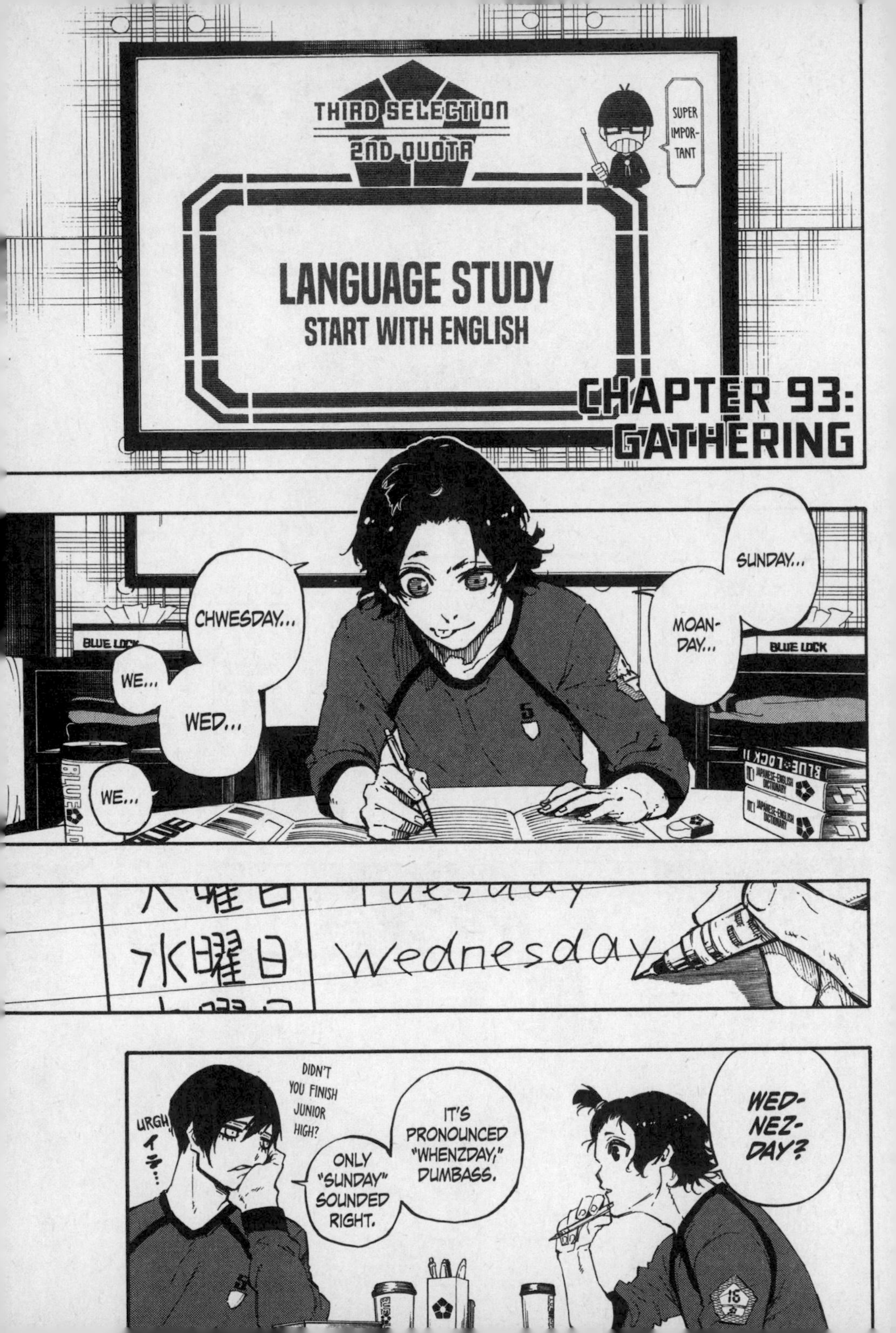
THIRD SELECTION
2ND QUOTA
SUPER IMPOR-TANT
LANGUAGE STUDY
START WITH ENGLISH
CHAPTER 93: GATHERING
SUNDAY...
MOAN-DAY...
CHWESDAY...
WE...
WED...
WE...
BLUE LOCK
JAPANESE-ENGLISH DICTIONARY
水曜日
wednesday
WED-NEZ-DAY?
IT'S PRONOUNCED "WHENZDAY," DUMBASS.
ONLY "SUNDAY" SOUNDED RIGHT.
DIDN'T YOU FINISH JUNIOR HIGH?
URGH
イテ…

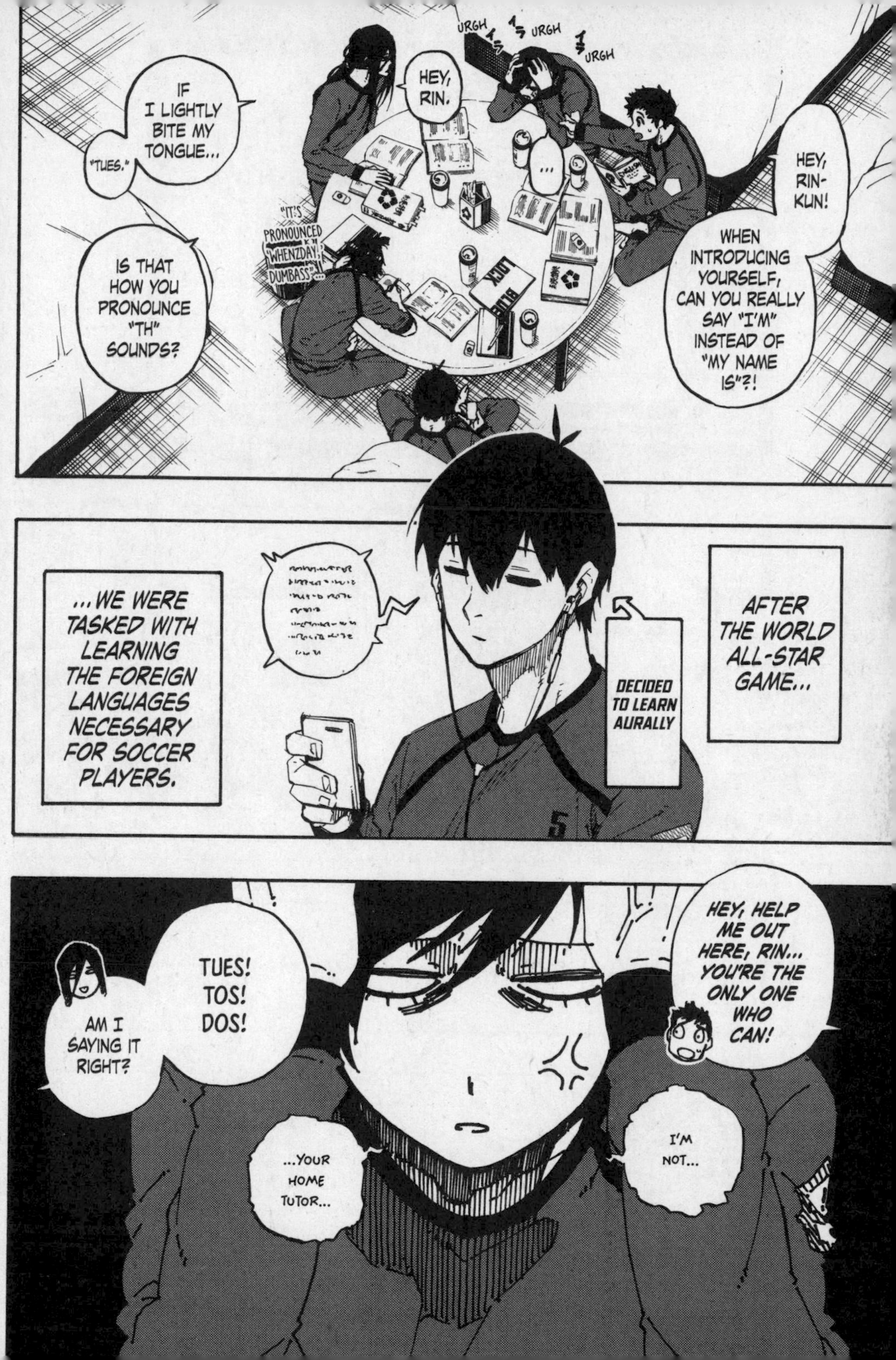
URGH
URGH
URGH
HEY, RIN-KUN!
WHEN INTRODUCING YOURSELF, CAN YOU REALLY SAY "I'M" INSTEAD OF "MY NAME IS"?!
HEY, RIN.
...
IF I LIGHTLY BITE MY TONGUE...
"TUES."
IS THAT HOW YOU PRONOUNCE "TH" SOUNDS?
"IT'S PRONOUNCED 'WHENZDAY,' DUMBASS"...
AFTER THE WORLD ALL-STAR GAME...
DECIDED TO LEARN AURALLY
...WE WERE TASKED WITH LEARNING THE FOREIGN LANGUAGES NECESSARY FOR SOCCER PLAYERS.
HEY, HELP ME OUT HERE, RIN... YOU'RE THE ONLY ONE WHO CAN!
I'M NOT...
...YOUR HOME TUTOR...
TUES! TOS! DOS!
AM I SAYING IT RIGHT?

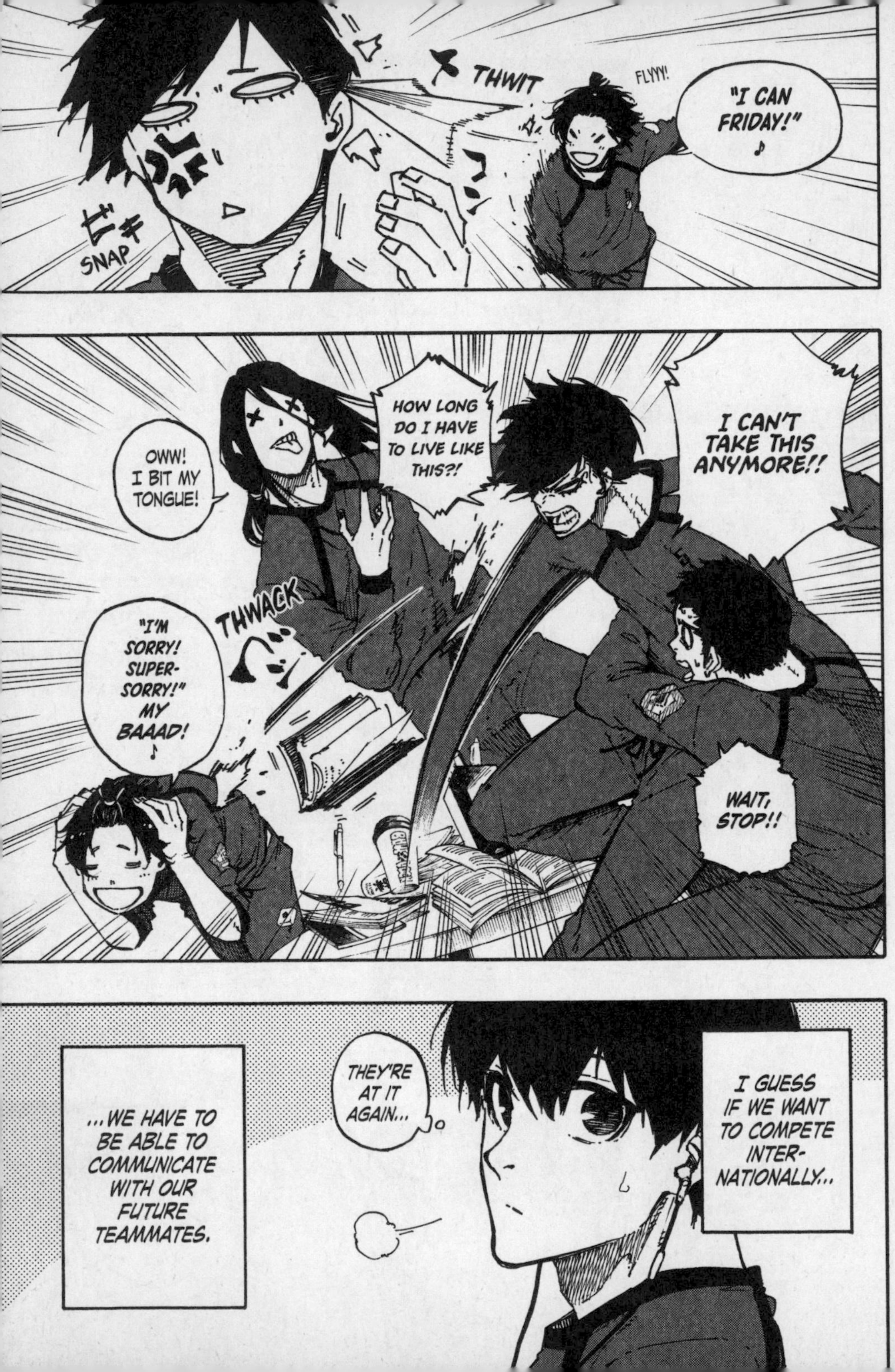
"I CAN FRIDAY!" ♪
FLYYY!
THWIT
ビキ
SNAP
I CAN'T TAKE THIS ANYMORE!!
HOW LONG DO I HAVE TO LIVE LIKE THIS?!
OWW! I BIT MY TONGUE!
WAIT, STOP!!
THWACK
"I'M SORRY! SUPER-SORRY!" MY BAAAD! ♪
I GUESS IF WE WANT TO COMPETE INTER-NATIONALLY...
THEY'RE AT IT AGAIN...
...WE HAVE TO BE ABLE TO COMMUNICATE WITH OUR FUTURE TEAMMATES.

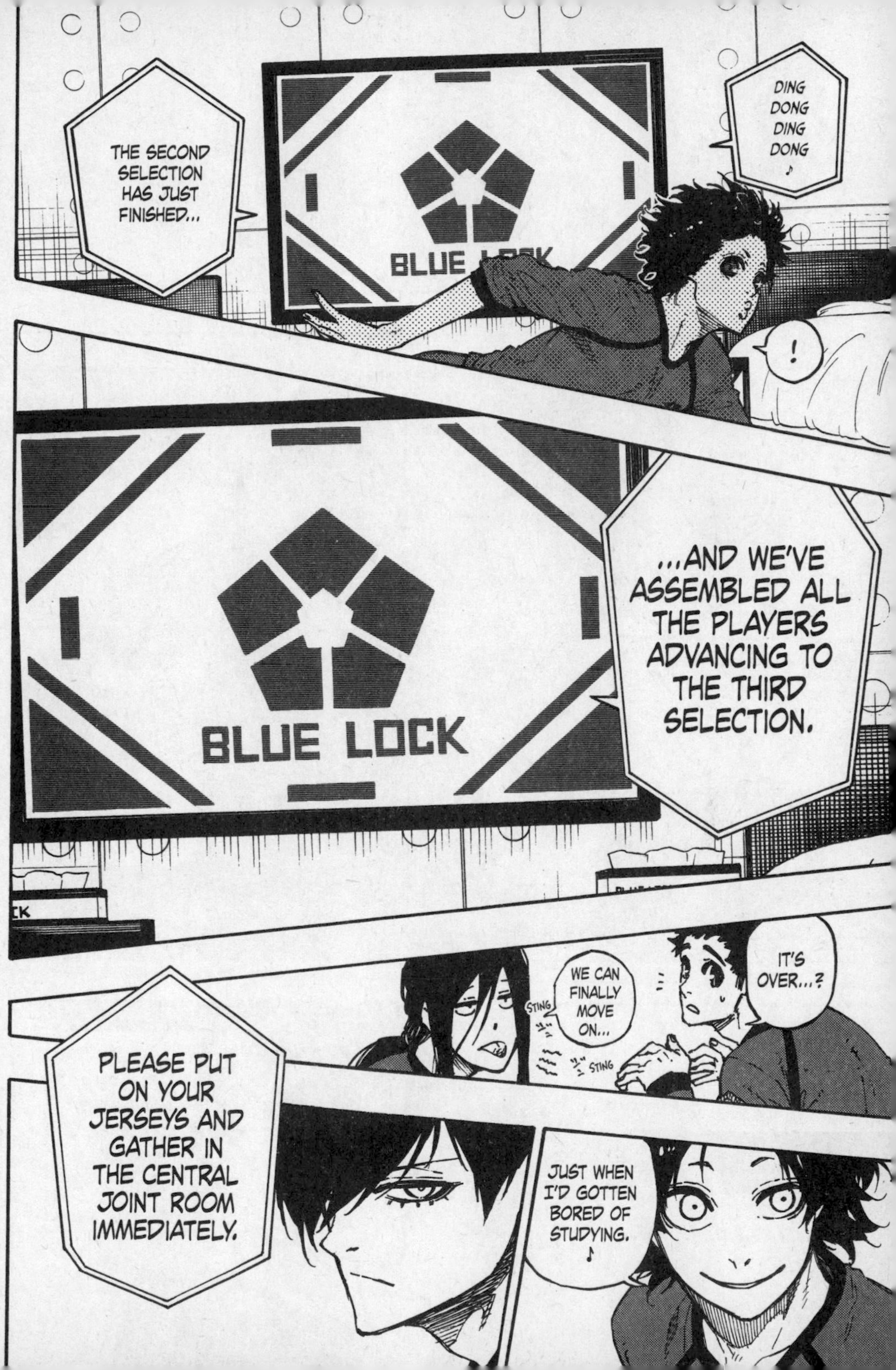
DING DONG DING DONG ♪
THE SECOND SELECTION HAS JUST FINISHED...
BLUE LOCK
!
BLUE LOCK
...AND WE'VE ASSEMBLED ALL THE PLAYERS ADVANCING TO THE THIRD SELECTION.
IT'S OVER...?
WE CAN FINALLY MOVE ON...
STING
STING
PLEASE PUT ON YOUR JERSEYS AND GATHER IN THE CENTRAL JOINT ROOM IMMEDIATELY.
JUST WHEN I'D GOTTEN BORED OF STUDYING. ♪

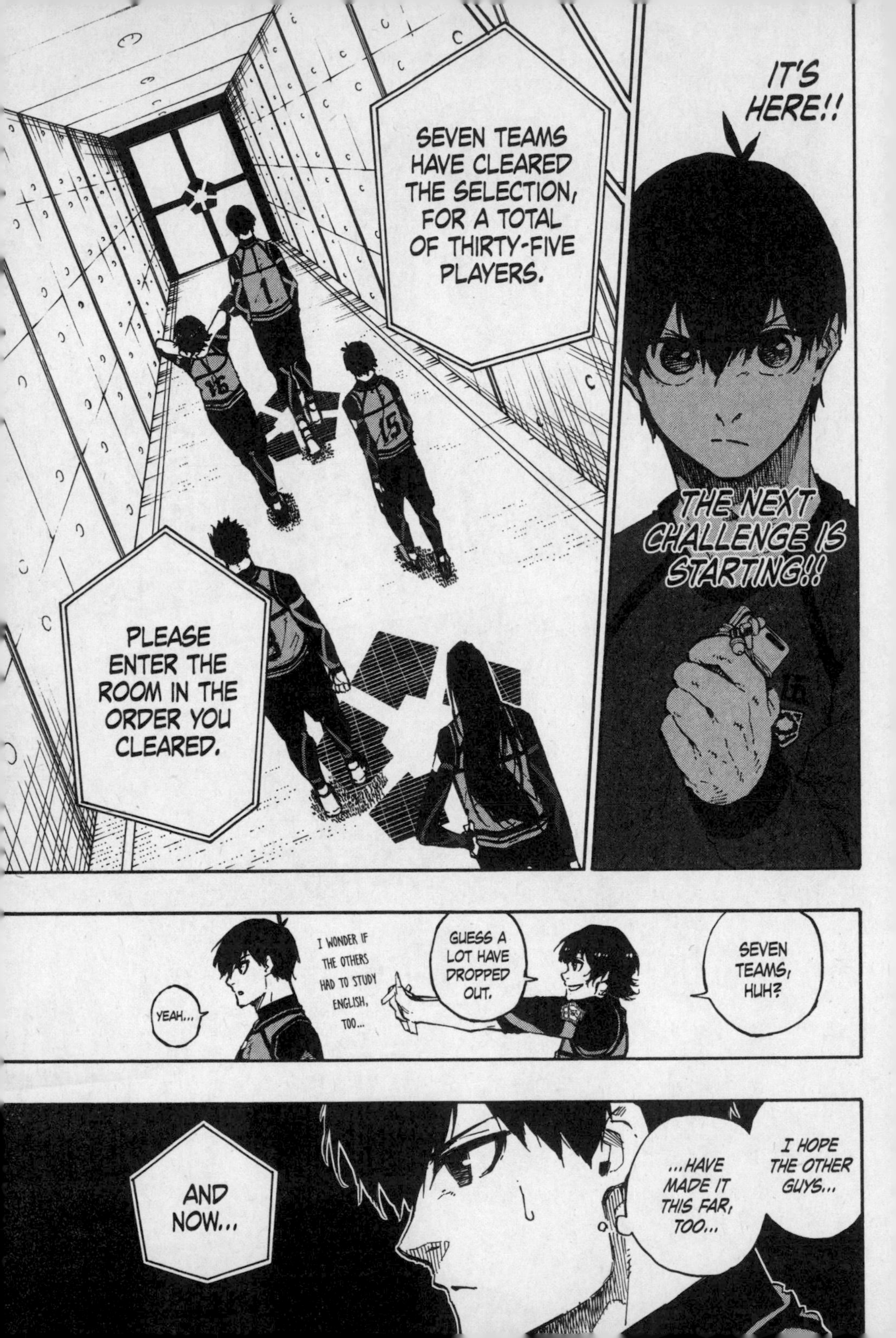
IT'S HERE!!
THE NEXT CHALLENGE IS STARTING!!
SEVEN TEAMS HAVE CLEARED THE SELECTION, FOR A TOTAL OF THIRTY-FIVE PLAYERS.
PLEASE ENTER THE ROOM IN THE ORDER YOU CLEARED.
SEVEN TEAMS, HUH?
GUESS A LOT HAVE DROPPED OUT.
I WONDER IF THE OTHERS HAD TO STUDY ENGLISH, TOO...
YEAH...
I HOPE THE OTHER GUYS...
...HAVE MADE IT THIS FAR, TOO...
AND NOW...

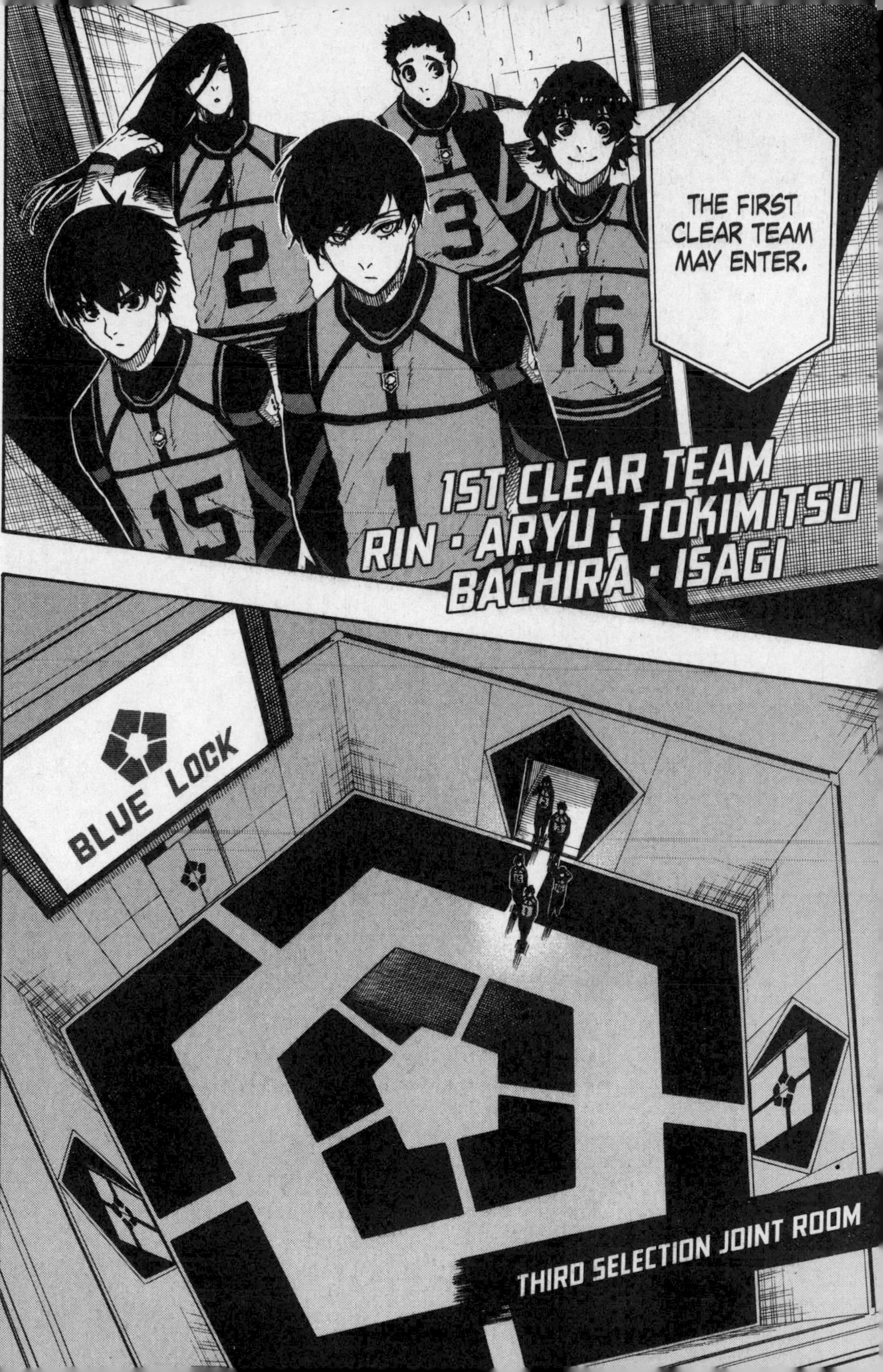
THE FIRST CLEAR TEAM MAY ENTER.
1ST CLEAR TEAM
RIN · ARYU · TOKIMITSU
BACHIRA · ISAGI
BLUE LOCK
THIRD SELECTION JOINT ROOM

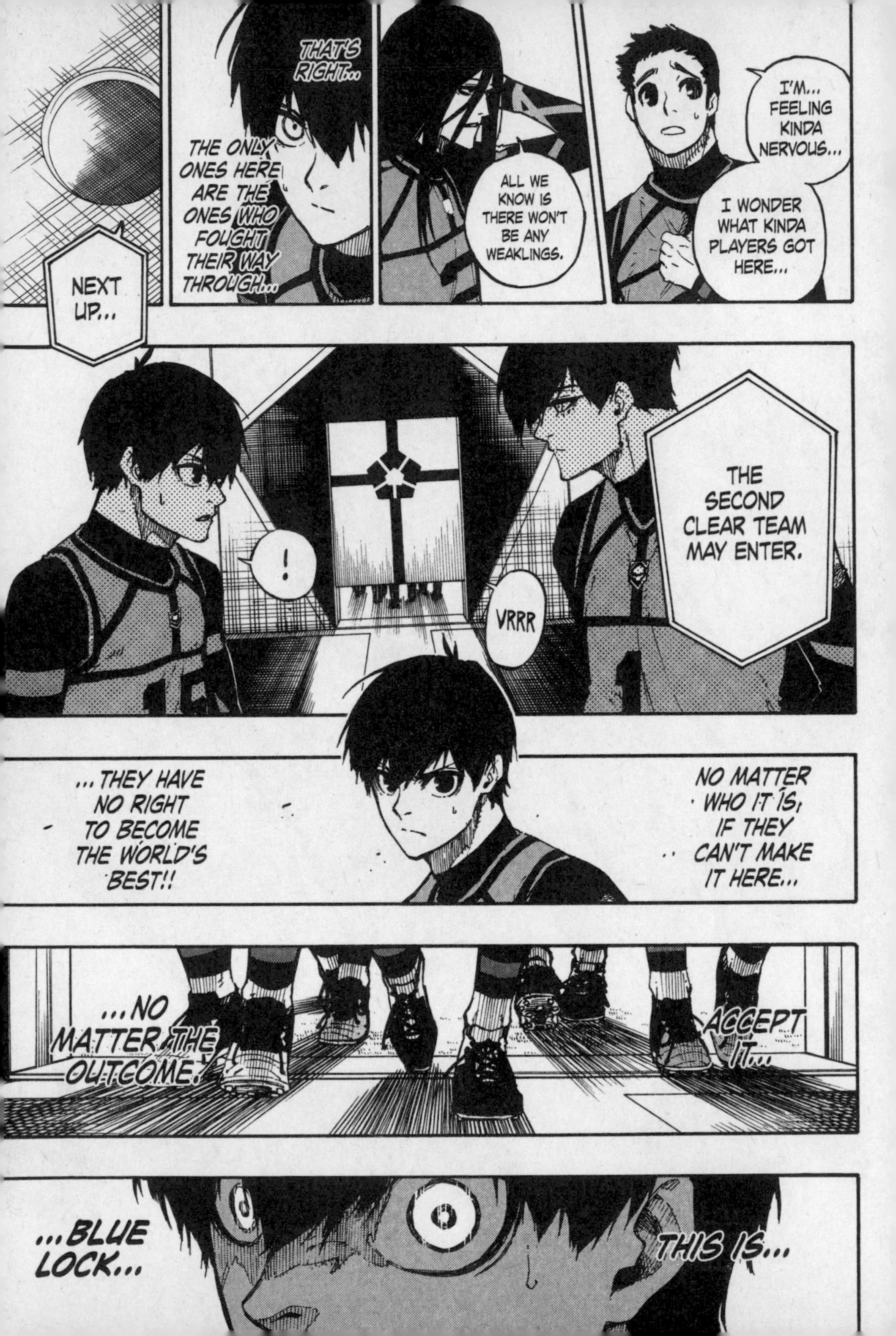
I'M... FEELING KINDA NERVOUS...
I WONDER WHAT KINDA PLAYERS GOT HERE...
ALL WE KNOW IS THERE WON'T BE ANY WEAKLINGS.
THAT'S RIGHT...
THE ONLY ONES HERE ARE THE ONES WHO FOUGHT THEIR WAY THROUGH...
NEXT UP...
THE SECOND CLEAR TEAM MAY ENTER.
VRRR
!
NO MATTER WHO IT IS, IF THEY CAN'T MAKE IT HERE...
...THEY HAVE NO RIGHT TO BECOME THE WORLD'S BEST!!
ACCEPT IT...
...NO MATTER THE OUTCOME.
THIS IS...
...BLUE LOCK...

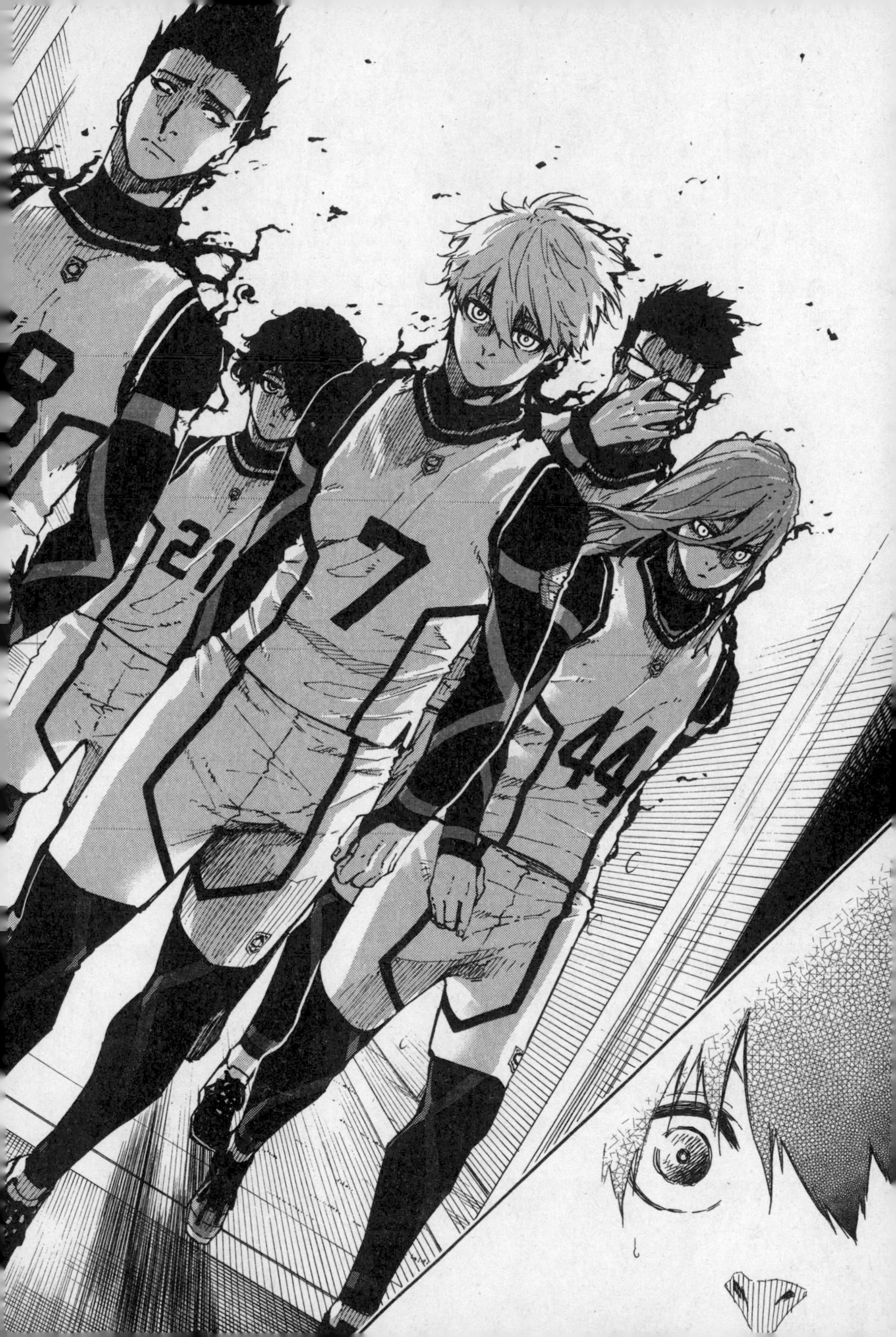

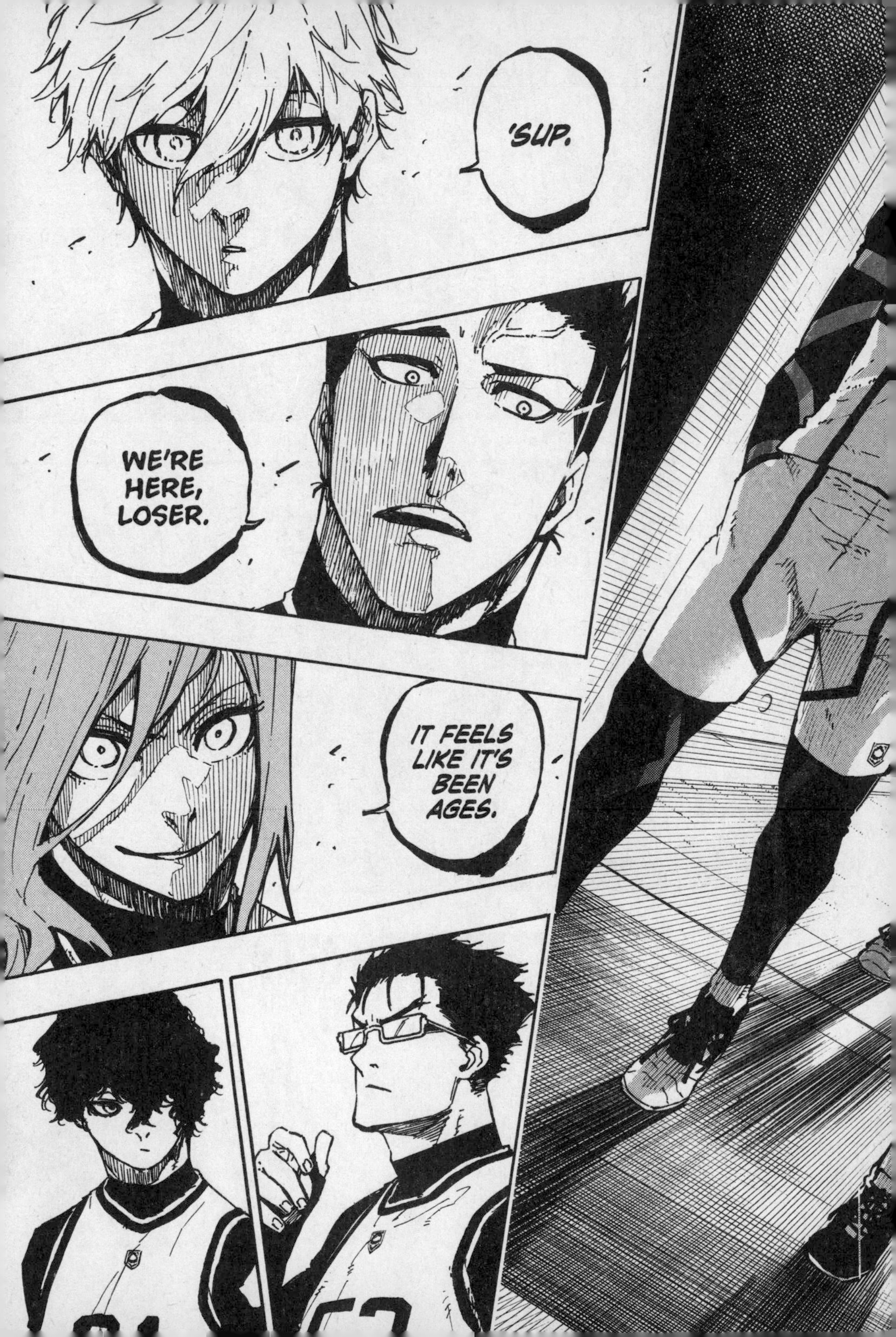
'SUP.
WE'RE HERE, LOSER.
IT FEELS LIKE IT'S BEEN AGES.

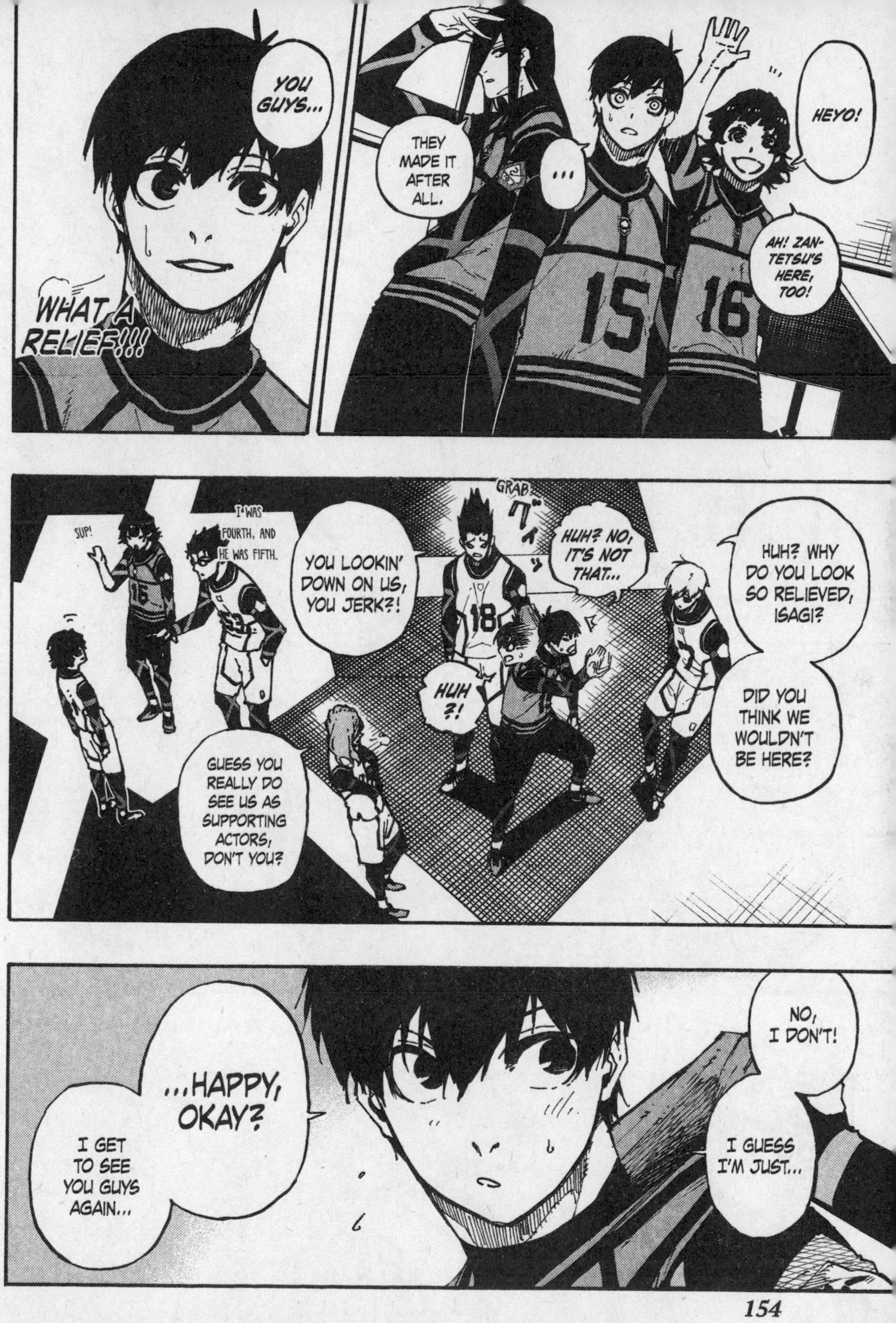
HEYO!
AH! ZAN-TETSU'S HERE, TOO!
...
THEY MADE IT AFTER ALL.
YOU GUYS...
WHAT A RELIEF!!!
HUH? WHY DO YOU LOOK SO RELIEVED, ISAGI?
DID YOU THINK WE WOULDN'T BE HERE?
HUH? NO, IT'S NOT THAT...
GRAB
HUH?!
YOU LOOKIN' DOWN ON US, YOU JERK?!
GUESS YOU REALLY DO SEE US AS SUPPORTING ACTORS, DON'T YOU?
I WAS FOURTH, AND HE WAS FIFTH.
SUP!
NO, I DON'T!
I GUESS I'M JUST...
...HAPPY, OKAY?
I GET TO SEE YOU GUYS AGAIN...

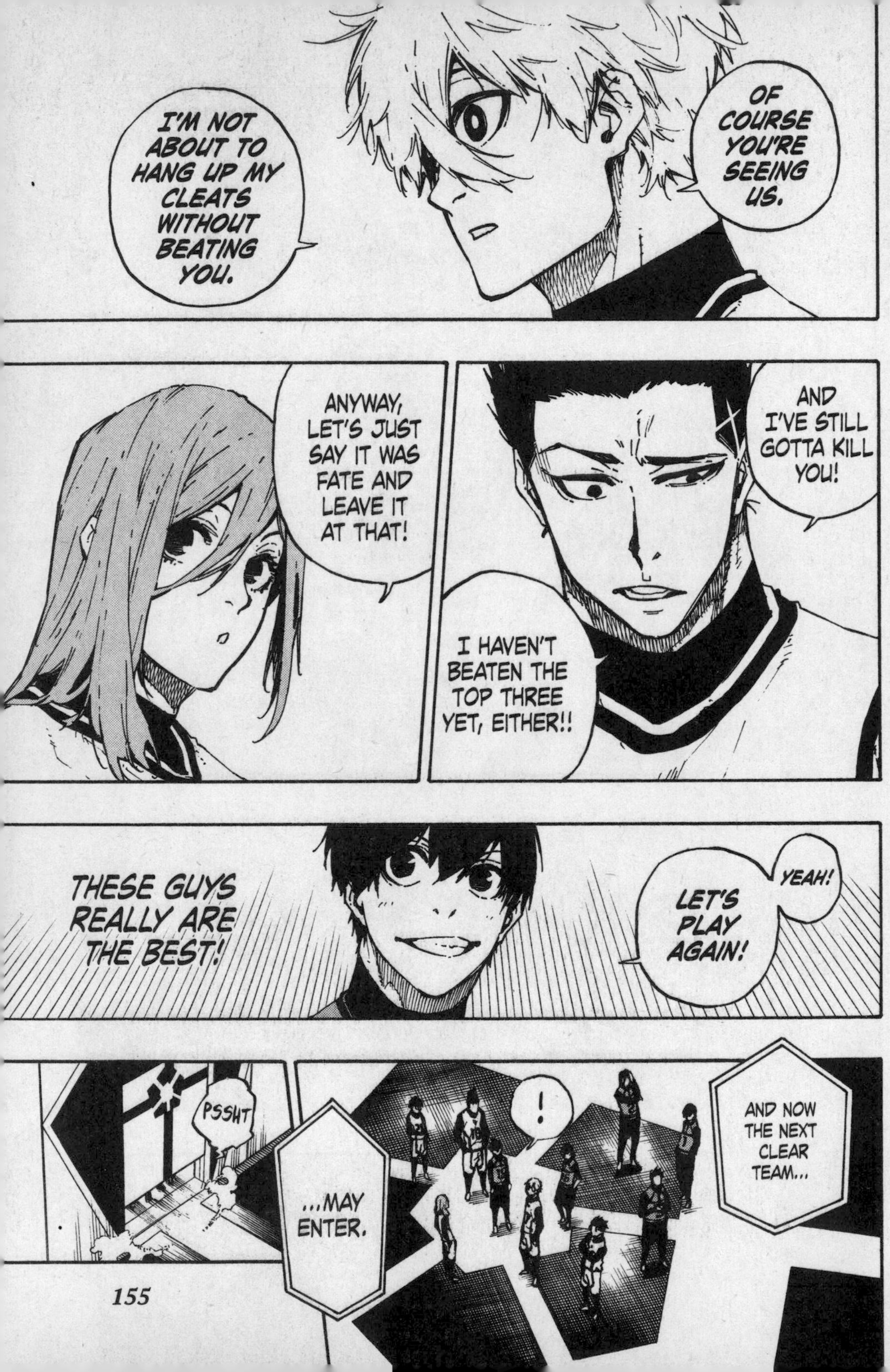
OF COURSE YOU'RE SEEING US.
I'M NOT ABOUT TO HANG UP MY CLEATS WITHOUT BEATING YOU.
AND I'VE STILL GOTTA KILL YOU!
I HAVEN'T BEATEN THE TOP THREE YET, EITHER!!
ANYWAY, LET'S JUST SAY IT WAS FATE AND LEAVE IT AT THAT!
YEAH!
LET'S PLAY AGAIN!
THESE GUYS REALLY ARE THE BEST!
AND NOW THE NEXT CLEAR TEAM...
!
...MAY ENTER.
PSSHT

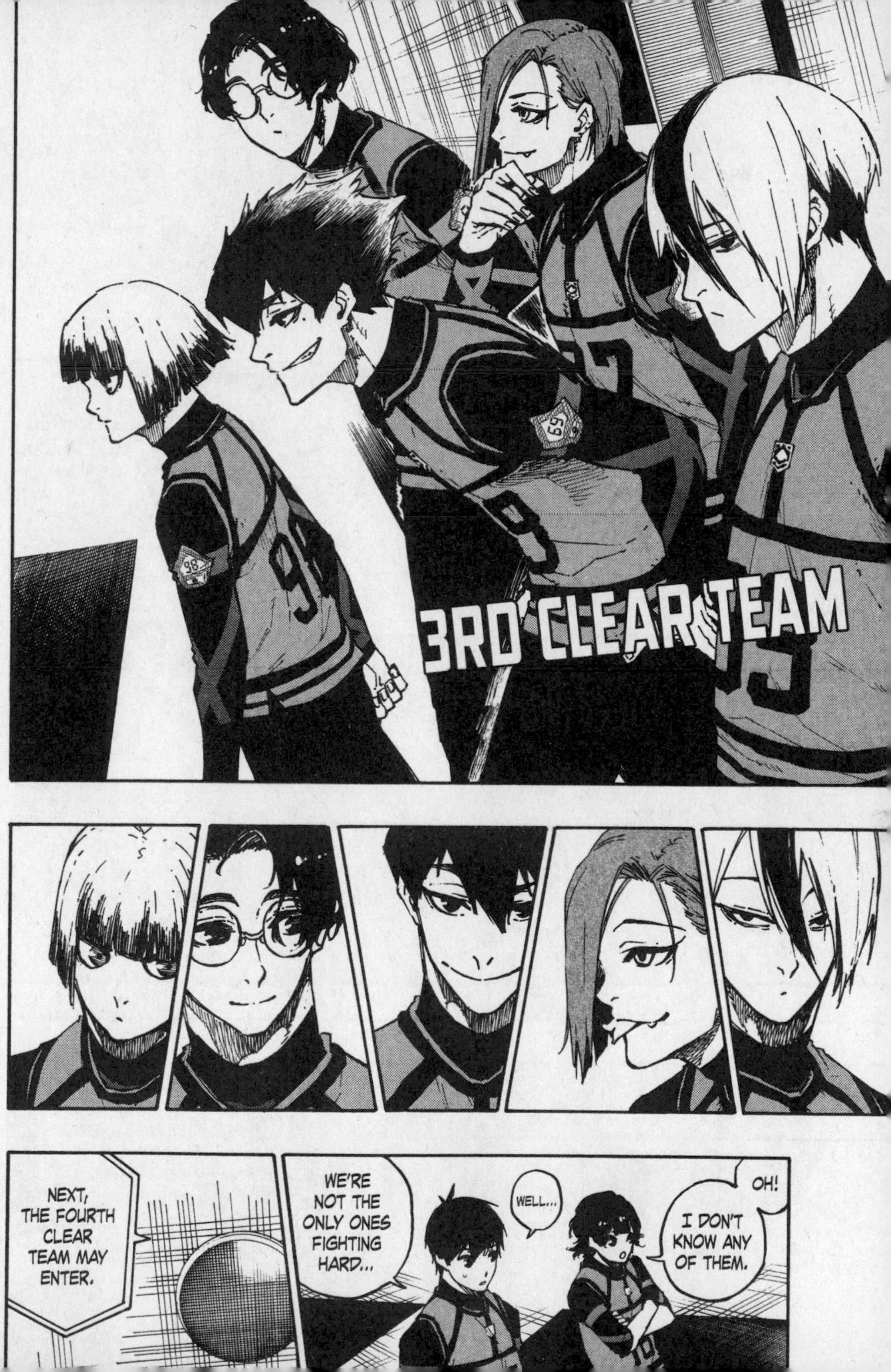
3RD CLEAR TEAM
OH!
I DON'T KNOW ANY OF THEM.
WELL...
WE'RE NOT THE ONLY ONES FIGHTING HARD...
NEXT, THE FOURTH CLEAR TEAM MAY ENTER.

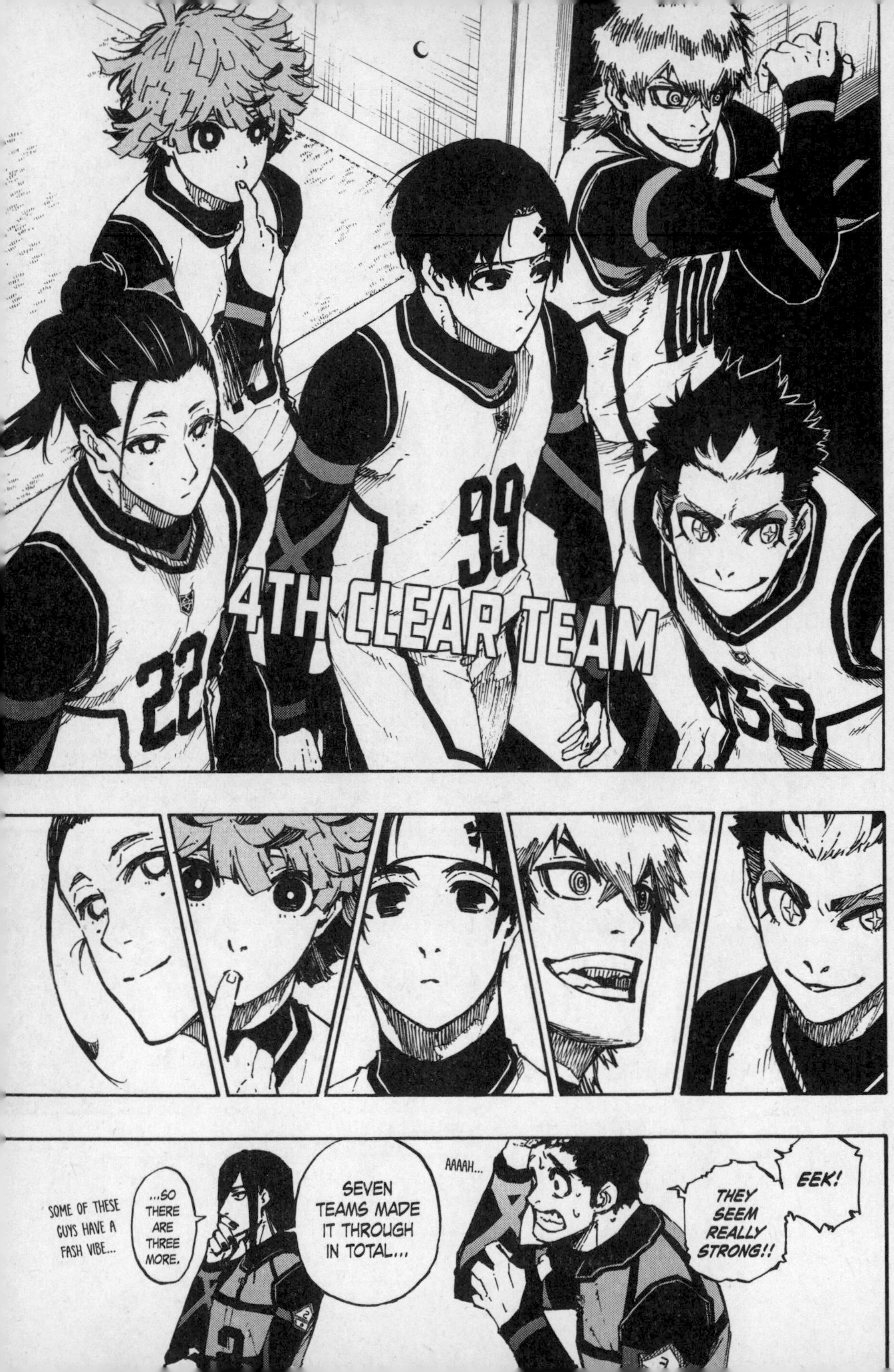
4TH CLEAR TEAM
EEK!
THEY SEEM REALLY STRONG!!
AAAAH...
SEVEN TEAMS MADE IT THROUGH IN TOTAL...
...SO THERE ARE THREE MORE.
SOME OF THESE GUYS HAVE A FASH VIBE...

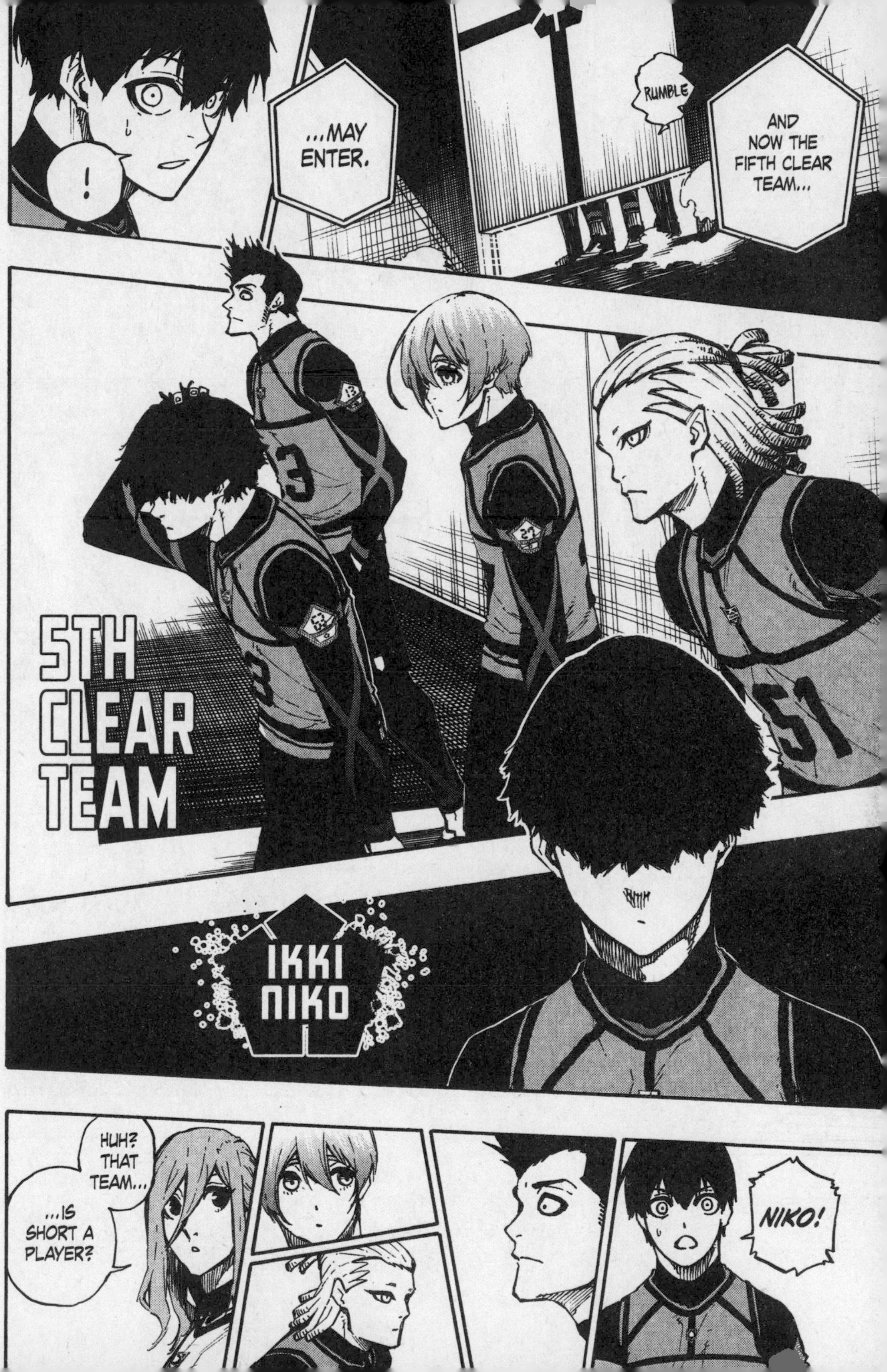
RUMBLE
AND NOW THE FIFTH CLEAR TEAM...
...MAY ENTER.
!
5TH CLEAR TEAM
IKKI NIKO
NIKO!
HUH? THAT TEAM...
...IS SHORT A PLAYER?

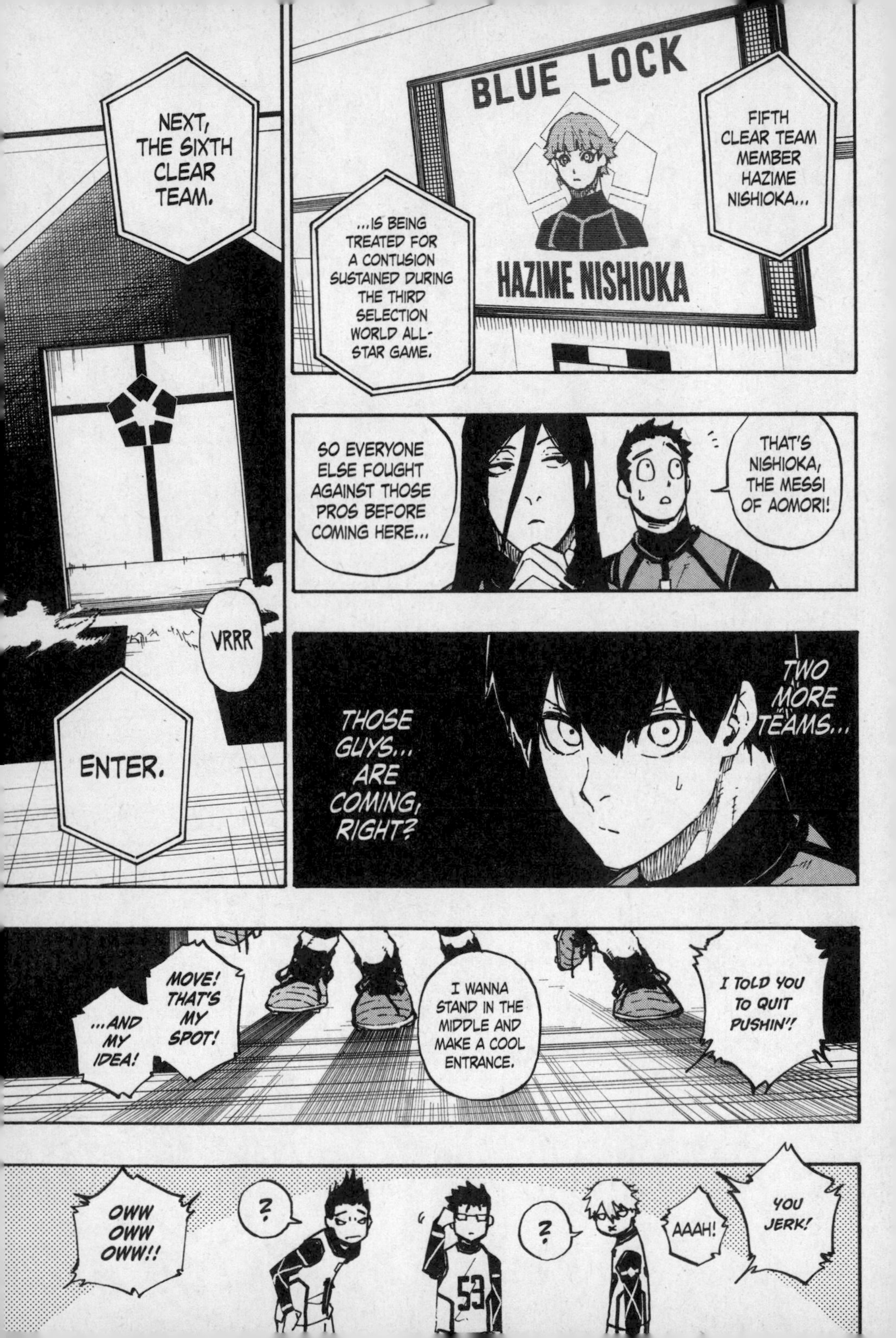
BLUE LOCK
FIFTH CLEAR TEAM MEMBER HAZIME NISHIOKA...
HAZIME NISHIOKA
...IS BEING TREATED FOR A CONTUSION SUSTAINED DURING THE THIRD SELECTION WORLD ALL-STAR GAME.
THAT'S NISHIOKA, THE MESSI OF AOMORI!
SO EVERYONE ELSE FOUGHT AGAINST THOSE PROS BEFORE COMING HERE...
TWO MORE TEAMS...
THOSE GUYS... ARE COMING, RIGHT?
NEXT, THE SIXTH CLEAR TEAM.
VRRR
ENTER.
I TOLD YOU TO QUIT PUSHIN'!
I WANNA STAND IN THE MIDDLE AND MAKE A COOL ENTRANCE.
MOVE! THAT'S MY SPOT!
...AND MY IDEA!
YOU JERK!
AAAH!
?
?
OWW OWW OWW!!

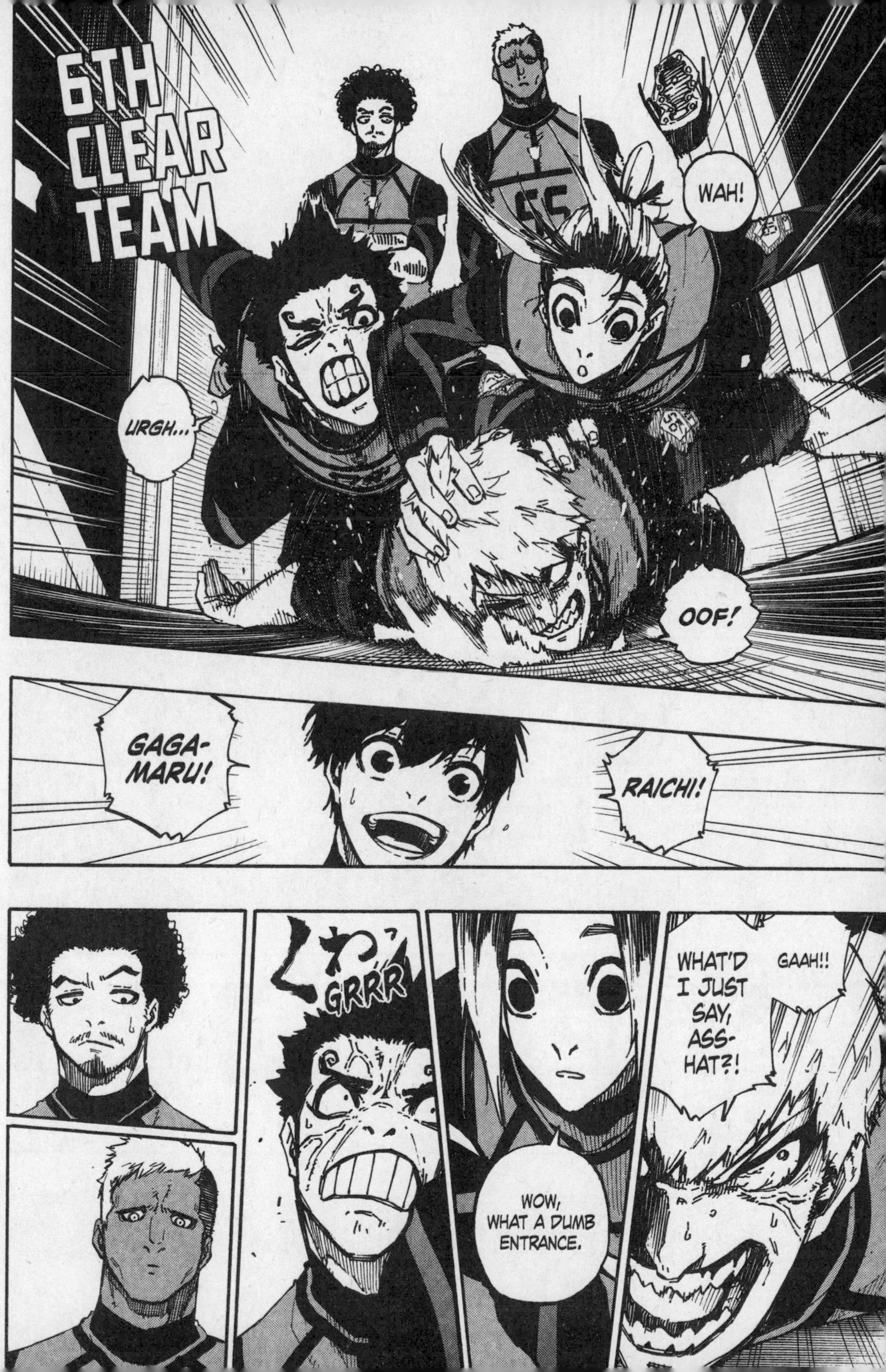
6TH CLEAR TEAM
WAH!
URGH...
OOF!
RAICHI!
GAGA-MARU!
GAAH!!
WHAT'D I JUST SAY, ASS-HAT?!
WOW, WHAT A DUMB ENTRANCE.
くわ
GRRR

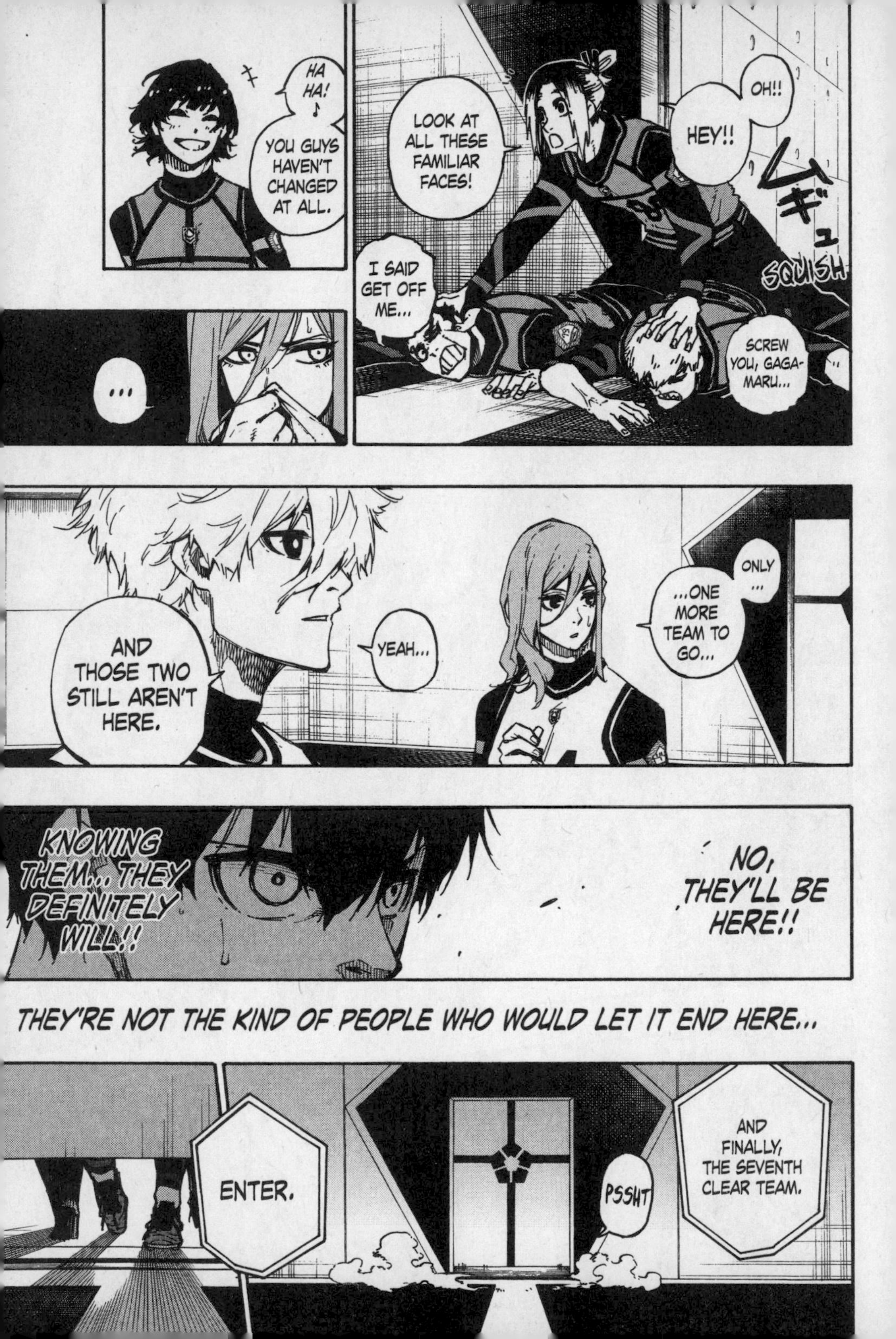
OH!!
HEY!!
ギュ
SQUISH
LOOK AT ALL THESE FAMILIAR FACES!
SCREW YOU, GAGA-MARU...
I SAID GET OFF ME...
HA HA! ♪
YOU GUYS HAVEN'T CHANGED AT ALL.
...
ONLY ...
...ONE MORE TEAM TO GO...
YEAH...
AND THOSE TWO STILL AREN'T HERE.
NO, THEY'LL BE HERE!!
KNOWING THEM... THEY DEFINITELY WILL!!
THEY'RE NOT THE KIND OF PEOPLE WHO WOULD LET IT END HERE...
AND FINALLY, THE SEVENTH CLEAR TEAM.
PSSHT
ENTER.

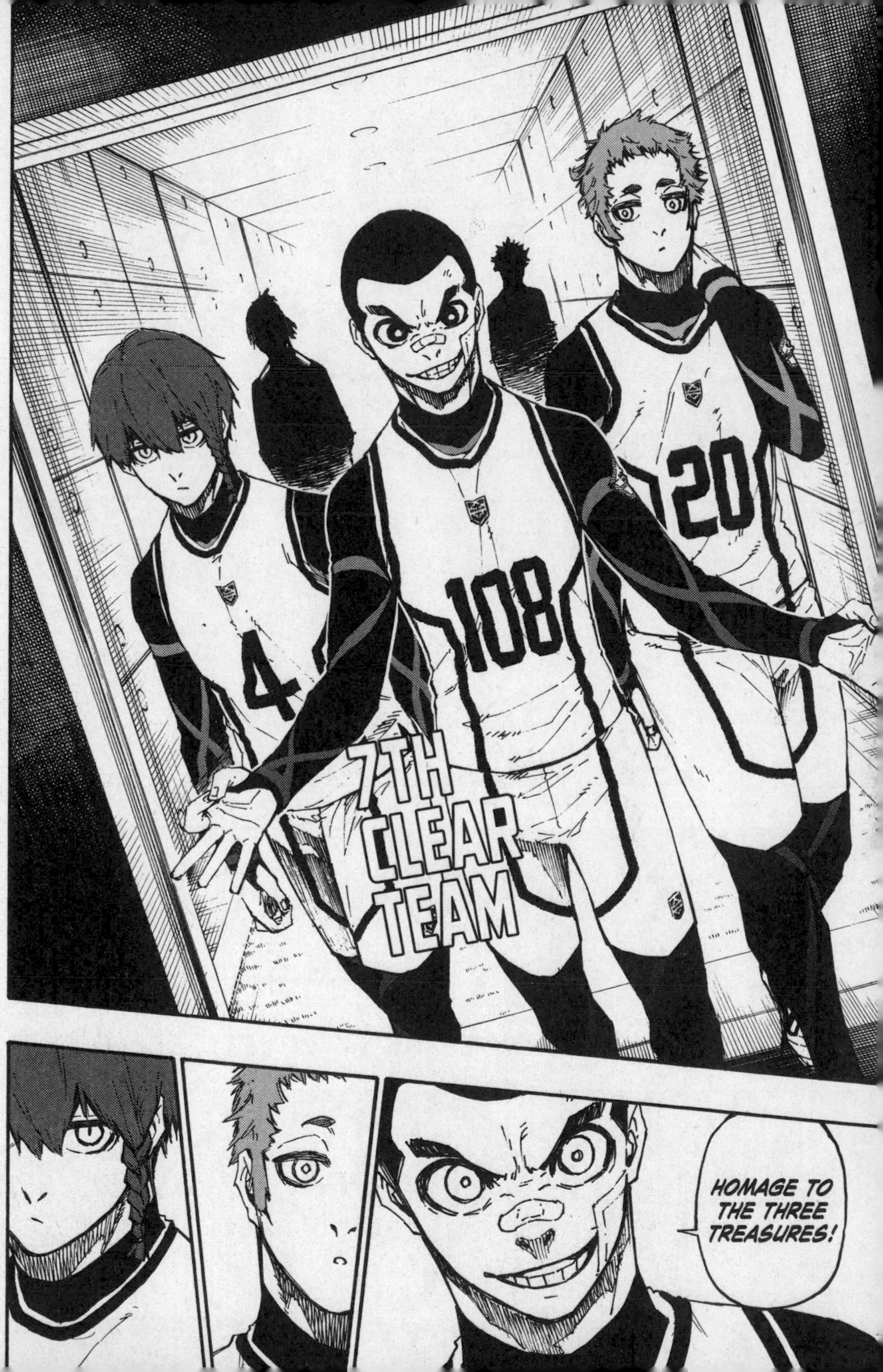
7TH CLEAR TEAM
HOMAGE TO THE THREE TREASURES!

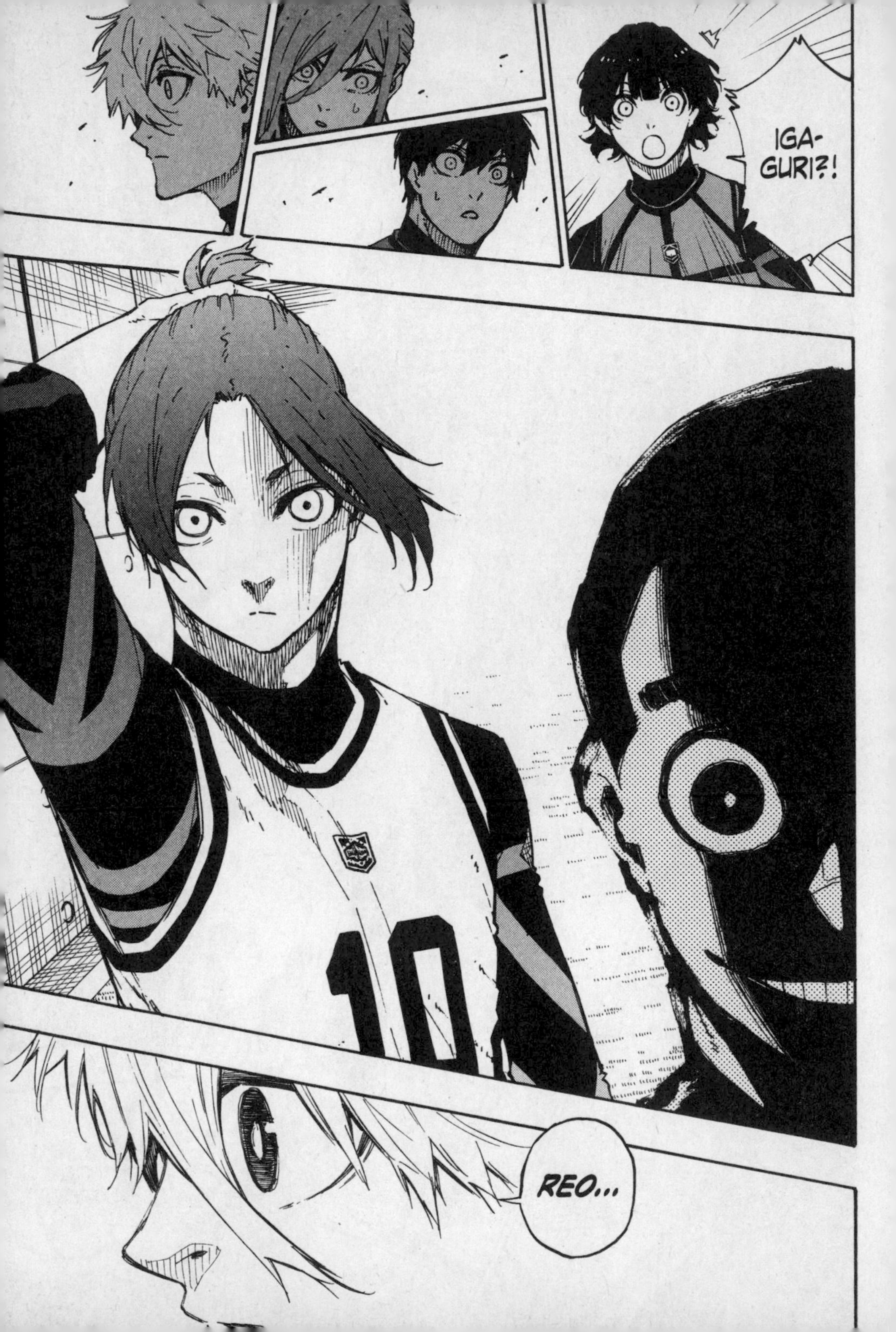
IGA-
GURI?!
REO...

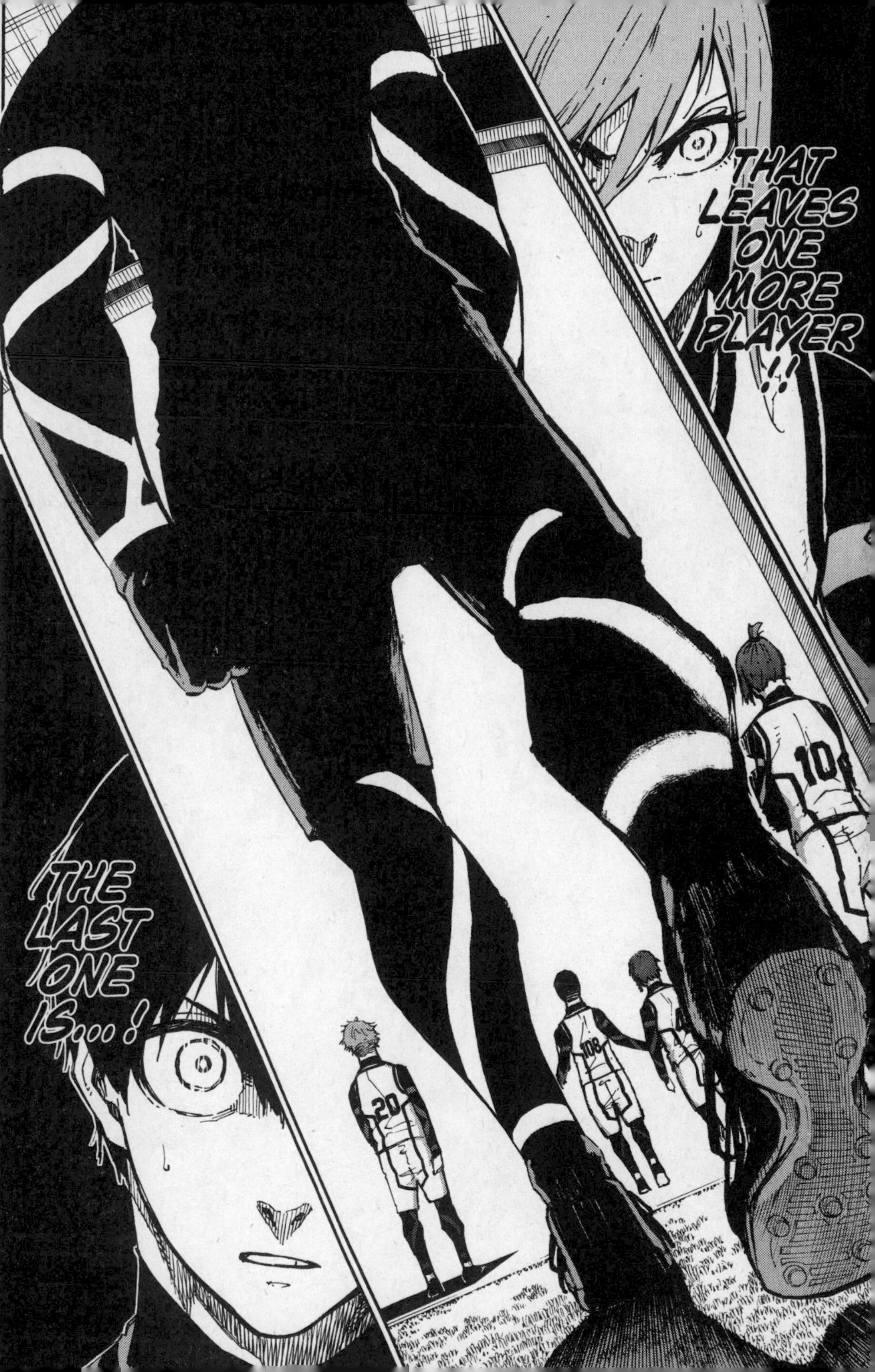
THAT LEAVES ONE MORE PLAYER!!
THE LAST ONE IS...!

CHAPTER 94: THE TIME HAS COME

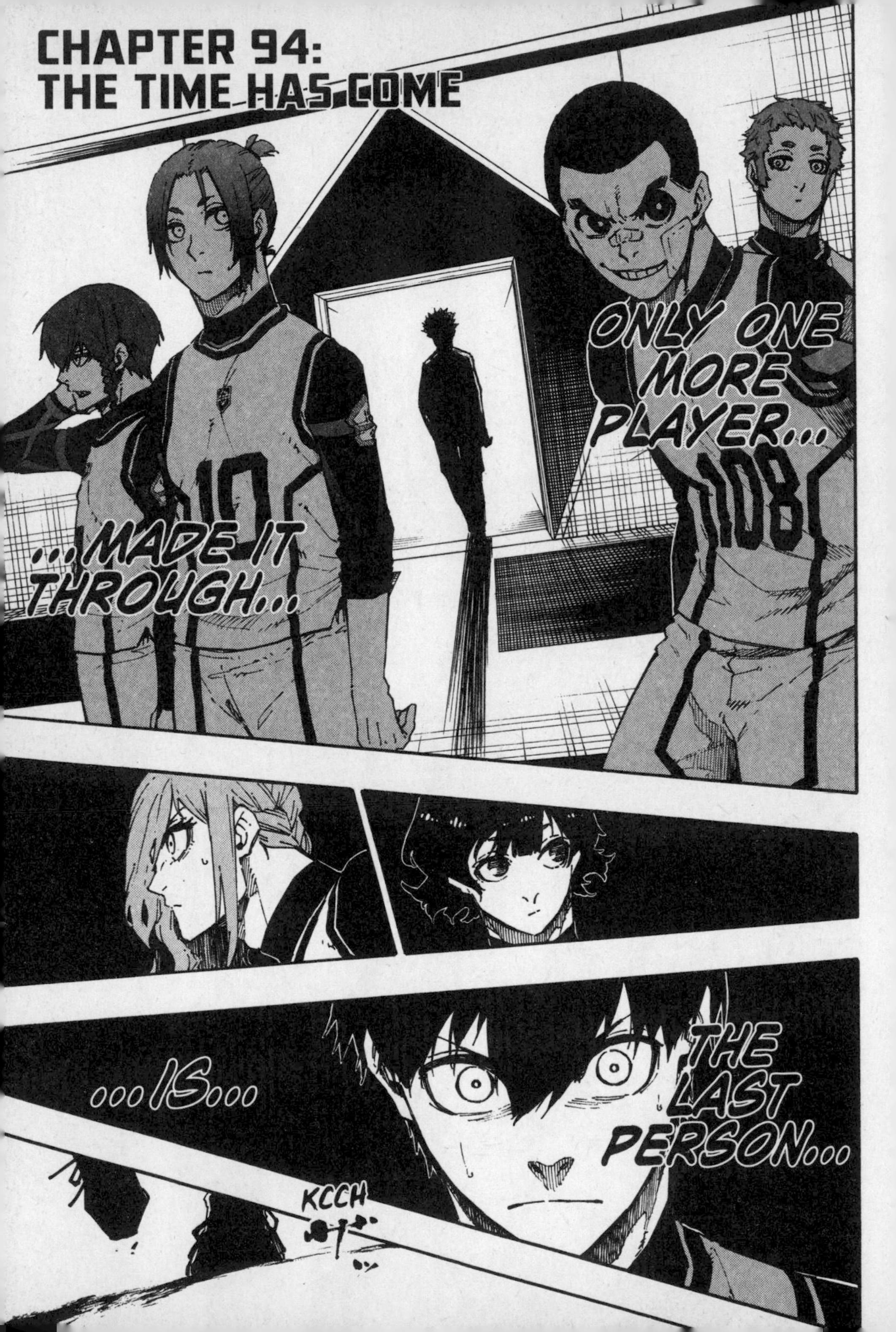
ONLY ONE MORE PLAYER...
...MADE IT THROUGH...
THE LAST PERSON...
...IS...
KCCH

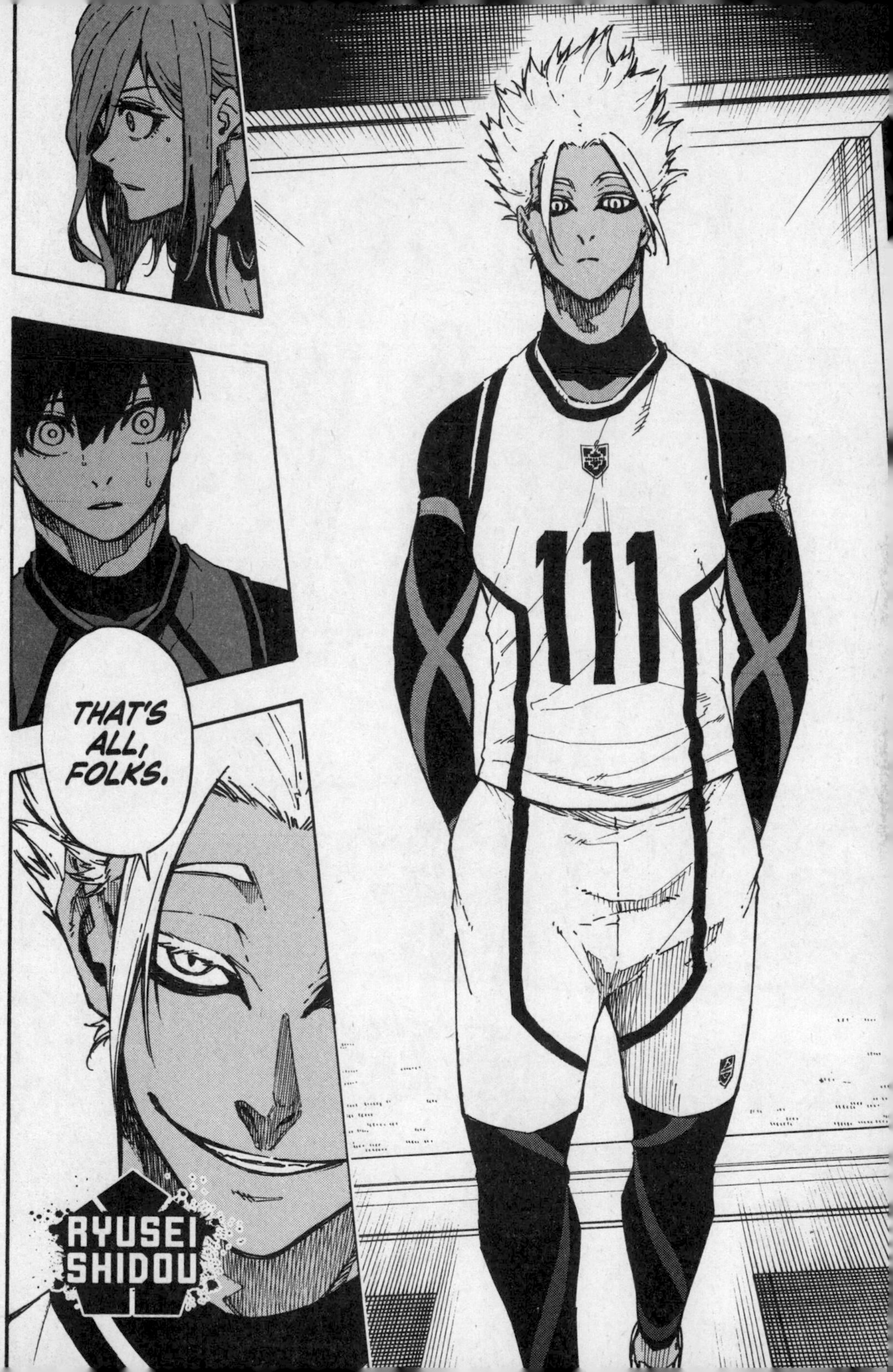
THAT'S ALL, FOLKS.
111
RYUSEI SHIDOU

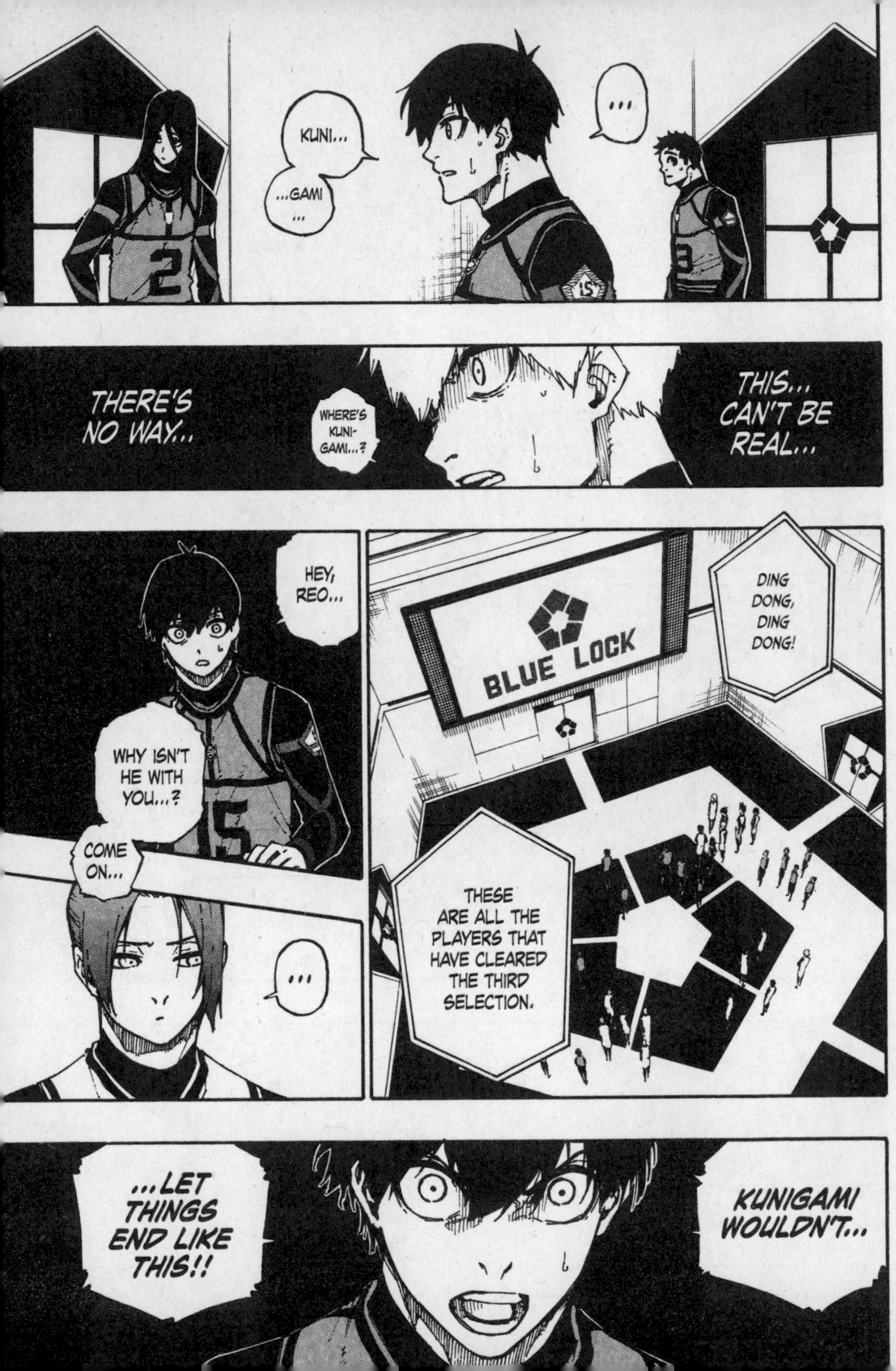
...
KUNI...
...GAMI...
THIS... CAN'T BE REAL...
WHERE'S KUNI-GAMI...?
THERE'S NO WAY...
DING DONG, DING DONG!
BLUE LOCK
THESE ARE ALL THE PLAYERS THAT HAVE CLEARED THE THIRD SELECTION.
HEY, REO...
WHY ISN'T HE WITH YOU...?
COME ON...
...
KUNIGAMI WOULDN'T...
...LET THINGS END LIKE THIS!!

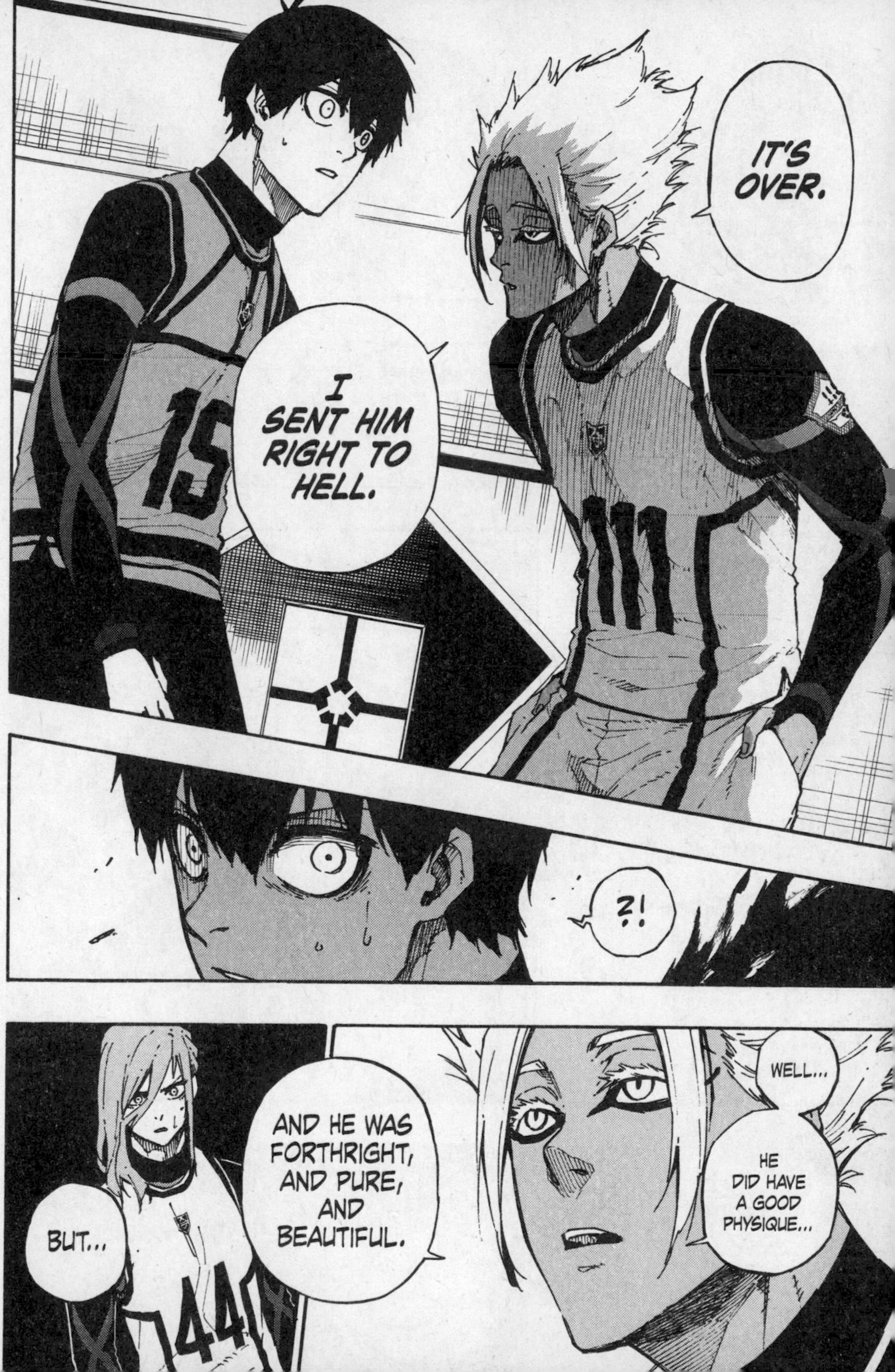
IT'S OVER.
I SENT HIM RIGHT TO HELL.
?!
WELL...
HE DID HAVE A GOOD PHYSIQUE...
AND HE WAS FORTHRIGHT, AND PURE, AND BEAUTIFUL.
BUT...

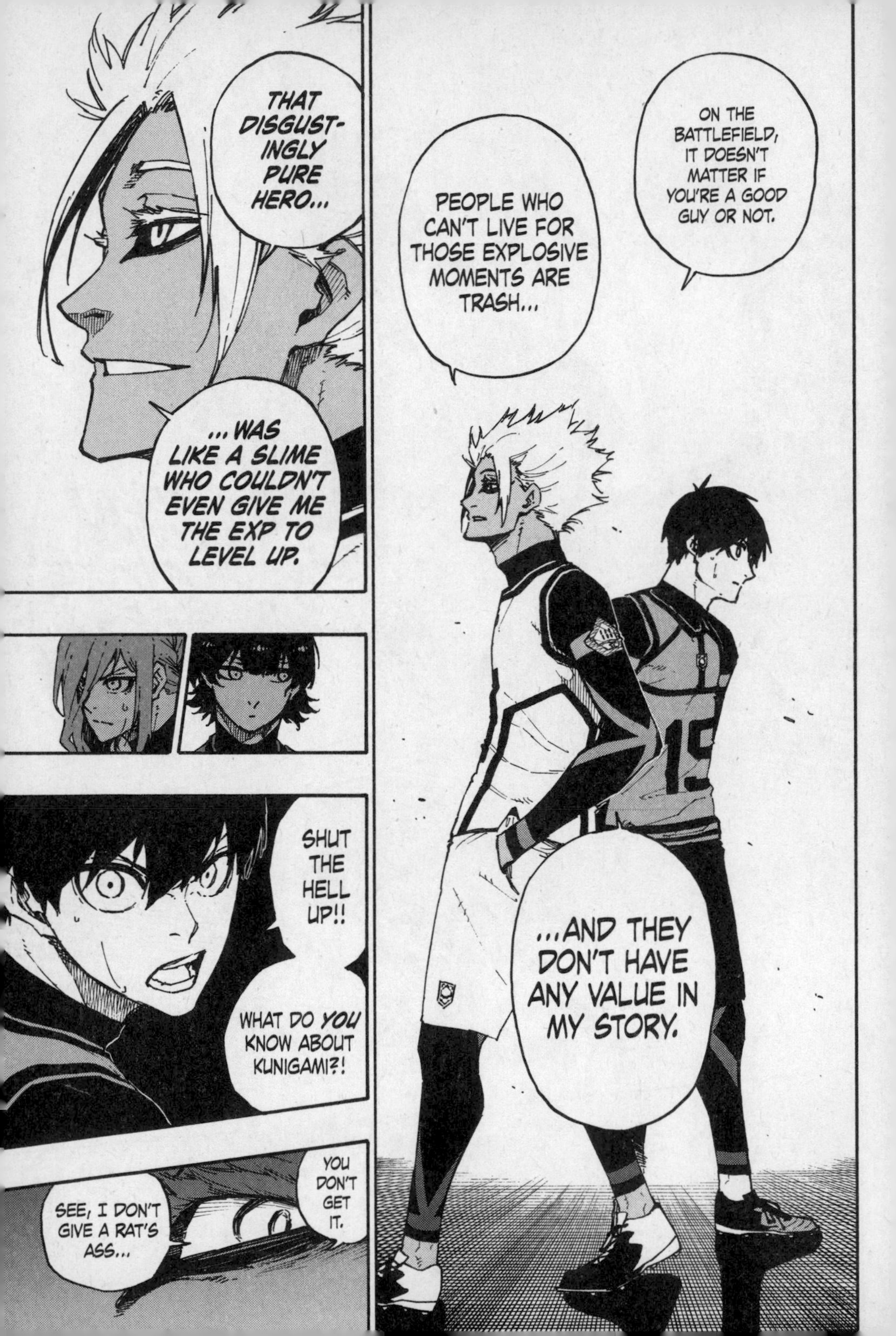
ON THE BATTLEFIELD, IT DOESN'T MATTER IF YOU'RE A GOOD GUY OR NOT.
PEOPLE WHO CAN'T LIVE FOR THOSE EXPLOSIVE MOMENTS ARE TRASH...
...AND THEY DON'T HAVE ANY VALUE IN MY STORY.
THAT DISGUSTINGLY PURE HERO...
...WAS LIKE A SLIME WHO COULDN'T EVEN GIVE ME THE EXP TO LEVEL UP.
SHUT THE HELL UP!!
WHAT DO *YOU* KNOW ABOUT KUNIGAMI?!
YOU DON'T GET IT.
SEE, I DON'T GIVE A RAT'S ASS...

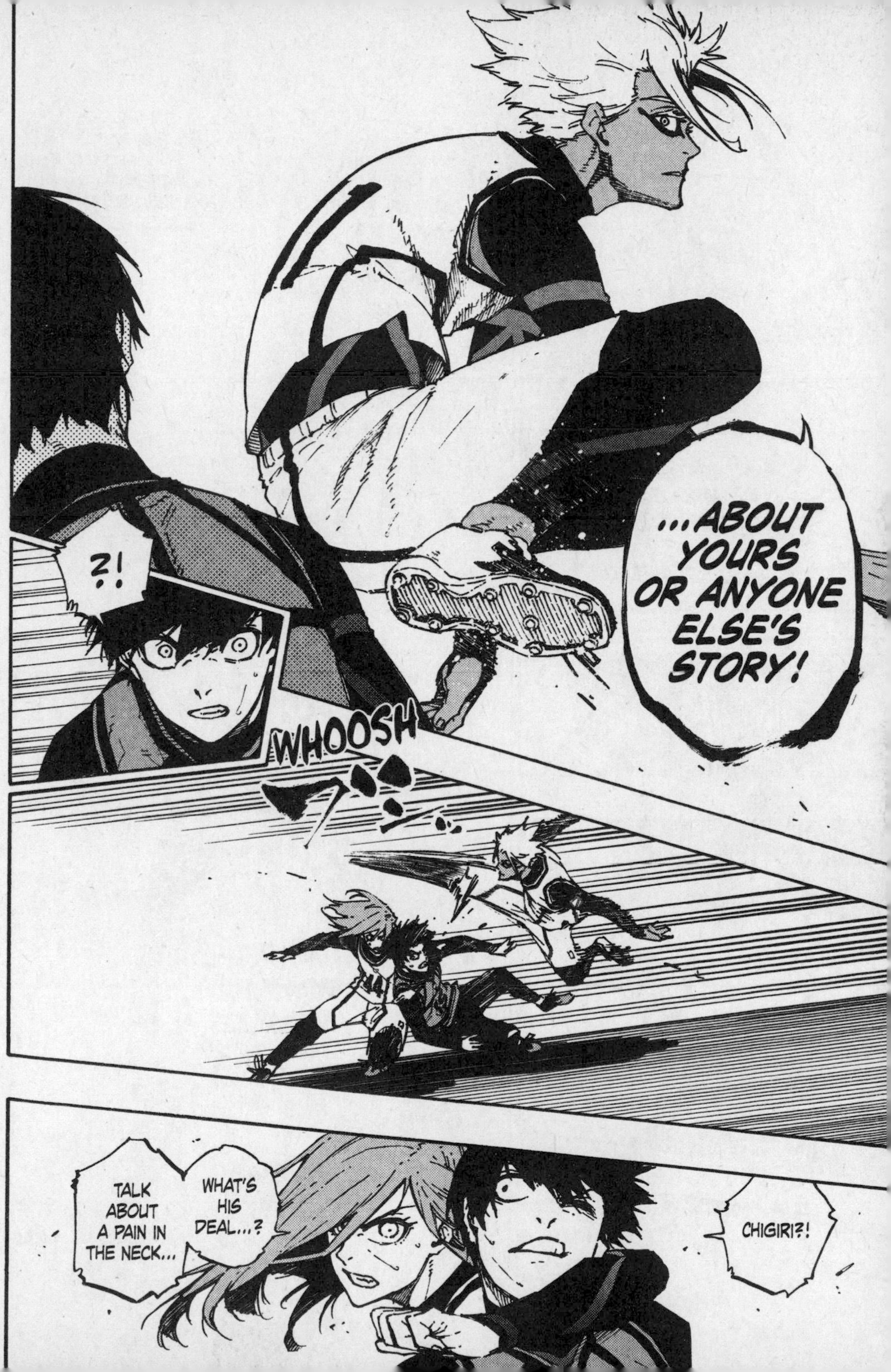
...ABOUT YOURS OR ANYONE ELSE'S STORY!
?!
WHOOSH
CHIGIRI?!
WHAT'S HIS DEAL...?
TALK ABOUT A PAIN IN THE NECK...

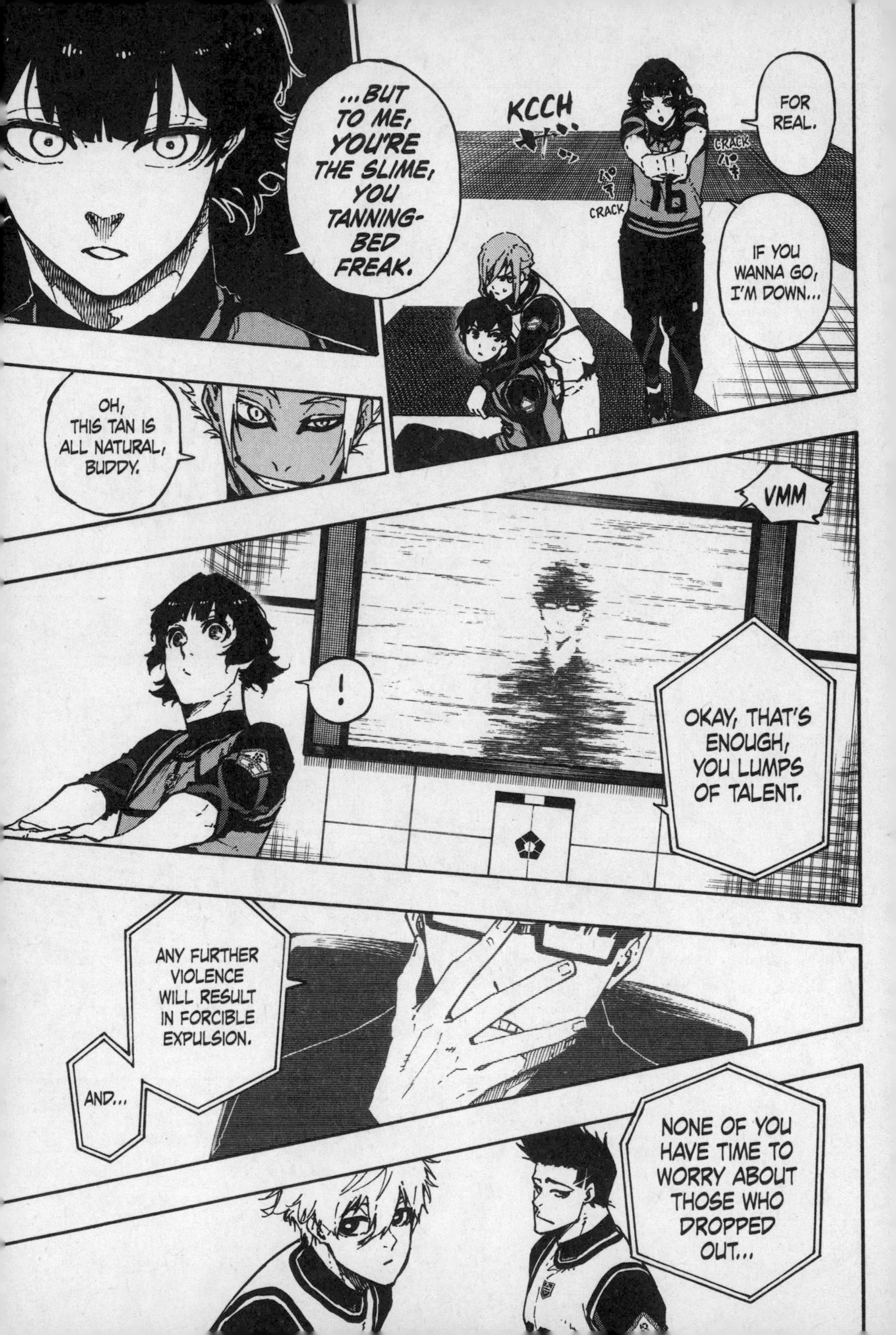
FOR REAL.
CRACK
CRACK
IF YOU WANNA GO, I'M DOWN...
KCCH
...BUT TO ME, YOU'RE THE SLIME, YOU TANNING-BED FREAK.
OH, THIS TAN IS ALL NATURAL, BUDDY.
VMM
OKAY, THAT'S ENOUGH, YOU LUMPS OF TALENT.
!
ANY FURTHER VIOLENCE WILL RESULT IN FORCIBLE EXPULSION.
AND...
NONE OF YOU HAVE TIME TO WORRY ABOUT THOSE WHO DROPPED OUT...

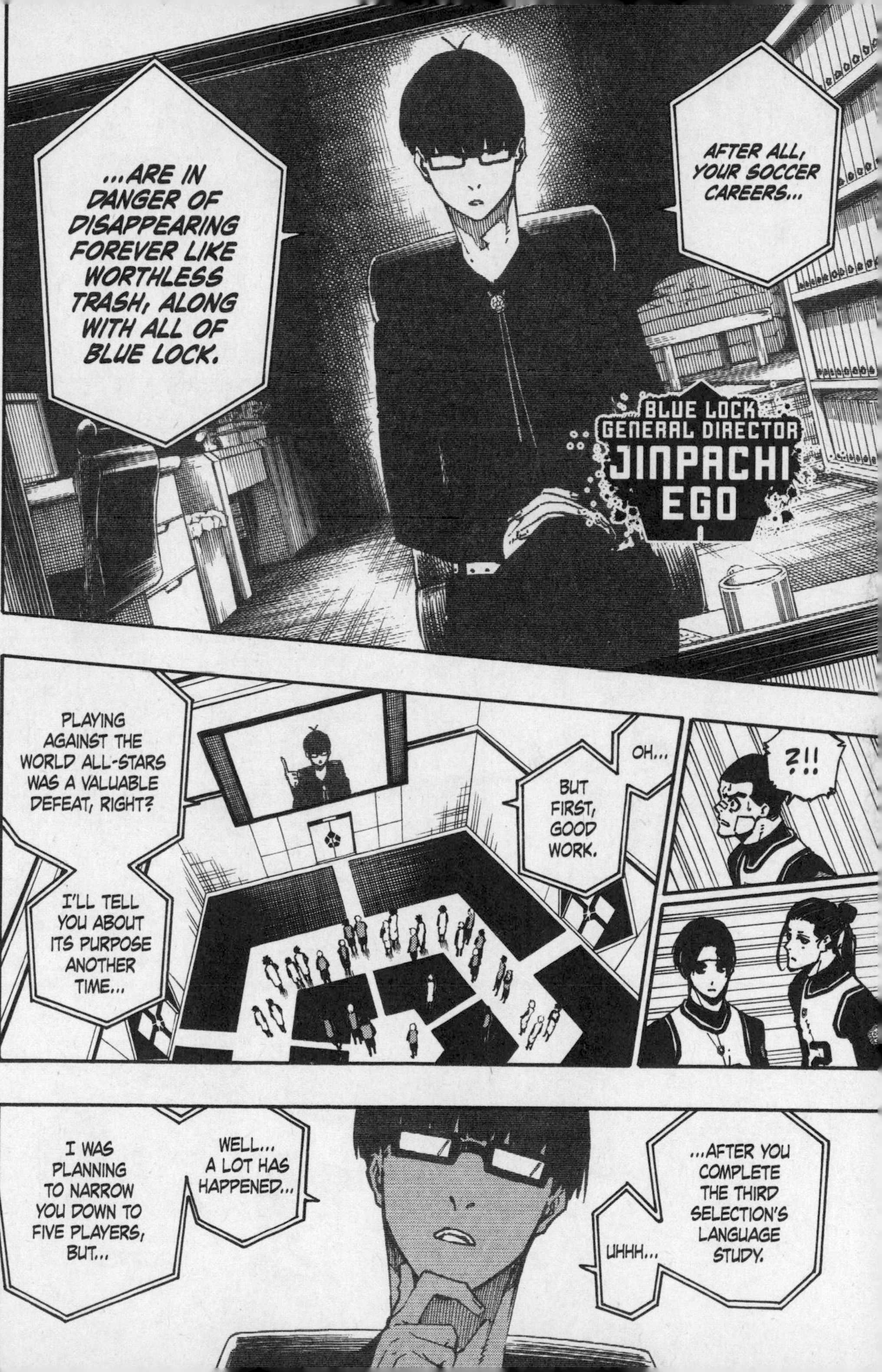
AFTER ALL, YOUR SOCCER CAREERS...
...ARE IN DANGER OF DISAPPEARING FOREVER LIKE WORTHLESS TRASH, ALONG WITH ALL OF BLUE LOCK.
BLUE LOCK GENERAL DIRECTOR JINPACHI EGO
?!!
OH...
BUT FIRST, GOOD WORK.
PLAYING AGAINST THE WORLD ALL-STARS WAS A VALUABLE DEFEAT, RIGHT?
I'LL TELL YOU ABOUT ITS PURPOSE ANOTHER TIME...
...AFTER YOU COMPLETE THE THIRD SELECTION'S LANGUAGE STUDY.
UHHH...
WELL... A LOT HAS HAPPENED...
I WAS PLANNING TO NARROW YOU DOWN TO FIVE PLAYERS, BUT...

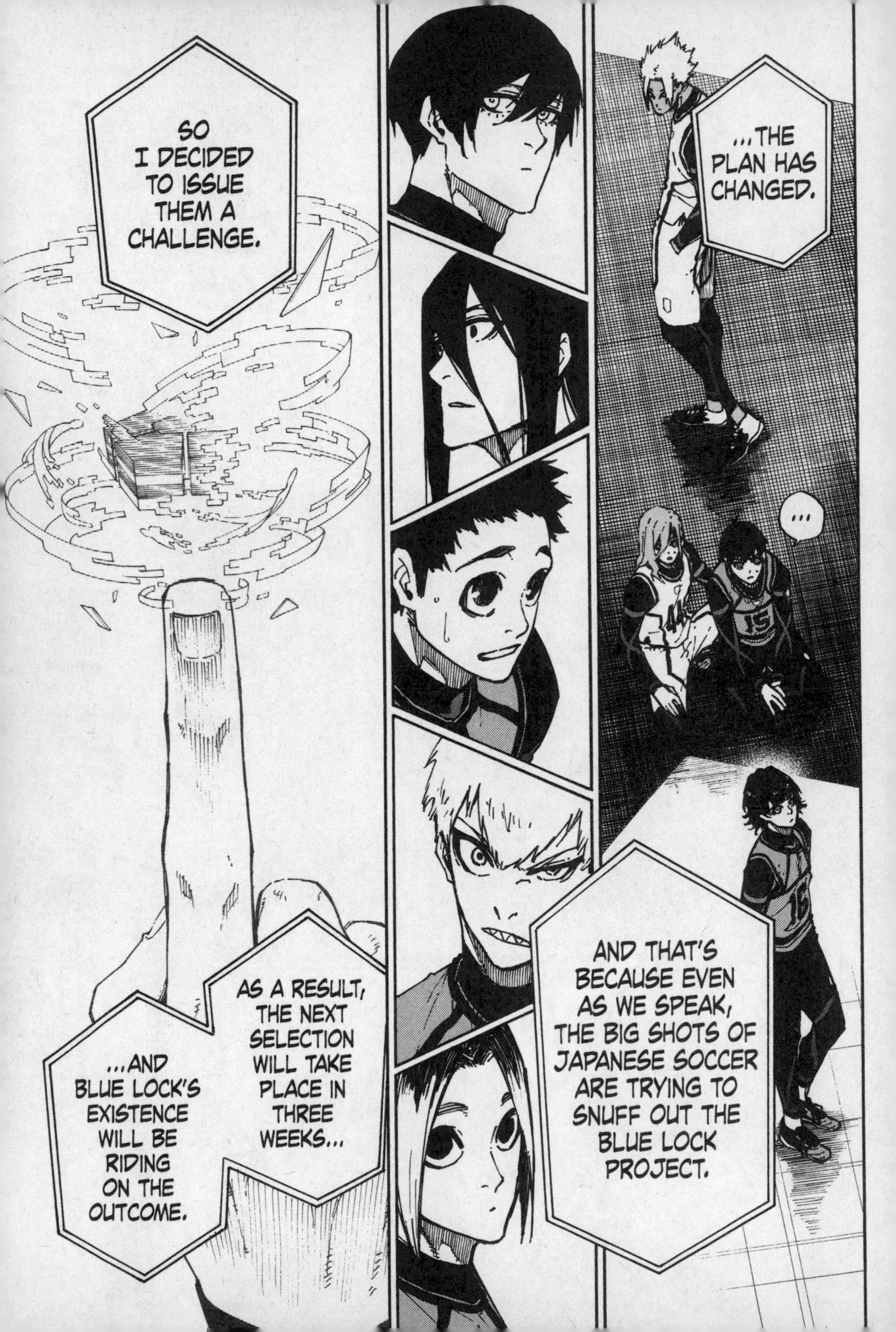
...THE PLAN HAS CHANGED.
...
AND THAT'S BECAUSE EVEN AS WE SPEAK, THE BIG SHOTS OF JAPANESE SOCCER ARE TRYING TO SNUFF OUT THE BLUE LOCK PROJECT.
SO I DECIDED TO ISSUE THEM A CHALLENGE.
AS A RESULT, THE NEXT SELECTION WILL TAKE PLACE IN THREE WEEKS...
...AND BLUE LOCK'S EXISTENCE WILL BE RIDING ON THE OUTCOME.

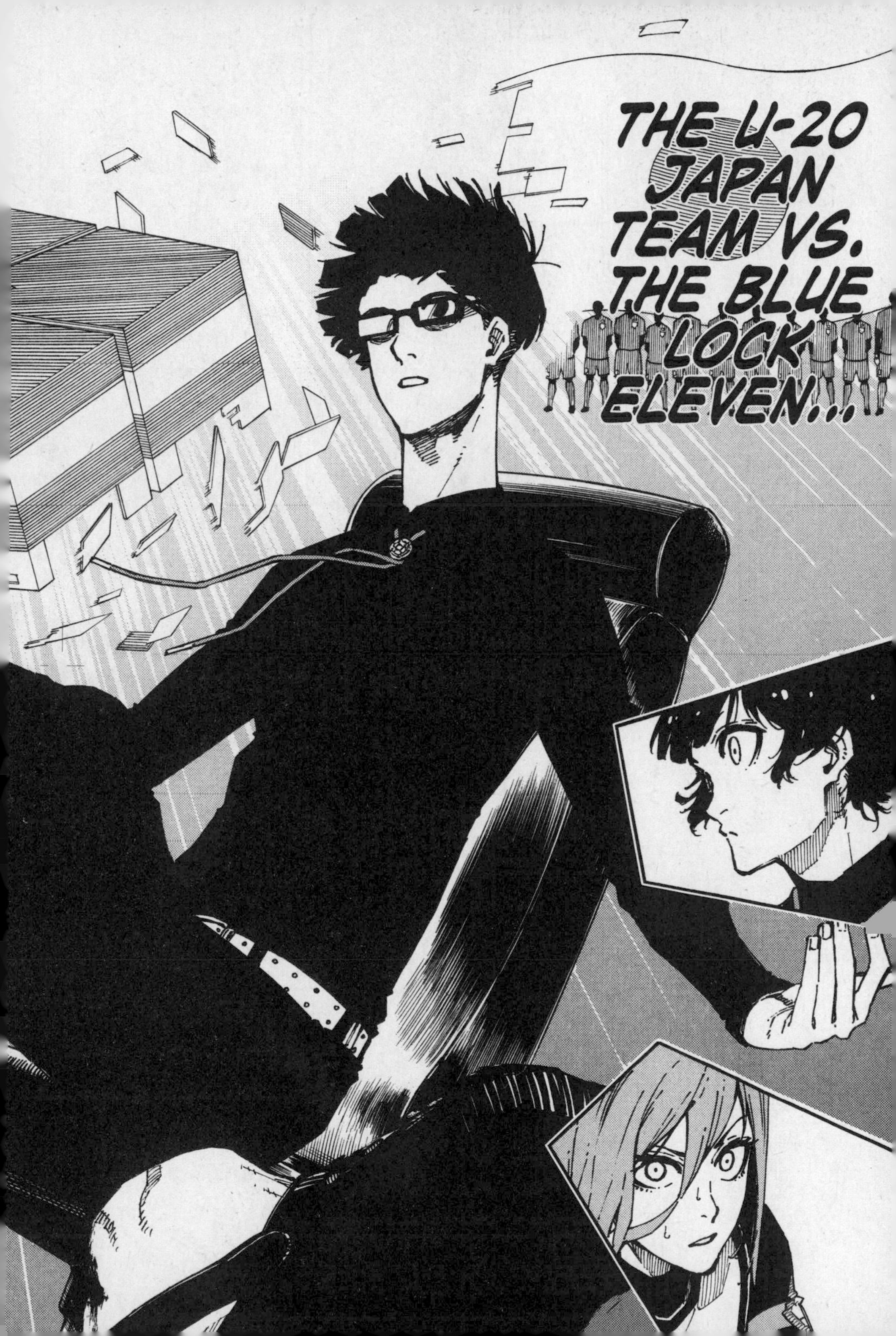
THE U-20 JAPAN TEAM VS. THE BLUE LOCK ELEVEN...

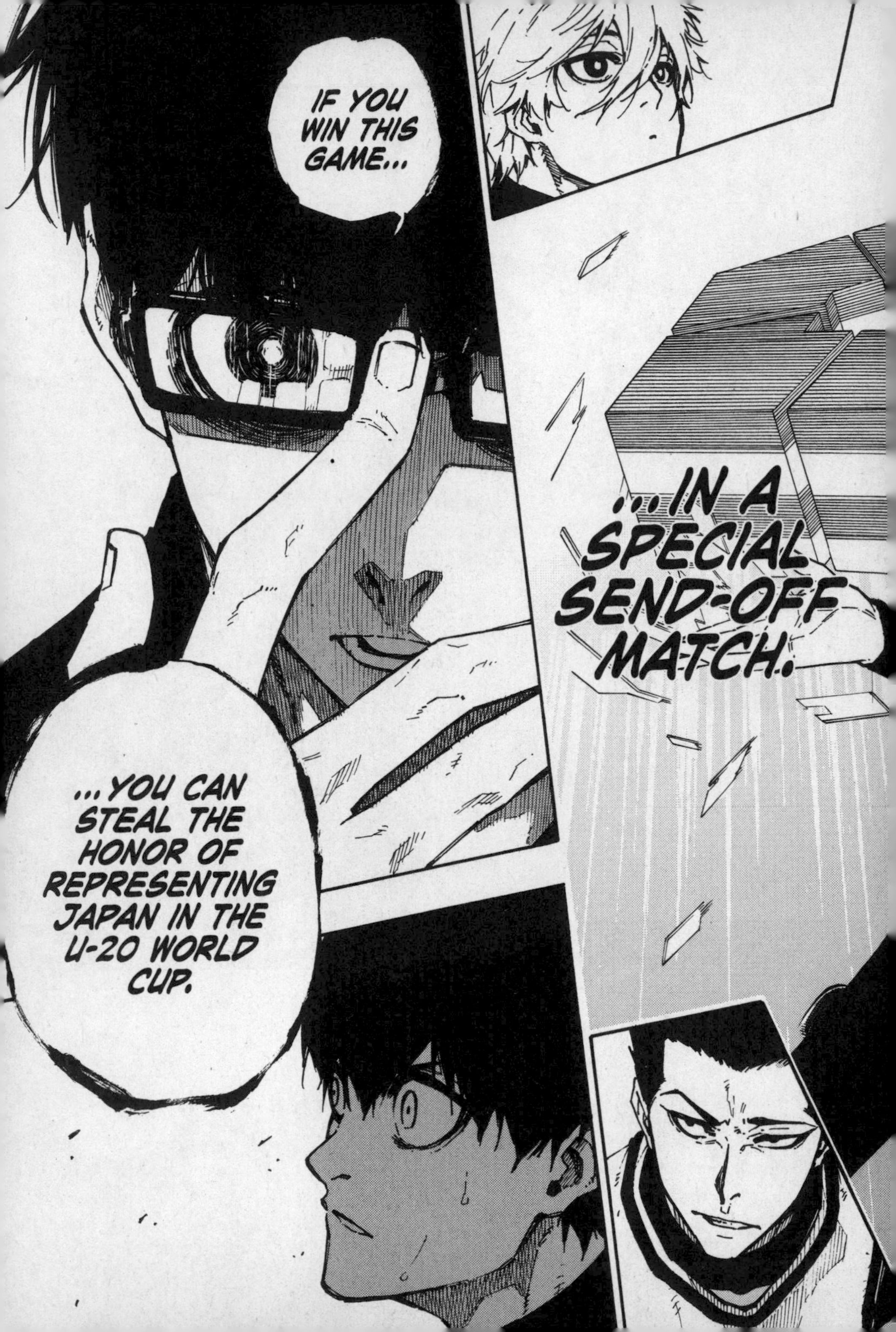
...IN A SPECIAL SEND-OFF MATCH.
IF YOU WIN THIS GAME...
...YOU CAN STEAL THE HONOR OF REPRESENTING JAPAN IN THE U-20 WORLD CUP.

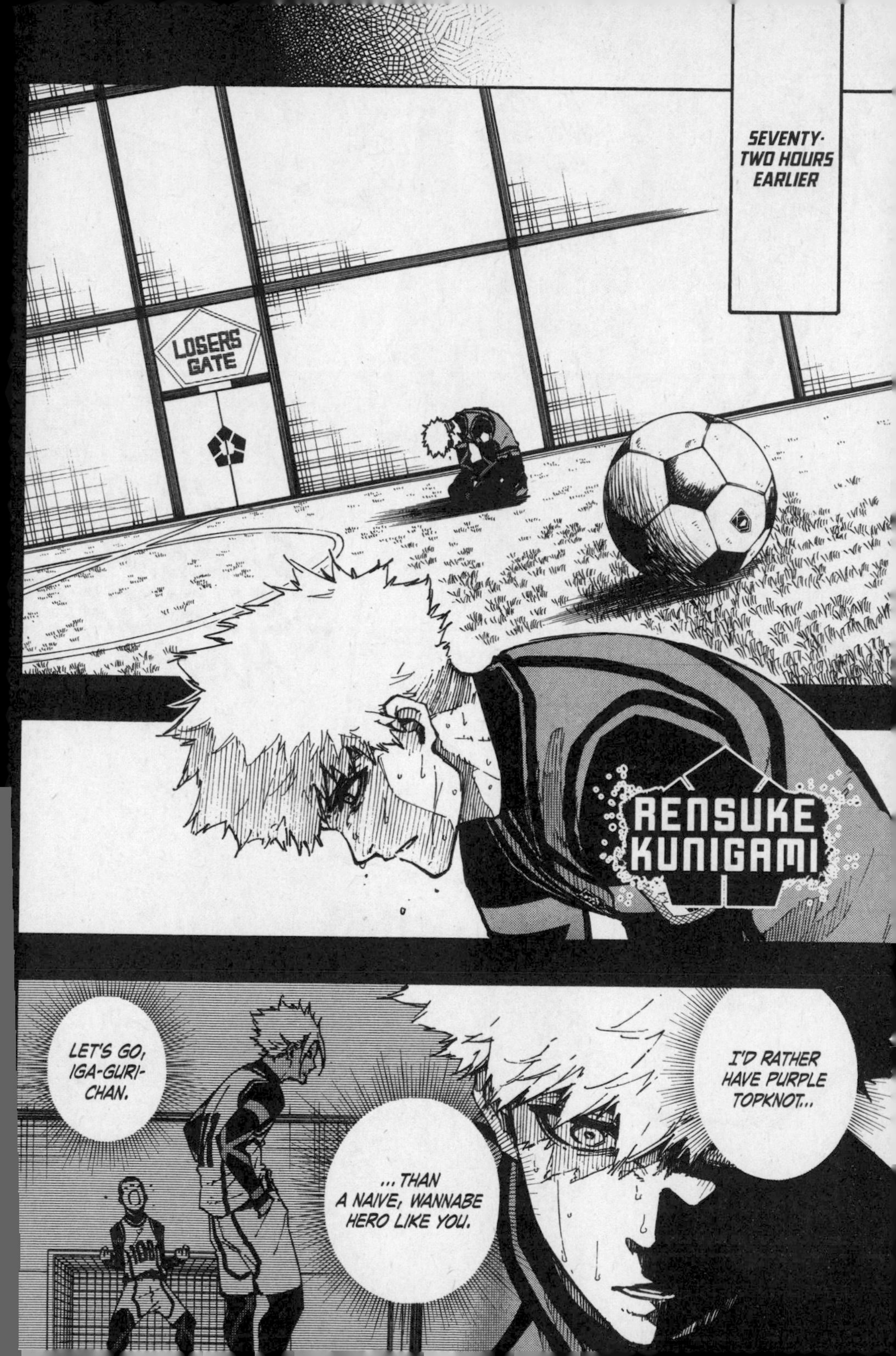
SEVENTY-TWO HOURS EARLIER
LOSERS GATE
RENSUKE KUNIGAMI
I'D RATHER HAVE PURPLE TOPKNOT...
...THAN A NAIVE, WANNABE HERO LIKE YOU.
LET'S GO, IGA-GURI-CHAN.

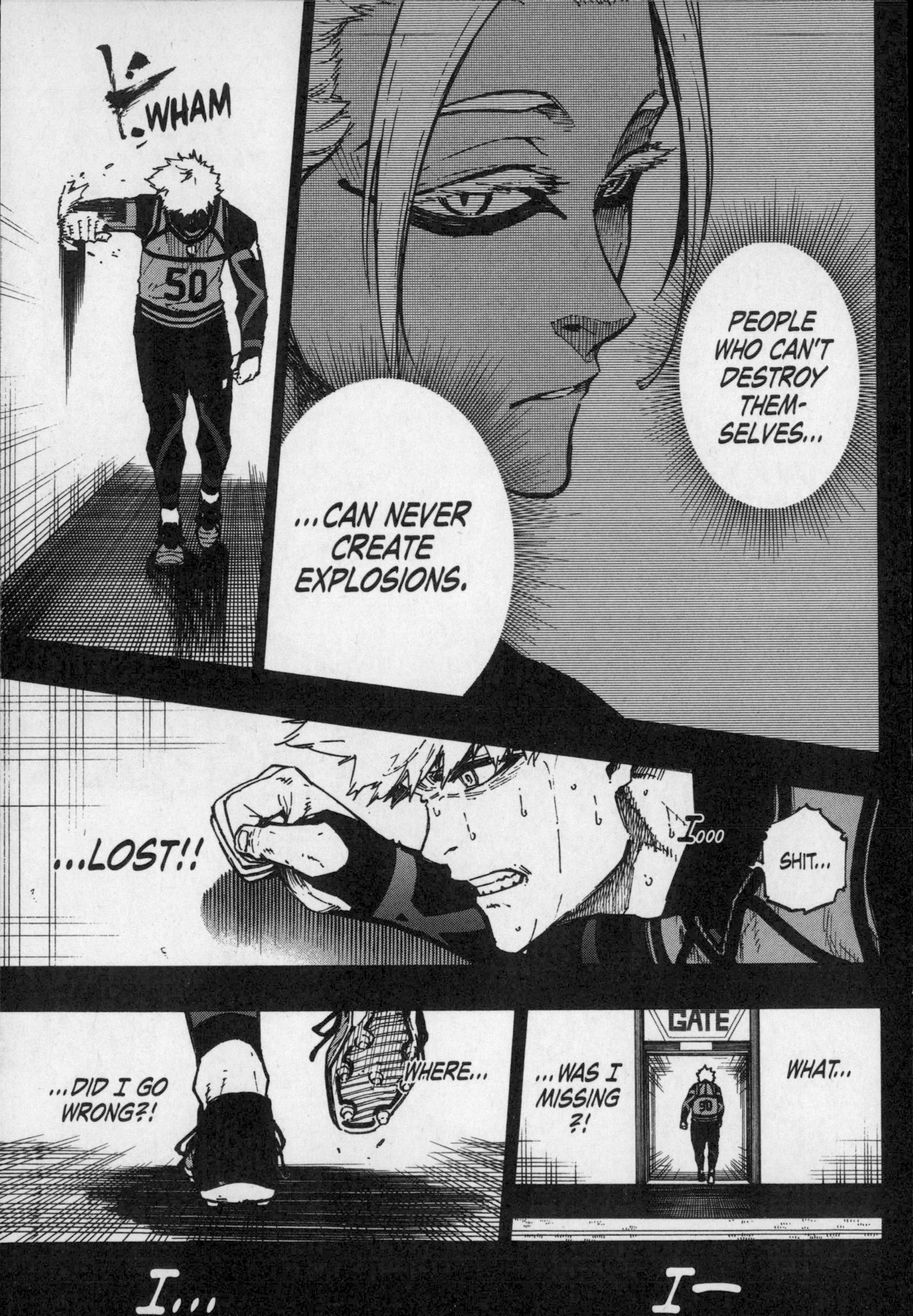
PEOPLE WHO CAN'T DESTROY THEM-SELVES...
...CAN NEVER CREATE EXPLOSIONS.
WHAM
SHIT...
Iooo
...LOST!!
WHAT...
GATE
...WAS I MISSING?!
WHERE...
...DID I GO WRONG?!
I—
I...

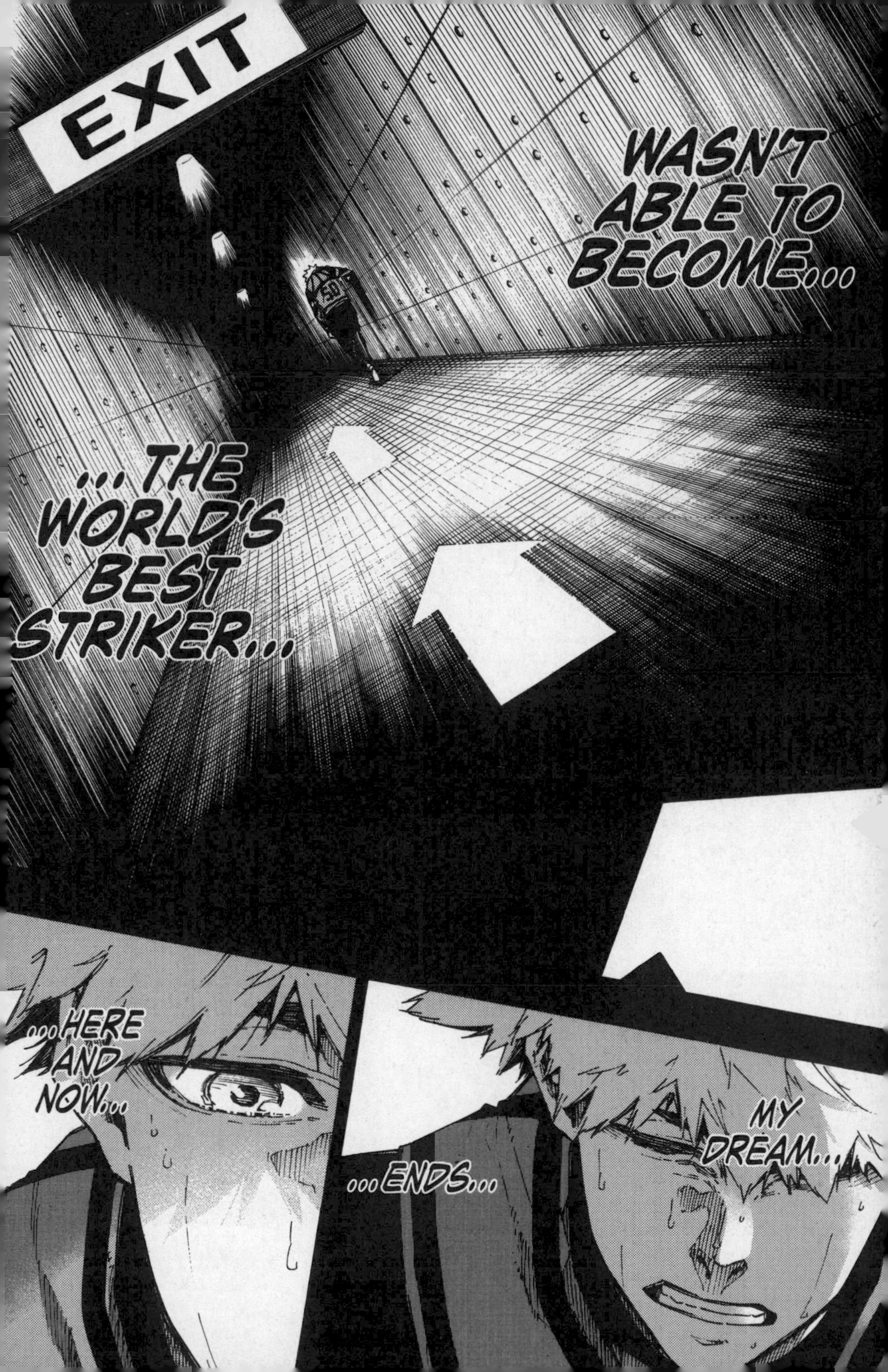
EXIT
WASN'T ABLE TO BECOME...
...THE WORLD'S BEST STRIKER...
MY DREAM...
...ENDS...
...HERE AND NOW...

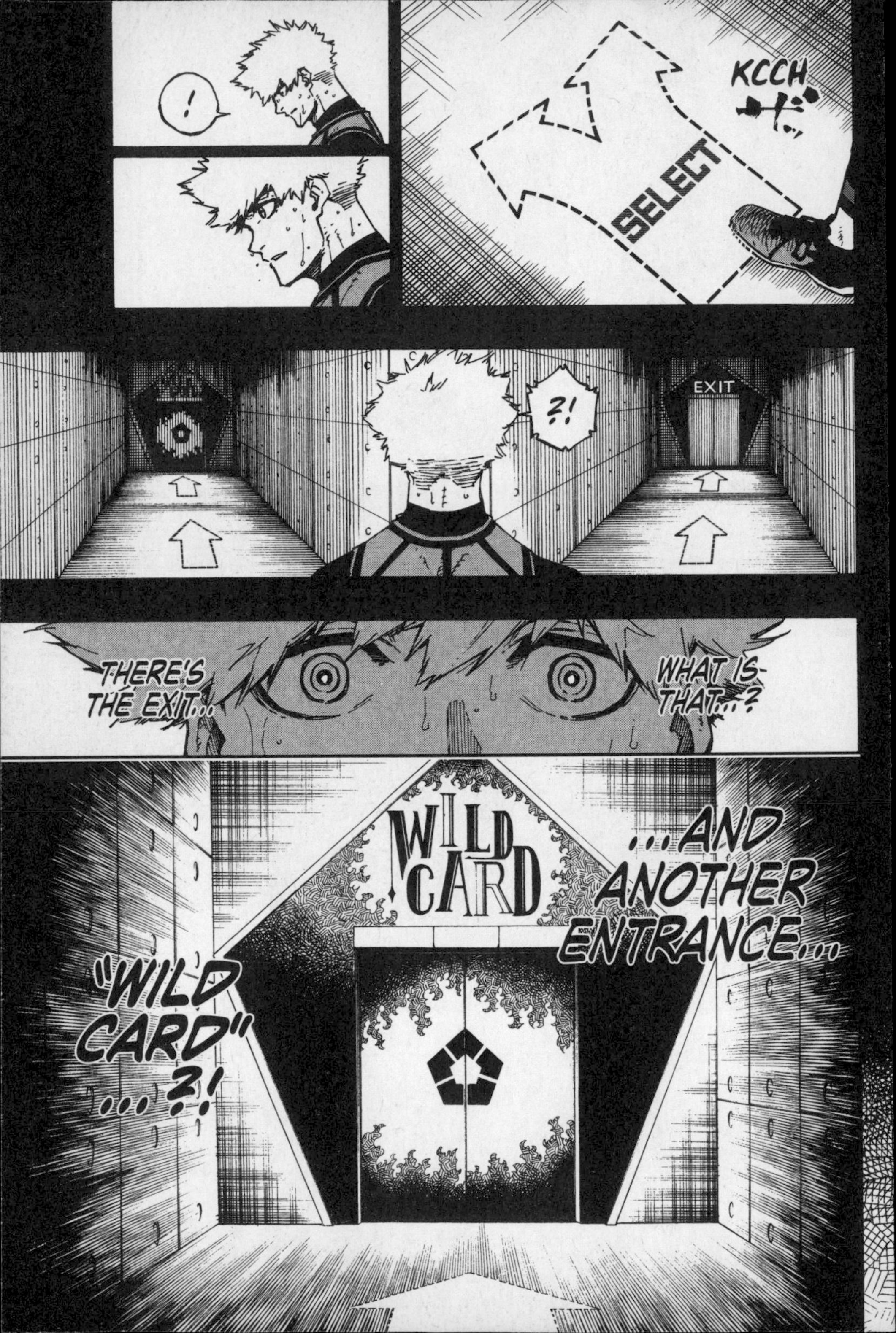
KCCH
SELECT
!
EXIT
?!
WHAT IS THAT...?
THERE'S THE EXIT...
...AND ANOTHER ENTRANCE...
WILD CARD
"WILD CARD"...?!

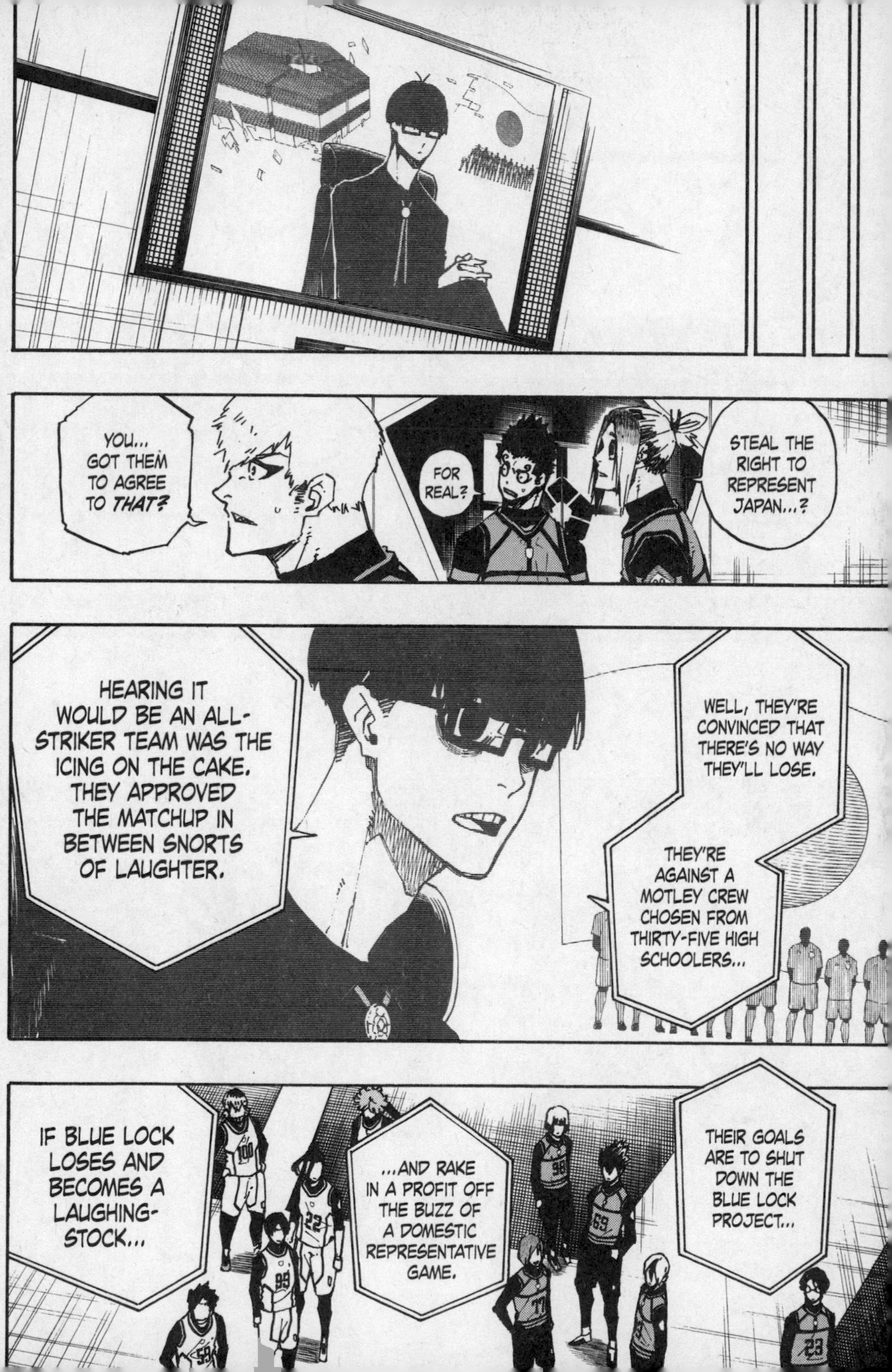
STEAL THE RIGHT TO REPRESENT JAPAN...?
FOR REAL?
YOU... GOT THEM TO AGREE TO *THAT?*
WELL, THEY'RE CONVINCED THAT THERE'S NO WAY THEY'LL LOSE.
THEY'RE AGAINST A MOTLEY CREW CHOSEN FROM THIRTY-FIVE HIGH SCHOOLERS...
HEARING IT WOULD BE AN ALL-STRIKER TEAM WAS THE ICING ON THE CAKE. THEY APPROVED THE MATCHUP IN BETWEEN SNORTS OF LAUGHTER.
THEIR GOALS ARE TO SHUT DOWN THE BLUE LOCK PROJECT...
...AND RAKE IN A PROFIT OFF THE BUZZ OF A DOMESTIC REPRESENTATIVE GAME.
IF BLUE LOCK LOSES AND BECOMES A LAUGHING-STOCK...

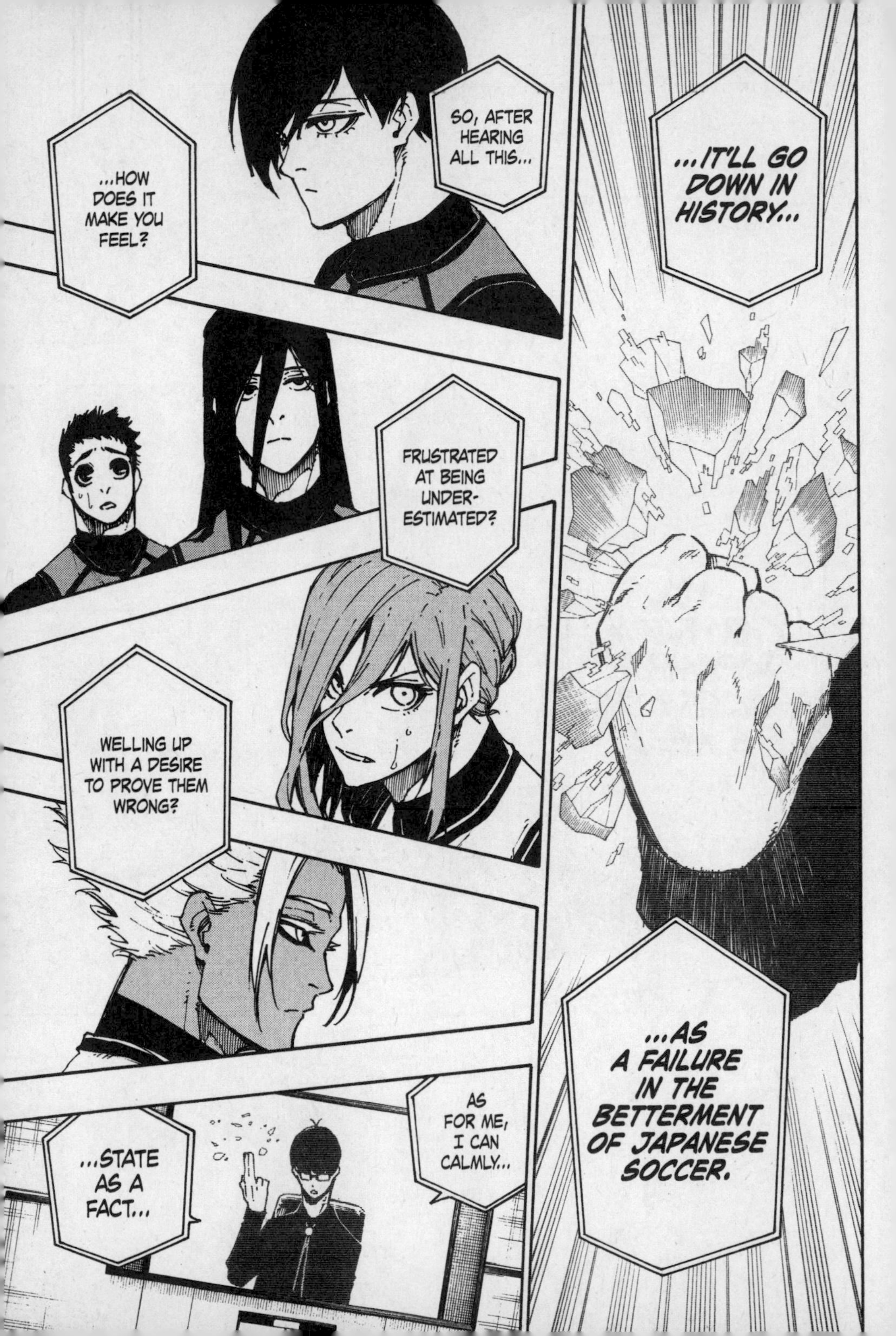
SO, AFTER HEARING ALL THIS...
...HOW DOES IT MAKE YOU FEEL?
FRUSTRATED AT BEING UNDER-ESTIMATED?
WELLING UP WITH A DESIRE TO PROVE THEM WRONG?
AS FOR ME, I CAN CALMLY...
...STATE AS A FACT...
...IT'LL GO DOWN IN HISTORY...
...AS A FAILURE IN THE BETTERMENT OF JAPANESE SOCCER.

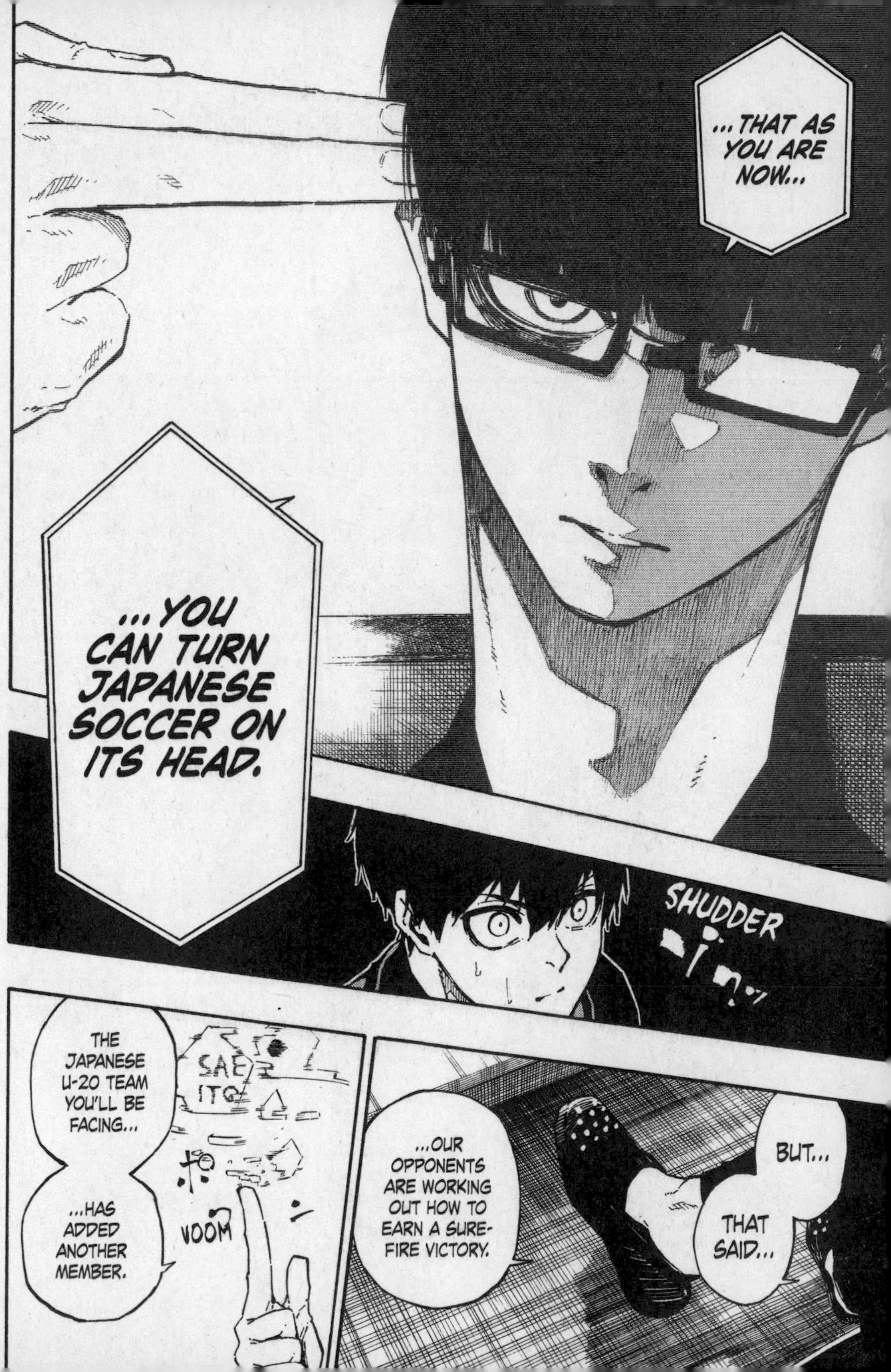
...THAT AS YOU ARE NOW...
...YOU CAN TURN JAPANESE SOCCER ON ITS HEAD.
SHUDDER
BUT...
THAT SAID...
...OUR OPPONENTS ARE WORKING OUT HOW TO EARN A SURE-FIRE VICTORY.
THE JAPANESE U-20 TEAM YOU'LL BE FACING...
...HAS ADDED ANOTHER MEMBER.
SAE ITO
VOOM

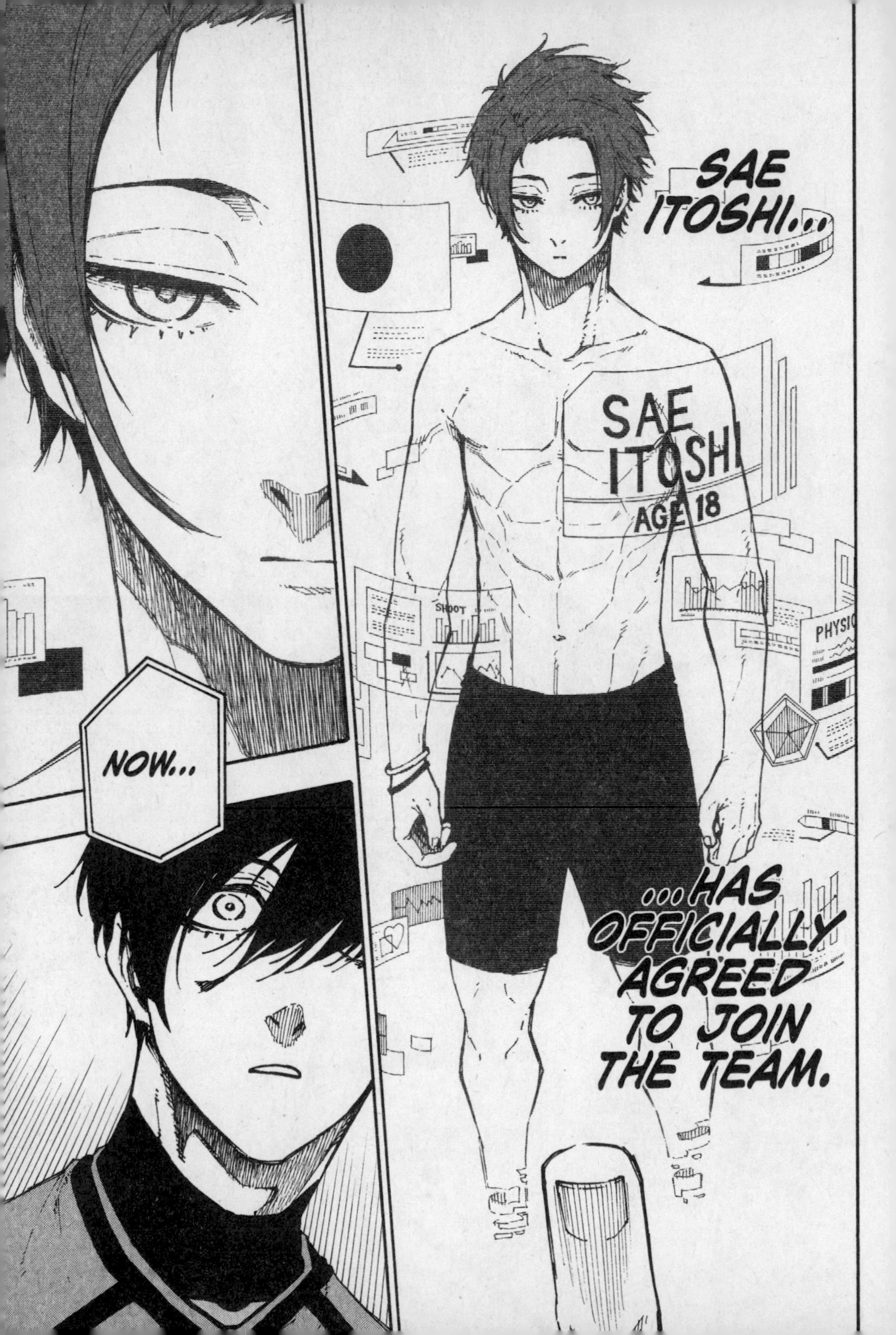
SAE ITOSHI...
SAE ITOSHI
AGE 18
SHOOT
PHYSIC
...HAS OFFICIALLY AGREED TO JOIN THE TEAM.
NOW...

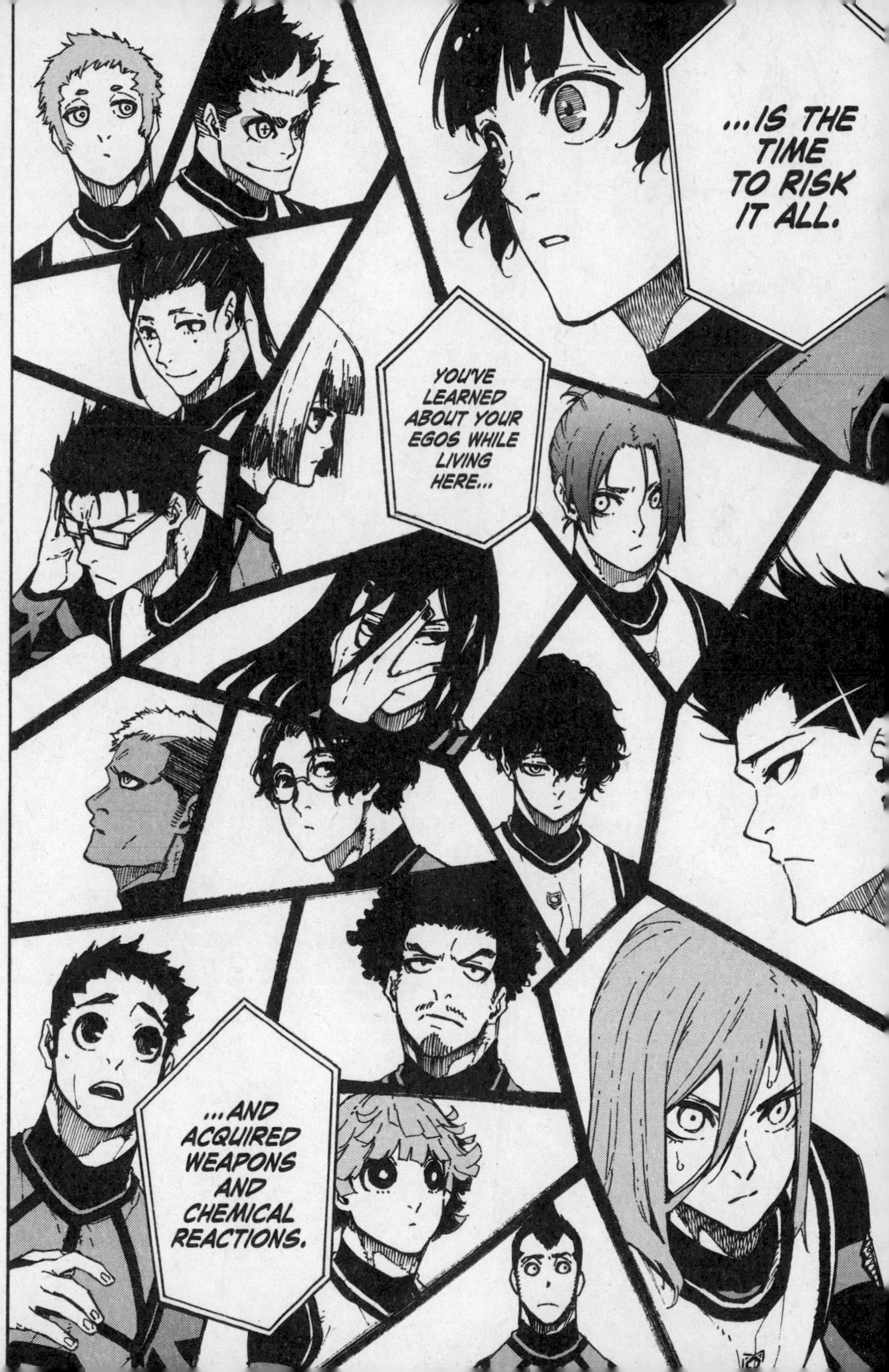
...IS THE TIME TO RISK IT ALL.
YOU'VE LEARNED ABOUT YOUR EGOS WHILE LIVING HERE...
...AND ACQUIRED WEAPONS AND CHEMICAL REACTIONS.

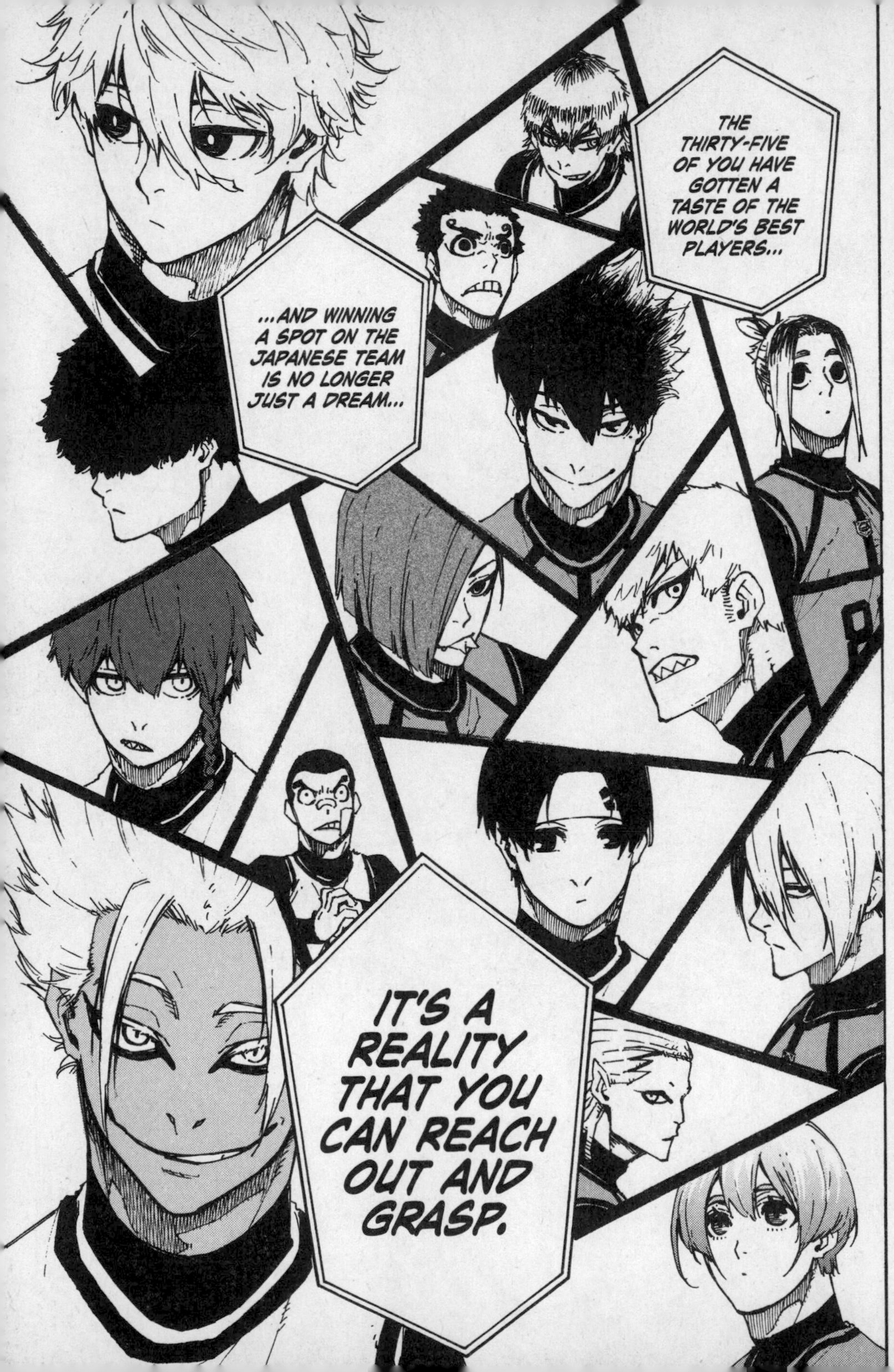
THE THIRTY-FIVE OF YOU HAVE GOTTEN A TASTE OF THE WORLD'S BEST PLAYERS...
...AND WINNING A SPOT ON THE JAPANESE TEAM IS NO LONGER JUST A DREAM...
IT'S A REALITY THAT YOU CAN REACH OUT AND GRASP.

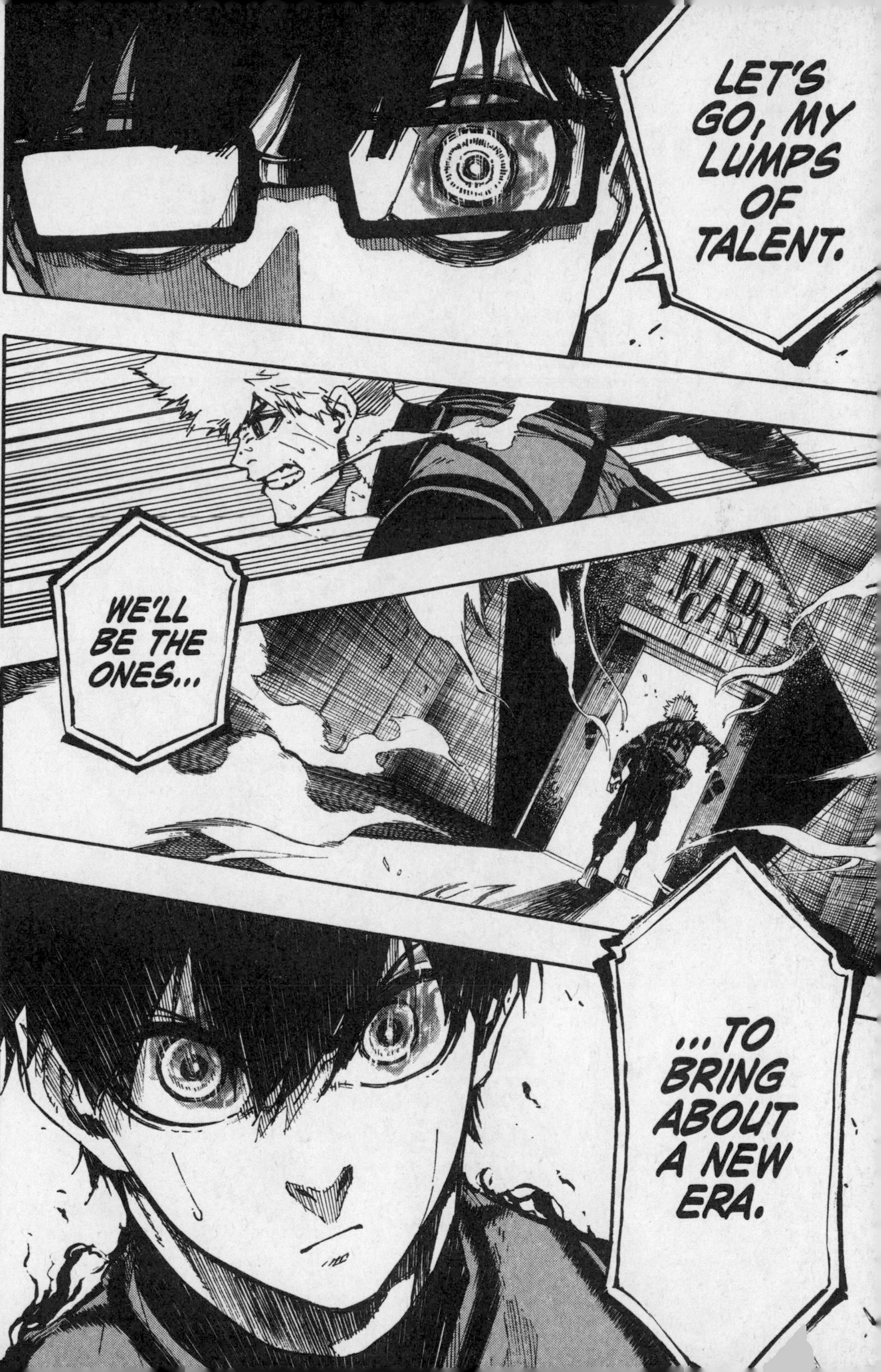
LET'S GO, MY LUMPS OF TALENT.
WE'LL BE THE ONES...
WILD CARD
...TO BRING ABOUT A NEW ERA.

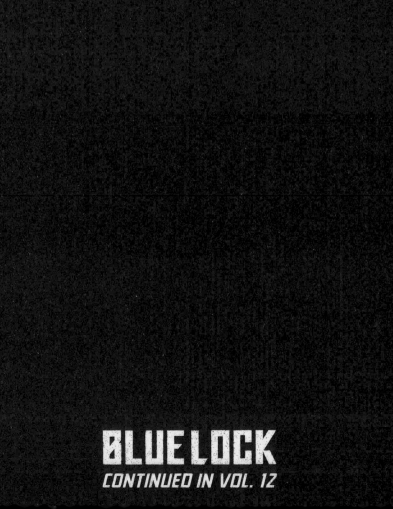

BLUE LOCK
CONTINUED IN VOL. 12

BONUS SECTION

INTRODUCING EVERYONE WHO PASSED THE BLUE LOCK SECOND SELECTION!

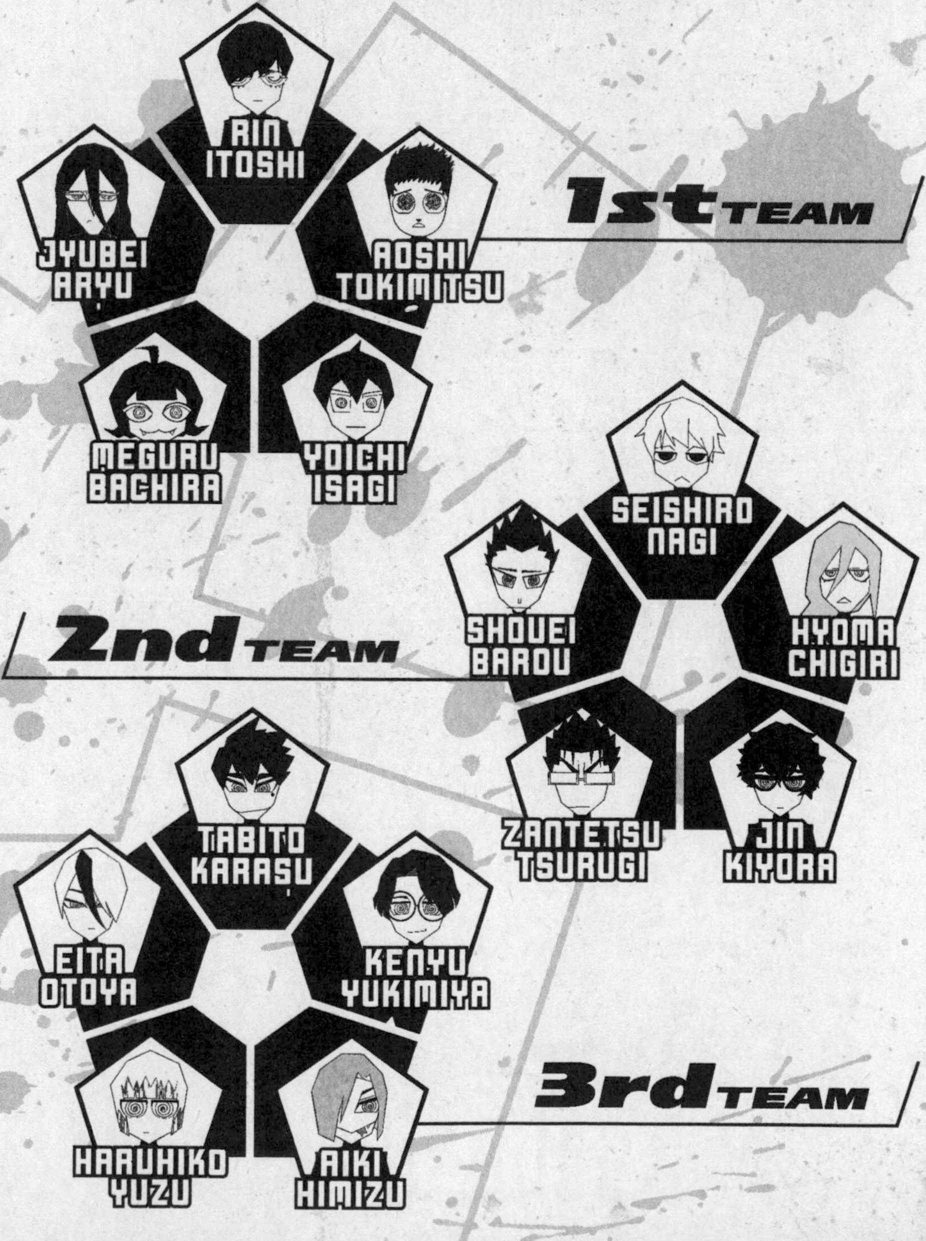
1st TEAM
RIN ITOSHI
JYUBEI ARYU
AOSHI TOKIMITSU
MEGURU BACHIRA
YOICHI ISAGI
2nd TEAM
SEISHIRO NAGI
SHOUEI BAROU
HYOMA CHIGIRI
ZANTETSU TSURUGI
JIN KIYORA
3rd TEAM
TABITO KARASU
EITA OTOYA
KENYU YUKIMIYA
HARUHIKO YUZU
AIKI HIMIZU

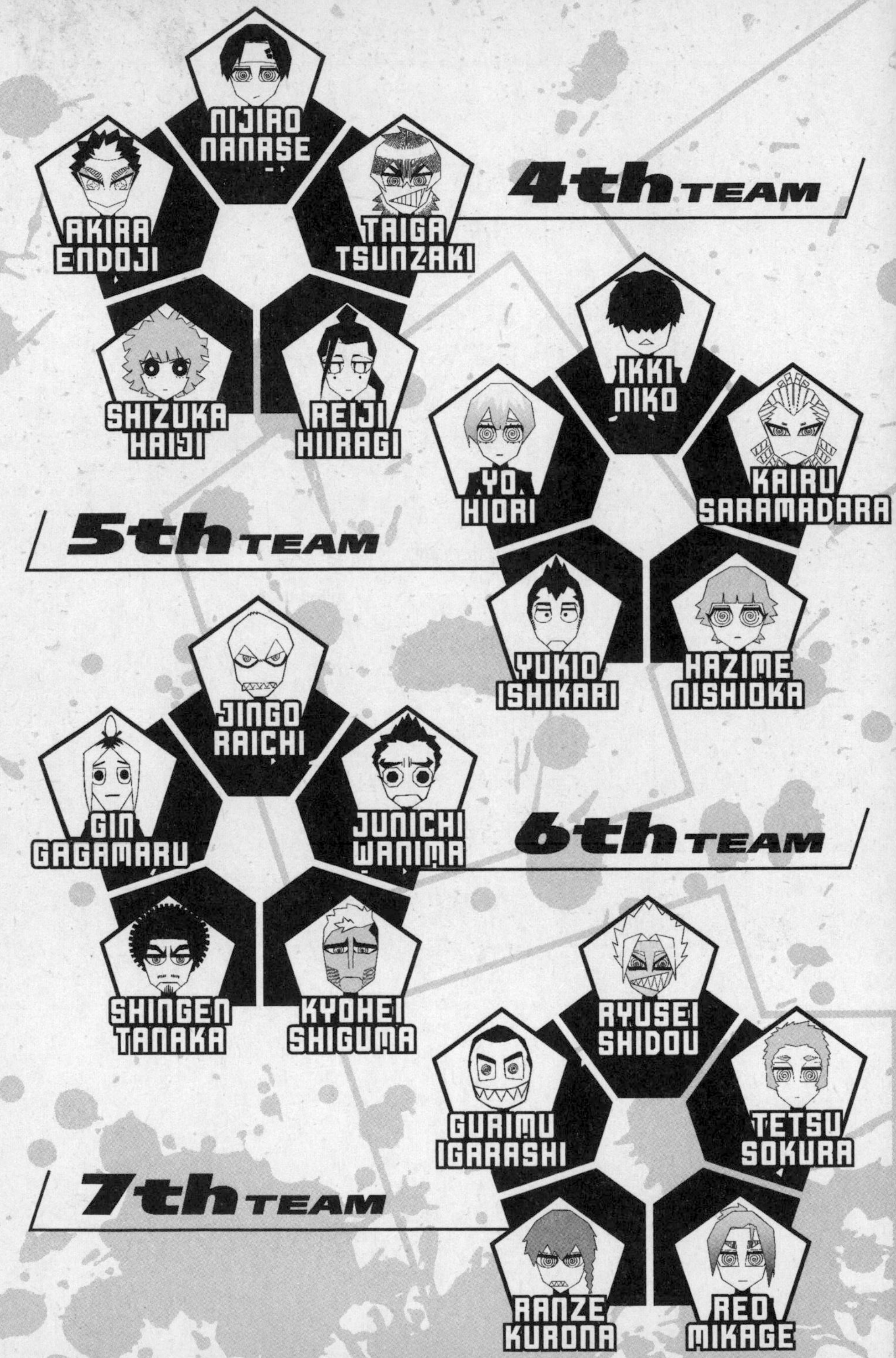
NIJIRO NANASE
AKIRA ENDOJI
TAIGA TSUNZAKI
SHIZUKA HAIJI
REIJI HIIRAGI
4th TEAM
IKKI NIKO
YO HIORI
KAIRU SARAMADARA
YUKIO ISHIKARI
HAZIME NISHIOKA
5th TEAM
JINGO RAICHI
GIN GAGAMARU
JUNICHI WANIMA
SHINGEN TANAKA
KYOHEI SHIGUMA
6th TEAM
RYUSEI SHIDOU
GURIMU IGARASHI
TETSU SOKURA
RANZE KURONA
REO MIKAGE
7th TEAM

◉ STORY   **MUNEYUKI KANESHIRO**

◉ ART   **YUSUKE NOMURA**

◉ ART ASSISTANTS **TAKANIWA-SAN   AYATSUKA-SAN**

                 OTAKE-SAN   HARA-SAN

                 HARADA-SAN   MUTO-SAN

                 KAWAI-SAN   SANNOMIYA-SAN

                 AOI-SAN

                 SPECIAL THANKS

                 SUEHIRO-SAN   KABAYA-SAN

                                  (LISTED RANDOMLY)

◉ DESIGN   **HISAMOCHI-SAN**

                 OSOKO-SAN

                 (HIVE)

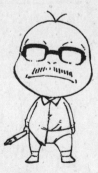

THANK YOU VERY MUCH FOR PURCHASING VOLUME 11.
I KNOW I'M LATE, BUT I'M WATCHING *BREAKING BAD*.
SORRY IT TOOK ME SO LONG! IT'S AWESOME!!
THE BOYS IS AWESOME, TOO!!

BLUE LOCK

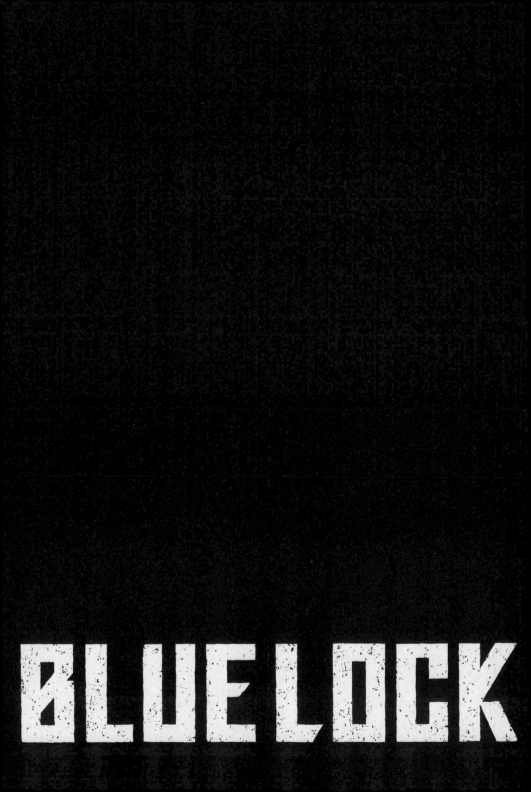

BLUE LOCK

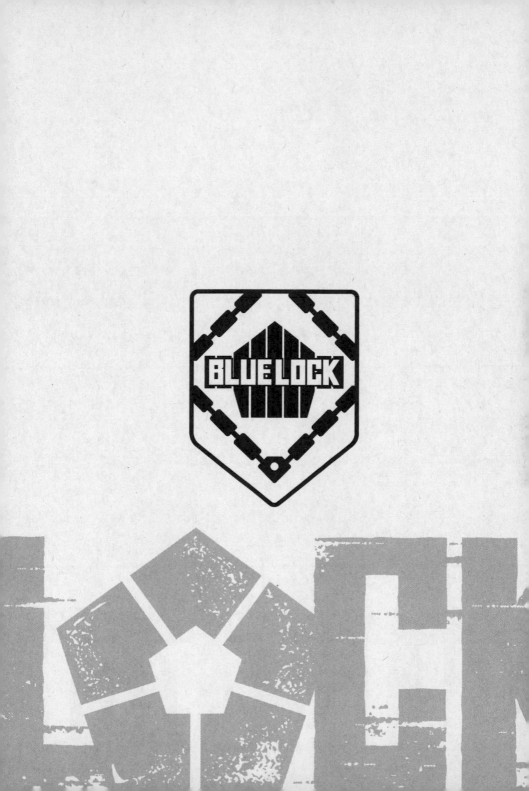

11

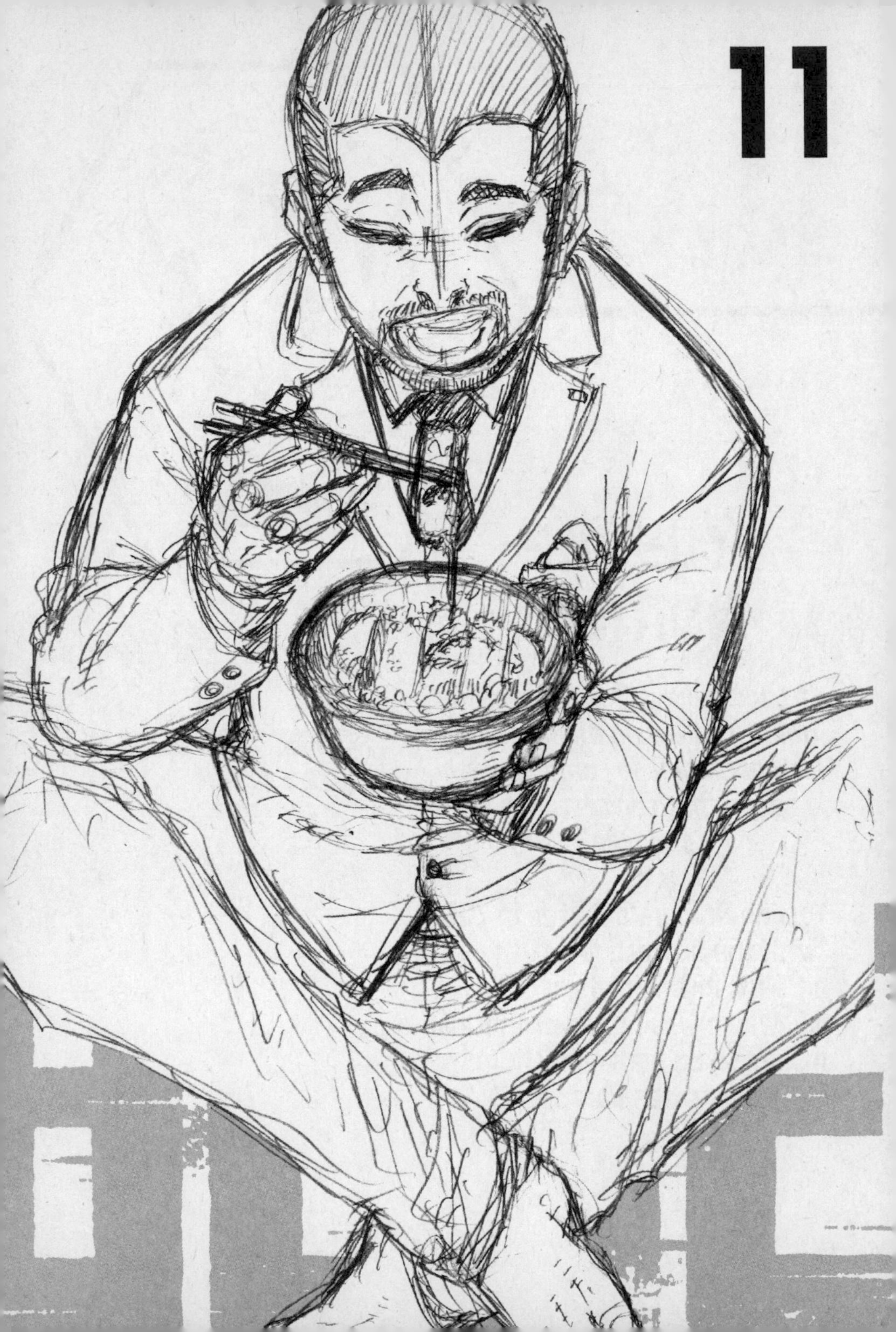

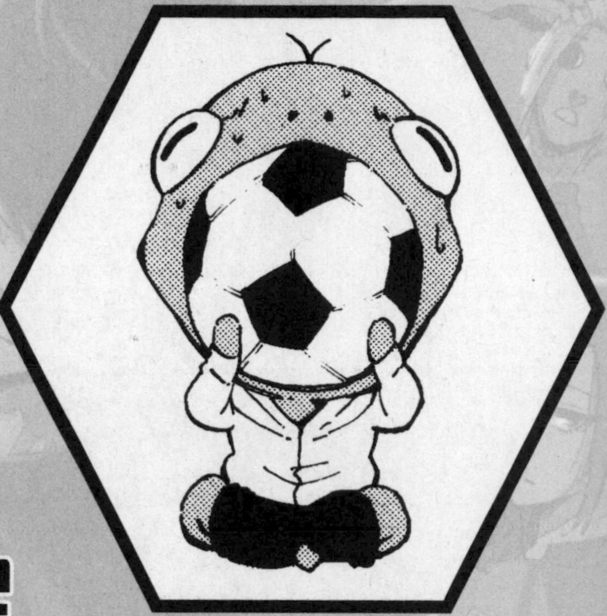

Yusuke Nomura

"I truly believe 3-6 AM is prime time for drawing manga. Could someone please come up with a space that can recreate that stillness?"

Yusuke Nomura debuted in 2014 with the grotesquely cute cult hit alien invasion story *Dolly Kill Kill*, which was released digitally in English by Kodansha. Nomura illustrates *Blue Lock*.

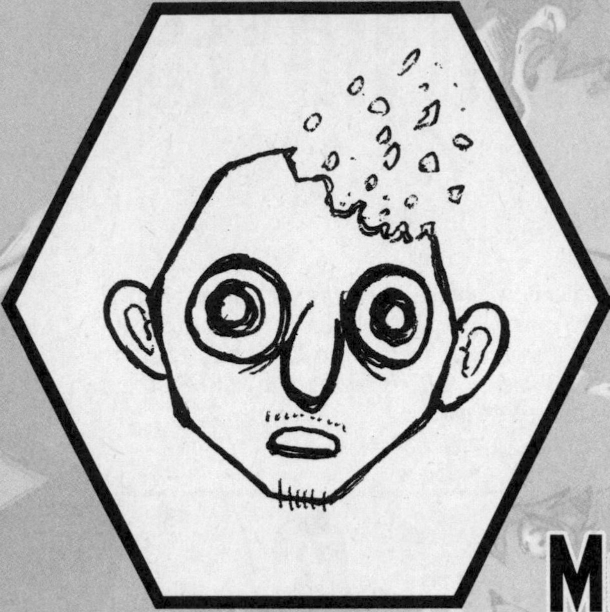

Muneyuki Kaneshiro

"I love backing characters into a corner. Those who rise above adversity, particularly in the most dire of circumstances, are the ones who keep a story moving. Probs."

Muneyuki Kaneshiro broke out as creator of 2011's *As the Gods Will*, a death game story that spawned two sequels and a film adaptation directed by the legendary Takashi Miike. Kaneshiro writes the story of *Blue Lock*.

TRANSLATION NOTES

Luck...is shit?

page 26

Aryu notes the similarity between the word for luck ("un") and the word for shit ("fun"), but that may not be the only reason Ego uses this particular metaphor. As he alludes to later in his analysis, there is a cultural notion in Japan that being pooped on by a pigeon is actually a sign of good luck, which may explain why Rin is described to go where the "pigeon shit lands" to get lucky enough to score a goal.

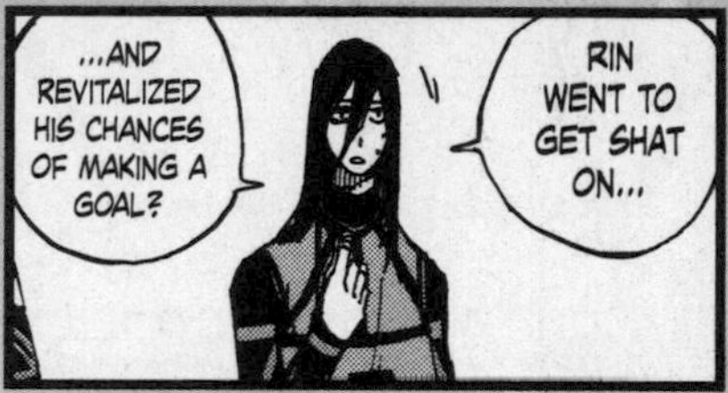
RIN WENT TO GET SHAT ON...
...AND REVITALIZED HIS CHANCES OF MAKING A GOAL?

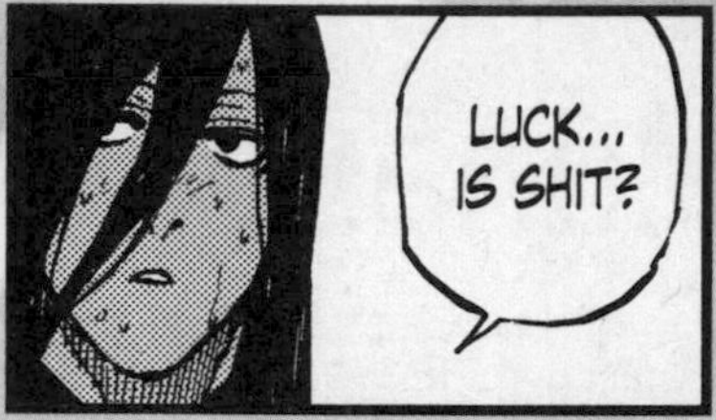
LUCK... IS SHIT?

Chestnut head

page 59

Igarashi's nickname is the term for a chestnut still in its burr. It is also the shortform of the term "igaguri atama" ("chestnut burr head"), which is used to describe a close-cropped hairstyle, not unlike the look Igarashi is sporting.

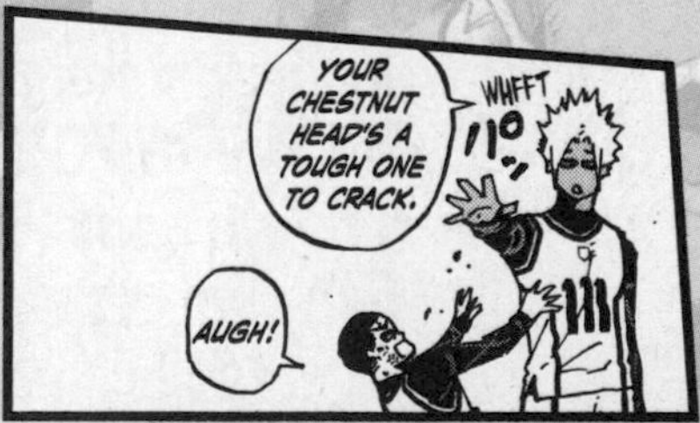
WHFFT
YOUR CHESTNUT HEAD'S A TOUGH ONE TO CRACK.
AUGH!

The vices of Buddhism

page 75

Igarashi frequently references the Buddhist traditions he learned at his family temple, and his jersey number is no exception, even if it wasn't quite his choice. The 108 vices [or defilements, among other terms] of Buddhism refer to the earthly desires one must overcome to achieve enlightenment. The term "klesha" is often used in the Japanese tradition.

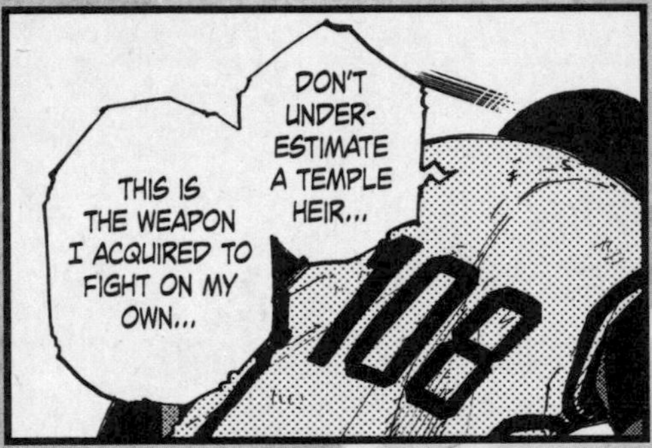
DON'T UNDER-ESTIMATE A TEMPLE HEIR...
THIS IS THE WEAPON I ACQUIRED TO FIGHT ON MY OWN...
108

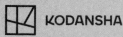

Fire Force Omnibus

Created by
Atsushi Ohkubo

600 pages each—blaze past the anime!
In the year 198 of the Solar Era, the
city of Tokyo is plagued by a deadly
phenomenon: spontaneous human
combustion! The only ones who
can stop it are the Fire Force!

RATED: 16+

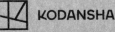

Break of Dawn

Created by
Tetsuya Imai

A coming-of-age sci-fi story
Yuma is obsessed with the impending return of the SHIII-Arville Comet. One day, he sneaks onto the roof of an apartment building and finds something not from this world...

RATED: 13+

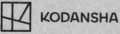

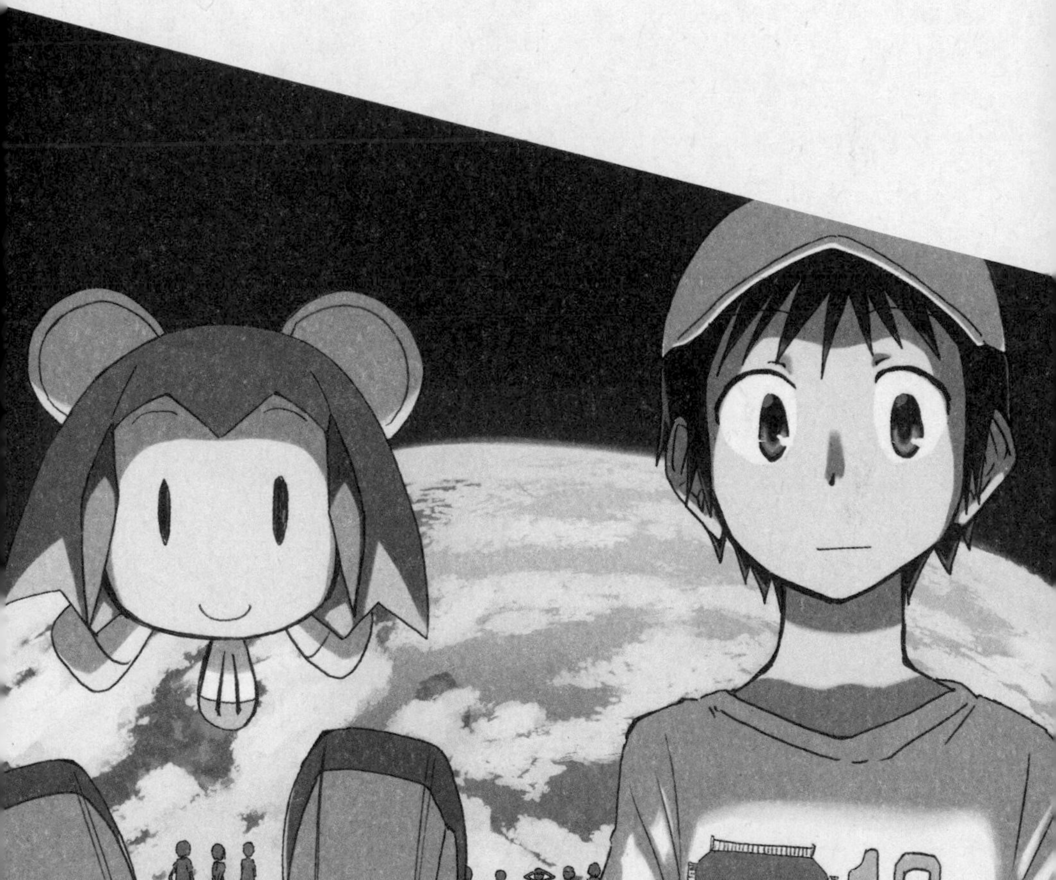

KODANSHA

In the Clear Moonlit Dusk

Created by
Mika Yamamori

Push past appearances in this teen romance!
Yoi Takiguchi is resigned to being the hero—not
heroine—in her life, until Ichimura-sempai shows her
what it feels like to be seen for her true beauty...

RATED: 13+

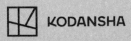

KODANSHA

Penguin & House

Created by
Akiho Ieda

Pen is a penguin who likes pancakes.
Pen the penguin lives with his friend
Hayakawa, a human. The only way
for Pen to express his love is by
doing chores and getting deals at the
supermarket. This is their life together.

RATED: 8+

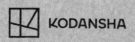

Wandance

**Created by
Coffee**

Get up and join the Wandance!
A boy named Kaboku sees a girl named Wanda
dance, and suddenly burns with a need to join in. A
new, inspirational manga for fans of *Blue Period* and
Your Lie in April.

RATED: 13+

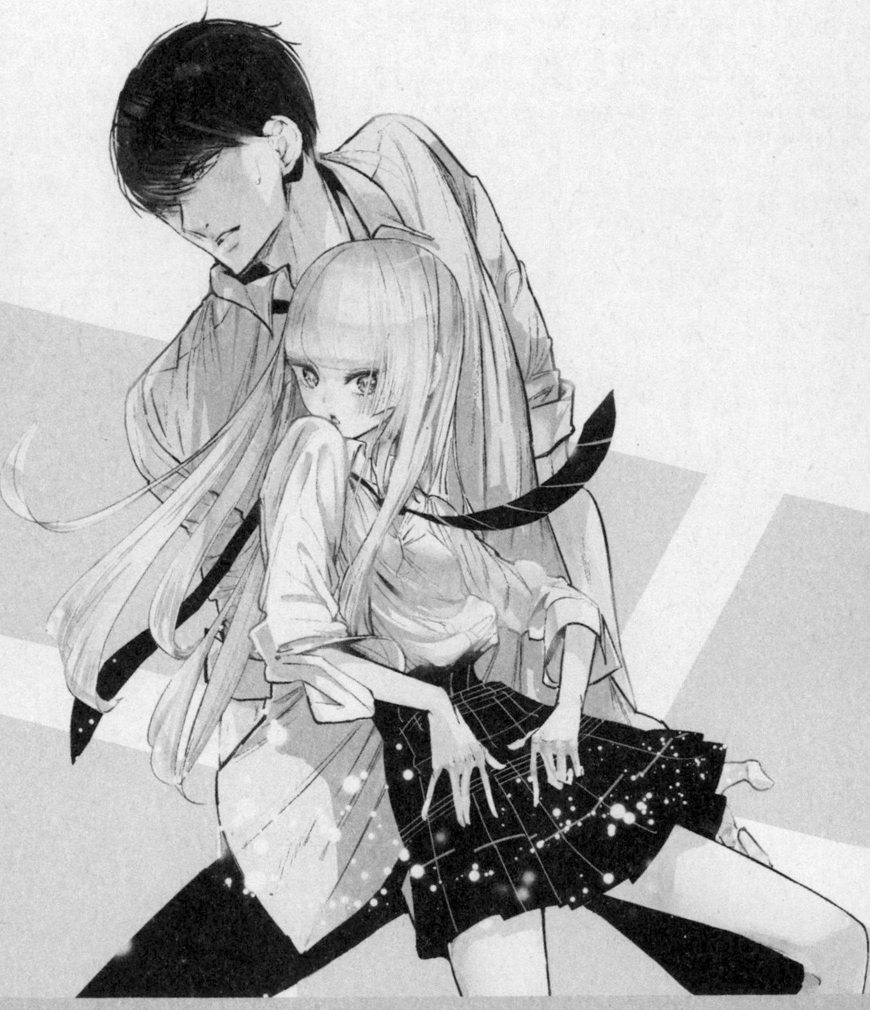

KODANSHA

Parasyte Full Color Collection

Created by
Hitoshi Iwaaki

The sci-fi horror classic returns in color!

They infest human hosts and consume
them. The parasites are everywhere,
but no one knows their secret except
high schooler Shinichi. After preventing
his own infection, can he find a way to
warn humanity?

RATED: 16+

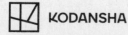

KODANSHA

Tsugumi Project

Created by
ippatu

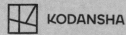

Peach Boy Riverside

Story by Coolkyousinnjya
Art by Johanne

**The bloody fantasy that
inspired the anime!**

There's demon-slaying action
galore in this stylish update to
a Japanese folktale from the
creator of *Miss Kobayashi's
Dragon Maid*! A rambunctious
princess is fed up being
trapped behind walls. But
walls keep out monsters...

RATED: 16+

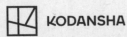

KODANSHA

A Kodansha Trade Paperback Original

Blue Lock 11 copyright © 2020 Muneyuki Kaneshiro/Yusuke Nomura
English translation copyright © 2024 Muneyuki Kaneshiro/Yusuke Nomura

Published in the United States by
Kodansha USA Publishing, LLC, New York.

Publication rights for this English edition arranged through
Kodansha Ltd., Tokyo.

First published in Japan in 2020 by Kodansha Ltd., Tokyo
as *Buruu rokku*, volume 11.

ISBN 978-1-64651-668-1

Printed in the United States of America.

9 8 7 6 5 4 3 2 1

Original Digital Edition Translator: Nate Derr
Original Digital Edition Letterer: Chris Burgener
Original Digital Edition Editor: Thalia Sutton
YKS Services LLC/SKY JAPAN, Inc.
Print Edition Letterer: Scott O. Brown
Print Edition Editor: Vanessa Tenazas
Managing Editor: Alanna Ruse
Production Manager: Meg Gugarty

Kodansha USA Publishing edition cover design by Matthew Akuginow

Publisher: Toshihiro Tsuchiya

Director of Publishing Services: Ben Applegate
Director of Publishing Operations: Dave Barrett

KODANSHA.US

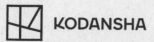 **KODANSHA**